For Simon
from the authors. W9-CPT-797
Robin   Mary

Christmas, 1987.

Penguin Books

The Living Past of Greece

Andrew Robert Burn was born in Shropshire in 1902. He was
educated at Uppingham and Christ Church, Oxford, where he took a
First in Greats. His enthusiasm for Greece dates from earliest
childhood, and while still an undergraduate he won the Charles
Oldham Prize with an essay on the early Greek lyric poets.
During the war he was the British Council's representative in Greece,
1940-41. He then served in the Intelligence Corps, and from
1944 to 1946 was Second Secretary in the British Embassy in Athens.
From 1946 until 1969 he taught ancient history at the University
of Glasgow, and to young Americans in Athens between 1969 and
1972. His other books include *The World of Hesiod, The Lyric Age
of Greece, The Modern Greeks, Persia and the Greeks,* subtitled *The Defence of
the West,* and *The Pelican History of Greece.*

Mary Burn obtained a Diploma in Classical Archaeology at Oxford,
and won a travelling scholarship to the British School at Rome,
with a visit to the British School at Athens. She later became an
Assistant Keeper at the Victoria and Albert Museum, until her
marriage in 1938. She was with her husband in Greece and Crete in
1940-41, and continued her war work with him in the Middle
East. In 1943 she joined the British Embassy to the Greek
Government in Cairo, returning to Athens in 1944 as Third Secretary
until 1946. She worked on excavations at Paphos, Cyprus, for
four seasons between 1950 and 1953, and has taught Greek and
Byzantine Art to American students in Athens as well as lecturing
at summer-schools.

Mr and Mrs Burn continue to travel widely in Greece whenever
possible, for both work and pleasure. *Still true, 1987,*
tho' more slowly.

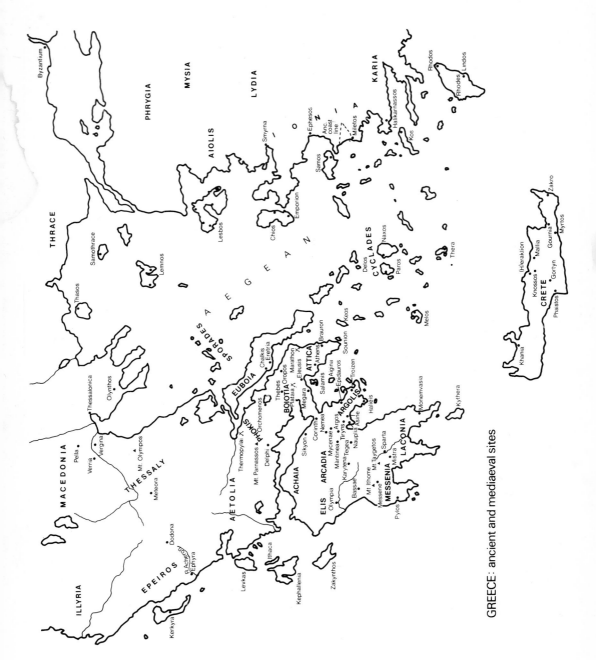

GREECE: ancient and mediaeval sites

A. R. AND MARY BURN

THE
LIVING PAST
OF GREECE

A time-traveller's tour of historic and prehistoric places

Foreword by Lawrence Durrell

Penguin Books

To Ismene and Nike
and our students in Greece *Whereof we chose Mollie to receive a specimen copy.*

Penguin Books Ltd, Harmondsworth, Middlesex, England
Penguin Books, 625 Madison Avenue, New York, New York 10022, U.S.A.
Penguin Books Australia Ltd, Ringwood, Victoria, Australia
Penguin Books Canada Ltd, 2801 John Street, Markham, Ontario, Canada L3R 1B4
Penguin Books (N.Z.) Ltd, 182-190 Wairau Road, Auckland 10, New Zealand

First published by the Herbert Press 1980
Published in Penguin Books 1982

Copyright © A. R. and Mary Burn, 1980
All rights reserved

Maps and plans drawn by Bill Hawker

Made and printed in Great Britain by
Mackays of Chatham Ltd
Set in VIP Baskerville
Designed by Judith Allan

Acknowledgements for photographs
Mary Burn, pp. 35, 53, 91, 96, 123, 173, 178, 181, 183, 187, 201, 211, 213, 223, 236, 247, 261, 269, 273; Camera Press, pp. 12 (Ken Lambert), 47 (Alex Starkey), 125 (Alfred Gregory), 146 (Patellani), 204 (Richard Harrington); Christopher Chalk, pp. 38, 43; Alison Frantz, p. 70; David Herbert, p. 120 and cover; N. Mavrogenis, p. 252; National Tourist Organization of Greece, pp. 58, 66, 134, 198, 207, 220, 229, 238, 243, 267.
Cover photograph: Temple of Aphaia, Aigina (David Herbert).

Contents

Foreword

Thoroughness of scholarship and warm sympathetic insight have always marked the books of A. R. Burn. Greece is his favourite subject, and there is no corner of Greek history that he is not fully at home in—which is to say a lot, for to deal with a matter so complex as Greek pre-history or even early history one must be something like a water-diviner or a soothsayer. The evidence we have upon which to build a picture of those forgotten epochs may be both conflicting and ambiguous. It can also be meagre in the extreme, or else recorded in alphabets to which we as yet have no key.

Despite the difficulties, Burn treads his path confidently among these shards and crumbs of knowledge, and never fails to present a convincing and intriguing picture of his subject matter; out of it he evolves a narrative which recreates vanished cities and the cultures to which they gave rise, conveying a feeling of complete authenticity. Moreover he is fully abreast of the latest findings in this field and is able to weigh up and present contending views with balance and ripe scholarship. In the present volume he has once again (this time with his wife as co-author) produced a work of finely-wrought scholarship extremely rewarding for the armchair reader as well as for the traveller.

Lawrence Durrell

Preface

We wish to thank our original publishers (The Herbert Press) for the idea of this book. It is *not* another guidebook. The public is well provided with these, and for up-to-date travel information one must in any case consult travel agents. Here we describe sites where what is to be seen best illuminates Greek history (including prehistory), adding brief accounts of what, in history or according to mythology, happened there, and with maps and plans which may, we hope, make this a useful companion to Greek history even for the 'armchair traveller'. Concentrating on the prehistoric, Hellenic and Byzantine ages we omit, for economy's sake, some Roman and most Frankish sites, as well as some where, as at Sparta, little that is informative remains above ground.

To the problem of order of presentation there is no perfect solution. We have chosen a historical order, that of the ages or events represented by the chief visible remains, or for which places are most famed. But many places have long histories; *e.g.* Orchomenos in Boiotia, like Athens, has remains prehistoric and classical and Byzantine, and to separate these would involve excessive fragmentation. We hope that the order adopted may have produced both a readable book and one in which, using the index, readers can easily turn up either, say, early Christian remains in Crete or Mycenaean at Athens.

The spelling of Greek names is a subject on which any form of consistency leads to some intolerable results. We have in general transliterated, keeping the more euphonious endings *-os, -on*, rather than the heavy Latin *-us, -um*; but we have left the familiar 'c' (Gk. 'k') in such names as Pericles, Socrates; and Athens, Corinth, Rhodes are English words, as is, unfortunately, Byzant*ium*. We do not use 'i' for long 'e' in ancient names; the ancient *eta* (written H) was a lengthened *epsilon* (E), pronounced like the vowel in *bay*, or French *è*; and with this vowel Socrates would have written his name. Imperial Athens did not use *eta* at all. Modern Greek, which pronounces six different ancient vowels and dipthongs all as *i* (as in mach*i*ne), has profoundly changed its pronunciation, though Greek school-masters hotly deny this.

Conversely, we do not use letter 'z', foreign to the Latin alphabet, in words of Latin derivation, *e.g.* 'colonise', 'civilise'; though it is acceptable in Greek words, such as 'emphasize'. Similarly, 'connexion' (from Latin *-nexum*) is correct, as is 'correction' (from *-rectum*).

For personal guidance on sites treated in this book, we would particularly thank Homer Thompson and Judith Binder in Athens; A. H. S. Megaw in many Byzantine churches; Charles Williams at Corinth; S. Dakaris at the Oracle of the Dead on the Acheron; the late S. Marinatos at Marathon; Peter Green at Marathon and Salamis; and the last, and also W. K. Pritchett and E. Vanderpool, for gifts of their works on the topography of Persian War battlefields. But it is literally impossible to thank adequately all those who have helped us in our travels. We remember particularly the British School of Archaeology at Athens, repeatedly our secure base; its directors and (one name) Jane Rabnett, its secretary for many years; scholars of the American, French and German Schools; and numberless Greeks, from ministers and renowned archaeologists to site-guardians who know and love their antiquities, and the people who in remote places have shown us the immemorial Greek hospitality.

A. R. Burn
Mary W. Burn
Oxford, 1979

I Historical Outline

Greece, said Aristotle, is geographically intermediate, between Europe, apparently incapable of civilisation, and south-west Asia, where only the King of Persia was fully a free man; and the Mean, or medium, to him was best. Modern geologists add that the Aegean basin is a slab of the earth's crust which has sunk and tipped, leaving only a rim (the Greek peninsula and Crete) and mountain tops (the other islands) above sea-level. Greece can therefore support a population, on its small though fertile plains, only much smaller than that of the adjacent 'slab' of Asia Minor; a fact which affects the whole of Greek history. Greater wealth must be found overseas, by trade or colonisation; and when adjacent powers in Italy or Asia are strong, Greece is threatened. Persia attempted conquest; Rome, the Franks and Turkey achieved it.

On the other hand, Greece enjoys, with its variety of scenery, clear air and summer heat tempered by north winds, an intensely stimulating environment; and when free, three times it has produced great art: the bronze-age Minoan–Mycenaean, the Classical and the Byzantine; all completely different, all unique. This is not to assert geographical determinism. There is no evident economic reason why bronze-age Cyprus and Sicily produced nothing to approach the art of Crete. Three times, groups of people *invented* and larger groups carried on and perfected great art; and once, contemporarily with the first philosophers of India and China and with the Hebrew prophets, Greece produced a literature and philosophy ancestral to all that of the modern west. This is why the classical age (in the wider sense, from Homer to the Stoics, 8–3CC BC) is rightly considered the most important of all.

Prehistory

Man, the 'naked ape', was from the first, it appears, a swimmer, and early a raft- or boat-maker; and by 7000 BC, before they even had agriculture, hunter-fishers in Argolis were fetching obsidian, volcanic glass for knife-blades, from Melos island, eighty miles oversea. But Aegean fine art does not antedate *c.* 3000, with the marble figurines of the Cyclades and stone bowls in Crete. In Crete after *c.* 2650 large houses, dominating settlements, appear, developing by 2000 into palaces; and the maritime Minoan civilisation (named by Sir Arthur Evans, after the legendary King Minos of Knossos), with its gay, naturalistic art, develops with increasing elaboration down to *c.* 1400. After *c.* 1600, Cretan culture was adopted and adapted by warlike Greek (Indo-European-speaking) chiefs on the mainland; and their civilisation, called Mycenaean after their richest settlement (Homer's 'Mykenai rich in gold'), spread widely. Mycenaeans probably occupied Knossos *c.* 1450; they traded with northern Greece and, via the Lipari Islands, with Italy; they were in touch with Egypt, like the Cretans before them, and with the Hittite empire in Asia Minor. But frequent wars strained their resources; the palace-people probably lost the loyalty of their exploited peasants, and could no longer rely on them; and despite the impressive fortifications of Mycenae and its neighbour, Tiryns, their palaces and others perished by violence *c.* 1200 BC and after.

Thucydides, who may be right though disbelieved by some modern scholars, speaks here of an invasion and takeover by the Dorians, rougher Greeks from the north, led by exiled Mycenaean princes, the Children of Herakles. Dorians in historic times did occupy precisely the chief centres of the old civilisation, including Crete. They were distinguished by their Doric dialects, with north-western connexions, and by the articulation of their people everywhere into the same three Doric tribes. Meanwhile the west coast of Asia Minor was occupied by Greeks: according to Greek tradition, by refugees, many of the expeditions being organized by Athens, which, alone on the mainland, had outridden the storm. It is a fact that the Ionic dialects of the central part of the coast and adjacent islands resembled that of Athens, and that the city-state populations, at least in several cases, were articulated, as at Athens, into four Ionic tribes.

A turning-point in the history of the impoverished post-migration Greek world comes when, perhaps first at Athens before 1000 BC, the debased 'sub-Mycenaean' style of pottery-painting gives place rather suddenly to a new and fine abstract art called Protogeometric, very Greek in its sense of pure form. This develops by the 8C into mature Geometric, in which, still with great precision, no square inch is left undecorated. In some of the latest and finest vases, which were set up as grave-markers, little, stylized human figures appear: funerals, with mourners and chariots in procession, and occasionally a sea-fight. In this age comes also a major development: the adoption of the Alphabet, with the Phoenician names of its letters, into a Greek society long illiterate; and in Ionia, the production of the two great epics attributed to one Homer, in which, though burial customs and many features of daily life are those of the poet's own day, the geographical settings of the stories, orally handed down, are those of the Mycenaean world, before Ionia was founded—and remarkably accurate. Homer sings (and writes?) for a confident audience, in which tales of the gods can actually be used for comic relief; a society in which later materialistic philosophy would be possible. Historic Greece starts its career already sceptical, at least in some upper-class circles; individualistic, and detribalised.

The rise and fall of classical Greece: *c.* 730–330 BC

Population had increased again, from a low level; and guided by merchants who had gone west in search of metals, states short of land at home poured out thousands of colonists to south Italy and Sicily, an America to Greece's Europe. Aristocratic governments encouraged it, to allay peasant discontent; but when the practice developed of importing food instead of exporting hungry men, the rise of trading classes led, in the maritime states, to a crop of revolutions. The 7–6CC are called the Archaic period, in contrast to the following Classical (5–4CC); also the Age of the Tyrants, revolutionary leaders, usually dissident aristocrats them-selves, who broke the power of traditional governments, though democracy was *not* usually the sequel to their fall. In art, the Geometric styles give place to Orientalising: opulent, curvilinear, with scenes from myth, beasts real and fabu-lous, and vegetable filling-ornament derived from Assyrian textiles. In literature, songs and personal poetry begin—not, surely, to be composed, but to be written down and preserved: Archilochos, Alkaios, Sappho. Monumental stone sculpture begins, influenced by what Greeks had seen in Egypt. Brightly painted, it would have given to Greek sanctuaries a, to us, startlingly colourful appearance. The agrarian rituals of Demeter and Dionysos, givers of bread and wine, 'come into town', and inspire new religious ideas of immortality, heaven and hell; and simultaneously in Ionia the first 'physicists' or natural philosophers dispense with mythology and dare to express rationalist thought. Colonisation extends in the west, and also opens up new sources of food and raw materials in the Black Sea.

This age of confident growth was ended by the rise of the Persian empire, and by Carthage, which united western Phoenician colonists to check Greek expan-sion. Ionia suffered irreparable damage in a brave six-year revolt against Persia (499–4); but Athens beat off an attack at Marathon (490), and the massively organized invasion of Xerxes (480–79) was beaten at Salamis and Plataia by the southern Greeks, led by Sparta, and the great new Athenian navy, brain-child of the democrat Themistocles. This achievement provided Greece with a national epic, told, in prose, by Herodotos, and set the stage for a tragic sequel.

Mountain-girdled Sparta, when others colonised oversea, had expanded by conquering the rich, low-lying plain of Messenia, across her western mountain range. The Messenians became Helots, serfs tied to the land and ruthlessly taxed in kind; but they never forgot that they had been free. Already lords of thousands of serfs in Laconia, as well as non-voting freemen in outlying villages who swelled their army, the Spartiate ruling class was now very rich; but with an irreconcilable 'Ireland' two days' march away, its members lived in perpetual anxiety. To secure their hold on their subjects, they revived or preserved an archaic military form of society, dining in their army 'messes' and living frugally; and they looked askance at any growth of democracy, though they co-operated with Athens against the Persian invasion.

Athens, largely through sensible concessions by her aristocracy, had come through the 'age of the tyrants' with little bloodshed, and emerged with a prosperous economy, a teeming population, and a modernised constitution; though the Areopagus, a council of ex-officers of state, of the richer classes, retained a veto on legislation until *c.* 462. After the defeat of Xerxes, when Sparta thought that the newly liberated Asia Minor Greeks could not be protected, Athens took the lead in doing this, and organized them in the League of Delos (Apollo's sacred islet), with contributions for common defence. The League became an Athenian empire, and about 455 Athens seemed set fair to become the super-power of all Greece, with the support of local democratic parties. But a large League fleet, sent to support a rebellion in Egypt against Persia even while Athens was at war in Greece, was trapped in the Nile and lost (454); mainland allies broke away, preferring independence to Athenian-backed democracy; and though Athens kept her Delian League, she lost that too in the Peloponnesian War of 431–404; once more, through sending a great expedition far afield while enemies were still powerful in Greece—this time to Sicily, in 415–13.

Athens failed to unify Greece; but, as her great liberal leader Pericles (d. 429) claimed, she was 'an education' to it. The Parthenon and the great ceremonial gateway to the Acropolis were built, mostly in time of peace, 447–31. The latter was a new departure, the first of many great colonnaded secular buildings; and the movement that led every Greek city of any pride to give itself a planned and monumental town-centre begins here. Only Sparta chose to remain an overgrown village. The detailed local-government regulations necessary for a city, a more prosaic by-product of civic growth, were also first worked out in Athens, and much copied elsewhere. In literature, Tragedy was the gift to the world of the imperial democracy. Other cities had developed Dionysiac drama; only Athens made it serious; and while three great men wrote all the thirty-one tragedies that survive out of hundreds, one must remember that a dramatist needs an audience. The great movement spans almost exactly the age of the empire, of confidence, when all things seemed possible. The oldest extant play, Aeschylus' *Persians* (472), does not even treat of a mythological subject, but of the repulse of Xerxes. What men living had done had no need to fear comparison with Homer. Aeschylus himself had fought in the war. Young Pericles, the man of the future, paid for the production. At the latter end, Sophocles and Euripides, the other two of the Great Three, both died in 405, just before the empire ended in irretrievable defeat; and though tragedy was still written, it was felt, even at the time, that it was an anticlimax. One may feel the same about later Greek history in general. As Pericles had once said of young men killed in a war, the spring is gone from the year.

Art follows a strikingly parallel course. Sculpture of the early 5C, contemporary with early, lost works of Aeschylus, is in a severe style, while developing towards humanism. The 'archaic smile' disappears; life is serious. In mid-century the Parthenon sculptures, by several hands, said to have been directed by Pheidias, whose own masterpieces are known only through copies, achieve a 'Sophoclean' perfection of humanist idealism. In later work, as in Euripides, there is a descent or development into greater realism, culminating in the 4C, just when tragedy died and the drama was best represented by the social New Comedy of Menander. In vase-painting (to the ancients, merely a poor relation of major painting, of which little survives), early 5C Red-Figure, which was exported even to Phoenicia, Carthage and Etruria, also has its 'severe style'. Full classical mastery is attained in the generation beginning *c.* 470–60. After *c.* 425, in the war years,

Athens: the Acropolis from the S.W.

there is a movement towards floridity or mere prettiness; and by 400 the spirit has gone out of these workshops too. It was noticed at the time. Attic vase-painting lost its foreign markets, and some of these (e.g. in South Italy) developed rather nasty florid styles of their own.

4C Athenians felt that they had lost some of the spirit of the brave days of old. Demosthenes, the war-hawk orator (son of an arms-manufacturer, 384–322), explicitly says so. But the tragic history of the imperial democracy left much food for thought. This is the background to the work of Plato (428–348), who had fought in the last years of the Peloponnesian War, and could not forgive the democracy for losing chances of peace, fighting on to disaster, and especially for executing, in 399, his master Socrates, whose self-taught dialectic had deflated alike pretentious rhetoricians, the unco' pious, and members of the democratic establishment in the days of its pride. (Plato, to do him justice, makes it quite plain that Socrates could have escaped; but, considering that he had a mission from God to make Athens face facts, he would not go!)

Plato's Dialogues give a portrait of Socrates in action, and expose popular fallacies; *he does not claim more for them than that*—as his admirers have often forgotten. His deepest convictions were mystical, not communicable in words; though a disciple, after long living together, might 'catch' the flame. Even his doctrine of Forms or Ideas (meaning ideal *species*, supposed to be eternal) as the ultimate reality—evolved in opposition to materialism—is provisional; in *Parmenides*, he himself criticised it—and left the dialogue unfinished. Politically, being anti-democratic, he appears as an extreme reactionary, proposing government by a dedicated and puritanical *élite*; but his picture of the typical revolutions of a class-state, from military aristocracy through plutocracy to democracy and finally despotism, in his *Republic* (viii–ix) is a passage which, from his impressionable schooldays, deeply influenced the young classical scholar Karl Marx. Plato's disciple Aristotle (384–22) pointed out that his Decline of the Class State was too schematic; history is full of exceptions. Aristotle himself formulated the rules of the logic or dialectic, which Socrates had already employed in argument, and set in order the science of his day; but his detailed study of the (city-)state was delivered in lectures (it is ironic) just when such small, independent republics were being left no longer viable by the rise of a superpower: the work of Philip of Macedonia, who had once employed Aristotle to tutor his son Alexander.

Ancient Greece never achieved unity in freedom. Sparta, victorious over Athens in 404, tyrannized over her late allies, ended a war with Persia by ignominiously ceding Ionia (387), and then, in 371, unexpectedly suffered a major defeat by Thebes. Athens reconstituted a rather half-hearted naval league, with safeguards against imperialism. Thebes liberated Messenia, halving Sparta's resources, but then proved unable to dominate even her own neighbour, Phokis, which used the treasures of Delphi to hire mercenaries; and it was this quarrel which let Philip enter central Greece, as liberator of the holy place.

When Philip was murdered in 336 (probably by an agent of his estranged wife, in the supposed interests of her son Alexander), he was supreme in Greece,

Captain-General of a Hellenic League aimed at an attack on Persia, and his advanced troops had already crossed into Asia. Alexander, as the world knows, after a year spent in suppressing rebellions—he destroyed Thebes as a frightful object-lesson—took up the project and in ten years carried his arms to the Indus, founding Greek colonies from Alexandria in Egypt to a group guarding Persia's north-east frontier in Afghanistan. The dispersal of Greek man-power so far afield was, in the long run, a disaster; it might have been better if Philip, who would only have been fifty-eight when Alexander died, had lived, and been content with a more realistic frontier, perhaps at the Euphrates.

The Hellenistic Age and the Roman Conquest

When Alexander, who while continually risking his life had never provided for the succession, died of a fever and probably the after-effects of his many wounds, in 323, his generals held together just long enough to suppress a rebellion in Greece. Their Levantine fleets crushed the last Athenian navy off the island of Amorgos, a little-mentioned decisive battle. But they were soon fighting each other; and a generation of wars left the empire divided between the Ptolemies in Egypt, Antigonids, descended from two other generals, in Macedonia, the House of Seleukos in the rump of the Persian empire, and several secondary kingdoms in northern Asia Minor. One of these, Pergamon, prided itself especially on friendship to Athens. Athens, after buying-out a Macedonian garrison-commander when Macedonia was invaded by barbarians in 229, renounced foreign policy and became what it remained for 750 years, the premier university-city of the classical world; the city of the philosophers, where the long-lived schools of Plato (the Academy) and Aristotle (the Lykeion or Lyceum) were joined by others. For long the most influential were those of Epicurus (Epikouros; 341–270) and Zenon, a Phoenician from Cyprus (335–263). The latter were called the Stoics, after the Painted Stoa or colonnade, where Zenon discoursed in his younger days, when he was too poor to hire a place of his own. Neither probed the secrets of the universe; both adopted Ionian, pre-Socratic scientific theories as a background to what interested them and their hearers; ethics, with special reference to how a free man should live, in the shadow of the superpowers. Quietists and activists, they were still arguing when St Paul visited Athens about AD 50.

This age after Alexander is called Hellenistic, the age of the Hellenizers, not necessarily of Greek descent (e.g. Zenon), who adopted Greek culture. Great scientific work was done at Alexandria, where the Ptolemies founded their own Institute for Advanced Study; though moral philosophy preferred the free air of Athens. In Greece politics, aimed primarily at freedom from Macedonia, produced two federal states, transcending the city-state; but too late. These were the Aitolian League, centred in formerly backward mountain country in the north, and the Achaian League, which added Arcadia and Messenia to Achaia proper (the north coast of the Peloponnese) and, with Corinth for its chief city, dominated the south. Unfortunately, they were always hostile to each other. Sparta, under two progressive kings, carried through the revolution that she had resisted

300 years before and, freeing helots and redistributing land, emerged once more as a major force; again, too late. For fear of revolution, the Achaians called in the Macedonians, from whom they themselves had liberated the Peloponnese; and together they crushed the revolution in 222.

The Hellenistic Age ends under the domination of Rome. This giant state, head of a league covering all central Italy, inevitably clashed with the Greek colonies in the south; these also clashed with each other, and some sought Roman protection. Pyrrhos, King of Epeiros (north-west Greece), of Alexander's mother's family, thought to build up a western empire by protecting the other side; but 'Pyrrhic' victories (280–79) drained his manpower, while heavier losses did not exhaust that of Rome. This pattern was repeated on a more terrible scale in Hannibal's invasion of Italy (218–202); that war left even victorious Rome's manpower grievously thinned; and Hannibal had made an alliance with Macedonia. Rome parried that threat by sending modest support to the Aitolians; but the traumatic experience seems to have left her with an irrational fear of Hellenistic kings, which found expression in 'preventive' wars. Macedonia was humbled in 197, and Greece liberated, quite genuinely, from all foreign garrisons; but the Aitolians, dissatisfied with Rome's settlement, called in the great Seleukid Antiochos III, who had restored his house's authority over Iran. He in turn was routed, and deprived of his territory in Asia Minor, in favour of Pergamon (188).

Greece was still free. The following years saw Athens adorned with buildings donated, in symbolic gestures, by Hellenistic kings. But both kings and Greek politicians tended to seek advantage by complaining of their rivals to the super-power. Complaints by Eumenes of Pergamon, of Macedonian provocation in Greece, led to Rome's breaking up Macedonia into four republics (167), a 'liberation' for which the Macedonians were not as grateful as Rome expected. At the same time, in order to collect a bonus for the soldiers while treating the Macedonians gently, the Romans sold into slavery the whole population of central Epeiros, which had been no more than friendly to Macedonia in the late war; about 150,000 souls. They encouraged their friends in Aitolia to massacre their enemies; and they interned as suspects 1000 prominent men of the Achaian League, most of whom died in Italy. The survivors were released only in 150, largely through the mediation of one of their number: Polybios, son of a General of the League, and the last great Greek historian. He had been taken into the house of Scipio Aemilianus (son of Aemilius the conqueror of Macedonia, adopted by a cousin), and in his circle came to admire the strict honesty of the best Romans and their genuine devotion to Greek culture. But he was powerless to avert catastrophe.

There was much social unrest in Greece, where the gap between rich and poor had widened, ever since Alexander and his successors had dispersed the huge Persian bullion reserve in wages to mercenaries, producing a kind of inflation. A clamour for cancellation of debts, which both Polybios and the Roman Senate regarded as revolutionary, embittered Achaian politics and made parties more extreme. The popular party, of whose leaders Polybios has a low opinion, also tried to pursue an independent foreign policy; and when Rome forbade them to coerce Sparta, which had been forced into the League in 192 and wished to leave it, they went to war and invaded central Greece too. This finally brought the Romans down upon them. Rome had just had a final Macedonian war, when the country rose under an alleged son of its last king. She now placed Macedonia under direct rule, dissolved the Achaian League and, as an act of deliberate terror, destroyed Corinth and sold its people into slavery (146). This is the end of independent ancient Greek history. The city-states, weakened by war and emigration, still administered their parochial affairs; but everyone knew that to attempt anything 'revolutionary' was to court the fate of Corinth. The depression of the poor continued.

The Greek world was now infested by Italian business men, Roman citizens or 'protected persons', and sometimes agents for rich senators, who were not allowed to engage in trade, but often lent money under cover, at exorbitant interest, to Greeks who needed it to pay indemnities and, in Asia, direct taxation. In 133 Attalos III of Pergamon, childless and disliking his relations, left his kingdom by will to the Roman republic. If he hoped thus to secure orderly protection, it was in vain. The new Province of Asia, consolidated only after a fierce rebellion, was subjected, by a move in Roman party politics, to the iniquitous system of 'farming' the taxes, by which syndicates of rich Romans bid for the privilege of collecting them. The winners paid a lump sum to the Treasury and then set out to make a profit, with Roman troops to keep order. After a generation of this, when Mithradates, King of Pontus, whose kingdom was next in line for penetration, invaded Asia during a Roman civil war, the Greeks there massacred all the Italians they could catch. Mithradates' fleet also sacked Delos, which Rome, in a deliberate move to weaken Rhodes, the last independent Greek seapower, had made a protected free port. It became a horrible slave-market, claiming a capacity to handle 10,000 bodies in a day; and the elegant, mosaic-floored houses, prominent among the visible remains there, are largely those of Italians who throve on it. Peninsular Greece also welcomed Mithradates; even Athens, which Rome had treated as an ally. The result was a siege and sack (86) by Sulla. Many works of art went to join those of Corinth and scores of other cities at Rome. The famous Piraeus Bronzes in the National Museum, found together but of various dates, may have been saved for Greece and for posterity at this time, when a warehouse collapsed over them.

Greece under the Empire, c. 50 BC–AD 276

There were still the Caesarian civil wars to come, thrice fought out in Greece (48, 42, 31). In the last, Greeks were mobilised to carry their own corn when mules ran short, to feed Antony's forces, blockaded by the Caesarians in the Ambrakian Gulf. (The famous Battle of Actium was a sortie, by which the leaders escaped without their army.) But with the Caesars there came at least better order. Julius Caesar in 46 had refounded Corinth as a colony of army veterans. Growing rapidly more Greek, this became the Corinth of St Paul. Caesar Augustus and his general and son-in-law Agrippa gave Athens a new look, making it, as we shall see, more 'safely' academic. Students from all the Roman world came there for higher education. Rhodes and Greek Marseilles, both also nominally independent enclaves in the empire, were other well-regarded seats of learning. The great sanctuaries, especially Delphi and Olympia, where the Games (long since professionalised) were still held, attracted tourists. So did Sparta, preserved as a museum piece—to watch the celebrated whipping contests. Nero visited Greece in AD 67, raced at Olympia in his own chariot, crashed, and was given first prize 'for his courage'. He started work on a Corinth canal, and thought of liberating Greece (the Province of Achaia since 27 BC); but his fall in AD 68 ended all that.

Most of the other cities (Thessalonica in the north was a conspicuous exception) had sunk to country market towns. Plutarch, who lived from before AD 50 till after 120, a country gentleman of Chaironeia in Boiotia, educated (of course) at Athens, and a priest and functionary at Delphi, doubts, in a dialogue set there, whether all Greece could now raise 3000 armoured troops. This means young men of the landowning class; landless peasants did not count. So 3000 is an estimate of the number of landed families; some of them, we know from other sources, were enormously rich. The Roman peace meant that the normal economic tendency of the rich to grow richer was never reversed by political action. With mineral wealth becoming exhausted and much emigration, the country was in decline. The traveller Pausanias, fifty years later, found at Patrai a population two-thirds female, mostly textile-workers, and was embarrassed at the advances made to him. Plutarch and his friends discuss whether the whole world is not running down. Many ancient oracles had ceased to function; the dialogue is called *On the Defunct Oracles*, and Plutarch piously suggests that the divine presence had withdrawn from them simply because there were not enough people to need them.

The second century AD saw the last major building in ancient Greece. The emperor Hadrian (d. 138), a sincere philhellene, built especially in his beloved Athens; and after him Tiberius Claudius Herodes (101–177), an Athenian of vast landed wealth, whose father had already been consul (equivalent to a peerage), adorned the historic sites of Greece with his benefactions, as though trying to compensate in stone for the social vacuum which his class had created. He was the most prominent Greek of the Antonine Age, and typical of it. During his lifetime Pausanias, a Greek of Ionia, travelled meticulously to every corner of the central and southern Greek mainland and wrote his account of the antiquities, some already ruined but mostly in good order. His 'guidebook' has been of enormous value to classical archaeologists, enabling them to identify what stood in hundreds of places where there are now only foundations. He saw the buildings, and the statues, except those already carried off by Romans, just before the decline, which had already worried Plutarch, developed into a crash. The wars of rival emperors that spatter imperial history from 192–284 were followed by barbarian invasions. Athens, Corinth, Argos, Sparta and many island cities were sacked by the Heruli, a Gothic tribe from south Russia which had taken to the sea. A shrunken Athens with its 'university' revived; but the year 276 marks an epoch.

Christian Greece

Christianity, intermittently persecuted, was the new force in the world. In Greece, the generation in which the scales of power tipped in its favour is represented best at Thessalonica. The triumphal arch there, sculptured to celebrate a great victory of Galerius, fiercest of the persecutors, over the revived Persian empire in 298, adjoined a vast palace complex; but before 400 the great Rotunda, which he may have intended for his mausoleum, became a Christian church. So did, at an uncertain date, the Parthenon.

Christians took over many Greek temples; but these were not well suited for congregational worship; they were simply houses of the god and of the cult-statue; at a Greek sacrifice, the crowd mustered outside. To make room for a congregation to hear the Word and receive the sacraments, the Christians adopted the pillared-hall form of a Hellenistic-to-Roman law-court, *basilica*, meaning a 'royal [court]'. Hundreds of such early Christian basilicas of the 4–5CC were built, even in little Greece; some, as at Lechaion near Corinth, very large. Usually little of them remains above the foundations; though at Thessalonica one has survived (for a time, a mosque) until today, and another, over 100 × nearly 30m, burnt down in 1917, has been rebuilt on its ancient plan. Many are fairly large, even in country places. For a movement that cared for the common people, people were still there. The depopulation lamented by Plutarch can be misunderstood.

The Dark Age in Greece begins in the 6C. The emperor Justinian in 529 closed the heathen schools of Athens, another epoch-making date. He also fortified first Thermopylai and then the Isthmus of Corinth against the invading Slavs; but his system of static defence was nowhere effective, and through the 7–8CC the peninsula, the province of Hellas, was, except for Athens and a few coastal strong-points, in Slav hands and out of imperial control. Heathen, and perhaps culturally on a level with the first English in Britain, the Slavs built nothing durable and ruined much, especially the rural basilica-churches; though their virtual disappearance is probably due to later 'quarrying'. Only in the 9C did the empire regain control. The emperors then forced much re-colonisation by Greeks from other areas. Under the Slavs, the local Chronicle of Monemvasia assures us that no 'Roman', i.e. subject of the empire, could set foot in the interior of the Peloponnese; but, certainly in the southern Mani peninsula, in Tsakonia in the east, and probably in many mountainous areas, Greek villagers did survive, with the same toughness and capacity for disappearing and reappearing alive as in other bad times. After the reconquest, the Slavs were (very slowly in some parts) pacified, Christianized and Hellenized; and Slavonic speech has disappeared south of Macedonia, leaving only a scatter of place-names, which Greek governments in the last hundred years have been assiduously labouring to eradicate from the maps.

The 7–8CC thus form a chasm between the early Christian Roman period and the Byzantine—a name commonly given to the culture of the continuing empire, whose own historians, writing purist Greek as much like Thucydides as they could, called Constantinople by its old name, Byzantion. Byzantine church-building was introduced into Greece ready-made, as it had developed in the east, normally with a cross-in-square plan, a central dome, and sometimes, especially later, four subsidiary domes on the corners; sometimes even two more on the narthex, an enclosed west porch. The earliest such church to be exactly dated, by a building inscription, is that at Skripou (Orchomenos; AD 874). The three greatest (described later), all monastic churches, belong to the 11C, which saw the climax of Byzantine grandeur and the beginning of its decline. Their mosaics, still splendid in the fragments that remain, are probably the work of metropolitan teams of artists, sent by emperors. Few of the little churches, sometimes the thank-offerings of prosperous families for benefits received, can be dated closely, and most are probably 13C or later. They imitate larger churches, sometimes in almost doll's house fashion; but their charm is all their own.

Another class of building, conspicuous in many Greek landscapes, commemorates the aftermath of the disastrous Fourth Crusade of 1204, when Frankish knights borne in Venetian ships, taking advantage of a Byzantine struggle for the throne, achieved an end long dreamt-of by the Normans in Italy: to sack Constantinople and plunder its empire. Castles, of indifferent masonry except when they are Venetian, and usually losing rather than gaining impressiveness on closer inspection, crown many ancient Greek acropoles and other heights. Often, as on Acrocorinth and Acronauplia, one can see in the foot of the wall the much finer, ancient masonry; and re-used classical blocks are often in evidence as corner stones. One tower on Paros island, run up in haste, uses the material of a whole Greek temple. Yet the knights seem to have caught the imagination of their Greek subjects. A kind of epic, the *Chronicle of the Morea* (the Peloponnese), tells their story in vernacular Greek and, unexpectedly, very much in their favour; it was ever a weakness of the empire that its depressed primary producers often preferred invaders to the local tax-man and landlord.

Nevertheless, Frankish power was unstable. The emperor Michael VIII Palaiologos, who from Asia Minor recaptured Constantinople in 1261, also recovered Laconia; and Mistra, a Frankish hill-fort replacing Sparta in the plain, became the last Byzantine provincial capital. Mistra was a centre of that Palaiologan art and scholarship which flourished so amazingly in the last century of the empire and influenced the Italian Renaissance; and from it the governors or Despots of the Morea campaigned against the Franks. But it was not until 1430 that the peninsula was wholly cleared; and by that time the Turks had reached the Danube, encircled Constantinople and taken (1429) Thessalonica. Mistra fell to them in 1460, one year before the last Byzantine outpost in distant Trebizond.

For events in later history, see date chart, page 275.

II Prehistoric

1 Dawn in the Islands

It begins in the islands: that is, a characteristically Greek culture, maritime from the first and soon artistic. On the mainland, in the Chalkidic Peninsula, Dr Aris Poulianos discovered in 1976 in the stalactite cave of Petralona a skeleton, embedded in stalagmitic deposit, some 400,000 years old; the oldest human remains yet found in Europe. Fire, moreover, was being used at Petralona for ages before that. This great discovery concerns the whole history of Man, rather than that of Greece as a separate area; and the cave, where work continues, is not on view. In times modern by comparison, after 8000 BC, the first European mixed farming, with its near-eastern grain-crops and legumes, sheep and goats, seems to have spread from the Bosporus into Bulgaria, south-west to northern Greece and north-west to the Danube. This too is part of the common heritage, the economic foundation of Europe. But evidence of Aegean navigation comes from much further south; and the first direct evidence is again from the mainland.

On the south coast of Argolis, north-west of Porto Kheli (the classical Halieis), the Franchthi Cave was for millennia the home of mesolithic people, fishers and food-gatherers. Here American archaeologists discovered among the food débris of *c.* 8000 BC the bones of large fish, which must have been caught well out at sea, and then, sensationally, blades of the volcanic glass, obsidian. Obsidian, formed by rapid cooling of viscous lava, is relatively rare, even among volcanic rocks. The nearest source of it to Franchthi is Melos island, 120km south-east across open sea, or further if the sea passages are kept shorter by 'island-hopping'; and analysis of trace-elements confirms that the obsidian at Franchthi is actually from that source. This is the earliest direct evidence in the world of deliberate and repeated seafaring. With Melos, then, we may start our survey of historic Greek places.

MELOS

Melos, famed for a shocking tragedy in classical times and for the recovery, in serio-comic circumstances, of a famous statue in AD 1819, is more important in prehistory, beginning with the startlingly early export of its obsidian.

Melos is the south-westernmost of the central Aegean islands, now the Province of the Cyclades; though the ancients called it and the other isles outside the 'circle' of the dozen Cyclades proper the Sporades or 'scattered isles'. Starkly volcanic, it is not one of the most beautiful islands. Its central bay, an unrivalled harbour, of local importance in many wars, is itself a crater, flooded and broken open to the west, like that of Thera but much ólder; its convulsions were before any human presence. Its mouth is dominated on the south side by the grim, black cone of a later volcano, now long dormant. On the north, Plaka, the chief village, partly on the site of the classical city, stands above cliffs broken by steep gullies with paths; the only road for wheeled traffic descends to Adhamas ('adamant'!) further inside the bay. Probably the classical city had a small harbour, now silted up, at the foot of one of the gullies. Mines and quarries for various minerals (sulphur, barium, kaolin, alum, etc.) scar the landscape. But, with an area of $c.$ 160km^2, the island had enough arable land to support by 3000 BC some thousands of neolithic farmers, at a time when its only visible export was still the much-desired obsidian, found at two places called Nychia ('finger nails' and then, secondarily, 'gun-flints') west of Adhamas and near the east coast.

A recent British archaeological survey has confirmed that neolithic pottery is to be found at many points adjacent to possible arable land; i.e. the population, whose huts have perished without trace, lived in scattered farmsteads. Then, some time after 3000, there was an 'urban revolution' when some potentate, having perhaps 'cornered' the obsidian trade, caused people to move into town, walking out from it (the distances are not intolerable) to till their fields.

The new settlement was at a place called Phylakope. The official modern Greek transliteration is Filakopi; the first British excavators of 1896 adopted a hybrid form, Phylakopi, no doubt to avoid having it rhymed with 'telescope', and this has become the established spelling. The site, marked by a massive, much later, bronze-age defensive wall, appears an odd one to choose; defensible, on top of an 18m cliff, descending to a beach on the east; but it is a stony beach, unsuitable for drawing up boats, and the whole site is exposed to the often fierce north winds. The explanation is that in over 4000 years the coast has altered considerably. The cliff itself has been eroded, carrying away probably at least half of the settlement. The same *may* have happened to some sheltering headland to the north; some rocks, out at sea, are no doubt the remains of formerly more extensive islets; and the beach, certainly extending further out, may for all we know have been sandy. The advantage over a site on the great inland bay was that ships from the Cyclades or Argolis could be seen approaching. The very name, which may be ancient, means something like 'sentry-post'. The chief who founded Phylakopi knew his business, which was to keep the obsidian trade in his own hands.

The nearest quarry was an hour's walk to the south, and not far from the east coast. There, large nuggets were plentiful, and innumerable splinters and useless knobs, struck off, show that they were roughly trimmed on the spot, to reduce weight. But the workshop where the tools—razor-sharp, straight blades and some arrowheads—were made was inside the settlement, just inside the west corner of the massive wall and perhaps also of a slighter predecessor. Fortunately for us, the sea has just not yet brought down the cliff at this corner; and on its very edge, to this day or at least within recent years, a small 'snowdrift' of spoilt or even quite serviceable blades marks the place where the skilled knappers practised their craft. The chief skill lay in shaping a core, a few inches in each dimension, with a

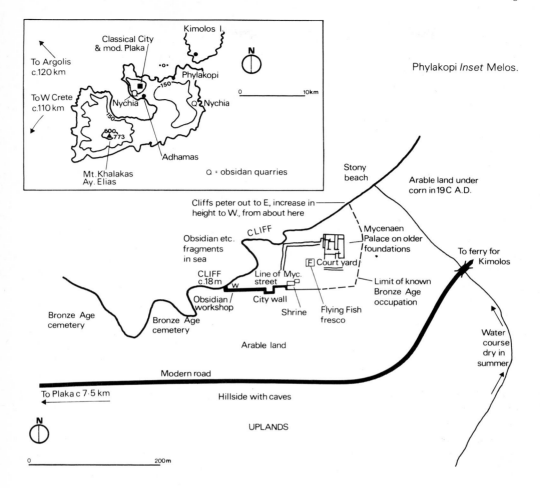

Phylakopi *Inset* Melos.

flat top at right-angles to its sides. This done, the knapper, very likely using a wooden mallet, as in flint-knapping, could strike off blades from successive corners at twenty to the minute, until the core was narrowed to a mere stick and a new one was needed. Free trade in obsidian could have made it cheap; but it was only to be had (short, at least, of the Lipari islands north of Sicily) in Melos; and controllers of a rare commodity have seldom needed book-learning to teach them the advantage of monopoly. Hence perhaps even the gathering of the whole population of Melos into one settlement.

Partly at least thanks to its unique mineral, Melos, though outlying, had its share in the Cycladic culture of the third millennium, with its agreeable and characteristic pottery and (a unique 'hallmark') its marble figurines; some perhaps idols, others, such as two fantastically skilfully-wrought musicians from Keros, south of Naxos, certainly not. The best were made of Parian marble and smoothed down with Naxian emery. Hundreds have been found, largely in graves, in the inner Cyclades, and scores (at least) forged in modern times. A few found their way to Melos in the way of trade or, in the ancient manner, 'gift-exchange'. Other Melian imports included early copper daggers; perhaps also objects of gold and silver, now being mined in the Cyclades, but these have not survived.

In the second millennium, with the rise of the Cretan palaces, the princely culture of that great island overtook and surpassed that of the Cyclades, which becomes relatively provincial; while the prestige of Cretan art is shown by exports. At Phylakopi the larger houses too were now rebuilt in a Cretan style, with internal columns making possible wider rooms; and their walls were deco-rated, as in Crete, with frescoes, often of marine life. Many scattered fragments were found; and of one work, enough to give it fame: the Flying-Fish fresco (National Museum, Athens). It seems quite possible that Cretan princes took over the lordship of Melos; but if there was anything like a Minoan palace, its lay-out is obscured by later buildings. For after 1400, and after another appar-ently rather abrupt change, we find another lordly building-style, mainland Mycenaean. Of the 'Mycenaean' townplan, with straight though narrow streets or passages between the houses, a good deal can be made out, including, at the east end of the rising ground above the slope down to the beach, a typical Mycenaean chief's house. The central *megaron* or hall is entered from the south, through a porch of its full width, from an open court, beyond which a street led off, parallel to the town wall; and the hall is surrounded on the other three sides by passages and rooms, probably stores for the lord's heaped-up wealth. The whole reproduces the plan of the grander palace at Pylos. Below its floor, a tablet with five signs in the older Cretan Linear A script was found in 1974.

Further west, just inside the walls and near the old obsidian-knappers' work-shop, renewed British excavations in 1974–7 discovered a Mycenaean shrine-complex resembling that found by the Americans on Keos. It may have been in use for 200 years, pre-1300 to pre-1100, restored after an earthquake latish in its life. Special finds indicating its sacred character (not yet on view, but destined for the island's museum) included eleven seals, fragments of ostrich-egg, a small human face, *repoussé* in sheet-gold, c. 3cm wide (did it decorate a figurine?), and a larger, wheel-made, pottery female figure 45cm tall, which may be an import from the mainland. Such relatively large idols are now known to have been a feature of late Mycenaean palace-culture.

The massive town-wall, with offsets, and with some of its stairs still in place, is also of this period. All over that world, city-kings were improving their defences; but their society had passed into a terminal, warlike phase (glorified long after by Homer), which, in the end, neither gods nor walls could save. Before 1100 Phylakopi, like Pylos before it, was left uninhabited for ever; and when, long after, town life is discernible again in Melos, it is on a new site.

Re-colonised, according to its own tradition, by Dorians from Laconia before 1100, classical Melos was not a negligible state. Little remains of the city, north of the great harbour-mouth; but its early vase-painting shows distinction, especially exuberant scenes from heroic saga on large wine-amphoras, and several of its statues are in the National Museum. It sent two fifty-oared longboats—small warships, already obsolescent—to the fleet that fought Xerxes; but cherishing its Spartan connexions, it refused to join Athens' League and, when the great war broke out in 431, made a modest contribution to Sparta's war-fund. Probably, too, its great bay was used by privateers and blockade-runners. Athens attacked it in vain in 426, and in 416, when at peace with Sparta, determined to make an end of it. A large force was sent; and Thucydides pauses in his narrative to relate the dialogue in which, he says, the Athenians preached nakedly the doctrine that might is right, and the Melians, vainly offering neutrality, put their trust in the gods and refused to surrender. After a brave and active defence, the city fell; and the Athenians 'put to death all the males above puberty, sold the women and children as slaves, and later sent out 500 colonists' [i.e. families] 'and occupied the city. And in the same winter the Athenians decided to try to conquer Sicily . . .' Thucydides' irony is never more telling than here.

With Athens defeated, Sparta turned out the colonists and restored such Melians as had survived. With some immigration, the island gradually revived, and to Hellenistic times belongs its most famous statue, the Aphrodite or 'Venus de Milo' (= Melos). Under the Roman empire it contained a considerable number of Jews. On the slope below the city, a Roman theatre has been partly restored; and to the south-east is an early Christian catacomb, with remains of painting in some burial niches.

On the same slopes, below a ruined corner-tower of the city wall, is shown the find-spot of the famous Venus, now in the Louvre. How it got there is a story whose details, at the time, had to be hushed up. A farmer, excavating squared stones for field-walls, found it in an ancient *cache*, roofed with a slab. He removed the upper half (it was carved from two blocks) to his store-shed, and showed it to Brest, a resident French consular agent, and to Dumont d'Urville, a young naturalist and ensign in the French navy. Brest bought the statue for 600 piastres (then = 24 gold £) and took it secretly to his house; but on a Greek island the movements of a foreign naval officer naturally became a subject of gossip.

Bound for Constantinople, d'Urville there informed his Ambassador, Marquis de Rivière, who at once decided to buy it for King Louis XVIII, and instructed Captain de Marcellus of the sloop *Estafette* to collect it on his way home. D'Urville, in a published account of the find, says that he heard that de Marcellus arrived just in time; he found the statue about to be shipped to 'another destination', but 'after various difficulties . . . succeeded in saving [it] for France.' Brest's account, long *un*published, explains. News of the statue had reached the Sultan's governor, the Greek Prince Mourousis; and the 'other destination' was the Seraglio, where it might have disappeared from view until the fall of the empire. Mourousis had seized it, despite Brest's protests, when the *Estafette* arrived and, alerted by him, landed a lieutenant and twelve sailors, who retook this 'French property' hard by the jetty, after a brisk skirmish with cutlasses!

And then, after Turkish blood had apparently been shed, though not lethally, on the Sultan's territory, the matter was hushed up! One can but guess that de Marcellus used the ambassador's money in *bakshish*; perhaps also to repurchase half the statue, which may have been already in a Turkish ship's hold. Since that ship's company were not likely to report that they had actually had the prize, and had been first intimidated and then bribed, this secret was faithfully kept.

What a tale for a film!

Pre-Palace Crete

VASILIKI

Before 3000 BC the Cyclades had the most interesting and enterprising culture in the Aegean world. After 2000, Crete of the palaces holds a commanding lead. From the intervening millennium, Crete has yielded many fine works of art, in pottery, polished bowls in hard stone, using the marble-like grain to decorative effect, gold jewelry; but nearly all of it from graves. Later the habitation sites commanding the best arable land were normally occupied by palaces or 'manor houses', and though older remains exist under most of them, they cannot be fully revealed.

The first accessible 'desirable building site' to be explored, by the American R. B. Seager in 1904–6, is on a hill some 3km south of the Minoan township of Gournia, in the narrow part of the island known as the Isthmus of Ierapetra; and though it is a 'horizontal' site, showing only foundations, its chief building, called the House on the Hill, is a unique example of what preceded the palaces.

The hill's sides were occupied by many other houses, with paved streets between them, though less packed than at later Gournia; but erosion on the slopes and cultivation have left very little of these. Many of their stones can be seen built into modern field-walls. On the top erosion was less severe, and the hard ground less attractive to farmers; and Seager was able to reveal the plan of an L-shaped

Central and Eastern Crete, with modern roads

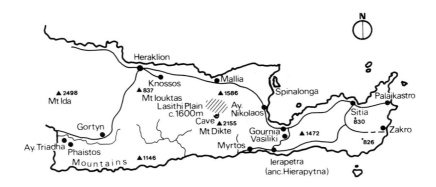

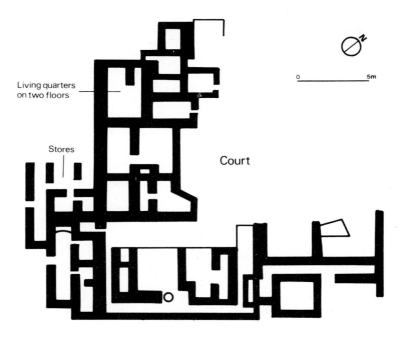

Living quarters on two floors

Stores

Court

Vasiliki: 'The House on the Hill'. The earliest known Minoan large house

house of many rooms, its wings probably built at different times, with its *corners* oriented to the cardinal points of the compass (as often in Asia Minor) and a paved court to the north. Its period is Early Minoan II (*c.* 2650–2200), a time when a new, larger-boned and broad-headed, immigrant element from Asia Minor was already settled among the descendants of the neolithic Cretans; this may, as we shall see, have affected the characteristic Vasiliki pottery-style. Under the foundations of the big house Seager found the slighter ones of an older, smaller house differently aligned, and above the bedrock pottery of the final neolithic stage, though he failed to detect traces of the makers' habitations.

The superstructure of the big house was, at least largely, of brick, made with straw, and the walls strengthened with beams. Ceilings of the visible basement rooms, which supported at least one upper floor, were of reeds set in clay plaster, supported on cross-beams. When the house ultimately perished by fire, around 2200, the bricks and plaster fused into an intensely hard mass, which as it fell protected the stone foundations and some fragments of pots that fell with it; while the beams themselves, burnt to fine ash, poured out of their holes when parts of the mass were moved, leaving hollow casts.

The peculiar Vasiliki pottery, which has become diagnostic for dating when found on other sites, is commonly called 'mottled', though 'blotchy', if less polite, perhaps suggests better the fairly large size of the irregular, curvilinear, black to dark green areas on the orange or reddish ground-paint. It looks as if invented by accident, through irregular firing, but was then certainly continued on purpose. The effect is not unlike some army camouflage. It first appears before the great house was built, and the pot-shapes include some with analogues in Asia Minor. It was exported locally, but did not survive the end of Vasiliki.

The mixture of cultures after the EM I immigration probably did help to break the 'cake of custom' of neolithic Crete, and quicken development; and the great house has suggested to many the rise of a dominant class. There may also have been some violence, on the scale of local feuding rather than war. No regular fortifications appear in Crete; but the situation was one in which, as R. W. Hutchinson says, 'The big man, whoever he was, grabbed the best site and built his palace or large house there, and his relatives or dependents built houses round it.' (*Prehistoric Crete*, Pelican, 1962, p. 162). The House on the Hill perished in a fire of great violence, after nearly all metal objects had been removed, though obsidian blades were left, discarded. Reoccupation was inferior; Seager says, of a 'squatter' character. There was never a great house on that hill again, rather curiously; but probably local lordship now passed to the chiefs of Gournia.

MYRTOS

Vasiliki was long almost the only Early Minoan habitation-site exposed; with palaces to be found, little time and money was diverted to less exciting projects. But in 1962 three British archaeologists of a new, distinguished generation set out to search for pre-palace sites in the most promising area, the isthmus of Ierapetra; and they selected for excavation one 2km east of Myrtos, on the south coast, on the end of a ridge dropping steeply to the sea and to a valley on the east, and less steeply on the west. Arable land was available up the valley. The place was known locally as one where prehistoric remains existed, and the schoolmaster of Myrtos gave much help. It is called Fournou Korifi, 'Kiln Hill' (classical Phournou Koryphe; but the transliteration used this time for publication is the official modern Greek one).

Two seasons of hard and meticulous work under Professor Peter Warren, one of the discoverers, revealed the first known Early Minoan village, occupied from *c.* 2600–2200 (EM II), with a remodelling *c.* 2460. The Phase 2 settlement was much the larger, extending for 50m along the top of the ridge and 25m to the west, where wall-ends fade out through erosion. In its west centre it faced on to an open space, over the levelled-off foundations of buildings of Phase 1. The earlier date of these was shown by differences in the pottery, including absence of the mottled Vasiliki ware, common here later.

There seemed to be no separate houses. The whole settlement was 'agglutinated', with rooms built on as wanted, using existing walls. Walls are not always straight, but follow the lines of the rock, especially at the southern end (Phase 2), where the hilltop slopes down. Rooms were small, for lack of beams to roof a larger span than *c.* 2.5m; and some, with walls standing up to 50cm high, have no apparent doorway. They may have been entered by ladders from above, as in the

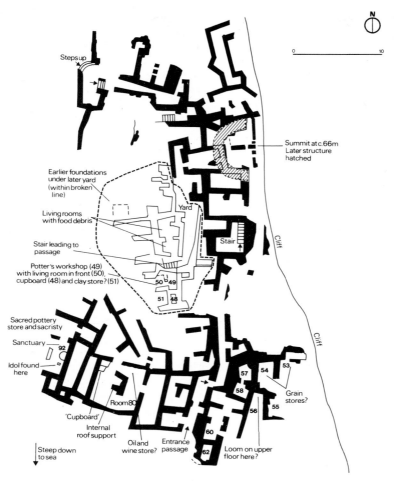

Myrtos (Fournou Korifi); an Early Bronze-Age settlement.
(After P. Warren, *Myrtos* (1972), Thames & Hudson for BSA)

much larger and older human ant-hill of Chatal Hüyük in Turkey. Some floors
were of the natural rock, only approximately flat, as in the caves which many
neolithic Cretans had inhabited in Crete; though others had been levelled up with
flat stones and earth, and even plastered. The first impression is of people living
hugger-mugger; but it would be wrong. The walls, 50cm–1 m thick, are well-built,
of flat, unworked stones, and were often coated with lime plaster, which might
then be coloured red with a pigment made from iron-rich earths. Many small cells
were cupboards or stores. Rooms at a higher level may have opened on to the roofs
of lower ones, as still in some Cretan villages; and if some rooms are so cluttered

with large storage-vessels as to leave little space to move or lie down, it is likely that sleeping-space was above, in rooms perhaps of lighter structure or, in summer, when Myrtos is very hot and dry, on the open roofs, as still in Greece generally.

Already in Phase 1 there is evidence of contact with a wider world, and long technical traditions. Obsidian cores from Melos were imported, perhaps via Mochlos (now an island, then perhaps a peninsula north of the isthmus; a flourishing settlement, known only from the jewelry and fine stone vases in its graves); and among other finds from Fournou Korifi 1 is a primitive, triangular metal dagger of copper alloyed with lead. It seems surprising that a metal object should have been allowed to go missing; but perhaps, as bronze technique advanced, this one had lost in estimation. Baked clay loom-weights, disc-shaped with two holes for hanging, and spindle-whorls indicate the manufacture of cloth from the community's sheep's wool; and its potters, or potter, had a rich lore on how to produce, with subtle differences of clay, fine or gritty, large *pithoi*, the great Cretan storage vessels, cooking-pots to go on the fire, large jugs that would stand up to the hazards of daily journeys to the springs below (there is no sign that there was ever one on the hill) and finer, smaller jugs, one-handled 'tea-cups' and bowls, for eating and drinking. The finer ware was usually highly polished ('burnished'), and decorated in red or brown paint with hatched triangles or lozenges or grass-like 'bunches' of radiating lines; and the potter knew too how to produce grey ware, sometimes preferred, by firing in a 'reducing atmosphere', i.e. with some smoke in the kiln.

Most interestingly, one room in the Phase 1 area (demarcated on the plan by a broken line) was the local potter's workshop, the earliest identified in the Aegean world. On its floor were eight baked clay discs, *c.* 20cm broad, flat on one side, convex on the other. They are the potter's turntables, on which, convex side down, he stood his plastic clay while he moulded his pot, to facilitate turning it by hand; a first step towards the spindle-mounted 'fast wheel' which appears later. One disc, of Phase 2, found in one of the north rooms, has a depression in the middle of its convex side, for mounting on a rudimentary spindle. The Phase 1 potter's shop, a little room 2.08 × 1.08m, was entered through a larger one, *c.* 3 × 1.5m, with ashes against its north wall (a cooking place?). The master did not wish to be interrupted. East and south of the workshop were two tiny cells, storage places; and west of the second was a larger one containing three *pithoi* which held earth that might well have been the potter's clay. Soaked in the winter rains of 4000 years, the clay seemed to have re-connected with the bases of the *pithoi*, causing them to rot away; a rare phenomenon. West of here, erosion of the slope had removed all traces.

Of Phase 2, much the best preserved remains are at the south end, where some walls abutted on small rock faces. Here, south west, was the largest room in the complex, the excavators' Room 80, *c.* 5m very roughly square, with plastered walls and a ⊐-shaped piece of walling in the middle, probably as a roof-support. By the door, in the north-west corner, was a compartment bounded by stone slabs set on edge in clay, with others forming an internal partition; it was probably open-topped, at its surviving height of *c.* 50cm. In it were kept some of the finer painted jugs and an 'incense'-burner. At the back of the room, *pithoi* and large amphoras stood against the south wall and that of the central roof-support, along with jugs for dipping up liquids from them; and in one *pithos*, grape-pips and the identifiable remains of pressed skins (matched elsewhere on the site) showed that wine was among the liquids. The fragments of jugs, bowls and cooking-pots, one of them three-legged, were scattered over the floor. The room contained remains of fifty-three pots of all sizes, and in a smaller, irregular-shaped room outside the main door were forty-four more, including two *pithoi*, two amphoras and a large water-pot; only a small space round the door was clear. There were yet more in a long, narrow room through another door on the east side of Room 80. Several of these could be put together, complete, from fragments found in the 'fill', well above the floor; they appeared to have fallen, with the roof, in the final destruction by fire, and strongly suggested that while Room 80 and its surroundings were a working area for the storage and preparation of food and drink, meals were taken 'upstairs'. Walls below, set near together, would have strengthened the floor.

The south wall of Room 80 was part of the continuous wall of the settlement, broken perhaps only at the main south entrance, where a socket for a door-pivot was found. Up to it led a flagged path; a path unprotected would have become a water-channel. East of the passage, which led from the door right through the south range, with a 'jog' half-way, another storage and working area was identified. Two rooms in the south-east corner (54, 53, the latter with outer walls eroded away) contained more *pithoi*, but probably not for liquids; one, at least, had its foot, which had been 'rotted' by acids or salts in some previous contents (wine, or olives in brine?), roughly plugged with a worn-flat potter's turntable. It would still have been good for holding grain—and the impressions of grains of barley and wheat have been found on the clay of a coarse pot, and those of barley chaff in mud plaster, which was regularly mixed with straw. The final fire had been particularly fierce here (a grain store?) and in Room 80, where the combustible might have been oil. Near the probable grain store, there was a scatter of heavy loom-weights in the fill (58; one in 56); and the fact that some of them too were not actually on the floor suggests that the loom was set up on a floor above, where the light would be better. Near by, down on the rock, was a large tub, propped up level with flat stones; and analysis of grease which had soaked into its clay suggested animal rather than vegetable origin. It may have been used for washing the grease out of the wool, afterwards to be spun and woven.

Examination thus revealed to the excavators, in the apparent 'hugger-mugger', a tidy specialisation of functions in different quarters; and last on the south-west corner, just before all traces of walls run out on the slope, well-earned luck gave them the oldest known Cretan household shrine, and its idol, intact.

This image is a unique object. Cycladic potters, through millennia, added pairs of nipples to their jugs and jars, 'for luck', or to suggest to the powers that yield plenty that there should always be plenty here; just as Mediterranean sailors from the earliest known times until this day paint eyes on their boats. But this little idol, 21cm high × 16.35cm maximum width, has no practical use. It is vaguely —deliberately vaguely—anthropomorphic, female. It consists of a crinoline-shaped body, and a neck, 8.4 × 2cm, ending in a head no thicker, but with nose pinched out, eyes and eyebrows painted, ears and a chin added before firing. The left arm embraces a miniature, typical Myrtos painted jug, communicating by a hole with the inside of the 'body'. (Were token offerings poured into it?) Hatched rectangles on the 'skirt' may represent woven cloth, and fringe-like painting at the sides, stitching; but an inverted triangle below centre may be meant to emphasize (though clothed) the pubic region, as on Cycladic figurines. The 'goddess of Myrtos' seems to represent a Lady of Plenty or (like the Roman Penates) spirit of the stores. She had probably fallen off a roughly semi-circular stand or 'altar' of flat slabs set against the east wall. A communicating room, 2 × over 3m (west wall lost), contained sixty-six smashed vases of fine ware, many of them jugs or bowls; a store of pottery, no doubt, for sacred use.

The settlement looks like the home of a close-knit unit, perhaps an extended family, of up to about a hundred people, with no chief; at least, there is no sign of specially fine rooms, though some on the highest ground in the middle, over Phase i foundations, are more accurately rectangular than most. But EM ii society, as at Vasiliki, was moving towards chiefdom, even monarchy. (EM iii is a short transitional period, leading on to the rise of the first palaces.) In their time the Fournou Korifi 2 folk were conservative, perhaps belated 'primitive communist' people. Did they quarrel with their neighbours? Was their way of life considered a bad example to the considerable numbers of subject peasants, who must have contributed their social surplus to the upkeep of the rising big houses? Not that big houses were exempt from aggression; Vasiliki was burnt about the same time. But it certainly looks (here I theorize) as if someone marched on Fournou Korifi and took the people away. There was no slaughter; at least, no bones in the wreckage. All that superior force, a few score men, needed to do was to block the access to water. But certainly the people went, and the place was burnt; and the state of some vases with pieces widely scattered over floors, looks as if there was some vindictive smashing. Afterwards (how long after?) a semi-circular stone wall with a built-in bench, facing east, was built over the ruins at the top of the hill. It is unique, and no 'properties' were found to suggest a hill-top sanctuary; but it surely commemorated and marked in some way a ban on the hill being ever again inhabited. It never was. In the following centuries its lands must have been farmed from Pyrgos, another hill only 1km west, near modern Myrtos.

Pyrgos too has now been 'dug', by G. Cadogan, one of the original explorers; and it proved to have been inhabited as early as Fournou Korifi, and burnt about the same time. Whether the two settlements were similar, later buildings and erosion do not permit us to say. Pyrgos was reoccupied, perhaps not at once, but within EM iii, when a fine paved way led from seaward along one side to a revered, stone-built tomb. Later there was a smart country house on the top. But at Fournou Korifi not only a hamlet but a way of life had perished for ever.

GOURNIA

Small towns and the small 'palaces' of local Cretan rulers must long have
preceded great ones like that of Knossos; and at Knossos itself they are buried
beneath the foundations of the earlier great palace, which preceded that which we

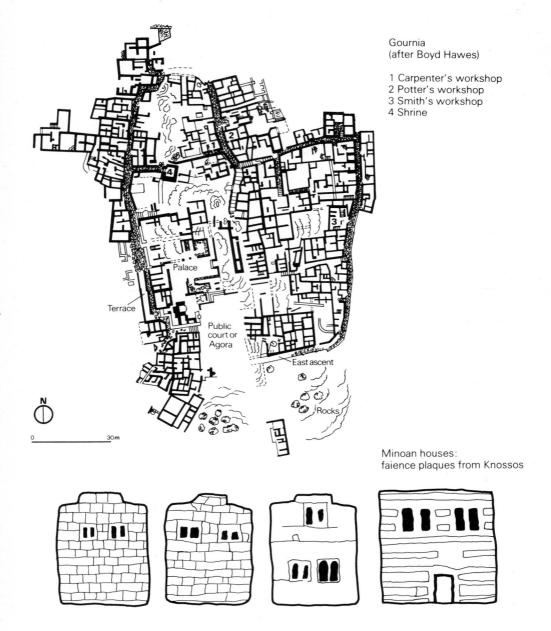

Gournia
(after Boyd Hawes)

1 Carpenter's workshop
2 Potter's workshop
3 Smith's workshop
4 Shrine

Minoan houses:
faience plaques from Knossos

can see. The little town of Gournia, 85km to the east, is in fact, as we see it, not older than the visible palace of Knossos; but from the fact that it remained small, it may serve as an example of what the first towns in Aegean Europe were like. Excavated in 1901–4 by a remarkable American lady, Mrs H. Boyd Hawes, it remains the only fully-excavated, visible example of a Minoan town.

Gournia has an area of only about six acres (*c.* 200 × 125m, omitting salients); yet it is definitely not rural. The houses stand shoulder to shoulder along the cobbled or sometimes flagged and stepped lanes on the slopes of a small hill; and among them could be distinguished the workshops of specialised tradesmen: the carpenter (1 on plan), with sets of bronze saws, at a corner on the central alley; the potter, with his wheels, just opposite (2); and the smith (3) at the east foot of the hill. All had sites handy for access by country people who needed skilled services. Re-surfacing had caused the street or lane surfaces to rise above the level of the house floors, leaving many rooms semi-basement; but probably most houses had an upper storey, like the quite small houses depicted on a series of faience tiles (from a mosaic of a city?) from Knossos in the Heraklion Museum.

The Palace, or Big House, with an area of *c.* 50 × 30m, occupied the highest ground, and its south wall, partly a retaining-wall, is of fine masonry. It overlooks an open court or *agora* to the south, and an L-shaped stair, a small relation of the grander ones at Knossos and Phaistos, could have served as a platform where the local ruler or his officers could address the people. Further up, an inner, columned court is flanked by the magazines, with their great storage-jars containing the produce delivered in rents or taxes. The residential rooms were further up again; and, by-passing the palace, a cobbled road on the west and north led to what seems to have been the town's public shrine just beyond the top of the hill.

2 Crete of the Palaces, and after

KNOSSOS

The Labyrinth of Knossos, pre-eminent in size among the Cretan palaces, is for ever associated with the name of Sir Arthur Evans, who devoted to it his wealth and the latter half of a long and active life (1851–1941). Evans was not the actual discoverer. In 1878, when the Turks conceded to Crete some local autonomy, Minos Kalokairinos of Heraklion, whose baptismal name is not without significance, inspired by the work of Schliemann, first dug on the hill called Kephala, the Head. He discovered the huge storage *pithoi* still standing in the west magazines, presented smaller vases to several European museums, and named the vast building, of which he had evidence, the Palace of Minos. Schliemann himself then proposed to buy it; but the Turkish owner, knowing Schliemann's reputation for finding gold, supposed (wrongly) that there must be much gold here too, and asked such a high price that Schliemann's business sense was aroused and the deal fell through. But after Schliemann's death, when the Turks withdrew in 1899, Evans had already arranged to purchase. At the same time other archaeologists set to work on other 'Minoan' sites.

Knossos: Central Court, W. side (much restored)

Knossos had been occupied by neolithic men since *c.* 6000, and by 3000 the debris of successive houses had raised the ground level in places by 8.5m; but classical Greeks had avoided the ruins; and only a shallow layer of earth covered them. Evans' success was rapid and sensational.

The visible remains are those of a Second Palace, rebuilt after destruction by an earthquake *c.* 1700, and especially as occupied by mainland Greeks after *c.* 1450. Architecturally, it is a vast agglomeration. On the west side of the Central Court, *c.* 45 × 23m internally, lie the great magazines with, in front of them, the famous though modest-sized Throne Room (a feature of the latest period), with its upright gypsum throne, carved to imitate wood, and flanked by frescoes of couchant griffins (now gaily restored). A stone bench runs round the walls, and a small adjacent room, which could be reached by a private stair from the *piano nobile* above, contained a basin for lustral water. The great staircase, approached from the western entrance along the Corridor of the Procession, lay further to the south.

East of the court, the north corner was a workshop area. In one shop one of the splendid stone vases, a glory of Minoan as of Egyptian art, was found, left unfinished when the final disaster struck. Further south, an easy stone stair with low treads—though hardly as 'grand' as its usual name implies, or as some of the broad flights west of the court—goes down the east slope towards the brook Kairatos, turning right-angled corners and lit by a light-well, to reach comfortable suites of living-rooms. A Hall of the Double Axes (a sacred emblem) gave access to another pillared hall, which Evans called the King's Megaron; and south across a colonnaded passage a smaller but dignified suite was called the Queen's. The principal room had next to it a bathroom, then a treasury, and at the end of the passage a water-closet, no less, flushed by water brought down beside the stairs in paraboloid sections of piping, which broke its rush and prevented it from gaining too great velocity.

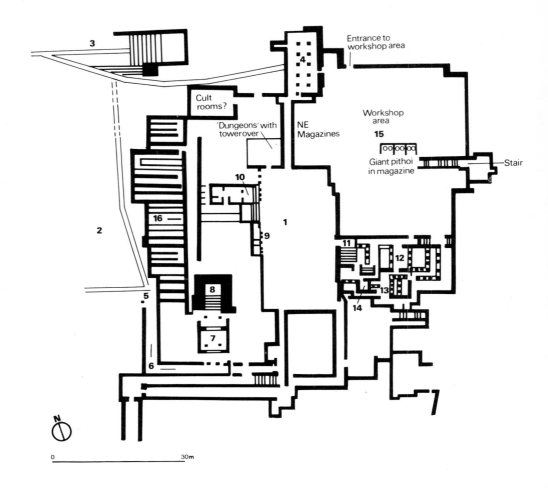

The Palace of Knossos

(simplified plan)

1 Central Court
2 West Court
3 'Royal Road' and Theatral Area
4 Pillar Hall
5 West Entrance
6 Corridor of the Procession
7 South Propylon, leading to (8)
8 Great staircase (to Reception Hall, above?)

9 Shrine
10 Throne room
11 Grand staircase to Royal (?) Apartments
12 Hall of the Double Axes ⎫
13 'Queen's Megaron'   ⎬ State and private
14 Bathroom   ⎪ apartments over?
15 Workshops   ⎭
16 Storerooms (archives and offices over)

But these identifications belong to the early years of Evans' great work. Pleasant as they are (and cool on a hot day), the rooms scarcely seem to have the grandeur appropriate for a High King, lord of the south Aegean. One may be permitted to express a lingering doubt as to whether these are not rather the apartments of important—perhaps noble—palace officials, living close to their work. The *piano nobile* was, rather, up the much grander stairs of the west wing.

So were some administrative offices. Many of the clay tablets, inscribed in the Linear B script of the mainland (found, in Crete, only here) which kept the palace accounts, were found among the *pithoi* in the oil stores. Some no doubt were labels, and belonged there; but others had probably fallen down through the upper floor when the palace was burnt soon after 1400 (the final destruction, except for some 'squatter' reoccupation); preserved, indeed, by their hard baking in the fire.

The whole agglomeration had grown, *ad hoc*, as required; the earlier palace had even grown together out of originally separate blocks. Foundations of some rounded, external corners have been found, now inside. It must have looked a monstrosity, though, from sheer bulk, impressive to bronze-age eyes. Perhaps the most dignified view of it would have been seen by travellers from the south, following the road, with bridges and culverts, that crossed a tributary of the Kairatos on a viaduct. From across the gully, where what looks like a guest-house (the Caravanserai) may have been used by privileged foreigners, the façade, with its walls crowned by pairs of 'horns of consecration' as shown on Minoan frescoes of buildings, may have looked truly monumental.

From the north, where the bronze-age city spread, enormous for its time (the palace alone covered an area as big as Gournia), there was some planning of the approach. A neatly paved path—it has been called 'the oldest road in Europe'—came in from the west, branching from one leading from the south into the town. It passed between the fresco-decorated villas of grandees and a building that has been called the Arsenal. Here were found the Chariot Tablets, describing chariots wheelless or otherwise defective; evidently those 'in workshops' awaiting repair or cannibalisation. Approaching the north-west corner of the palace this 'Royal Road' splits into three. One branch turns south into the West Court; it leads to a side door, into the Corridor of the Procession: a fresco-painted procession of servitors, of which the famous Cup-Bearer, represented by a copy *in situ*, is the largest surviving fragment. The original is in the Heraklion Museum. A second branch approaches the north entrance at a slant, as it were informally; the third goes straight on into what Evans named the Theatral Area, heading for a flight of broad and easy stone steps. On its right is another flight, at right-angles; and in the angle a built-up stone base, level with the top of the steps, might, Evans suggested, have held a Royal Box, where the king greeted important visitors. Proceeding to the north entrance, one entered a large pillared hall and thence, turning right, through a long, curiously mean though frescoed passage (*c.* 26 × 3m), reached the Central Court. The palace was not fortified; evidently 'Minos'' internal supremacy and sea-power left no fear of war; but all its entrances were narrow; eminently defensible in case of a riot.

Knossos: Royal Road and Theatral Area

This apparently secretive and reserved attitude to the outside world is a characteristic of a palace entrance which reappears at Phaistos. It may be natural to holders of enormous riches; but it is not attractive. Knossos however, in its last luxurious phase, which we see, was more alien to the rest of Crete than earlier palaces. In that phase, when the other palaces had been destroyed, it is now generally accepted that Knossos was ruled by Greeks from the mainland. Its last pottery 'palace style', found only here, shows mainland influence; and some archaeologists had already suggested that there was a Mycenaean takeover, even before the late Michael Ventris' study of the Linear B texts had led to the conclusion that they make sense as Greek, unlike the earlier Cretan Linear A. The latest princely or aristocratic burials, further out from the palace than the earlier, are different too. They are warrior graves of chiefs buried with their weapons, as on the mainland; another new development. A warrior nobility might have felt secure; but perhaps they were few in comparison with their subjects. One famous palace fresco shows a white captain leading a file of black spearmen; slave mamelukes? Evans, who resisted the theory of a mainland domination, himself suggested that the final destruction, *c.* 1380, might have been due to a rebellion of 'submerged elements within the island'. Much remains obscure; but Homer makes Idomeneus, leader of the Cretan contingent at Troy, a grandson of Minos. This would make Minos himself, even if some links in Idomeneus' pedigree have been forgotten, a Greek Achaian. It is time to look at the body of Greek mythology that centres on the Labyrinth.

No Greek story is more familiar than that of how Minos ruled the waves (a tradition, in which Herodotos and Thucydides believed as history); how he took Nisa, the predecessor of the city of Megara, and took tribute of Athens in revenge for the murder of his son, in the form of seven youths and seven maidens each year to be fed to his monstrous beast, the Minotaur; and how Prince Theseus volunteered to be one of them and slew the Minotaur, by the help of Ariadne, Minos' daughter, who fell in love with him and gave him the Clue—a literal clue, a ball of wool to unwind behind him—with which to find his way back out of the labyrinth. But only since the archaeological discoveries has it been noticed how many elements in the story seem to be garbled reminiscence of facts about ancient Crete. The word Minotaur means, literally, just 'Minos' Bull'; and Minoan art shows the importance in Cretan life of a bull-leaping sport, watched by crowds including richly dressed ladies in special stands; a sport that seems to have become hieratic,

The Knossos area, to show relative position of archaeological sites

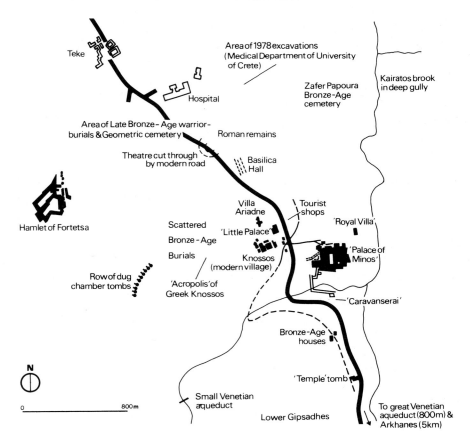

and was also very dangerous. Young athletes, boys and girls, seized the horns of a charging bull and somersaulted over its back, to be received by a comrade behind the bull. How many died in the attempt? And did 'Minos' import young slaves to be trained for this terrifying sport? Minos himself, in the *Odyssey*, is described as a king who 'reigned for nine seasons' (whatever that means) and 'held familiar converse with great Zeus' ('knew God face to face', like Moses). This sounds more like a reminiscence of an ancient sacred monarchy than of a mere grandfather of a Homeric hero. Ariadne, in other myths, was a bride of Dionysos, the very important vegetation-deity; and this made it necessary for Theseus, whose story includes relatively late Athenian embroidery, having fled with her, somehow to get rid of her. He was said to have 'forgotten' her (!) and left her in Naxos, where Plutarch in his *Theseus* mentions a semi-dramatic religious ritual in her honour. Even her name ('Very Holy' in Greek?) might be an epithet of a goddess (or The Goddess, dominant over a young god in Cretan and near-eastern religion), whose real name might be too holy for common use.

As for the Minotaur as a monster, its shape does appear just once in palace-period art. Among other fantastic monsters on seal-impressions from Zakro, one shows a horned beast head on a human body.

Lastly, the Labyrinth. There is little doubt that it once meant the palace itself, the Place (*-nth*, cf. Corinth p. 234) of the Double Axe. *Labrys* was an Asia Minor word in historic times, meaning an axe, especially the weapon or symbol of Zeus Labraundeus, Zeus of the Axe, at Labraunda in Karia; and many place-names support a Greek tradition that a common language was spoken on both sides of the south Aegean in pre-Hellenic times. That the double axe was, along with the (bull's) Horns of Consecration, a religious symbol is shown by many appearances of it both in the palace and elsewhere in Crete, from masons' marks to double axes set up on bases as cult objects.

How then did 'Labyrinth' in Greek come to mean simply a maze? The change came about probably on the spot. After the great sack, the palace was reoccupied, at least by squatters; but after several more dark and turbulent centuries the Dorian Greeks avoided the ruins, *though they lived close by*. When the great stucco relief of a bull, which had stood above the north entrance, at last fell down, it fell actually on top of some 9C Geometric pot-sherds; household rubbish, thrown out against the old wall. High walls would have fallen; the magazines, which stood, under a mass of wreckage, were dark and mazy indeed; uncanny; dangerous, too; liable to further stone-falls and perhaps, as in modern times, a haunt of poisonous tarantulas. Herodotus uses the word labyrinth of 'labyrinthine' buildings in Egypt; and soon after his time a design of a square, conventional maze became a regular badge on the reverse side of coins of Dorian Knossos.

PHAISTOS

In contrast to Evans' brightly coloured reconstructions at Knossos, the southern palace of Phaistos stands unadorned, almost as the Italian archaeologists found it, with minimal necessary shoring up and restoration. The ground floor and some basements remain visible. It is well-sited along the end of a ridge, some of which has fallen away, with fine views over the fertile plain of the Mesara to the surrounding mountains. The excavated area is much smaller than at Knossos, though the Italians are continuing to dig down the south west slope, where the town was. Like Knossos, Phaistos had two harbours fairly close (the sea has since receded), naval stations and for trade with Africa and Egypt. It also was inhabited in the neolithic era.

As at Knossos, and at Mallia and Zakro, the general plan centres on a large rectangular court (51.50 × 22.30m; identified as 170 × 80 Minoan feet), running north and south, with many small rooms grouped round it. Along the west side are rooms for religious use, including a pillar crypt where cult objects have been found, though Phaistos does not boast a 'Throne Room'. Behind these are rows of magazines for the large *pithoi*. East of the Central Court, as at Knossos, are some workshops. A room at the north-east end was a pottery, and south of it, now fenced off in an open area, a horseshoe-shaped place is identified by fragments of

The Palace of Phaistos

1 Theatral area	6 Stone platform
2 Cultrooms—First Palace	7 Pillar crypt
3 Grand staircase	8 Bathroom
4 Propylon	9 Phaistos Disc found here
5 N. Entrance	10 Foundry

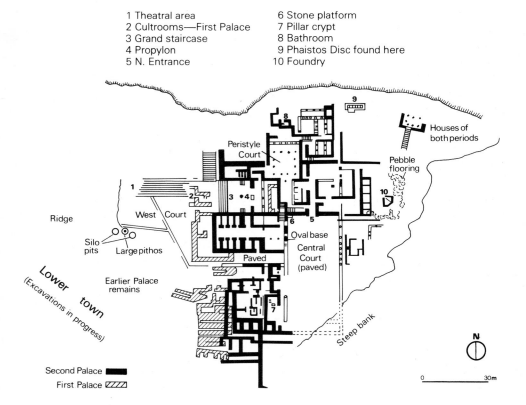

copper and bronze as a foundry. Both palaces were approached across a paved West Court with a raised causeway leading to a west entrance and forking part way along its course. Both have a theatral area to the north of this. Here the main similarities with Knossos end and the special features begin.

The most striking are the two imposing flights of steps at the north side and the north-east corner of the West Court. A wide flight descends in front of a later retaining wall, probably for spectators to watch religious or royal ceremonies, ritual dances or athletic contests. It is more imposing than the smaller theatral area at Knossos. These steps belong to the First Palace, as do the foundations and low walls of small rooms where cult objects were found near the foot of the Grand Staircase, and a stretch of the façade of the court *c*. 8m in front of that of the Second Palace, with some of the magazines behind it. More of the First Palace remains visible than at Knossos. It, like those of Knossos and Mallia, was destroyed by an earthquake *c*. 1700, but here also a larger palace was built on the same site, showing that the vitality of society was unimpaired.

The Grand Staircase belongs to the Second Palace. Its comfortable steps are cambered, and flanked by walls of ashlar masonry. They lead up to the principal entrance, the *propylon*, which is divided into three small and narrow anterooms. The first has a single central column between piers to support an upper floor, the next three piers, and the last three columns, which open onto a light well. Below are magazines of the First Palace with large *pithoi*. In contrast to the spacious stairs the eventual entrances into the palace are, here too, rather small and mean, perhaps intentionally so, to check visitors arriving close to the royal apartments. From here there are two small exits, one leading by a dog-leg course to the Peristyle Court, the other finally emerging, down a few steps, into the north-west corner of the Central Court.

As at Mallia, there are some pier bases for a colonnade along the sides of the Court. It has two unique features at the north end. The main north entrance is adorned by two wooden (restored) half columns on stone bases, and curved niches in the wall. The latter may be simply for guards beside the way into the royal apartments, but the general effect is that of a planned architectural façade, unlike any surviving in the other palaces. The second special feature is a stone block in the north-west corner. Scholars have evolved various theories about its purpose. Professor J. W. Graham of Princeton, who believes that the famous bull games took place on the Central Courts, suggests that it served as a vaulting platform for the somersaulting athlete, and he cites a gem depicting precisely this manoeuvre. Not all scholars, however, accept this theory. Another suggestion is that the block was an altar, or even a stand for flowers for the flower-loving Minoans.

Another feature, so far unique, is the Peristyle Court in the royal apartments. In several ways the Minoans anticipated the Romans, on a small scale, in their attention to road systems, viaducts, conduits, baths and drains—and here too we find a 'Roman' feature. The Peristyle Court is roughly square, surrounded by pillars and open to the sky. The rooms at this north end are well placed to catch the prevailing north-west summer breeze, with a splendid view across the plain to

Pnaistos: West Court, theatral area with ceremonial stairway on right, remains of First Palace at base

Mount Ida, and with the modern conveniences of bathroom and lavatory at a lower level. Normally visible from here is a dark patch on the mountain. It is the Kamares cave, a sanctuary in which fine pottery of the First Palace period was found in such quantity that the name Kamares was given to the style. It has polychrome painting on a dark ground on vessels of many different shapes, decorated in a variety of abstract, floral and occasional marine designs. It appears to be a southern manufacture. Examples were found in the magazines of the First Palace, and some, found at Knossos, could have been imported. A few Kamares vases have even been found in a tomb in Egypt.

In another room, at the north-east of the site, yet another unique and enigmatic object came to light, the famous Phaistos Disc, inside a mudbrick box. It is made of clay, stamped with pictograms running in a spiral from the rim to the centre. Some of the characters resemble those of the first, hieroglyphic, form of Cretan writing. Both are so far undeciphered.

The Second Palace at Phaistos was destroyed by fire *c.* 1450, perhaps following an earthquake, or in the general destruction after the eruption on Thera. It was never reoccupied.

Phaistos is a pleasant palace from its position, not so overwhelming as Knossos, interesting for its unique features, and impressive, in a civilisation of many miniature masterpieces, for the monumental element of the theatral area and the Grand Staircase.

AYIA TRIADHA

A paved Minoan road connects the palace of Phaistos in *c*. 3km with a pleasant site nearer the sea, called, as its ancient name is unknown, Holy Trinity after a chapel nearby to the south-west. It was clearly a dependency of Phaistos; perhaps a Summer Palace by the sea, or a Royal Villa for another member of the royal family. The site has produced an unique wealth of works of art, such as are conspicuously missing at Phaistos.

The Villa has no clearly defined Central Court. It is L-shaped, built along the west and north sides of an open court, with the main rooms in and near the angle. The rooms are small, but well arranged. An inner room with wall benches has in front of it a portico opening on to a pillared hall, or terrace, with a fine view. Beside this suite is an 'archive' room where 168 Linear A tablets were found, and many clay impressions from sealstones. In a narrow treasury close by lay nineteen ox-hide-shaped bronze ingots, weighing 29.5kg and hall-marked—the unwieldy form of bronze-age currency also found at Zakro, and in Cyprus, the source of supply. Next door was one of the best Minoan frescoes, showing with characteristic observation and delight a cat stalking a pheasant among bushes. A second fresco shows a woman seated in a garden.

From this wing also come three famous, black serpentine stone vases carved with scenes in relief: the 'Chieftain Cup', with a Minoan prince receiving an armed warrior; a pointed vase (rhyton) with bands of athletic scenes; and the small globular 'Harvester Vase', with a joyous procession of men singing on their return from harvest—a masterpiece of miniature art.

In the north wing there is another suite of Minoan rooms near a flight of steps leading to the east exit and the road to Phaistos. The middle of this wing has been disturbed by later building resembling a Mycenaean *megaron* and a length of stone drain protrudes, now above ground. In the short east end of the site was a small shrine with a unique, painted plaster floor, now at Heraklion, showing sea creatures in relief.

Stretching to the north, at the back of confusing ruins of two periods, is a row of shops with a columned portico in front of them, a lone forerunner of the classical stoa, and so far unique in Minoan architecture.

Further north are the cemeteries, including remains of two early, stone-built, domed tombs. A rock-cut tomb yielded the famous Ayia Triadha painted stone sarcophagus, with a seal of the Egyptian Queen Tyi (1411–1375). It gives along its sides two fascinating pictures of sacrifices at a dead man's tomb, by priestesses accompanied by male musicians, and a procession to the tomb with offerings, including a model boat. At the ends are women in chariots, one drawn by dark horses and the other by griffins. This and all the other treasures from this Royal Villa are in the Heraklion Museum.

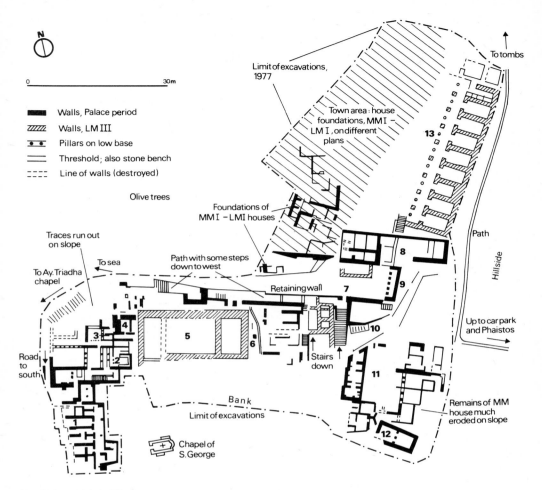

N

0 ————————————— 30m

Walls, Palace period
Walls, LM III
Pillars on low base
Threshold; also stone bench
Line of walls (destroyed)

Olive trees

Limit of excavations, 1977

Town area: house foundations, MM I – LM I, on different plans

13

Foundations of MM I – LMI houses

Traces run out on slope

To sea

To Ay. Triadha chapel

Path with some steps down to west

Retaining wall

Path

Hillside

7

8

9

Road to south

3
4
2
5
6

Stairs down

10

11

Up to car park and Phaistos

1

Bank
Limit of excavations

Remains of MM house much eroded on slope

12

Chapel of S. George

To tombs

The Palace of Ayia Triadha

1 Storerooms
2 'Sitting-room' with view
3 Archives
4 Treasury
5 (?) 'Mycenaean' Megaron over older foundations of storerooms
6 LMIII water-pipe, now above ground
7 LMI open space

8 Warehouse?
9 Loggia?
10 Retaining walls and steps down to west
11 Courtyard
12 MM Shrine with painted plaster floor (in Heraklion) and LM 'properties'
13 LMIII shops with colonnade of piers and posts in front

MALLIA

An extensive settlement with a palace has been excavated by the French School on the coast, *c.* 40km east of Heraklion, at Mallia ('the levels'—ancient name unknown). The palace history follows that of Phaistos, with two destructions, *c.* 1700 and *c.* 1450 BC. The general plan is similar to that of the other palaces, though it is less spectacular, and unrestored. It has no theatral area, nor Grand Entrance, but unobtrusive entrances north and south leading to the north-west and south-west corners of the Central Court. The north corridor passes between a building with very thick walls, which perhaps carried a tower, and a large pillared hall which probably supported large upper rooms. Mallia has several special features.

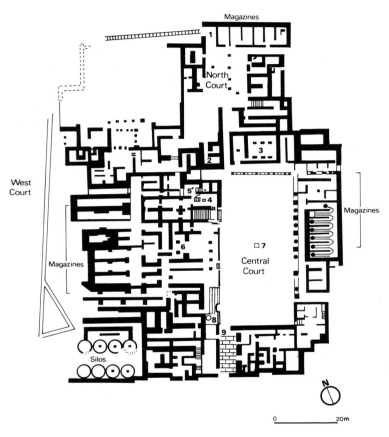

The Palace of Mallia

1 N. Entrance	6 Pillar Crypt
2 Tower	7 Altar pit
3 Pillared hall	8 Kernos
4 Loggia	9 S. Entrance
5 Room of the ceremonial weapons	

The thin line in the E. storage magazines represents a drainage channel conducting spillage to small collecting tanks.

Mallia: ruins of palace with giant *pithos*

Bases for columns along the north end of the Central Court and for piers and columns down the east side imply colonnades. The west side is devoted to rooms of ceremonial and cult importance, as in the other Cretan palaces, but Mallia has elements of its own. There is a platform or 'loggia' jutting out slightly on to the Court, presumably for the ruler to use in public appearances. A staircase beside it indicates an upper floor. Behind the 'loggia' some splendid ceremonial weapons were found: an incised stone axehead in the shape of a leopard's head and forepaws, and a large gilded bronze sword with rock crystal and amethyst pommel. A second sword has a gold ring round the hilt, with an acrobat's curved body filling it, his feet touching his curly head—a masterpiece of repoussé work. These, and a third sword here, are the longest found in Crete. South of the loggia is an anteroom with a pillar crypt behind. In line with this, and exactly in the middle of the Central Court, is a pit *c.* 25cm deep in which burnt wood was found, suggesting that it was an altar. This has not been found on other palace courts. Further south, at the top of a few steps, is set a round stone dish, with thirty-four small hollows round the rim and a large central one. This type of dish is called a *kernos*. Other less grand ones have been found. They are generally taken to be for token offerings of first-fruits.

In the south-west corner of the site is a group of eight large round pits in two rows. In five a central stone pier survives. They are thought to be grain silos, as were perhaps similar pits at Knossos and Phaistos. There are many magazines on the east side, with special channels in the ground of the oil storerooms to take the spillage into collecting hollows; and more storerooms behind the cult rooms on the west, and some on the north. More space is given to storage in this palace, suggesting a more rural character than the others. Perhaps it had a closer connection with the people who worked on the surrounding plain.

Round the palace several large houses are being explored by French archaeologists. A market place has been located, and cemeteries with tombs of different ages stretch out to the sea. In one, known as 'the pit of gold', was found the most famous object from this site—a gold pendant of two bees or hornets clasping a round piece of honeycomb, with granulated and appliqué work of great technical excellence.

Low-lying, palace and town were probably finally destroyed by the tidal wave of the Thera catastrophe.

ZAKRO

In a seaward-facing valley, a little way up from a good, shingle beach, sheltered north and south by headlands, lay Crete's eastward-facing port, Zakros or Zakro (the s is omitted in Greek speech; but the name, which may be ancient, is feminine, not neuter). Its palace flourished from c. 1600 to 1450, with some rebuilding c. 1500, perhaps after an earthquake. Any earlier occupation levels would be under water, the silt from gorges in the surrounding hills having raised the level of natural drainage to the sea.

This palace is only about one third the area of that of Knossos, but extremely interesting, partly because of the fact that the early pioneers missed it. D. G. Hogarth, a contemporary of Evans (and the archaeological trainer of T. E. Lawrence in Syria) explored the area and found some interesting seal-impressions in clay—but not the palace. That was reserved for Dr Nikolaos Platon after 1960, who, already an expert on Crete, having been earlier Director of the Heraklion Museum, and with the experience of others behind him as he generously emphasizes, knew exactly what to look for.

In front of the town, whose blocks and alleys spread up the slopes inland, the palace lies with its corners, not its sides, roughly to the cardinal points of the compass, and the road from the beach comes up to its east corner and turns left into the principal entrance passage, with a bathroom off to its right. On this side of the palace were the royal residential apartments, facing into a Central Court, again about one third the size of that of Knossos. Traces of column bases suggest that the upper rooms had balconies. Much of this south-east wing, on ground sloping up, has been 'ploughed out' or severely damaged by later agricultural operations; but one unique feature was a colonnaded hall c. 13m square, with a central circular tank, constantly fed by a spring from the hillside. The spring also fed a main cistern below and to the south-west, beyond indications of a stair leading to the *piano nobile* and itself approached by a separate stair leading down.

Service quarters were in the north corner, and here Platon identified by bones

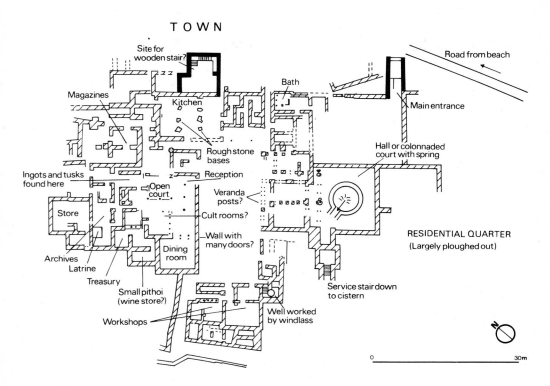

T O W N

Site for wooden stair?

Road from beach

Magazines

Kitchen

Bath

Main entrance

Rough stone bases

Hall or colonnaded court with spring

Ingots and tusks found here

Reception

Open court

Veranda posts?

Cult rooms?

Store

RESIDENTIAL QUARTER
(Largely ploughed out)

Wall with many doors?

Archives

Latrine

Dining room

Treasury

Small pithoi (wine store?)

Service stair down to cistern

Well worked by windlass

Workshops

0   30m

The Palace of Zakro (after N. Platon)

on the floor, coarse pottery and an absence of decoration, the large kitchen; no wall foundations separated it from the courtly areas, but he was able to infer a wooden partition, of which no visible trace remains, from the way in which the kitchen-floor débris ends abruptly up against a line. Off the other end (south-west) of the central court were the palace workshops, and here he distinguishes those for specialised workers in stone, crystal, ivory, pottery, even perfume-making (from the small vessels for holding it). Many of their products were found, neatly stored in small rooms and cupboards, in the large west wing, facing the residential quarters across the courtyard, which was devoted to ceremonial: a small shrine, a banqueting hall with a light-well, where many cups lay scattered, with stores and treasuries behind. Many walls here were decorated with the sacred design of the Double Axe.

The finds from this wing, now on view at Heraklion, include many of the most exquisite products of Minoan pottery and fine stone-vase making; for after its sudden destruction the palace had never been reoccupied, and nothing had been touched since then. The archive cupboard was found, stacked with tablets in the Linear A script, in a language still undeciphered, though an attempt has been made to read it as Semitic. Hopes of a massive discovery—perhaps even of enough for a decipherment—were high; but unfortunately only the top few could be carefully lifted off. They had not, like those at Knossos, been hard-baked in a conflagration; and all the rest, in the wet seasons of 3400 years, had reverted to a single mass of grey clay. Lying in disorder, by contrast, having probably fallen through a floor from above, were six large ingots of copper from Cyprus, and three massive elephant tusks, perhaps from the herds that still existed in north Syria.

Platon was able to discern beyond doubt the cause of the destruction that came suddenly, *c.* 1450. The whole place had been smothered in ash, like Pompeii; and among the stumps of walls of the store-rooms and inside great storage *pithoi*, it had not been washed away or absorbed into the soil. Even after long settling down, it lay four feet deep, and in it were sizeable lumps of pumice and similar volcanic material. Here, more clearly than anywhere else in Crete, were the traces of the final and most terrible eruption of Thera in that age; a catastrophe which, it is thought, must have rendered the whole of eastern Crete uninhabitable for a considerable number of years.

Post-Minoan Crete

GORTYN

Post-Minoan Crete never again led the Aegean world. Cretans travelled, as colonists, as pirates, as holy men, as artists, as famous mercenary archers; but the cities corporately preferred isolation, especially when Knossos and Gortyn, the two largest and most central, in classical times reached an understanding and imposed on the island a *modus vivendi* which has given us the word *syncretism*, observing certain laws of war even when, inevitably, local fights did take place. In the 8–7CC 'Greek Renaissance' Crete, in touch with the Levant, showed artistic precocity; but its classical culture was undistinguished, probably because, as at Sparta, the Dorian aristocracies were primarily concerned with keeping a large subject population, the *Mnoitai* ('Minoans'??), in their 'proper place'. One of the laws of war was that in no circumstances would the master class encourage rebellion by another city's serfs. Aristotle refers to Cretan city constitutions as all much alike, and like Sparta's, with the master class eating together daily in common messes, and the subjects forbidden to bear arms or to engage in gymnastic exercises. This gives added interest to the largest of all Greek inscriptions: the Laws of Gortyn.

Gortyn, dominating the fertile Mesara plain, is the best representative site for post-Minoan Crete. Knossos was as large; in the *Iliad* it is still listed first and Gortyn second; but of Dorian Knossos little of interest remains. The remains of Gortyn, by no means fully excavated, are scattered over a kilometre, north-north-west to south-south-east, from an acropolis on a foothill to a classical stadium beyond the city wall. The acropolis bore a classical temple standing on a late Minoan site, and votive offerings, buried on the east slope, run from immediately post-Palace to Roman imperial times. As its foot was a classical (4C?)

theatre and, across the Lethaios torrent, the Agora. Just north of this, perhaps about 450, was set up a round building with, inscribed on its wall, the famous laws.

This huge inscription runs to some 17,000 letters, arranged in twelve columns 3m high, and the whole measuring 9m from end to end. Reading starts in the top right-hand corner, and the lines run in alternate directions, 'ox-plough fashion' as early Greeks called it, to ease eye-movements. The Phoenicians, who invented our alphabet, wrote always from right to left; Athens, after experimenting, had long since settled for left to right; but, if a round public building may be a tribute to the prestige of 5C Athens, Gortyn's inscription positively asserts its Cretanness. It is, naturally, in broad Cretan Doric, and in a highly idiosyncratic alphabet. An Athenian would have had difficulty in reading it; but foreigners were not expected to want to. The laws are not a full code; they presuppose a traditional common law that was generally known; but they codify regulations on such subjects as were felt to need it, including questions of status among the lower classes and disposal of property on death; there is no free testation. A wife's property is not merged with her husband's. Slaves are more severely punished than citizens for the same offence; but they have recourse to the courts for injury by a citizen, even their own masters; they can contract a legal marriage and, surprisingly, if a slave marries a free woman, the children are free.

The building underwent several vicissitudes, and the curved wall ended up as that of a Roman-period Odeion (covered theatre); but it was always preserved, with its inscription intact. Gortyn was evidently proud of its historic past.

After falling out with Knossos and fighting several wars after 300 BC, Gortyn emerged as the leading Cretan city, and after a fiercely resisted Roman conquest in 67 BC (provoked, it must be said, by Cretan piracy) it became the seat of the Roman governors. Their Praetorium has been identified, along with a second theatre and a temple, among others, of Isis and Serapis, in a new city centre south-east of the old one; and an amphitheatre (meaning a 'double theatre', a closed oval) shows that the Romans introduced their barbaric customs; there are few such in the Greek world. At Gortyn would have been the See of St Titus, consecrated by St Paul as Bishop ('Overseer') of the churches in Crete; and a 6C basilica-church with apse was built over his reputed tomb. The apse remains in good condition. Its preservation, like that of the nearby theatre wall with the great inscription, is due to the fact that after the city was abandoned in face of Arab raids and, after AD 823, Arab occupation, the whole site was buried in earth washed down from the hills, already badly deforested; and naturally the parts nearest the hills were buried deepest. When F. Halbherr, an Italian archaeologist with a German name, first realised that there was an important building (the Odeion) under the surface, he was washing his feet in a millstream which ran actually above the level of the top of the wall!

Just east of the former city is another relic of early Christianity and the end of the ancient world. The hamlet of Ayioi Deka, 'the Holy Ten', is named for its aisled Byzantine church, dedicated to ten martyrs executed there under Decius (c. 250) and built largely of material salvaged from the ruins of Gortyn.

Thera

The island-group of Thera (also called Santorini since Frankish times, after its patron St Eirene) is one of the most fantastic places in the world. Navies could shelter in its lagoon, over 12 × 7.5km internally; but no ship casts anchor. Not far from the brown volcanic cliffs, which rise 100–200m on all sides, the water is too deep, reaching over 200 fathoms in places; and where it is shallower, near the active volcano on the central 'New Burnt Island', anchors can be lost, caught in the eccentric shapes of underwater pumice. We are inside a crater, or *caldera* as geologists now say, using for large craters the Spanish instead of the Greek word for a bowl. Its rim, the existing islands, consists of *tufa*, volcanic material including much ash, and porous; so no rain-water stays on the surface unless in cisterns (every house has one), and there are no springs, except under an older outcrop of limestone in the south-east, where the classical city stood. Otherwise, the rain soaks down fast. Only the vine, whose capillary roots are able to reach surprising depths, has the power to fetch it up again. The island's exports are the tufic dust itself, which, suitably mixed, can surprisingly make a water-resistant cement, and its wine, sweet and potent; too sweet for some tastes but unique in flavour *in situ*; unfortunately, it does not travel well.

When neolithic men first built their stone settlements and carved their figurines of Cycladic marble, Thera was probably a large island, covering the whole *caldera* and rising in the centre to a volcanic cone; but for millennia the volcano gave no cause for alarm. By the middle Bronze Age there were at least two towns. In AD 1860 workers quarrying the tufa on the south coast of Therasia, the smaller western island, for the Suez Canal Company, were surprised to find walls under-

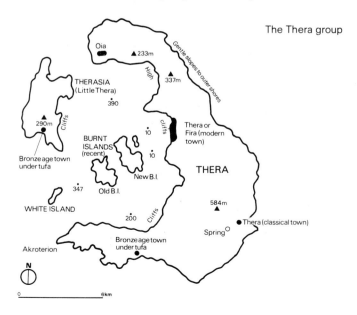

The Thera group

The cliffs of Thera

neath it. They were examined by the local doctor and the landowner, and later by the French vulcanologist F. Fouqué. Fouqué also encouraged two young archaeologists of the French School to examine (1869–70) similar accidental finds south of the village of Akroteri(on), named after the south-west peninsula of the main island. Working in from the side of a ravine cut through the tufa by the rains of thirty-five centuries, they found evidence of a high civilisation, including a fresco-painted room. Left as they found it, it soon collapsed; a warning that conservation cannot simply be ignored. Bronze-age Thera had been put on the map and the existence of a flourishing culture, and its destruction by the volcano which also blew out the centre of the island, dated, though somewhat earlier than is now believed. To uncover either of the towns fully would have meant removing thousands of tons of tufa; and there matters rested for a century, until the campaigns of S. Marinatos in 1967–74.

Only one street of the town on the Akroteri had been dug out when Marinatos was killed, late in 1974, by the collapse of an ancient wall on which he was standing. But the finds have been sensational. To avoid moving a great depth of tufa Marinatos, like the Frenchmen long before, tunnelled in from a ravine; he discovered houses standing three storeys high, with their stone door and window frames intact; kitchens, with their cookers and identifiable remains of food; fresco-painted rooms; even a detailed cast of a piece of wooden furniture. This was found when a keen-eyed archaeologist observed four holes going down into the tufa. It was decided to fill them with liquid, hard-setting plaster-of-Paris; and they swallowed a considerable quantity of it. The surrounding tufa was then very carefully removed, to reveal the cast of a bedstead, with even some folds of a rug, roughly thrown back when the last occupant rose, perhaps in a hurry. Both the cast and a wooden facsimile now stand in the National Museum in Athens.

There was another problem about this bed. It stood in an exquisitely painted room, and seemed unworthy of it. It now seems, from this and other indications, that a few squatters had returned to the abandoned town, in a quiet interval of some years, before it was buried. This is part of the evidence for a catastrophe in two stages, several decades apart, which, though problems remain, not least about its exact dating, would suit some of the evidence from Crete.

The art of Thera, contemporary with the Second Palaces in Crete, has been a revelation. Enough remained of many wall-paintings, now at Athens, to make possible confident restorations. Large blue monkeys riot round two walls of one room; a woman makes offerings at a shrine in another. Two little boys seem to be boxing, each with a 'pillow' glove on the right hand only. Two young, naked, redskinned fishermen bring home their catch. In the room with the bed, swallows fly and 'kiss' in mid-air (courtship feeding), above red lilies that bend in the Aegean sea-breeze. Particularly fascinating is a long band of miniature frescoes from three sides of a room in the rather grand though scarcely palatial West House, freestanding behind those on the street: on the north, a city on a hill, from which soldiers march out, while below there is perhaps a sea-battle—though others think that the 'casualties' in the sea are pearl-divers! On the west, a blue river winds through a tropical landscape; are we in north Africa? On the south, two more cities are seen; a lion chases deer on the hills behind one of them; and between them, august persons sitting under awnings on deck are ferried in several many-oared ships, while smaller craft ply between them. It looks like a narrative composition, if only we had the key to it; perhaps the autobiographical Odyssean reminiscences of an island admiral.

The pottery-painters lay on their strokes with a heavier hand than those of Crete; the 'island school' is definitely provincial. But at the same time, they know exactly what they intend to do, and much of their work, variously decorated with spirals or with marine life, bunches of grapes, flowers, grasses making a criss-cross pattern, has a charm all its own.

The town has inevitably been called a 'bronze-age Pompeii'; but Herculaneum is a closer parallel, buried *not* under ash, which could be dug out with a shovel, but under tufa, volcanic ash compacted into a rock, albeit a soft one. This has preserved what is under it even better; but it renders excavation laborious. Even of Ercolano not half has yet been uncovered; and Thera still requires many years of expensive work. As at Herculaneum, no bodies lay in the ruins; and no wealth of jewelry was found. Evidently the catastrophe was preceded by shocks sufficiently menacing to cause an evacuation. (The heavy loss of life at Pompeii was due to the fact that, further from Vesuvius, the eruption did not *look* dangerous. People stayed indoors and waited for the rain of ash to stop; but it did not, until many were trapped.)

The latest imported Cretan pottery in Thera was of Evans' Period LM 1a, *c.* 1550–1500 BC; consistent with a carbon-14 date from wood of a tree found standing buried in the quarries below Phira town, which in several samplings gave dates centring *c.* 1560, with possible errors of up to forty-four years. Nearer the centre of the island, it may have been killed in an eruption some time before the flight from a town on the south coast. But the great destruction in Crete comes at the end of LM 1b, a period in which a distinctive pottery style arose, definitely *succeeding* 1a, and was widely exported. On Thera the empty town stood half buried in pumice, solidified lava; and the pumice surface showed rain runnels and other signs of weathering before it in turn was covered by a new deposit. As we have seen, a few squatters, probably fishermen, came back and patched up some rooms. There was quite a long, quiescent interval between two convulsions, which are dated *c.* 1520 or 1500 and *c.* 1470–1450. Then came the huge disaster, in which the whole cone, covering the centre of the *caldera*, disappeared, blown into the sky or with its shell, left hollow by the ejection of cubic miles of matter, finally collapsing into the sea. The disappearance of all but a stump of Krakatoa, west of Java, in the eruption of 1883, has provided scientists with a comparison; but the amount of matter displaced in that of Thera has been calculated to have been four times as great.

Vast clouds of dust darkened the sky, especially, driven by a strong north-west wind, to the south-east, as is shown by the depths of it in cores extracted by researchers from the sea-bed. Some of those who play the ever-enthralling game of seeking scientific explanations for ancient tales of marvels have identified this with the Mosaic Plague of Darkness in Egypt, which would involve re-dating the Exodus. It was now that all eastern Crete was probably rendered uninhabitable for years; though Knossos, near the edge of the blasted area, was soon occupied by Greeks from the mainland. The greatest immediate damage would have been done by a colossal seismic (miscalled 'tidal') wave, set up by the backlash when the volcanic cone collapsed and the sea rushed in to fill the 90km^2 *caldera*. Masses of pumice, which would be floating everywhere, are found in the valley heads on Anaphe island, 24km away, at heights up to 250m; and many comparable figures have been collected as to the height and devastating power of *tsunamis*, as such seismic waves are called in the Pacific.

Thera seems to have been quiescent in early historic times, when the Dorian city grew up on its limestone outcrop. To relieve population pressure after a severe drought, its people founded Cyrene. It also produced some of the earliest known Greek alphabetic writing: male names, with obscene epithets, deeply carved on the outcrop, behind the gymnasium! Most of the extensive visible remains, however, are Hellenistic, from a time when the Ptolemies made Thera a naval outpost. A violent eruption took place in 197–6, when 'flames rose from the sea' in the middle of the *caldera*, and a new island rose there, now called the Old Kaimene, or Burnt Island. Other islands have appeared and disappeared in later eruptions; but a Little Kaimene appeared in 1570 and remains, and between the two a New Kaimene in 1711. Since an eruption in 1925–6 the last two have been joined in one, with, in its centre, a crater, most of the time quietly smoking: a safety valve which merely keeps the sea around it at hot bath temperature; though a violent quake in 1956 did much damage both on Thera and other islands. Many inhabitants then emigrated; but the small, white town still crowns the cliff overlooking the *caldera*.

THE ATLANTIS LEGEND

Atlantis is not to be found on maps of Greece; but attempts to identify it with the 'lost world', recently of Minoan Crete, and now of Thera, have been so persistent that it seems necessary to say something about it.

Plato in the dialogues *Timaios* and *Kritias*, a linked sequel to his *Republic*, introduces the name, short for 'an Atlantic island', a phrase used earlier in full. Kritias, who tells of it, is probably not the one infamous as the ruthless, doctrinaire head of the government imposed by Sparta upon defeated Athens, but his uncle or grandfather; a very old man, whose great-grandfather, Dropides, had been a friend of Solon, the lawgiver of 594–2. Kritias tells a story that he had heard when he was ten from *his* grandfather, another Kritias, then about 90, who had heard it from Dropides, who had heard it from Solon, who had heard it from priests at Säis in Egypt, who had contemporary records of the events of 9000 years before. They included details of the constitution of the kingdom of Atlantis, an island in the Atlantic 'larger than Libya and [south-west] Asia put together', and of the republic of Athens, where (Plato says) everything was then much better, before deforestation and consequent loss of soil ruined the environment. Attica then included all the border lands, lost in Plato's time to Boiotia; and its constitution has a marked resemblance to that of the imaginary Republic which Socrates had been describing to his friends the day before. (How wonderful, says Socrates, to find that it really did exist!) The story culminated in a war, in which Athens' specialised military aristocracy beat off the forces of Atlantis; but the detailed account of this, and of the subsequent earthquake and flood, in which Atlantis sank into the sea and the military class of Athens also perished, was never written by Plato. He gave it up, at a point where Zeus has just convened a council of the gods, to point out that since the lords of Atlantis have sunk from Utopian justice to greed and aggression, something must be done about it.

All this, even omitting many details, is much for a boy of ten to have taken in (though to remember what he did take in as a child is, Kritias remarks, not surprising). But there are more serious reasons for doubting the whole 'Säis' story. Firstly, Herodotos says that he had questioned priests at Säis; he heard about the source of the Nile and formed theories about an Egyptian origin of Greek mythology. From other sources he tells of the conquests of 'Sesostris' (Senosret), said to have marched to Asia Minor; so he was interested in such things; but he has not a word about Atlantis or any similar story. Secondly, if Solon had heard of a great exploit of ancient Athens, and talked about it at home, we would expect it to be treated in Attic drama, which has a good deal about Egypt; but again not a word, not merely in the forty-three plays that survive, but in the quotations by learned Greeks from hundreds of others; nor is there any theory of an earlier stable civilisation in Thucydides' introduction on 'ancient history'. Thirdly, in the quite considerable remains of ancient Egyptian literature that have been recovered, there is no foreign geography or history, nor trace of an interest in foreign parts except when foreigners attack or trade with or are attacked by Egypt; nor in foreign religions or forms of government, even then. No: Plato did not only add details (such as the 9000 years), as even the most enthusiastic modern 'Atlantians' admit. There is no reason to believe that any part of the story, hanging on a (surely deliberately) tenuous thread of alleged oral tradition and apparently unknown to any other Athenian in the two hundred years since Solon, is anything but one of Plato's 'myths', which are light-hearted inventions with a serious purpose. The detail about bull-worship first caused some scholars before 1914 to speculate as to a 'core of truth' about Atlantis, referring to Crete, which had traded with Egypt and then been lost to sight. Now the enthralling search for a lost land has been transferred to Thera; but though the Greeks were familiar with volcanoes (Etna, Stromboli; not Vesuvius, then dormant, but other phenomena in the Bay of Naples), there is nothing about them in either Plato's or any other of their tales of ancient catastrophes.

3 The World of the Heroes, and after

RICH MYCENAE

The Lion Gate has become the symbol of an age, a region, a whole culture, the final phase of the brilliant Aegean Bronze Age; an age, too, of importance in the rise of the Hellenic classical civilisation ancestral to our own; for Homer's 'Mycenae rich in gold' is the leading city of that heroic world to which refugees in Ionia wistfully looked back. To them, their own Iron Age seemed degenerate. The corruptible, base metal had driven out the nobler, as rough Dorians had, they said, driven out the grandson of Agamemnon; but out of their songs of a lost land, they gave us Homer.

Homer in turn gave us back the idea of the Hero—an ideal grand, but limited;

Mycenae: grave circle A

Homer himself sees how its unbridled individualism could lead to disaster. He also gave us back some understanding of Mycenae; for it was Homer who fired the young Heinrich Schliemann, first to make himself rich—the essential preliminary—and then to go and find Troy, and dig at Mycenae too; as he did, to the dismay of the scholastic establishment, which had its own doctrine of the Heroes as pure myth, and would fain have explained away Schliemann's gold as deposited by the Goths!

The Lion Gate is impressive, almost daunting. It is meant to be. Most of the fortress wall is massively built, but of rough stone; huge stones; 'Cyclopean' work as marvelling peasants later called it, imagining it 'piled by the hands of giants, for godlike kings of old'. But the gate and its approaches were ashlar-built, for dignity, though also for defence. A feature is the contemporary bastion, built out so that an attacker would have to approach under a cross-'fire' both from the wall on his left and from the tower on his right, unshielded side.

Above, the heraldic lions stand with their fore-feet raised on a plinth, 'supporters' to the sacred pillar between them. Their heads are missing; but cuttings show that they were made separately; one may guess, of some more valuable stone, perhaps facing the approach with glaring, crystalline eyes.

Immediately inside, on the right, is the grave-circle, surrounded by a double circle of standing slabs, with others, mostly now missing, laid across the tops. Here, in 1876, Schliemann dug, and at once discovered six royal shaft graves, with nineteen interments, and the greatest treasure of gold ever found in Greece. It looks like a diviner's flair, but really it was the simplest common sense. Pausanias, the 2C AD traveller, had been shown the circle, said to contain the graves of 'Agamemnon and those slain with him'; anyhow, the orthostats had clearly been placed to demarcate something special, and he would find out what it was.

The Shaft Graves are some 300 years older than the Lion Gate. Mycenae as we see it was not built in a century. The Middle Helladic Bronze Age on the mainland (c. 2000–1600) had had an unspectacular culture, distinguished by the use of fine, smooth, wheel-made pottery, conventionally called 'Minyan'; and the hill of Mycenae had held one of the hundreds of villages. Then the brilliant Mycenaean or Late Helladic flowers swiftly; we do not know why, nor where the gold of Mycenae came from. Greek legends told of the arrival, at the beginning of the Heroic Age, of strangers from oversea: Danaos in Argolis from Egypt, Kadmos from Phoenicia at Thebes, Pelops later from Asia Minor, going to the western Peloponnese, whence his descendants supplanted the Danaid House of Perseus at Mycenae; and serious scholars have believed that there may be some truth in this. There was no massive invasion; but whether under foreign or native leaders, what happened was the rapid and no doubt competitive rise of a group of wealthy monarchies. Thucydides speculates on Pelops' success being due to 'the treasure that he brought with him to a poor country'. Or was the new wealth simply due to the concentration in the hands of a few great dynasts, with professional war-bands, of all the gold already present in Greece, which previously had rarely, but not quite never, been committed to tombs?

An earlier grave-circle, designated Circle B, discovered outside the walls only in 1952, shows the transition. (A 19C Greek archaeologist had made soundings down to bedrock in the area, but by pure bad luck twice narrowly missed the graves.) It contained twenty-four graves, of which the earliest ten are simple Middle Helladic cists. Larger shaft graves and the wealth of gold then begin; also buried are bronze spearheads of a Cretan type, and long, thrusting swords with blades strengthened by a rib and hilts weighted with a pommel to give balance. These, too, were a Cretan invention. Three, the earliest known, come from the earlier palace at Mallia; but in that peaceful society they remained rare. Now they become the regular Mycenaean sword for such as could afford it. The new kings

Mycenae: Citadel and immediate
surroundings
Inset Citadel and southern approaches

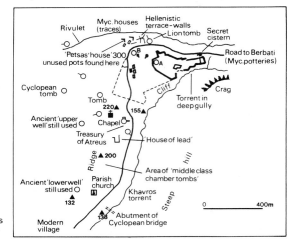

○   `Beehive' tomb without dromos
-○   `Beehive' tomb with dromos

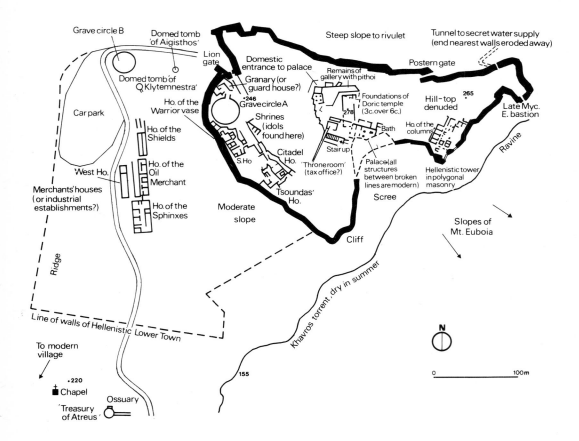

owed their supremacy to new, superior weapons; and strong hands to fence with the heavy but well-balanced swords were not lacking. One of the kings buried in Circle B was over 2m tall.

Circle A, which follows B with no time-lag, probably marks a 16C change of dynasty. Long after, when the Lion Gate was built, the newly extended walls enclosed Circle A, but not B, as if the kings considered A the resting-place of their founding fathers. Meanwhile, they themselves had adopted a more spectacular type of monument: the domed tombs, resembling in shape the old modern beehive 'skep'. Older examples of these have been found in the south-west Peloponnese, and one, actually Middle Helladic, in western Thessaly. They are corbel-built, with circles of masonry narrowing upwards until the final hole could be covered by a slab. There is no vertical keystone; they were prevented from falling in by the *lateral* pressure of stone on stone. The most magnificent of nine scattered west and south-west of the citadel was called by later Greeks the Treasury of Atreus, father of Agamemnon; the modern popular title, 'Tomb of Agamemnon', is equally fanciful. Too conspicuous to escape notice, it was looted in early times, which prevents accurate dating; but as the finest, it is presumed to come late in the series, and still at the height of Mycenaean magnificence; perhaps *c.* 1300. Its dome, over 13m high by 14.5m in diameter, is the widest single-span chamber known ever to have been built before Hadrian's Pantheon. Driven into a hillside, this, like others of the grander 'beehive' tombs, was approached by a *dromos* or passage, unroofed but with masonry walls; and the inner lintel of its door, 5.40m high and narrowing upwards from 2.70 to 2.46m, is a huge slab measuring 8.50 × 3 × 1.22m, calculated to weigh nearly 120 tons.

The palace stood on the top of the hill, with a fine view over the Plain of Argos to the sea. To the south-east the ground drops steeply to a torrent-bed, and on that side the processes of nature have carried away a corner of the palace, its approaches and the town wall below. (All have lately been rebuilt.) When new, it was approached by a grand stair from the south, leading to the central courtyard with an altar in the middle and, on the left, an anteroom and 'throne-room'. From the fact that, as at Knossos, the magazines with their *pithoi* lie behind this, one may infer that this was where the King or a great official sat to receive his taxes or tribute in kind. East of the court was the Great Hall, approached through an outer and an inner porch, very much as one may picture an homeric *megaron*. The main hall was *c.* 12 × 13m, with a central hearth; bases remained for three of the four timber columns supporting a louvre over it; the fourth has been restored.

Lost, if it existed (as one would expect from Homeric usage and from the analogy of Tiryns) is a bathroom *off the porch*, the convenient place in which to offer the facilities to a dusty traveller, with, if he was a truly VIP, the king's daughters to minister to him. (This arrangement had various possibilities: when Minos went to Sicily, the local princesses had private instructions to keep him under.) The Mycenaeans were, however, not so uninhibited about nudity as classical Greeks. This appears even in Homer, where the athletes wear loincloths; and the murder of Agamemnon, mentioned in the *Odyssey*, seems from Aeschylus to be that of a man entangled in a bathrobe with a hole for the head when his wronged and unfaithful wife did him to death with an axe. A room with a bath-tub in it was indeed found behind and north of the megaron, where remains, probably of private apartments, are weathered almost to nothing in their hill-top situation; but it seems more likely that the scene of the crime, the most famous of Mycenaean bathrooms, was on a site now a few paces out into thin air, south of the porch.

It is easy to imagine ghosts haunting the grey hill of Mycenae, just as the doomed, fey, captive prophetess, Kassandra, sees and scents them in Aeschylus' play; but it was not only family crime that brought down the palaces. If there was an Agamemnon—and there pretty certainly was a mid-13C siege of Troy—then he lived in an age when other sites, too (Tiryns, Athens) were strengthening their defences. They were also seeking to secure their water supplies; a siege had become a possibility. So, east of the palace, half-way between the east postern gate and the massive tower that blocks the ridge where the ground outside is highest, a tunnel was driven under the wall, turning east and descending to tap the water of the spring Perseis—a name cognate with that of Perseus, the legendary re-founder of Danaid power. The shaft is still there, though erosion has left its opening above ground, and a gap between it and the hole under the city wall, as well as lowering the water level. When it was new, clearly the whole of it must have been hidden.

Space does not permit us to discuss the various large houses, presumably of nobles and officers, with some fine fragments of frescoes, within the walls; nor those of palace suppliers, south of the Lion Gate—one of them, on the reading of Linear B tablets, a spicer. They were burnt around 1200. The citadel survived, with debased vase-painting as a sign of the times, for another century; then it, too, was sacked, and for a time may have been deserted. Centuries later a Doric temple, whose foundations remain, was built on a north-south alignment, its south end partly overlying the site of the palace.

HIGH-WALLED TIRYNS

'Hollow Lakedaimon' (where Menelaos' palace has not yet been found); 'Mycenae rich in gold'; 'sandy Pylos'; 'Tiryns of the mighty walls'. All Homer's epithets are extraordinarily apposite, when we consider that it was centuries since the poet's probable ancestors fled, leaving their country to the Dorians. The walls of Tiryns are even more massive than Mycenae, and quite different in style. All the outside walls are immensely thick; at the south end they have chambers in their thickness; and huge stones, the chinks packed with smaller ones, are hoisted in as though with glee; it was of them that the word 'Cyclopean' was first used. These particular Kyklopes were said to have been brought in by the Danaid founder, Proitos, at war with his brother Akrisios, grandfather of Perseus at Mycenae. The existence of these two co-aeval but not twin fortresses at opposite ends of the plain, not three hours' walk apart, is indeed so anomalous that it looks as if, like the frontiers of Belgium, they might very well have been the result of wars that neither side could win outright. Even in Homer, though Agamemnon is

overlord, Tiryns, with Argos and the Argolic peninsula, is still a separate province; but at the head of its contingent two descendants of kings of Argos are
accompanied, and overshadowed in prowess, by Diomedes, son of an exile from
Aetolia, a faithful baron who is dependent upon Agamemnon and never crosses
him in debate. Argos is the natural centre of the plain, and has a good citadel; but,
though inhabited in Mycenaean times, it was never the capital until the coming of
the Dorians.

The entrance to Tiryns was up a long ramp under the east wall, exposing all the
way the attackers' unshielded side to defenders above. It led to an opening 4.5m
wide through the walls (here 8m thick), later reduced by rougher stonework to
2.5m; but even this led only into a passage, continuing south and uphill under an
equally massive inner wall, to a gateway between huge, square, monolithic
doorposts. Here, in contrast to the first entrance, can be seen the holes for pivots
for double doors, and sockets in the gateposts for a heavy bar; and then there is
still another gate, 45m further on.

Only inside the inner gate, where surely no open enemy ever penetrated, does
the atmosphere relax somewhat; but this is still a 'service' area. The outer wall,
here at the top of the low hill, is hollowed out into the famous chambers (so-called
'casemates'); and east of the space fronting the entrance to the palace courtyard is
a fortuitously famous place: a passage with high, corbelled roof, in the thickness of
the wall, with the upper part of the stonework curiously polished, and with six
sizeable pointed-topped doorways, through which one can step out into the open
hillside! The fact is that one should have been stepping into one of six (store-?)
chambers, c. 3.30m square; but denudation has undermined and brought down
the relatively thin outer wall of the chambers, and the slope of the hillock is strewn
with large fallen stones under the ramping weeds and scrub. The polish was
administered by sheep, after the wall had fallen, when the gallery, half filled with
rubble but open to the world, was long used by shepherds as a fold.

What the chambers would have been like can be seen at the south end of the
fortress, down a stair from the court. Here a row of five chambers is intact, though
walls above them, perhaps more chambers, have fallen. Cisterns lay at the end of
each row of chambers, probably with towers above, at the south-east and south-
west corners of the fortifications. Slight traces remain of another row, west of the
court; probably much of its stone went into a Byzantine chapel, built in the court
but now removed.

The courtyard itself was entered from the direction of the ramp through a
ceremonial portal, no doubt gaily decorated. Stone bases show the positions of its
internal wooden columns. One passed through an outer and then an inward-
facing porch. Off the inner one, on the right, a door gave on to a long, narrow
passage with a 'jog' half-way; it leads to two smaller, secondary *megara* with their
own small inner and outer courts; and here at least one can feel fairly sure that the
archaeologists have been right in identifying the Queen's and princesses' private
apartments.

Visitors to the King crossed a corner of the Great Court, 30m wide, with service

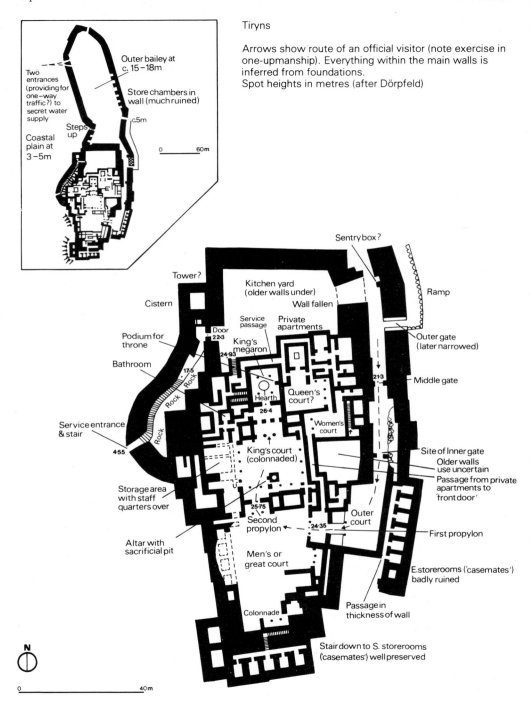

Tiryns

Arrows show route of an official visitor (note exercise in one-upmanship). Everything within the main walls is inferred from foundations.
Spot heights in metres (after Dörpfeld)

Outer bailey at c. 15–18m

Store chambers in wall (much ruined)

Two entrances (providing for one–way traffic?) to secret water supply

Steps up

Coastal plain at 3–5m

c.5m

0   60m

Sentry box?

Tower?

Kitchen yard (older walls under)

Ramp

Cistern

Wall fallen

Service passage

Private apartments

Outer gate (later narrowed)

Podium for throne

Door 22·3

King's megaron

24·93

Bathroom

17·5   Rock

Rock   Rock

Hearth

26·4

Queen's court?

21·3

Middle gate

Women's court

Service entrance & stair

4·55

King's court (colonnaded)

Site of Inner gate

Older walls use uncertain

Passage from private apartments to 'front door'

Storage area with staff quarters over

25·75

Second propylon

24·35

Outer court

First propylon

Altar with sacrificial pit

Men's or great court

E.storerooms ('casemates') badly ruined

Passage in thickness of wall

Colonnade

Stair down to S. storerooms ('casemates') well preserved

N

0   40m

rooms off it, and turned north through a second propylon into the Inner Court (over 20 by nearly 16m). The entrance is off-centre, to clear the centrally-placed round altar near it, where the King would sacrifice or pour a libation before he went out on any enterprise; the altar called in the *Odyssey* that of Zeus Herkeios, God of the Fenced Court. Stone bases indicate that the court was surrounded by a colonnade of wooden posts; and 'under the echoing colonnade' is where guests in that poem are given beds. (It does not sound comfortable; but the epithet is conventional; no doubt it was quiet by night.) To the north, finally, lay the twin-columned entrance to the royal megaron; the customary outer and inner porch leading to the Hall, just under 12 × 10m, with a central hearth surrounded by column bases for the posts of the louvre, and the place for the royal throne on the right. Off the inner porch was the door, left, leading to a passage to the essential bathroom; a splendid place, even with only its floor left; for that floor consists of one huge limestone slab, just sufficiently tilted to let splashed water and the contents of the tub when emptied run off tidily to a drain, through a hole bored in the far corner. On a flatter hilltop than at Mycenae, and no doubt artificially levelled, this palace is above all the place where a reader of the *Odyssey* feels on familiar ground.

Traces of earlier fortifications of a smaller castle have been found under the inner propylon. Naturally, the place underwent various alterations during the centuries. Its pre-palace prehistory goes back, indeed, to the Neolithic Age, when the hillock may have been almost an island in the coastal salt marsh. We see the groundplan of its last and grandest phase (13C?). A stout, transverse wall across the hill was added after the main walls, as the joints reveal, and the space between it and the back wall of the palace became another and humbler court. From it descends on the west a curving stair; hardly 'secret' as some have said, since its presence is advertised by a pronounced bulge of the main wall; rather a 'servants' entrance'. Later, again, but still before 1200, there was a major extension; the whole north end of the hillock was taken in, doubling the area within the walls and providing space for a considerable population and their animals, in case of danger; and here, as at Mycenae, a secret access to water *was* found as lately as 1962, and then by accident. In the extreme north-west of the new 'outer bailey', where there was supposed to be nothing of interest, two passages under the wall gave access to cisterns fed by springs at the hill-foot.

But Tiryns, too, fell, earlier than Mycenae. Greek tradition ascribed the whole Mycenaean collapse to the Return of the Herakleidai, exiled descendants of the hero, Herakles, at the head of Dorian hordes from the Pindos—foreshortening into one event, as epic and folk tradition both do, at least a century of wars and artistic decline. Herakles himself was said to have been born in Tiryns—but also in Thebes, which casts a mist of doubt over whether he was born in either. He is, in fact, a much more mythical character than the besiegers of Troy. He is made out to be a vassal of Eurystheus of Mycenae, and his famous Labours begin in the Peloponnese; but they continue to the ends of the earth (the Gardens of the Hesperides), and even to Hell. His Theban connexions were explained by saying

that first his mother and then he, long after, lived there in exile. Learned Greeks built up a whole biography about him. Sometimes he is an aggressive conqueror (remembered by Nestor in Homer); sometimes a culture hero. It is best to regard *him* at least as mythical; a hero who became a god, which is very rare; a god or demigod common to Peloponnesians and northerners. Indeed, the whole story of a *return* of the Herakleidai, necessitating their previous exile, may have been invented by poets to account for the fact that, while he was claimed as ancestor by all Dorian aristocrats, it appeared even from Homer that he and several of his descendants lived in the Mycenaean world.

ASINE

Asine is a small rocky headland (*c.* 350 × 140m, rising to the south to 51.9m) of the bay of Tolon, and about 8km south-east of Nauplia. It has the charm of a miniature and the fascination of a place where life has gone on for many centuries in a little room. Swedish archaeologists excavated it, first from 1922–30, on the initiative of the then Crown Prince Gustav, who participated, enjoying roughing it in camp life and eating sardines straight out of tins; and work has been resumed since 1970. Abundant evidence of very early occupation was found; foundations of houses long before the Mycenaeans, some with apsidal ends, and hand-made pottery dating back as early as *c.* 2800–2500, giving way to wheel-made *c.* 2000. Early Cretan seals and obsidian from Melos have been found in graves. Three artificial terraces were excavated on the acropolis. On two, foundations of pre-Mycenaean houses were found, and on the third predominantly Geometric remains, with graves dug down among Mycenaean house foundations. About 150 graves were found on the peninsula, above, below and between the house founda-tions of all dates. Mycenaean houses—one with at least nine rooms, two column bases and a cult ledge—graves and much painted pottery were found. This little town gets just a mention in the *Iliad* (ii, l.560) together with Hermione, 'holding the deep bay', in the ships' muster, among the far grander cities of the Argolid. Its name is not forgotten. There are a few scanty remains from the post-Mycenaean age. Even hand-made pottery and apsidal-ended houses reappear, then evidence from houses and much pottery of Protogeometric and Geometric settlement, *c.* 1000–700. A few Archaic figurines have been found, but, after 2000 years of continuous occupation, the little town was abandoned and there are no remains at all of the classical age. The people had allied themselves with Sparta against their powerful neighbour, Argos. Argos destroyed the city, and 'when the wall was taken they put their women and children into ships and left home'. The Spartans gave the refugees a place to settle in Messenia, another headland resembling their old home, at 'Rhion opposite Tainaron', on the east side of the south-west peninsula of the Peloponnese. This port, classical Asine, is now called Korone.

Asine by Tolon was reoccupied in the Hellenistic age (from about 300) and to

Tiryns: 'casemate' in S. wall

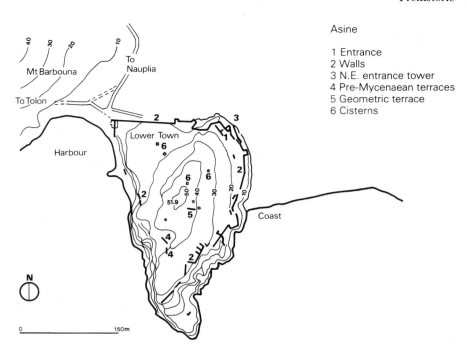

this time belong the imposing walls and towers which are visible along the north, landward end, and up the east side. On the west the rocks are precipitous and only the north-west corner and three small gullies needed walling up. At the entrance to the Lower City in the north-east corner is a section of paved ramp and some steps. A deposit of twenty Geometric vases was found just above the entrance in such a position, close to the wall, that it must have been built before they were placed there. It is part of the buttress of the road which led south up to the acropolis in Geometric times, and the Hellenistic entrance is in the same place. The south-east entrance tower survives to a height of 9.5m. Its base is over 10m wide and the south side projects 7m. It is built of polygonal blocks laid in fourteen horizontal courses. Up from it fifteen steps survive; more, lower ones, were destroyed when a bath of typical Roman brick was built. A stretch of about 300m of the walls of the Lower City survives, mainly Hellenistic, but altered and improved in some places by the Romans, and also the Venetians, who landed at Tolon in 1686 and, under Morosini, captured Nauplia from the Turks.

The last use of Asine for coastal defence was by the Italians in 1942–3. They made a pebble mosaic floor for their gun position on the summit, and the Greeks have left their inscriptions, *Viva il Re, Viva il Duce*, a memorial to their short-lived presence.

The Swedes have dug many more graves, including seven Mycenaean chamber tombs, some containing gold jewellery, on the hillside of Mount Barbouna (91.5m) opposite the town, an extensive cemetery area with graves of all types of all these periods.

This miniature Mycenaean city, or 'kingdom', has in our days gained the fame of a fine poem. The late George Sepheris, Nobel Prize winner and Greek Ambassador in London, was inspired by the place and the slight passing mention by Homer, to write 'The King of Asine':

> We looked all morning round about the castle,
> starting from the shady side . . .
>
> . . . No living form, the wild doves gone
> and the King of Asine we've been after for two years now
> unknown, forgotten by all, even by Homer
> —just one word in the Iliad, and that uncertain,
> thrown in here like the gold mask in the tomb . . .
>
> . . . The King of Asine a void under the mask,
> everywhere with us, everywhere with us, under one name,
> 'Asine' . . . 'Asine' . . .

And, at the end:

> The sun came up like a shield-bearer to war,
> and from the depth of the cave a startled bat
> hit the light, like an arrow upon the shield.
> 'Asine' . . . 'Asine'. Suppose that that were the King of Asine
> we've been seeking so carefully on this acropolis,
> feeling sometimes with our fingers his touch on the stones.

SANDY PYLOS

For sandy Pylos, Homer's traditional epithet is as apposite as usual. When Telemachos landed there in his search for his father, he found Nestor and his people out on the beach, about to sacrifice to the Sea-god and feast on the proceeds. There is sand in plenty; when a wind blows, too much.

The local palace is two hours' walk inland, on a hill at 150m, dropping on all sides in short, steep banks. Inhabited since the Middle Helladic, it was cleared and its surface levelled, c. 1300 BC, for a fine new palace, that of a new dynasty. (Nestor's father Neleus came from Thessaly, in the north.) The Lower Town half encircled the south-west half of the plateau, where the palace stood.

Of the palace complex, the first part to be built may have been the smaller palace at the south-west end; perhaps first a temporary residence while the greater palace was abuilding, later a dower-house or prince's house. It had an exceptionally large porch, with two wooden columns supporting the beam across its 7m-wide open side, and 10m deep; and from it one turned (unusually) left into

Pylos: 'the Palace of Nestor', looking S.E. (before roofing over)

the principal hall, 10m by perhaps 12 or more. Natural erosion of the steep bank, and stone-robbing, not least when the adjacent modern road was laid, have done considerable damage to the outer south-west walls. It had some fourteen rooms on the ground floor, a separate wine store to the north (as had the main palace), and, as the beginning of a stair shows, an upper storey.

The greater palace itself is not photogenic. Only the foundations remain, and are now roofed, to protect them, with corrugated iron. But owing to the short life of the building (it perished in a violent conflagration *c.* 1200), the ample space available, and the fact that the site was never re-occupied and was excavated (1952 onwards) by Carl Blegen, one of the great American archaeologists of his day, these foundations give the most coherent and detailed picture of a Mycenaean palace that we have.

The overall plan is simplicity itself: the familiar Great Hall (12.90 × 11.20m, much the same size as at Mycenae), with its outer and inner entrance porch, and ancillary rooms grouped round it; but these are more regularly disposed than elsewhere, all opening off two corridors running the full length of the building.

That on the left as one entered was later divided by cross-walls into yet more rooms, some entered only from outside. Doors at both ends of the inner porch, as well as from the front court of the palace, gave on these corridors, and opposite to each of the former a stair led to the upper floor. What is unique is the mass of finds which have identified the use of almost every room, and the character of the great hall itself. This, like the other principal rooms and some out-door courts, was stucco-floored, and its floor was decorated by a division into squares in its inner half, each a little over a square metre, gaily painted with simple geometric designs. Between the door and the central hearth, however, the 'squares' are not exact. The lateral lines slant slightly inward from left to right; probably to guide the eye of one entering towards the middle of the right wall where, as usual, was the royal throne. (Were people expected to approach it with eyes to the floor?) In front of it was the only piece of more elaborate floor decoration: a true square, filled by the design of that favourite Minoan creature, an octopus. It reached nearly to the edge of the great plastered hearth, raised 20cm from the floor, with its vertical edge decorated, an attractive device, with painted conventional flames.

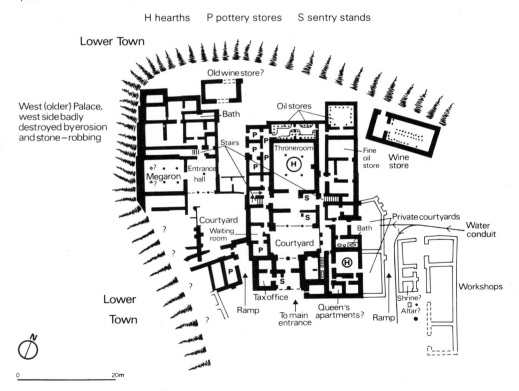

Pylos

H hearths   P pottery stores   S sentry stands

Round this, again as usual, four great posts on stone bases supported a clere-storey; and above, a detail not known before, two sections of large clay piping, found smashed on the hearth itself, must have formed a chimney carried through the roof.

Outside the front porch there was only a small courtyard, between forward wings of the palace which look like afterthoughts. At the north-east end of it, two bases for columns look like support for a balcony in what may have been the Queen's apartments, the east corner of the block. This had its own stair from the loggia, and in the centre of the ground floor a small but, it seems, elegantly decorated subsidiary *megaron* with hearth. There was no need for a larger internal court; for, beyond an outer gate (a simple door in a wall between inner and outer porches, with a stand outside it for a sentry and perhaps a sentry-box), the whole north-east end of the hilltop was open. One other door could be watched by the same sentry: that to a pair of rooms at the south corner of the main block, in which many Linear B tablets were found; presumably the tax office, or that to which workers brought their finished products, made from materials previously handed out to them. Many Linear B tablets, here and at Knossos, appear to be records of such materials, handed out to named individuals.

A large separate block of six rooms with clay floors stood a few paces away to the east; apparently the workshops. The largest room yielded fifty-six written tablets, many apparently specifying repairs in bronze or leather; some seem to name parts of chariots, and some might be 'indents' for material required.

What happened to the dues (taxes or rents, or however people thought of them), paid in kind by the people to the Palace, is revealed in the store-rooms off the corridors. All was neatly classified and put away: oil in large *pithoi* set permanently into stuccoed stands, in two stores backing onto the back wall of the throne room, and more in a still larger store built out at the north corner. Tablets apparently recorded the different kinds and qualities of oil; as it could only be drawn by dipping, and the *pithoi* would be refilled, it was important to know what oil went where. In a room nearby, off the corridor but only to be reached through a lobby, smaller, often artistically painted, three-handled jars probably held the finest oil, perhaps perfumed. South-east of this store, several rooms were found empty of any visible remains; they may have held stores that would not survive the fire, such as cloth. In one of them, however, were a number of small slivers of ivory in the débris, above floor-level. They had fallen down through the burnt upper floor, and may have come from the combs and boxes on a queen's dressing table.

Off the other corridor, and in the rooms into which it was divided, apparently to provide more storage space, with access from the west court, were found vast quantities of stored pottery: 2853 tall-stemmed goblets lay on the floor of one 'pantry' in fragments—but the stems could be counted; and the total number of pots of all shapes and sizes, in this corner of the block alone, is estimated at over 6000. The stores were full to bursting; which is probably why several hundred more wine-cups were found covering the floor, where they fell from the crowded shelves, in another pantry, adjoining a room off this end of the front courtyard;

probably an ante-room where visitors might wait for an audience. Wine was kept there too; a visitor might be offered refreshment; but why several hundred cups? One wonders whether the palace traded in pottery, or whether workers might draw it as part of their wages—until one remembers Maria Theresa's scores of teasets, decorating the walls of her apartments in the Schönbrunn, or the annual gift of a huge dinner-service from the Chinese Emperor to the Turkish Sultan, hundreds of which were found still crated up in the store-rooms of the Seraglio. Pottery, too, is among the commodities for which palaces seem to have an inexhaustible appetite.

The state rooms were decorated with frescoes, of which enough fragments remained recognisable to permit restorations, in the Pylos Museum at the neighbouring village. The royal throne was flanked by couchant griffins (as at Knossos), with, behind them, in a secondary position, lions; perhaps the paired beasts had some heraldic significance. Paintings of deer from other parts of the *megaron* walls remind us of earlier Thera; and here too, more recently restored, some paintings may refer to historical deeds of violence. In one, Mycenaean soldiers in helmets, kilts and greaves (but with no shields) are fighting or massacring men dressed only in skins: 'wild men of the mountains', like those whom old Nestor, in his first long speech in the *Iliad*, boasts of destroying in the days of his youth.

In the midst of all this prosperity, the palace was destroyed; we cannot say by whom, but the generation around 1200 BC was a time of widespread upheavals. Apart from devastation in the Mycenaean world, it saw the sudden fall of the Hittite empire in Asia; much destruction in Cyprus, and its resettlement by a new wave (the second Greek wave?) of migrants from the Aegean; and the great land and sea migration, whole tribes with their families in ships and ox-carts, which Rameses III beat off from Egypt, and which left the Philistines, also using Mycenaean pottery, to give their name to the land of Palestine. Nestor's palace was never inhabited again. The name Pylos survived, attached, indeed, to more than one place in the region; but no classical Greek, no-one indeed until 1939, knew where the palace had been.

Pylos, perhaps near the beginning of the chain reaction, fell in the midst of its prosperity, its store-rooms full, its scribes, almost to the end, still making notes of metal and flax handed out and work due in. Such records are not concerned with military dangers; but two tablets do perhaps give a hint of anxiety. John Chadwick, the colleague and heir of Ventris' decipherment, has translated five of the longest, of small-page size, as a list of coast watchers, some 800 of them, a large number for mere look-out duties, and widely spread; it looks as if there are dangerous people, 'sea peoples', abroad. And another (the last tablet?) hastily scribbled and apparently unfinished, is a list of offerings to many gods: to each a gold vase; but also, to each chief male deity a man, and to the female, a woman. Dedicated for service? Or for human sacrifice? There are tales of such sacrifice in Greek mythology. But the text shows such signs of haste that it may never have been promulgated.

One other detail dates probably from the very last day. In the bathroom, which was as usual near the main entrance, a wine cup lay actually *in* the built-in bath. Did the last Neleid king drain it before going to his last battle? In any case, no one ever tidied it up.

The fire was devastating. There was much timber in the palace, even in the main walls; also much oil. The perfume store may actually have exploded, pushing over a section of wall *en bloc*. The royal clan, if we may trust Greek legend, did not all perish; some Neleids, fleeing from the Dorians, appear and enjoy prestige in historic Athens and Ionia. But they never reigned in Pylos again.

MYCENAEAN TO MEDIAEVAL: ORCHOMENOS AND GLA

Boiotia (spelt Boeotia in Latin, but not 'Boetia', and pronounced 'Vee-o-tia' in modern Greek) is the land beyond the mountains, north of Athens and Eleusis. It was dominated in classical times by Thebes, whose citadel, the Kadmeia, occupied rising ground in the centre of a fertile plain; but the occupation of this site by the mediaeval and modern town has led to the 'quarrying' of all its buildings down to ground level, and to its presenting very little of historical interest. One building site, intended for a business block, was expropriated by the Greek archaeological service when found to overlie part of the Mycenaean palace. It revealed one major curiosity: a collection of Babylonian seal-stones, curiously miscellaneous, and unlikely to have been legible by its late-bronze-age owner. Some Mycenaean-age prince must have been an antiquarian collector; and his penchant for oriental antiquities may imply that he knew the tradition that Kadmos (the 'man from the east'?), legendary founder and ancestor of the house of Oedipus (Oidipous), came to Greece from Phoenicia. However, the large sums necessary to buy up adjacent blocks with standing buildings, for further exploration, are not at present available.

For a site presenting noteworthy remains of all ages from prehistoric to mediaeval, it is necessary to look further north, to an ancient city near the borders of Phokis, the land where a confederacy of small classical cities held the country under Mount Parnassos, from Delphi nearly to Thermopylai: Orchomenos, called Minyan, after its first legendary inhabitants, to distinguish it from Orchomenos in Arcadia.

Ancient Orchomenos occupied the foot of a long ridge, overlooking another good plain. Here neolithic men built a village of round huts of brick on stone foundations perhaps as early as 6000 BC, replaced by a different building style *c.* 3000, and again *c.* 2000, when there appears the Thessalian rectangular or apsidal-ended *megaron* or hall. With this appears the grey, polished, wheel-made pottery, with analogies in Asia Minor, which Schliemann designated 'Minyan'. Replacing earlier painted wares, and found widely in peninsular Greece, this pottery *may* represent the coming of speakers of an Indo-European language, ancestral or related to Greek.

The 'Minyan' Middle Bronze Age culture develops, here as elsewhere, without a break but under influence from Crete, into the Late Bronze Age or Mycenaean; and from this there survives a striking monument: a 'Mycenaean' domed or 'beehive' tomb, its roof fallen, but with a side-chamber (ossuary?), not rough-hewn as in the 'Treasury of Atreus', but with its stone ceiling elaborately carved with connected spirals, rosettes and a kind of palmette; a complete scheme of decoration, showing a skill which is represented indeed in Argolis, but only by fragments. Like the 'Treasury of Atreus' this tomb was known throughout classical times, but called the 'Treasury of Minyas', the eponymous ancestor. Homer described Orchomenos as fabulously wealthy; and one of the bases of its wealth was a remarkable engineering achievement.

The trouble about Orchomenos' plain was that it was liable to floods. The river Kephisos (one of three of that name in Greece) has no visible outlet to the sea. The water found its way out to the east through swallow-holes in the limestone; but these could prove insufficient in a wet winter, and might get temporarily blocked. The Minyans not only enlarged them when they could get at them in dry weather, but channelled the waters by means of canals, of which traces can still be seen. Traces have even been found of more ambitious attempts to tunnel through the eastern hills, but these were not completed. With the resulting resources, the kings of Orchomenos are said to have held Thebes tributary, until it was delivered by Herakles. There were numerous legends about wars between Thebes and her

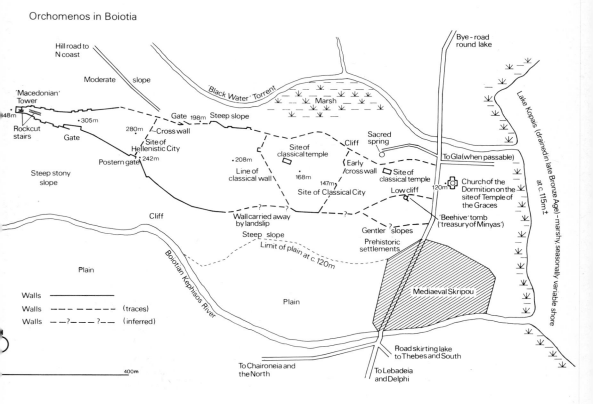

Orchomenos in Boiotia

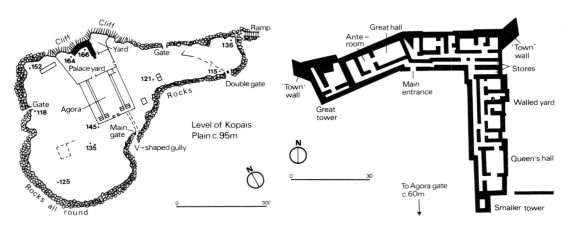

The Fortress of Gla (after A. de Ridder)
right The Palace of Gla

north-western neighbours; and the legends of Herakles, claimed by both Thebes and Tiryns, were compiled, as we saw, into a biography. But there is no doubt about the warlike character of the late Bronze Age. Material remains of it hereabout include the huge fortifications on the rising ground called GLA (Albanian for 'castle'?), a vast enclosure: massive walls, 3km round their irregular perimeter, and enclosing an area seven times that of Mycenae. Within, there are no signs of intensive occupation. Probably, like the 'lower town' at Tiryns, it was a place of refuge for use in time of war.

There was, however, a palace, on the highest point of the hill, which rises, a dome of rough pasture land above steep rocks on all sides, from a matter of 21m above the plain inside the south-east gate (a double gate) to over 70m at the palace. It is a thoughtfully planned building. Two wings run at right angles, one 80m long, backing on to the north 'town' wall, the other for 70m southwards. At the outer end of each wing, massive foundations suggest a tower, that on the fortress wall being much the larger. Near but not next to each tower is a *megaron* hall, reached through an ante-room from a corridor which runs the full length of the palace from a main door, the only entrance found, half-way along the north wing. The inner half, part of both wings, joining at right angles, is divided into smaller but quite commodious rooms, and these can only be reached from an inner, parallel, private passage in each wing, with two doors each from the outer, more public one. The south wing, whose lay-out is the more private of the two, including no apparent access from outside except by the 'front door' in the north wing, was surmised by A. de Ridder, who uncovered the foundations in 1893, to have contained the Queen's apartments.

The huge walls of the fortress, 5m thick, with some single blocks measuring 2 × 1 × 1m, curve or zigzag along the top of the steep rocks on all sides; the place looks as if it had been an island before as well as since they were built. Inside, some straight but much slighter walls perhaps demarcated areas for people apart from those for cattle; among them a large rectangular area, on the relatively flat top overlooked by the palace, could have provided an *agora* or place of gathering, where people could be marshalled; its long, parallel, side walls might have supported shelters. But there are no signs of houses; nor was the fortress very long in being. We do not even know its ancient name; several have been suggested, mostly from Homer's list of the contingents at Troy, but there are objections to all of them. The palace was built hardly before 1300, and burnt around 1200. Even the local Herakles legend may preserve a fact. He is said, in his war with Orchomenos, to have blocked the drainage system; and blocked, about that time, it was, turning most of the plain into the Lake Kopaïs (named for Kopai, a village that grew up on its shore), and leaving Orchomenos with greatly reduced resources.

The drainage system was not restored until modern times. Classical Greece never matched the greatest achievements of the Bronze Age in such utility matters as roads and drains—perhaps because the city republics could not marshal labour with the same authority as the old monarchies. Classical Orchomenos always ran second to Thebes; but tension was constant, straining the federal Boiotian League to breaking point, and at last in the 4C Thebes overcame and destroyed her old rival. However, most of the people escaped, and when the Macedonians destroyed Thebes they restored Orchomenos. Their work appears in the most striking classical remains on the site: the extension of the city wall in a pair of 'long walls' up to the top of the ridge, ending with a magnificent 'donjon' ascended by a rock-cut stair; one of the finest classical fortification works extant. Its site was evidently now regarded as an essential 'strategic point'; no doubt to secure the town from bombardment by catapult artillery, just then being greatly improved, from up the hill.

Many famous battles were fought in Boiotia, since all armies moving between north and south had to pass through it. Greeks called it the Dancing Floor of Ares, a more elegant equivalent of our ancestors' 'cockpit of Europe' for Belgium. The names of Koroneia, between the lake and mount Helicon, Chaironeia, across the Kephisos from Orchomenos, and Orchomenos itself, all recur. In the Dark Ages the place may have been abandoned; but, even with eels as the chief food product of Kopaïs, the site was too good not to be used, and a Slav village called Skripou occupied it. Here a famous church, once monastic, of the Dormition of the Virgin, paid for by one Leo the Protospatharios, or Guard Commander, and dated by his inscription to AD 874, marks the return of Byzantine civilisation. It is in a west Balkan style, paralleled at Ochrid (though to call it 'Bulgarian' does not really mean much; religious art was not ethnic); a Greek cross in plan, still with traces of the basilica about it. The low dome, on pendentives, is supported by very thick walls. Ancient columns, statue bases and inscriptions, built into the walls, reveal that it re-used material from a temple of the Graces on the same site; the Spirits of Beauty or givers of all good gifts. Their cult was very old at Orchomenos, and in their sanctuary a choir had once chanted Pindar's shortest but not least beautiful victory ode, for a boy runner at Olympia.

We are not in principle treating of modern times in this book; but in this bottleneck of communications the tendency of 'history' to repeat itself in the same place demands notice. The church of Skripou (now officially Orchomenos) contains a large ikon, commemorating a miracle of the Virgin in 1944. She appears in the sky, top right; and in the rest of the picture a German armoured column halts amazed, the officer in the leading vehicle shielding his eyes. The incident took place when guerilla raids on the Athens-Thessalonica railway had become so frequent that the Germans decided to destroy Orchomenos as a reprisal. An armoured column set out from beyond the Kephisos—and then came no further. A sceptic may be pardoned for thinking that it stuck in the mud; mud which had been fatal to armoured troops at least once before, in 1311, when the Catalan Company, a band of mercenaries, here destroyed the Frankish chivalry of the Duke of Athens and took over his duchy. In any case, Orchomenos was still undestroyed when the Germans left Greece.

BRONZE TO IRON AGE IN KEOS

One place where slightness of later occupation has permitted earlier remains to survive is the island of Keos (modern Kea, or in the vernacular Tzia, pronounced Djia); an island 20km east of 'Sunium's marbled steep', and famed chiefly as birthplace of the poet Simonides (c. 556–468). Pear-shaped, c. 22km long by 16km in greatest width, its rocky coast has three harbours sheltered from the often fierce north winds; and it is characteristic that in late classical times they belonged to three separate cities, each proudly striking its own coinage. In the south-east was Karthaia, at the mouth of a valley, where remains of walls and temple-foundations have been excavated; in the south-west Poieëssa, 'meadowy'. Its remains, on a steep-sided acropolis at a place where two valleys converge at the sea, have suffered more from erosion; but a few kilometres to the north, on high ground, a fine look-out tower over 10m square still stands four storeys high; the best preserved in all Greece, though now requiring attention. Two more, on the way down to Poieëssa, on eroded slopes, have fallen. The local schist, splitting into long slabs, is excellent building material, even for primitive architecture; some of the whitewashed farms dotted over the landscape still have sizeable main rooms roofed with it. A series of long slabs, called the 'teeth', is laid across the top of each of the thick side-walls, and then the gap is bridged with *dhonghi* (ancient *dokoi*, 'beams') of the same material. With a built stone bench, on which visitors are provided with bedding at night, running all round the walls, the general effect is something between megalithic and Mycenaean.

The largest bay is in the north-west, 2km across, and sheltered even *from* the north-west by a natural rock breakwater. It is dedicated today to Ayios Nikolaos, St Nicholas, patron of travellers. (It once took a miracle to save him from being wrecked at sea himself.) The ancient name of its port was Koressos. It was on the south side in classical times, and was not a state, but the harbour-town of Ioulis,

3km inland up a steep hill. This, in the undulating uplands, was largest of the island 'cities', and birthplace of its famous poets, Simonides and his nephew Bacchylides, a lesser Pindar, some of whose poems have been recovered on papyrus. The uplands still support many small oak trees, a local species whose acorns yield an oil used in tanning; still a significant export. Corn could be grown between the trees. But the Bay of St Nicholas has always been Keos' main 'door'; and here, so far as search has yet revealed, was its one significant bronze-age settlement. Here probably landed the first neolithic settlers, though they made their first home on a headland, still called Kephala, 1600m to the north. On the hill have been found the remains of their stone huts, and below it their graves; and among their artifacts two, not least among early Cycladic works in the island marble: a conical vase, and a male figurine in unusually naturalistic style. Since Kor- in many pre-Greek place-names seems to mean 'head', and -sos is the commonest place-name termination, one may guess that they were already called the Men of Koressos.

As their numbers increased, in the early Bronze Age Kephala was abandoned and they moved down to the bay. On its north side a cape, low-lying this time, is now named after a chapel of St Eirene. It ran out for 170m into the bay, and was 150m wide at its base. Since then the sea in all these parts has risen some 2m relatively to the land, encroaching by 10–15m, and leaving the foundations of a stout defensive wall visible at both ends, running out into the shallows. Many archaeologists had noticed them, and in 1960 Professor J. L. Caskey, with an expedition from the University of Cincinnati, devoted the first of many seasons to laying bare what has proved a highly interesting Cycladic small town. Wherever the excavators have dug, from the land-wall, which protrudes boldly in the central sector, down to two areas between the chapel and the point, the remains have been found of close-packed stone houses in regular Cycladic style. The area might have held 1000 inhabitants; a city, by the standards of the time. It flourished in the middle-to-late Bronze Age, the Second Palace period in Crete, when it imported much Cretan high-quality pottery. Bacchylides, writing a victory-ode for a boy boxer of Keos, tells that King Minos himself came with fifty ships, briefly (very briefly!) espoused a local princess, and departed, leaving half his men to protect her; presumably this was a local tradition.

What makes the Ayia Eirene site unique is the discovery of a temple, much larger than the familiar Minoan house-shrines. It is just inside the main gate, close to the east shore. Its original floor is indeed now below water-level, which gave the excavators much trouble. Behind the wall, on to which a row of rooms backed (not unparalleled in bronze-age fortification), a street or straight alley nearly 2m wide was cut through older buildings; and then, with its long axis parallel, came the 'temple', a structure of two rooms, *c.* 17 × 6m over all. It was destroyed, like the whole town, by an earthquake some time around 1300 BC, but was at once rebuilt, though on a smaller scale. In the ruins of the earlier walls were found the fragments of several female terracotta figures, of local clay, built up on wooden frames, of which the marks showed inside. The largest was nearly life-size, and has been restored almost complete. The exposed breasts (as in Minoan fashion) are large, as befits a mother-goddess, the waist small (Cretan style again), the skirt flaring. She wears round her neck a thick 'boa' or perhaps garland (the figure was no doubt painted); her head-dress or the top of her head is missing, but some of the other figures, about half life-size, show the hair coiled round the head in two heavy rolls. This is no doubt a cult-image, while the smaller ones may represent other goddesses or perhaps votaries. The face, large-eyed and gently smiling, is not without beauty; very different from the large idols of later Mycenae, which are consistently hideous, at least to our eyes. The find, in a place under strong Cretan influence, reminds one of similar, relatively large, late-Minoan idols lately found in Crete, and of a sheet of fire-damaged bronze from the palace at Knossos, which might have been a statue's hair. Statues of gypsum, a material popular at Knossos, but soluble in water, with wooden cores and metal accessories, might well leave no trace.

Across a narrower alley, south-east of the 'temple', and surrounded by similar alleys on all sides, is a self-contained block apparently comprising a single house, 'House A', measuring c. 30 × 20m, much the largest in the settlement. One may guess that its owners managed the shrine and were leaders of the community. It had no less than thirty-nine rooms (some must have been, or have had, light-wells) on the ground floor, and a *piano nobile*, as in the Cretan palaces, above, with painted walls. Fragments of a fresco of blue birds (rock doves) were thrown from it by the earthquake; some were found inside two great storage *pithoi* which survived, buried in the wreckage, near the east end of the ground floor. This was the grander end of the block. The east corner was rectangular, and framed a large room with a central pier. Off it and accessible only from it, a private stair led to the floor above, while another stair rose outside the door from this suite into the interior of the building. The rest of the block was of more irregular plan, no doubt following older lines. From near the top of the private stairs, there would have been a view over a small courtyard and along the street to the main gate. From the courtyard, just clearing the wall of the private apartment, a few steps led down into a basement; but a suitable 'front door' to the block has not been found. A stone outside stair that looked promising proved to be of post-earthquake construction. However, some sort of access from the gate, via the courtyard, seems to be postulated; *or* perhaps access to upper floors was regularly across other people's flat roofs, with bridges over the alleys, as it was still in the 19C AD in the village that now stands on the site of Ioulis.

The town was rebuilt upon the levelled-off ruins, which lay 2m deep, and survived through the Mycenaean age, probably less prosperous; but the chief reason why much less is known of it is that the new, higher stratum has been exposed to erosion. For the same reason, we have no details about its end; but by about 1000, with violence becoming, as it is for Homer's Achilles, a way of life, the site was abandoned. The people perhaps moved to Ioulis, a name which may mean 'shaggy', i.e. in the woods, at the top of the hill.

The presumably ancient name of Koressos was not forgotten, nor the fact that it

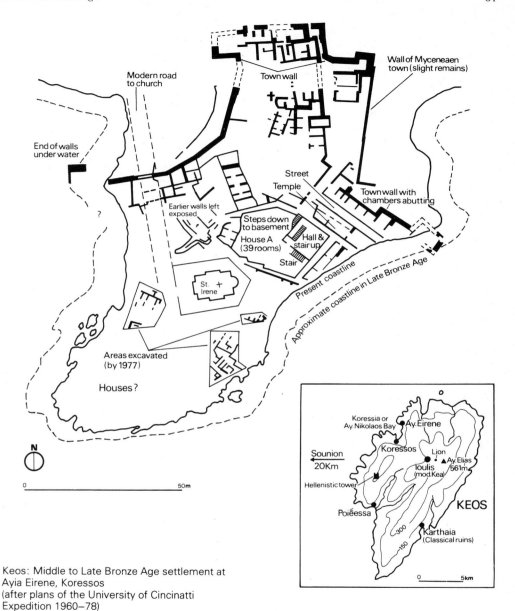

Keos: Middle to Late Bronze Age settlement at
Ayia Eirene, Koressos
(after plans of the University of Cincinatti
Expedition 1960–78)

Inset Keos island.
Contour lines given at (very roughly) 150
and 300m do not give a very good idea of the
shape of the relief, which usually consists of
steep slopes or cliffs rising from the sea, and
gentler undulations at higher levels.

had had a temple. When things were quieter, and renewed communication with Athens is showed by the spread of Protogeometric vase-painting—perhaps brought by emigrants, who were crossing even to Ionia—votive vases appear on the old site, though there was no settlement there. It was safest not to neglect the gods at a place where the ancients had worshipped them; and worship at Ayia Eirene continued through the centuries; indeed, to the present day. But the Keians, perhaps now largely emigrants from the mainland, were vague about just what deity to worship there. This is shown by one of the oddest finds: the head of one of the ancient statues, antique, therefore holy, set up on a new stand in Geometric times. The shattered trunk, which it joined, was found by the Americans over a metre further down. It is, we know, a female head; but when writing returned, in the shape of the Phoenician alphabet, *graffiti* on some sherds show that the deity worshipped was the male fertility god Dionysos! It has been ingeniously suggested that the image's Minoan-style pointed chin was taken for a beard. No site shows more emphatically the tenuous continuity and degree of discontinuity in the Greek society that survived the Dark Age.

Keos enjoyed some prestige at Athens as a place of simplicity and virtue. Aristophanes puns on the contrast between honest Keians and slippery Chians. It sent its contingent to the fleet against Xerxes: two triremes and two fifty-oared longboats, and these and the 560 men they carried earned the Keians their place on the muster-roll, on the memorial at Delphi. Herodotos names them as one community, and as one Athens afterwards assessed them for contributions to her Delian League; the three separate coinages begin in the 4C, when autonomy for every city was being written into treaties. The contribution was set at four talents, or 24,000 drachmas, top day-wages, which suggests a small but quite viable community; but on this and other small islands famines could occur. A Keian maxim is quoted: 'Whoso cannot live well shall not live ill'; and it was later alleged that they had a law prescribing euthanasia by hemlock for all, at sixty—the age, indeed, at which an Ionian poet had said he hoped he might die. Simonides, who did live to a great age, had long since emigrated. Another story has this decree promulgated only during a siege by Athens (4C?), and adds that in face of such resolution the siege was raised.

Keos has one more unique classical monument. *C.* 1km east of the town, in a valley-head, there is a splendid, rock-cut, couchant lion, over 9m long. It is difficult to date; weathering makes it look more archaic than it perhaps is. No ancient author mentions it; but there is a legend, reported by a pupil of Aristotle, that the island was once inhabited by nymphs, who were frightened away by a lion. Nymphs in Greek mythology are usually fairly benign; but was there some superstition that the spring in *this* valley-head was haunted by a malevolent presence, and was the lion (probably painted) executed to frighten it away?

III The making of classical Greece

1 The great sanctuaries

DELPHI

The 2457m gabled summit of Parnassos towers above the ancient Sacred Road from Athens: the beginning of the main Pindos chain. At the point where the old valley road turned west, to climb to a col, was the famous Parting of the Ways, where young Oedipus in the legend, disturbed by what he had heard from the Oracle and determined not to return to his supposed parents at Corinth, took the left fork: the road to Thebes. Over the col at 940m, the road descends to Delphi on its steep shelf, below the rust-red 'Bright Cliffs', the Phaidriades, and above a precipice, dropping from 550m to under 100 in the gorge at the bottom; in its mountain setting, the most numinous of Greek holy places.

There had been bronze-age occupation on that well-watered slope; it is attested by some burials above the classical town, and some votive figurines. Some 'Mycenaean' figurines, found by the French excavators near the Temple of Athena on the road from the east, had evidently been 'excavated' before, and reverently reburied—with Geometric pottery of the 8C BC! Men of that century, when Greece was recovering after the Mycenaean *débâcle*, were interested in the heroic past. Many Mycenaean tombs began in that age to receive cult as tombs of heroes, in the technical sense: superhuman beings, who had lived long ago, and talked with gods.

The feeling that inspired that modest reburial of ancient relics inspires also much the earliest literary text about Delphi, which is, as at Delos and Eleusis, a long narrative Hymn (the Greek word for it) in the Homeric metre and uncritically ascribed to the Bard himself. Apollo comes to Pytho (the older name of the place) from Olympos, seeking a place to please him. (Later, in classical times, he was said to have connexions with a land further north, with the mythical Hyperboreians, 'beyond the North Wind', and even left Pytho for three months in each year to visit them, leaving his half-brother Dionysos in charge.) At Pytho, in the Hymn, he slays a dragon (a deed treated as a 'murder' in a Delphic ritual drama in classical times); and the learned poet derives the place-name from a Greek word for 'rot', from the monster's rotting carcase. Apollo also takes over the spring Telphousa, dumping a mass of rock over it (the place is very liable to rock falls) when the spring nymph objects. All this could be epic working-up of a real arrival of Greek worshippers of Apollo, taking over a sanctuary devoted to older spring and serpent cults. Apollo then looks round for priests for his Oracle and, though there are already people living there, picks on a shipload of 'Cretans from Minoan

Knossos, who were bound for Pylos to trade'. In the shape of a dolphin (whence, we are told, the name Delphi), he sweeps the ship past Pylos to the port of Krisa; and the terrified sailors are consoled for not being allowed to go home by the promise of the great future awaiting them.

How old is this story? The word 'Minoan' here has no chronological reference; but Cretan wares had reached Krisa in the late Bronze Age, as well as in the 8C, which would be 'modern times' to the author of the Hymn (7–6CC BC?); and in the later age Pylos, which had had close connexions with Crete, had for centuries been lying waste. *Could* there have been a local poetic tradition, right through the impoverished Dark Age? Archaeological evidence of continuity of cult is lacking, although archaeologists of the French School have worked here since 1890, and would have been delighted to find it. That, however, is what classical Delphians believed about their origins.

Just how the place achieved its oracular fame is equally mysterious. The story that a herdman saw his goats jumping about more than usual, and found that they were intoxicated by vapours from a cleft in the rock—the same which later were said to intoxicate the Pythia (the 'Woman of Pytho', the Medium) seems to be a pure invention. We first hear of it from the last century BC; and no sign of such a cleft has been found, nor geological indications that there ever was one, though they have been diligently sought. However, oracles were given at many Greek shrines, so we need not really seek for a special cause here. What was unique was not the Delphic Oracle's existence, but its success. Its great fame dated from the age of colonisation, when several important expeditions set out from the Corinthian (also called the Krisaian) Gulf. Some of the stories are apocryphal; one, relating to the choice of the site of Byzantium, for example, simply appropriated an observation made by a Persian general 150 years later! Nor need we imagine the priests—though no doubt they did become well-informed—*systematically* collating information and running a safari office. Probably the answer was often contained in the question: not 'Where shall we go?', but 'Shall we have good fortune if we go *there*?'—for western trade had often preceded the flag. But perhaps, too, the Oracle's early reputation was built upon some spectacular successes in sheer clairvoyance; for clairvoyance or 'second sight', taking strange short cuts in space-time, is, even though most stories of it may be false, a phenomenon that does occur. It occurs, moreover, most often among highlanders and seldom among townees. All the freelance seers, too, who appear in Herodotos, 'retained' as advisers to army commanders, are from western Greece.

The Oracle was consulted about all manner of problems, public and private; and on occasions, it could act as a public conscience of Greece. A man who consulted it on whether he would succeed in an act of fraud was not only rebuked but, even when he had expressed repentance, told that to have approached the God about such a matter was itself a sin—and, we hear, his family died out. The adages KNOW THYSELF and NOTHING TOO MUCH were inscribed on the door-posts of the temple. But when the stakes were high and the question difficult, the priests, who 'interpreted' the frenzied utterances of the Pythia—a simple peasant woman, thrown into a mediumistic trance by suggestion, including ritual and the chewing of laurel leaves—tended to hedge their bets, not always honestly. The most famous ambiguous answer was that given to Croesus, the rich king of Lydia, who is said first to have tried out the Oracle's clairvoyant powers with a stiff test on a matter of no importance, and then sent it great gifts. He then put his great question: whether to go to war, to check the rising power of Cyrus the Persian. The Pythia's answer, as reduced to hexameter verse by the priests, was 'Croesus crossing the Halys [the frontier river] will destroy a great empire'. He did; but the empire was his own (c. 546).

Delphi had become an objective of Greek power politics some forty-five years before that. It was in the territory of the state of Krisa; but when it became rich and influential, this arrangement aroused envy, especially that of the horse-riding barons of Thessaly, who had embarked on a career of conquest. Krisa was accused of levying excessive tolls on pilgrims, and then (no doubt when already feeling threatened) of worse outrages. The Thessalians 'liberated' the sanctuary and put the port under siege; but they could not take it until Kleisthenes, dynast of Sikyon, west of Corinth, blockaded it from the sea. Krisa was then starved out, destroyed, and its territory 'consecrated' to Apollo. For the victors, its destruction unblocked a 'window' to the south.

The 'Sacred War', as it was called, was commemorated by the founding of the Pythian Games, or the reorganization of the local musical and athletic contests, which Delphi had probably long held (most places did). They were held with greater splendour every fourth year, half-way between those at Olympia, beginning in 582. Kleisthenes (probably) also rebuilt the Treasury of the Sikyonians at Delphi, one of a series of buildings like small temples, which city states were beginning to erect at the greater sanctuaries for their own glory and to protect specially valuable offerings. From this Treasury come some of the finest archaic sculptures in the Delphic museum. All are of mythological scenes; but one slab has an interest not only artistic. The *Argo* is about to sail on the quest of the Golden Fleece; and among the Argonauts, standing, with his lyre, is Orpheus; his name written beside him, in Doric, ORPHAS. This is of interest as showing that the mythic musician, who became the Prophet (never god) of a widespread Apolline and Dionysiac mystery cult, was known so early, and associated with the *Argo*. That story, which is quite overtly connected with myths about the clouds, the weather and seed-corn, evidently *was* a myth, and not only, like the *Odyssey*, heroic saga. The Grail legend, *vis-à-vis* the other Arthurian stories, is a parallel. Orphic initiators no doubt read into it further hidden meanings.

The Oracle had now become politically important. A northern Greek League of Neighbours, the Amphiktiony, which met for sacrifice in the Pass of Thermopylai and legislated to mitigate war between its member tribes, was now dominated by the Thessalians, and made Delphi its second, alternate meeting place. Athens and Sparta were later admitted by allotting to each of them one of the two votes long held by Ionians (perhaps of Euboia) and Dorians, of whom a few villages remained north of Parnassos. At the same time, increasing popularity had its embarrassments, with the prospect of increasing numbers of questions as weighty as that of Croesus. The Delphic authorities sought to stem the tide by reducing consulting days to one a month; which meant that consultants not enjoying the privilege of priority (presently given to Athens, Sparta and other important powers) might be kept waiting indefinitely. On the other days, however, an answer, respected though less impressive, might be obtained by offering the usual sacrifices and then drawing one of two lots from the altar. This restricted questions to such as could be answered Yes or No. This accounts for the remarkable story, preserved by Plato, that the God declared Socrates the wisest of men. Chairephon, the admirer of Socrates, did not ask who was the wisest of men. He asked, 'Is any man wiser than Socrates?'—and the God said 'No'. Socrates, who said that he knew nothing, was constrained after a long quest, in which he made himself very unpopular, to conclude that perhaps Apollo gave him credit for being, apparently alone, *aware* of his state.

Meanwhile, the sanctuary grew in splendour. The archaic temple, no doubt bright with painted wood and terracotta, was burned down in 548; but all the Greek world subscribed for its restoration, in stone. The great and turbulent Athenian family of the Alkmeonidai (maternal ancestors of Pericles and Alkibiades, and more than once in exile) took the contract; the later tradition that gentlemen did not engage in business was not yet; and they gained much prestige by going beyond their obligations and sheathing the façade in Parian marble, where the contract said *poros* (limestone). This was perhaps the first marble façade in Greece. It was the temple known to Herodotos, the Athenian dramatists, and Plato. It, too, was destroyed, by an earthquake in 373; but the third temple, of which the French have re-erected some columns, still stands on the ancient site. More 'treasuries' rose along the Sacred Way, which ascended the steep slope within the sacred enclosure in a long zig-zag. Most opulent of all was that of the Siphnians (late 6C), built next to that of Sikyon, from their wealth from a gold-mine on their island. It had, instead of the usual two columns, two plump and smiling damsels (so-called 'caryatids') supporting its porch. These, like all other surviving sculptures, are in the museum, now (1980) including an amazing wealth of sculpture sheathed in ivory and gold; even the great, throned Apollo, reassembled from fragments found reverently buried under the Sacred Way.

The oldest building still standing here is the simple Doric Treasury of the Athenians, in a fine position above the hairpin bend of the Way. It housed thank-offerings for the victory of Marathon; some of the spoils formed a trophy of arms on the triangular 'apron' in front of the façade. It owes its preservation to the fact that its well-built marble chamber was found useful throughout the centuries; in the 19C it housed the village pawnshop. When the French bought out and (not without police assistance) moved the whole village, which occupied the sanctuary, they found that all the stones were present except for most of the two marble columns, which had no doubt gone into a lime-kiln, and were able to restore it. Over 150 inscriptions (mostly honorary and complimentary) in small, neat, late- or post-classical writing, still cover its outer walls. Two, of special interest, have

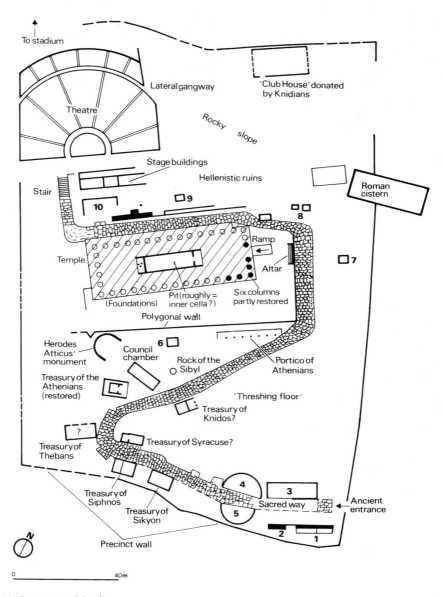

To stadium

Lateral gangway

'Club House' donated by Knidians

Theatre

Rocky slope

Stair

Stage buildings

Hellenistic ruins

Roman cistern

10

9

8

Temple

Ramp

Altar

Pit (roughly = inner cella?)

Six columns partly restored

(Foundations)

Polygonal wall

Herodes Atticus' monument

Council chamber

Rock of the Sibyl

Portico of Athenians

Treasury of the Athenians (restored)

'Threshing floor'

Treasury of Knidos?

Treasury of Syracuse?

?

Treasury of Thebans

Treasury of Siphnos

Treasury of Sikyon

4

3

Sacred way

Ancient entrance

5

2   1

Precinct wall

N

0 ——————————— 40m

Delphi: Sanctuary of Apollo

1 Aigospotamoi war memorial
2 Marathon war memorial
3 Tegean war memorial
4,5 Argive war memorials
6 Base of Naxian Sphinx

7 Site of allied Persian war memorial
8 Site of Syracusan (480) war memorial
9 Find-spot of Charioteer
10 Site of Alexander Monument

been placed under cover in the museum and replaced by copies. They are texts of 2C BC choral hymns to Apollo, with letters above the lines, evidently denoting musical notation. We do not have the key to it, but making certain assumptions, and working back from the earliest Greek church music, musicologists have tried to rediscover what ancient Greek song was really like.

Ten years after Marathon came Xerxes' invasion; and in the face of it the Oracle flinched, counselling submission or, to the maritime Athenians, emigration to the west. The Athenian envoys barely elicited, by a threat to 'fast to death' in the temple, a second answer, obscurely saying that 'a wooden wall' should survive and that 'divine Salamis shall destroy the children of women'. The Pythia, well forewarned, had greeted their first entry with a shriek, 'Fly to the ends of the earth'. What they extorted was probably permission to put their prepared question, *naming* Salamis, which their strategist Themistokles had in mind as Athens' last, island citadel.

Strangely, as it seems to us, the Oracle's faint-hearted advice shook men's faith not at all. The victorious allies came back with their thank-offerings, which clustered about the east end of the temple. Due east of the great altar of sacrifice (presented by Chios, and now rebuilt by modern Chians, some of them in America) the base has been found of the monument for the crowning land victory at Plataia. The scaly bodies of three snakes, twisted together as in a rope, rose vertically, and their heads, facing outwards with gaping jaws, supported the feet of a golden tripod. The gold was melted down during a war in the 4C, when the Phokians took over 'their own' sanctuary and were holding it against their neighbours. The serpent column was carried off by Constantine, and a stump of it still stands in the Hippodrome; one head survives in the Istanbul Museum. The coils bore the names of thirty-one cities, with the heading, drafted at Sparta, and truly laconic, THESE FOUGHT THE WAR. Somewhere nearby, a bronze Apollo was the offering for Salamis. Uphill from these was the more grandiose monument of Gelon and his brothers, dynasts of Syracuse, for their simultaneous defeat of an attack from Carthage. Below, backing onto the eastern part of the temple's terrace wall, a lightly-built colonnade bears an inscription in late-archaic letters, later re-cut, saying that the Athenians dedicated the ships' rams and *hopla* ('arms', or 'gear' or 'cables') of 'enemies', unidentified. It is an attractive guess that it held the master cables of Xerxes' bridge of boats across the Dardanelles; but experts think the lettering is too early. The colonnade came to hold spoils from several wars, mostly against Greeks.

The terrace revetment wall itself, of beautiful polygonal masonry and well-preserved, looks archaic; it is really archaistic, contemporary with the third temple, and (one wonders whether the architects knew) its avoidance of continuous joints between courses would help to make it earthquake-resistant. Opposite to it, across the Sacred Way, was the 'Threshing Floor', where the 'murder' of Python by the boy-god was enacted, once in eight years.

North of the temple, room was found for later dedications, cutting away the rock in places. From about 474 dated a bronze chariot group, commemorating a victory of Polyzalos of Syracuse, Gelon's brother, in the Pythian chariot race. From it survive, found buried in earthquake rubble, a few hooves and pieces of reins—and the famous Charioteer, at rest, impassive. His slightly elongated body may be a refinement, to make the statue *look* right, in its chariot, on a high plinth. East of its site, chance has spared the bases of monuments of Hellenistic kings: Eumenes and Attalos, benefactors of Athens, and the devious Prusias (of Broussa in Asia Minor), who in 183 betrayed the fugitive Hannibal. To the west, below the modest-sized and pleasing 4C theatre, was once a famous, no doubt very exciting, baroque sculptured group, Alexander's Lion Hunt; a hunt in Persia, in which his life was saved by his general Krateros. It was set up by Krateros, in the two years between Alexander's death and his own—killed in battle in the power struggle between the generals.

Up the hill some 250m is the running track, the best-preserved in Greece; its stone seating for about 7000 is perfect on the upper side. It was sheathed in marble in the 2C AD, by Herodes of Athens; but of that not a scrap remains. Its early-modern Greek name was Marmaria, 'the marbles'; and the peasants must have stripped it methodically, to burn for lime. Roman, too, is the arched entrance, behind the Olympic-type grooved starting line. The course is shorter than the men's Olympic *stadion*; only 160m, which was (is it accident?) the length of the older Olympic *stade*, for girls' races.

Here, says Pausanias, was 'the top of the town', and he turns back. Beyond was the cemetery, with graves from Mycenaean to Christian times. Pausanias, writing as a traveller coming by land, had dealt first with the second in importance of Delphic sanctuaries; another Marmaria, where a few pieces of marble, scattered under landslip débris, have survived.

This, below the road from the east, was the sanctuary of Athena Pronaia, 'before the Temple', *i.e.* that of Apollo. Later ancient writers turned it into Pronoia, 'Providence'. The easternmost building here was a small chapel of the hero Phylakos, 'Guard', who was said to have appeared with his comrade Auton-öos, two warriors of superhuman stature, to terrify one of Xerxes' columns, marching to sack Delphi. (Since the Oracle had counselled submission, one may surmise that the Persians, after ravaging Phokis with calculated frightfulness, turned back here by order; but that was the story.) Herodotos adds that there was a thunderstorm, and two huge rocks fell from Parnassos, crushing many; and, he ends, 'the rocks were still there in my time, lying in the precinct of Athena Pronaia'. That, at least, is no doubt true. One may be still there, lying among the altars east of the temple; but another, lying actually *in* the archaic temple, arrived there in 1905. The temple, Doric with 12 × 6 columns, was already in ruins in Pausanias' time. The French cleared it of rubble, but the rockfall of 1905 shattered twelve of the fifteen surviving columns.

The temple that Pausanias saw still in use is 50m further west. It is smaller, 22 × 11m, hexastyle, prostyle; that is, with six columns in front, but no surrounding colonnade. Only two Ionic columns, trisecting its inner doorway, relieve its Doric simplicity. Two rooms built on at the side look like a house for the priestess. It was built after the earthquake of 373; and it was impossible to build closer to the old site (perhaps reckoned unlucky?), because the ground was occupied. Two of the three buildings there are of the small temple or 'treasury' type; one 5C, of marble (very little left!), the other, *c.* 530, of stone. Its twin columns had foliage capitals (one is in the museum), of a style older than classical Ionic, called 'Aeolic' because first noticed in modern times at a temple in Aiolis, north of Ionia. It has been claimed as a Treasury of Massalia (Marseilles), furthest-flung of all the greater Greek colonies; though Pausanias only says that the Massalians had dedicated a bronze Athena outside her temple 'larger than the one inside'.

The third building, partly restored, is one of the most loved in Greece: a rotunda or *tholos*, *c.* 15m in diameter, with an outer ring of twenty Doric columns and an inner of ten Corinthian, engaged to a perhaps low wall. All are of Athenian Pentelic marble, and the wall (like the Athenian Propylaia) stands on a footing of dark stone. The materials, brought so far, suggest an Athenian dedication; but its use, like that of the *tholos* at Epidauros, is unexplained. Pausanias does not mention it (ruined already in his time?); and the date, if correctly given on stylistic grounds, *c.* 380, is too early for a monument to himself by Philip of Macedon, like that at Olympia. However, three columns and a piece of the entablature, restored by the French with the help of some patching, make a pleasing and romantic ruin amid the surrounding greenery.

West of the Marmaria the road to the main sanctuary bends in, to the ravine formed by water descending between the two 'Bright Cliffs'; and in the angle, just above the road, is the famous Kastalian Spring, where pilgrims purified themselves before approaching the Oracle. (That drinking of it conferred poetic gifts is a fancy of Roman poets.) The foundations of an archaic fountain-house, and rock steps leading up to a shallow tank (9 × 3m) below the seven spouts of a later one, cut into the cliff, are shaded by plane trees; it is a cool and pleasant place. Niches, cut into the rock-face, for offerings, may be of any age; the sanctity of the spring was preserved by a Byzantine and then a post-Turkish chapel, now removed. A rustic votive inscription on the rock gives the date 1824. There were other sacred springs on the main site, but Kastalia always kept its pre-eminence.

Just below Kastalia, nearer to it than to the Marmaria, was the Gymnasium or complex of athletic facilities, founded in the 4C BC, and maintained and variously improved through 700 years. A running track of 160m was paralleled by a long portico, where a runner could practise in shelter. Below was the colonnaded court of a Palaistra or wrestling school, and next to it the Baths. Water from the same sources that fed Kastalia was conducted to eleven spouts, where, with showers and bath-tubs handy, athletes could scrape off the oil with which they greased themselves and the dust that clung to it, before plunging into the neighbouring pool, 10m in diameter and 1.80m deep. The Roman age characteristically added facilities for a hot bath too. Here perhaps (as certainly at Olympia), athletes were

Delphi; the *tholos*

expected to pass a period of training and purification before competing in the Games.

Purified at Kastalia, people entered the precinct of Apollo from the bottom, where the remains of Roman-age tourist shops still stand; but the crowding monuments between there and the Treasury of Sikyon are the saddest in Delphi: victory monuments, mostly for wars between Greeks. Just inside the gate there was a second Athenian Marathon memorial, featuring the general Miltiades with Apollo, Athena and Athenian mythic heroes. If, as Pausanias says, Pheidias worked on it, it was set up long after the battle; probably promoted by Miltiades' son Kimon, to rehabilitate his father, who had died in disgrace, accused of misusing the fleet entrusted to him for a counter-offensive. Kimon was now Athens' chief general, when she was leader of a league of over 200 cities, liberated from Persia and fast becoming an Athenian empire. Athens' imperialism aroused bitter enmity; and when Sparta finally defeated her, she and her allies set up a huge group of statues next door to hers, or confronting them across the Sacred Way: the gods, with the admiral Lysander and all the contingent commanders, many of them from Athens' re-liberated subjects. A generation later, when Sparta in turn had won hatred and suffered defeat and invasion, Argos and the Arcadians, whom she had bullied, set up their own groups close by, to commemorate invading Sparta's homeland along with victorious Thebes. One of the artists had worked on the Lysander memorial thirty-five years before! (The statues were in bronze; the old man would not have been chipping marble.) Thebes herself built a treasury for her self-liberation, after a reactionary party had invited in a Spartan garrison, and subsequent victory. Syracuse had done the same, for the destruction of an Athenian armament sent to conquer Sicily in 415–13. Both were near that of Athens. So Greeks fought Greeks, until in 346 King Philip came to Delphi as liberator from Phokis, and in 168 Aemilius Paulus, as liberator of Greece from Macedonia.

Under the Roman Empire the Oracle still functioned. Even after Nero had carried off 500 statues (angered, the Delphians said, by Apollo's refusal to condone his murder of his mother), the number remaining was still put at 3000. Plutarch (c. AD 45–120), from Chaironeia east of Parnassos, was a priest and councillor of the Amphiktiony. The base for a bust of him survives in the museum; and many of his earlier works, written before the famous *Lives*, are the record of dialogues at Delphi. They breathe a gentle melancholy. Greece was suffering from depopulation. Indeed, was the whole world running down? The beginning of the end came when the place was sacked by the Gothic raiders of the 270s. Greek religion itself was giving ground before Christianity. About 361 the romantic, reactionary Emperor Julian 'the Apostate' is said to have evoked the last oracle, spoken among the ruins:

> Say to the King: In ruin the once gay courts of the Temple
> Lie; not a shelter of boughs has the God, nor speaks in the bay-tree
> Nor in the fountain; silent is even the voice of the water.

OLYMPIA

No change could be sharper than that from the austere grandeur of Delphi to the green lowlands of Olympia.

On the southern border of the land called Hollow Elis, which is Athenian for local Walis, the Vale, there was a place called Pisa, the Meadow. Olympia is the name of the sanctuary that grew up there. Round a copious spring at the foot of the conical hill Kronion, foundations have been found of a prehistoric settlement. It does not follow that it was a place of note; but it had its cults and, like all the great classical sanctuaries, Olympia arose in a place with some natural advantages. It was the classical age that made full use of them.

Olympia developed an enormously rich mythology, full of tales of competition and cheating—this last, a vice from which the historic Games remained largely free. The original, mythic chariot race was said to have been founded by King Oinomaos of Pisa, who loved his beautiful daughter Hippodameia ('Horse-tamer') so much that he did not want to lose her by marriage; so he required suitors to race against him, with death the penalty if they lost. One version added that if one got ahead of him Oinomaos felled him with a spear-cast from behind. A grave of eighteen unsuccessful candidates was shown in classical times. Pelops of Phrygia, who gave his name to the Peloponnese, outsmarted Oinomaos by bribing Myrtilos, Oinomaos' groom, who was also in love with the girl, with the promise of one night with her. Myrtilos took the linchpins out of Oinomaos' wheels, replacing them with clay. The wheels stayed on just long enough for the king to get up speed, and he was killed. When Myrtilos demanded his 'rights', Pelops threw him overboard at sea; but his dying curse rested upon the Pelopid house. The scene just before this race formed the subject of the pediment sculptures on the front (east end) of the classical temple, which survive.

There were also legends of Herakles; one, of how he cleaned out King Augeias' dung-choked byres by turning a torrent through them. Augeias then defrauded him; and Herakles gathered an army, sacked Pisa, marked out the site as a sacred grove, and held (the poet Pindar says) the first Olympic games as a victory celebration. But others put back the Foundation so much nearer the beginning of time, with gods competing in the games, that systematizers had to postulate an earlier Herakles, one of the Kouretes, or Youths of Crete, who hid the infant Zeus, drowning his lusty howls with the clashing of their arms, when his father Kronos would otherwise have eaten him. This is a good example of the complexities of Olympic mythology.

To the real evolution of Olympia, entirely post-Mycenaean, its institutions and the dates of its buildings give the best clue. The archaic Temple of Hera, close by the spring, was much older than the classical one of Zeus; but the Altis (local dialect for *alsos*, a sacred grove) had been sacred since before the age of written records, or of temple building. Its wall delimited an inexact square, with sides *c.* 160m, later extended a little; and it was the scene, not only of the great four-yearly festival of Olympian Zeus, but of that of Hera, in which the chief event was a foot-race for the local girls. Their course was just the length of one side of the Altis.

The race may well have begun as one of those in which young people ran, originally carrying something, *from* an altar on the occasion of a sacrifice. When men gained control (very likely it really was the result of a conquest of the south by Hollow Elis) they left the Heraian rites alone (they would have considered it very dangerous not to), but added their own festival, which became much grander. Its athletic element, too, was originally a simple foot-race; but the course was longer—192¼m, the classical Greek *stadion* (whence 'stadium'). A new stadium was laid out, originally beginning inside the Altis, but extending to the east, between earth banks. The spectators never had anything more luxurious to sit on, except for a later built-up box for the Presidents of the Games (obviously not judges!) half way along; opposite it was an altar, on which a woman sat, watching the Games from which the rest of her sex were rigorously excluded. She was the priestess of the earth goddess, Demeter, and she was there as of right; for the new Stadium cut slightly into her goddess's precincts. This, and the fact that the girls raced just the length of the Altis, are evidence that women and female deities, as in the old bronze-age religion, were in control here first, and that Olympian Zeus, from his mountain in the north, was intrusive.

Later, when Olympia became famous, it naturally attracted dedications from the whole Greek world. Among them were trophies of arms from many battles; not least, from the Persian Wars. A favourite place for these was along the banks of the Stadium, where they were probably supported on wooden crosses. When the posts wore out, they were apparently left religiously where they lay, and covered with earth in successive repairs to the banks. When the Germans, in recent decades, excavated the whole stadium from under thousands of tons of silt from mediaeval floods, they found enough Greek bronze armour to give the new museum the finest collection in the world. One conical helmet (an old oriental shape) bears the words 'the Athenians dedicated [this], taken from the Medes'; and a Greek one the even terser and even more intriguing 'Miltiades dedicated'. Probably this is the famous Miltiades, victor of Marathon; and it may be the helmet he wore in the battle, dedicated *ex voto*.

Meanwhile, more events had been added to the Games, mostly, we hear, in the 7–6CC; first a two-length race; later wrestling, boxing, the pentathlon (long jump, foot-race, discus, javelin and wrestling); all-in combat, in which nothing was barred except biting and gouging; and the horse events, both riding and driving. Most prestigious of all in classical times was to win with the four-horse chariot, which only dynasts and the very rich could afford—and they did not drive their own teams. The athletics, including events for boys under puberty, had now become the chief feature of the festival, and after a failure to complete the programme in daylight, it was extended to several days.

Gradually too grew up the first monumental building within the Grove. 'Grew' is the right word. Far back in the Dark Ages, according to the Eleians, a Temple of Hera had been built. It was near the spring; probably a simple wooden megaron to house the cult image of The Goddess, and later that of her husband too. After 700 BC, a more solid structure was built, with stone foundations; but the upper

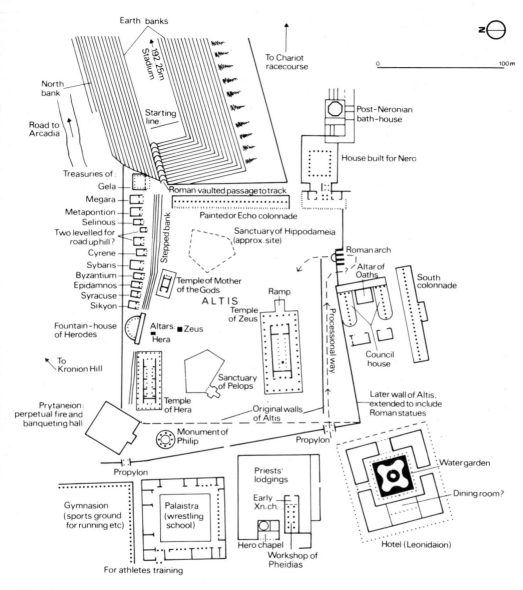

Olympia

walls were of mud brick. 'There are pillars all round it', says Pausanias, thanks to whose detailed description of the site the German excavators have been able to identify all the buildings. He does not say a regular colonnade; and we can see why. The Doric columns that stand there now are of all ages, from archaic to

Olympia: the Temple of Hera

Roman, and vary in shape. The earliest are thickest, with bulging 'cushion' capitals; and Pausanias adds that one pillar inside, at the west end, was of oak. Probably all the pillars, inside and out, had been of wood; the *cella* had simply been given very wide 'eaves', supported on wooden posts, to keep rain off the brick; and the posts had been replaced in stone as and when they wore out.

 We can see here the evolution of the classical Doric temple, which, even when built in marble like the Parthenon, preserved the marks of its wooden ancestry. The 'triple-grooved' *triglyphs* represent the ends of roof beams supported upon the architrave above each column and one over each space between; and *metopes*, later the stone slabs between the triglyphs, put to such fine use for sculpture, originally meant 'spaces between'. *Metope* as a surface to be decorated meant originally a slab of terracotta put in to block such a hole, to stop birds from nesting and making a mess. We do not know if the Heraion in its thousand years of use ever had painted metopes; but undoubtedly it would have been brightly painted. Archaic public buildings and stone sculptures always were. They would have been a surprising spectacle to viewers brought up on early-modern ideas of classical restraint.

The mud brick has been responsible for leaving the Heraion today the best preserved building at Olympia. When the site was deserted and its roof timbers gave way, the mud brick gradually melted and settled down in a mass, along with more mud from flooding, protecting the stone lower walls of the *cella*; and these remain, almost unworn. Into the mud also fell, its legs snapping probably in an earthquake, but not injuring even its nose, the most famous statue remaining at Olympia. Pausanias just mentions, here, among 'other dedications: a Hermes in stone, holding an infant Dionysos; work of Praxiteles'. If so, it is something unique; an original work from the hand of one of those reckoned by ancient critics the Great Six Masters of classical sculpture (Myron [of the Diskobolos]; Pheidias; Polykleitos; Praxiteles; Skopas, who worked on the Mausoleum with three others, and Lysippos, the portraitist of Alexander the Great), from whom otherwise we have only copies, of varying degrees of competence. Unhappily, most high authorities have now become convinced, often unwillingly, for a variety of technical reasons, that this is a copy too. Sleekly handsome and of wonderful 'finish', it remains, if it is a copy, uniquely good of its kind.

Meanwhile, the rest of the Altis was still a grove. North-west of its centre a pentagonal area some 40×30m across was demarcated by a low wall. It was the special grove of the hero Pelops, still distinguishable. East of it was another for Hippodameia, but this has disappeared. The altar of Hera was in the normal position east of her temple; and south of it developed the great altar of Zeus, never a built structure, but consisting of a huge mass of ash; one of the primitive features which Olympia preserved. As it constantly settled, it was kept up, between monthly sacrifices, by dumping on it the spare ash brought out from the Prytaneion, literally 'presidency', at the north-west corner. Here, as in city *prytaneia*, a perpetual fire was kept burning, and here the victorious athletes and horse-owners were entertained to dinner.

Stone buildings (stuccoed and brightly decorated) began to be seen, however, after *c*. 600, in the shape of the 'Treasuries', whose foundations remain at the top of a stepped bank (the foot of Kronos or Kronion Hill), lining the north wall of the Altis east of the spring. They were, as at Delphi, chapel-like buildings dedicated by cities, to house specially valuable offerings, often paid for out of spoils of war. Ultimately, there were twelve. Pausanias names ten; two, in the middle, may have been demolished before his time and their foundations hidden under a road up the hill. He names, from east to west, those of Gela in Sicily, the first and largest; Megara in old Greece; Metapontion in Italy; Selinous in Sicily; Cyrene; Sybaris in Italy; Byzantium; Epidamnos (Dürres in Albania); Syracuse, commonly called the Treasury of the Carthaginians, because it housed spoils from the defeat of their invasion in 480; and Sikyon, just west of Corinth. It is striking that all but two of the dedications are from colonial cities, and half from the opulent and powerful colonies in the west, Greece's America. Western visitors were prominent at this west-Greek pilgrimage centre. Actually, out of fifty classical or archaic bronze brooches found here before 1930, having been dedicated or merely lost, nearly half were of western colonial shapes.

The western connexion had a side effect with a long history in European literature: it must have been here that the Sicilians, rich townsmen—for the poor could not afford to come—discovered Arcadia. The Syracusan Theokritos (*fl. c.* 260) was to make of it a poetic dream-world, where the Nymphs (mountain, forest and spring spirits, thought of as lovely girls, but slightly uncanny) and Pan the goat-god, bringer of panic fear—were never far from the thoughts of shepherds and shepherdesses. This Arcady had nothing to do with the high-lying, war-ridden lands of eastern Arcadia; it began close to Olympia, in the green, better-watered west. Kronos Hill itself is a foothill of the Arcadian mountains.

After the repulse of Xerxes, the Eleians evidently began to think of giving Father Zeus a worthy temple, such as might be seen in many oversea cities. The bronze Zeus set up by the allied Greeks in thanksgiving stood inside the south-east processional entrance; perhaps the site for the temple was already chosen, or even occupied by some simpler edifice. The new one, on massive foundations, 200 Olympic feet along the top step by $86\frac{1}{2}$ (64.12×27.66m), with 6×13 stout Doric columns, is of local fossiliferous limestone, which would have been covered in smooth stucco. All the columns have been shaken down by earthquakes since the site was abandoned, and the squared blocks were built into a Byzantine fortification. Some of the columns, with their drums lying like fallen dominoes, are impressive even in ruin; but the weathered stone is unfortunately extremely friable, and to re-erect some of them would be a hazardous enterprise.

The temple was finished in 457; and its splendid gable-end (pediment) sculptures are largely preserved, through having been built into the Byzantine fort. They represent the fine flower of pre-Pheidian sculpture. But for their gold and ivory statue of Zeus, a work intended to match Pheidias' Athena, the Eleians decided, during the peace of 445–31, to charter Pheidias himself.

Pausanias was shown the Workshop of Pheidias, outside the Altis opposite the west front of the temple; and his information is right. In a space between later buildings, occupied for a time by a Byzantine basilica-church, were found clay moulds for casting the sheets of gold for Zeus' draperies (they were attached, piece by piece, to a wood and clay interior model); small slivers of ivory and even tinier particles of gold; goldsmith's tools, much worn, and, most precious of all, the bottom of a small black-glazed jug, inscribed beneath in a firm hand, 'I am Pheidias' [jug]'. So here, exactly, the prince of sculptors worked on his statue of the king of Olympos. His descendants, called 'the polishers', were charged with its maintenance 'for ever', oiling the ivory to avert cracking.

The throned statue rose forty feet from the pavement. There was a gallery for viewing it. We hear that its sheer size did worry some viewers, who reflected that if Zeus had stood up he would have gone through the roof. But the Roman literature teacher, Quintilian, said that by the benevolence of its expression it added something to the received religion. It was removed to Constantinople by a Christian emperor, and perished in a palace fire (c. AD 475).

During the 5C too, the starting line of the track was moved out of the Altis, and the East Colonnade, called later the Painted and the Echo Colonnade—it was said that a voice there echoed seven times—was built. The Grove was now on three sides a classical, columned quadrangle. Olympia, like Athens, had reached its zenith. Pindar, its greatest poetic celebrant, was an older contemporary of Pheidias. Late in the century something of its spring-time glory begins to fade. Semi-professional specialisation began to invade athletics; for, though the Crown of Wild Olive, cut by a boy with a golden sickle from a special tree south of the great temple, was still the only official award, cities rewarded the winners who brought fame to *them* with more tangible prizes. The right to dine at 'High Table' in the Prytaneion for life was often one. Already Xenophanes, an irreverent philosopher-poet who emigrated to the west, had mocked at the extravagant honours paid to athletes. Euripides later paraphrased him. But the tendency would not be stopped; and old-fashioned gentlemen-athletes, who could afford to compete for honour alone, had to admit that the new specialists were generally the winners.

Later buildings at Olympia were ancillary. To the west, outside the Altis, the Palaistra or wrestling-school and Gymnasion or general sports-field, where competitors had to spend the last month before the Games and the redundant were perhaps eliminated in 'heats', were surrounded by slender colonnades. The Palaistra had dressing-rooms round its central courtyard. In the 4C Leonidas, a rich man of Naxos, donated in the south-west another quadrangular building, probably a hostel for distinguished visitors. Its main entrance faced the temple and the Council House (south, outside the Altis), with its altar where competitors swore to play fair and observe the rules. Across the quadrangle an open-fronted, columned hall might have been for dining, while the rest is divided into rooms or suites. Lastly, in the 4C, the end of classical Greece is marked by the erection of a pillared rotunda, the Philippeion, promoted by the conquering king Philip of Macedon in honour of himself. The west wall of the Altis was slanted out from true north to make room for it. Philip and his immediate family, whose statues stood there with his own, were in with the gods; a step towards the divine pretensions and cult of his son Alexander, and of many Hellenistic rulers, and Roman emperors.

It is difficult for us to understand these ruler-cults; but it is certainly wrong to suppose that all those who took part in them were merely bowing in slavish adulation. People were, rather, in search of a saviour, a father-figure. The cult of Caesar sprang up when he was dead, and in face of official disapproval. Augustus was embarrassed by his own cult in Greek Asia; but it was impolitic to reject it. So with Philip; many Eleians and others, though by no means without 'a lively sense of future favours', probably were grateful to him for stopping the wars and bullying power politics of Thebes, Athens and Sparta. The Eleians had themselves fought a battle in the Altis itself, trying to recapture their own sanctuary from Thebes' Arcadian allies, in the middle of the festival!

Olympia survived; but it had to come to terms with the times. Romans, as at all Greek sanctuaries, had to be accepted as not barbarians. Among the proliferating statues—3000, we are told, by *c.* AD 70—many were of Romans, among them Q. Metellus, conqueror of Macedonia, and L. Mummius, destroyer of Corinth and of the Achaian League. The Eleians, who had favoured the rival, Aetolian League, were perhaps less shocked by this than some; and the south wall of the Altis in its turn was slanted outwards, to take in these and other statues of the new lords. Under the empire a small 4C BC temple of The Mother of the Gods (no doubt on a more ancient site), east of that of Hera, was used to house statues of the emperors; and Leonidas' hotel became the residence of the Proconsul of Achaia when he attended the Games.

The most famous Roman visit here was that of Nero, in 67. The Games were not due until 69 (since there is no Year 0, AD 1 was an Olympic year, and so on) but they were brought forward in his honour. A special house was built for him in the south-east corner; its brick walls look dull, but they would have been stuccoed and frescoed; and near it a triumphal arch leading into the Altis, whose abutments remain. He was said to have raced his own chariot, crashed, and been awarded the crown by acclamation, for his courage. It could be true; but stories against Nero proliferated.

Later, part of Nero's house was overlaid by one of the several Roman bath-houses. Olympia was being made more comfortable. The last classical building here was the elegant fountain-house of the ubiquitous benefactor Herodes of Athens, who laid on additional drinking water from a spring some 2km away.

There were still eighty four-year Olympiads to come. The athletes were now fully professional; they went round the numerous games held by cities of the empire on Olympic lines, expecting prize money from their native cities for crowns that they won. The emperor Trajan legislated, listing the games that were to 'count' for quasi-Olympic honours. But Olympia still attracted large crowds until in 393 the emperor Theodosios, much influenced by Bishop St Ambrose of Milan, forbade all pagan religious festivals. One of the objections of the Christians to Greek athletics was athletic nudity. The place decayed, though the church on the site of Pheidias' workshop still ministered to a village. Later a Byzantine fort took in the Temple of Zeus, and built the architectural sculptures into its other walls, thus preserving many of them. Lastly the rivers Alpheios and Kladeos, and rain-wash from Kronion hill, covered everything under 3–6m of earth.

From Mummius to Theodosios, the Roman period had run for over 530 years; but we, and indeed the Romans, have revered Olympia because of its brief classical flowering, when the temple was new and Pindar sang of a mythical ancient past—of Herakles' 'Olympiad', when 'the moon shone bright and all the holy place was filled with song of the feasters.'

NEMEA

Next in honour to the Olympic and Pythian Games ranked those of Nemea and of Isthmia, east of Corinth; Pindar wrote odes for the victors at all four.

Isthmia preserves little of interest to the non-specialist; the site is 'horizontal', and most of what shows even at ground level is Roman or later. The most prominent edifice is a Byzantine fort, without special features, built under Justinian at the east end of his unsuccessful Isthmus wall, largely of stone robbed from the classical site. Only the starting-line of the Greek running track may date from the days of Pindar; even there, the interesting fittings, apparently for starting *gates*, are probably later; and the line itself is under the foundations of a Roman *stoa*.

Nemea, on the other hand, about half-way in a direct line from Argos to Sikyon west of Corinth, has a temple of Zeus, of which three columns at one corner still stand. The drums of many others lie in series, orderly in ruin; only unlimited money would be required to put some of them up again. It was Doric, hexastyle (6 × 12), with columns exceptionally tall and slender for the Doric order; late classical, judged stylistically to date *c.* 340–320 BC. Inside its west end, behind or under the place where the statue would have stood, steps lead down to a chamber in the foundations; probably a treasury, and a very 'strong room' indeed. To the east, the sacrificial altar runs to the unusual length of 40m.

Nemea lies in a level, upland, intermontane plain, extending *c.* 4km north–south × 2km east–west, at a height of *c.* 364m. In the mountains was shown, inevitably, the cave of the lion killed by Herakles in the first of his Labours. The makers of the local, strong red wine call it the Lion's Blood. The plain belonged to Kleonai, a small inland city a few kilometres east, forced in classical times into dependence upon Argos, which took over the Games. These are dated, as a panhellenic event, from 573, and were held every two years. As a local festival of Kleonai, they are probably older.

Their legend is an odd one; they were said to have been founded by the Seven Champions from Argos, marching against Thebes, as a funeral rite in honour of the infant Opheltes, son of the local priest (but other parents are also named), who was killed by a serpent when his nurse had put him down for a few minutes while she showed the Seven where to find water. The child was posthumously named Archemoros, 'first to die', and the nurse's name was Hypsipyle, said to have been a princess fallen into slavery, and associated with another tale of death in Lemnos island. Her saga invoked pirates to get her from there to here. Was Hypsipyle, 'lady of the High Gate', originally an honorific name of the Queen of the Dead herself? We are told, in any case, the curious detail that the judges at the Games wore dark gray, not festal clothes, even in classical times when the Games were said to have been re-organized by Herakles, and when the temple had been set up to his father Zeus. It looks as if they did start as funeral games, a placation of the powers of death, and as if this character never wholly left them.

Recent American excavations have discovered traces of a much older temple on the site of the late-classical one; also, quite unexpectedly, evidence of a battle,

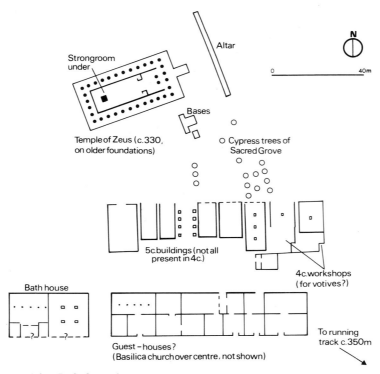

Nemea c. 330 BC (after R. G. Seager)

unmentioned by historians, some time in the later 5C. (Did Sparta's League try to liberate Nemea from Argos?) Many bronze arrow-heads and iron spear-heads were scattered in the earth, stratified under the immensely hard earth surface of the 4C piazza, south of the temple, and probably in this violence the temple was burnt down; accidentally, we must suppose, for nearly all classical Greeks would have shrunk from such sacrilege, as likely to provoke some appalling divine retribution; and this was a temple of Zeus the Thunderer himself. That there was a sense of shock, that a terrible sacrilege *had* taken place, whoever's fault it was, perhaps accounts for so much metal being left unrecovered. Most ancient battlefields were well stripped. People avoided this one.

Probably there were repairs. We can hardly imagine that Zeus of Nemea was left with no temple at all until the late 4C rebuilding. A large base was built, aligned with the south-east corner of the temple, presumably, from its shape, for a large statue and two lesser ones flanking it. The Games went on; in early 4C wars, the Argives took to announcing the Holy Month for them during which Greeks observed a 'truce of God', whenever a Spartan invasion was imminent; in the end, the Spartans complained to Zeus at Olympia and Apollo at Delphi about it, and ignored it. But there were still large fallen blocks lying near the temple; the archaeologists noted that when the piazza was resurfaced (it became so hard that it yielded only to a mechanical drill) the surfacing avoided them.

Across the piazza, the Americans traced the plan of two parallel rows of buildings, not contemporary. One, 120m from the temple, could have been a guest-house for important visitors (most people camped), with a bath-house west of it, in use during the life of the second temple. The other row, in front, consisted of eight separate buildings standing shoulder to shoulder, with a pillared passage between them near the middle. They may have been 'treasuries' like those at Olympia. Two blocks, re-used in an early Christian basilica, whose ruins overlie the site of the 'guest house', bear inscriptions, 'of the Epidaurians' and 'of the Rhodians'; so these two cities were represented; Epidauros, a neighbour with her own famous sanctuary, and Rhodes, an island proud to claim colonisation from Argolis, and where the three cities often spoke with one voice even before they founded their common capital. This row of buildings probably suffered in the sack, and in the 4C some were levelled, while the walls of two at the east end were adapted to house a workshop, with foundries for casting small metal objects: probably votive offerings, the counterparts of those in base silver—figures, often of children, limbs, eyes, burning houses, even motor-cars—which are still hung on the ikons in Greek churches in acknowledgement of answered prayers for deliverance.

The 4C running track has been found, utilising a natural hollow c. 500m south-east of the temple; but a block from a typical, grooved starting line, built into the basilica, may be a relic of an older one, closer in. In the 4C restoration, it was evidently also felt that the sanctuary ought to have a literal *also*, a grove of sacred trees; and a number of large holes, which disturbed the ground north of the workshop, were presumably dug to plant cypresses, concealing it from the temple; ancestors of those that Pausanias saw, 500 years on. But in his time Nemea was already in decay—eclipsed, perhaps, by Isthmia, which was handier for Roman Corinth, the capital. The temple roof had fallen in, and the cult image had been removed. Villagers 300 years later, now Christian, farming the plain, built their basilica and buried their dead near it. That phase will have ended with the Slav invasions. Only the tall columns of the temple still towered, presiding over a great silence, as they still do.

DELOS

Delos, 5km² and the smallest of the Cyclades, which encircle it, became in antiquity the most famous of them all, as the birthplace of Apollo, his seagirt sanctuary and oracle. By the 8C BC it had become a religious centre with an annual festival, the Delia, celebrated in an early Hymn. After relating the wanderings of his mother Leto and how only this barren islet took her in to give birth to her son, the poet describes the festival:

> Many are your temples and wooded groves;
> All peaks, lofty cliffs of high mountains

Are dear to you, and rivers flowing into the sea,
Apollo; yet in Delos does your heart take most delight,
Where the long-robed Ionians gather in your honour
With their children and modest wives.
Remembering you they give you pleasure
With boxing and dancing and song . . .
A man would say that they are immortal and age not
If he came upon the Ionians at this gathering;
For he would see the grace of them all,
And rejoice in his heart at the men
And women with their fine figures,
And their swift ships and many possessions.

It is interesting that here we find a family festival, unlike Olympia. The poet ends, unusually at this date, with a personal appeal to the girl singers of Delos to remember him, and if any stranger comes and asks:

'Who is the sweetest singer who comes here
And gives you most delight?'
—Then answer each and all together,
'He is a blind man, and lives in craggy Chios;
His songs are and for ever shall be best of all.'

These words were very soon applied to the great Homer. Delos is mentioned in the *Odyssey* (Book vi), where Odysseus compares the young princess Nausicaa to the beauty of the fresh young palm tree which he saw growing there by the altar of Apollo. In the *Hymn* Leto clung to a palm tree as Apollo was born, and many later writers refer to it. It is the God's sacred tree on Delos, as the laurel (or bay) was at Delphi, and a palm was kept growing and at least one of bronze set up in the sanctuary as a memorial of his birth.

Long before these joyful festivals Delos had been inhabited. There are remains of a settlement of c. 2000 BC on the 'montagnette' of Kynthos (112m) with its enchanting view—then, of practical importance! Later, a 'beehive' tomb was built, down in the area which became the sanctuary; and many Mycenaean offerings, including gold jewelry and ivory plaques which may have decorated a throne, were tidily deposited under a new Temple of Artemis, Apollo's elder twin sister, built in the age of Greek recovery (late 8C?). This was built partly over and on the same alignment as the foundations of a long, narrow building, c. 4 × 15.30m, which may have been the Mycenaean temple of the Archer-Goddess. Many bronze arrowheads were also found in the deposit. The new temple, which measured 8.60 × 9.60m, was large for its time. It stood in a walled precinct, c. 46 × 33m, in which were set up many archaic statues now (sadly worn) in the museum. Here, too, stood the plank-like Artemis (?) of the 7C now in the Athens National Museum, with a dedicatory inscription by its female donor, Nikandra, a landmark in art history, and the 6C Victory signed by the sculptor, Archermos.

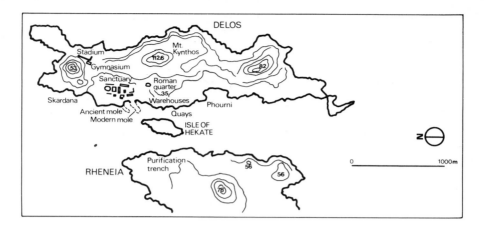

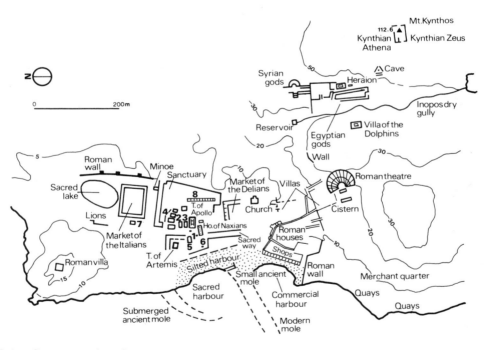

Delos: Sanctuary and southern area

1 Base of statue of Apollo   5 Altar?
2 'Poros' temple   6 Base of palm tree
3 'House of the Seven'   7 Temple of Leto?
4 Treasuries   8 'Monument of the Bulls'

The temple was carefully restored, incorporating the old walls, in the 2C BC.

Also *c*. 700, but on a virgin site on the slopes of Kynthos, was built a small shrine of Hera, 3.40 × 2.80m, which attracted dedications from far and wide in the Aegean. This archaeological evidence is all very unlike what we would expect from the *Hymn*, in which Artemis is barely mentioned, while Hera is a 'villainess'. The wife of Zeus, she jealously persecutes his paramour Leto and delays the birth of Apollo for nine days by keeping Eileithyia, the goddess of childbirth, up on Olympos, until other senior goddesses intervened! The Blind Poet of Chios and his patrons (in the 6C?) seem to have been supporting something of a revolution, in aid of a takeover by Apollo and, in effect, of male dominance; for even Leto seems to have had scant honour in what became a very crowded sanctuary. Only a small archaic temple to her stood near the south end of the Avenue of the Lions (see below). An inscription mentions, too, a Garden of Leto, perhaps along the south side of the Sacred Lake. If so, it was 'bulldozed' away before 100 BC, under Roman influence, when Italian merchants built a large paved market-place between the lake and the sanctuary. Near its south-east corner is a well, 4m deep, which never runs dry. It is significantly called Minoe, and may have been used in prehellenic times. The walls of the fountain-house built round it date from the later 6C and the masonry resembles that of the temple of Leto. The steps down to it have been restored. A single column remains on the third step which supported the roof.

The Ionians attending the early festival would have landed in the Bay of Skardana, where the rivulet Inopos ran out into the sea, and walked along the Sacred Lake (drained in 1925) where the swans and geese sacred to Apollo were kept. On its west side is an avenue of archaic, late 7C, weatherbeaten lions facing the lake, the only sculpture remaining *in situ*. They are of Naxian marble, made of one piece with their plinths. So was the colossal statue of Apollo in the centre of the sanctuary. Its base is inscribed in very archaic lettering, 'I am of the same marble, statue and base'. A much later 4C inscription added, 'The Naxians to Apollo'. These monuments show a strong, early Naxian presence. There was an early school of Naxian sculptors making colossal statues on their own island. Near the cult statue are the foundations of the 'House of the Naxians', an early 6C building with internal columns, built over an earlier, perhaps Geometric building, and nearby a primitive building, respected throughout antiquity, which may have been a Mycenaean temple.

The sacred precinct contains the ruins of a thousand years of worship. It has been subjected to sack and used as marble quarries. Most of our knowledge of the buildings and statues is gained from the great number of inscriptions which have survived.

The later Sacred Harbour has silted up and the breakwater, *c*. 150m long, is submerged. The modern mole is made from excavation debris. A Sacred Way, paved, *c*. 13m wide, lined with statues and stone, semi-circular seats, leads to the Propylaia (with Doric columns), set up by the Athenians in the 2C, replacing an earlier gateway. Originally the market place of the Delians had direct access to the

Delos: Avenue of the Lions

shore, but Hellenistic colonnades have been built here and in other parts of the sanctuary. At the centre of the sanctuary near the statue and altar of Apollo was a small building, referred to in inscriptions as the 'Poros', or limestone, Temple. The French archaeologists call this the first temple of Apollo, and date it to the end of the 6C.

In the year of Marathon the Delians fled to Tenos, but the Persian commander Datis respected the sanctuary. He kept his fleet under control, stationed off Rheneia, now called Greater Delos, separated by a channel only 1000m wide from the sacred island. Datis actually landed and made a huge offering of incense.

In the 5C Delos came under the domination of the Athenians, who, in 478, founded the First Delian (or Athenian) League, a defensive maritime alliance against Persia, centred on Delos, where the treasure was kept in the 'Poros' temple. In 454, the Athenians moved it to Athens, and the League became, in effect, their empire. The Great Temple of Apollo standing between the 'House of the Naxians' and the 'Poros' temple, with the statue of Apollo at its south-west corner, was started in 477, but the work slackened after 454. It was built up to the frieze and may have had a temporary wooden roof. The building was not completed until the 4C. It was Doric, 6 × 13 columns, with plain metopes and palm leaves on the architrave. The Athenians added another temple to this central group, in 425–17, called the 'House of the Seven', and placed a semi-circular base of marble from Eleusis inside it, and, it has been suggested, statues of gold and ivory on it. Near these temples to the north was a row of small buildings resembling the 'treasuries' at Delphi and Olympia, but here simply called 'Houses'.

In 426, the Athenians ordered a second purification of Delos. They had carried out one in the 6C, removing graves from the sanctuary. This time they removed *all* burials to Rheneia, and decreed that no one should be born or die on the sacred island. Those *in extremis* were hustled over to Rheneia. They restored the festival, which had lapsed, and instituted the Delian Games. In 417, they sent a very splendid embassy to Delos under the pious general Nikias. Previously the processions had been somewhat untidy affairs, with the choirs scrambling ashore from boats in some disarray. Nikias did it in style; he brought along brightly decorated boats for a pontoon bridge from Rheneia, where the procession formed up, and was then able to proceed with due solemnity across and up to the sanctuary. He may have 'opened' the House of the Seven. He brought with him a huge bronze palm tree to dedicate and it was set up close to the statue of Apollo. The base with a large hollow for it survives with part of his name on it. Later, Plutarch says, this blew down in a gale and knocked over the statue.

After the defeat of Athens in 404, Delos gained a short-lived independence, but in 378 a Second Athenian League was formed, this time purely defensive.

There is a curious late 4C building along the east side of the sanctuary, called, merely from its decoration, the Monument of the Bulls, *c.* 70 × 8m, a long gallery with a hollow floor over a partitioned framework, surrounded by a pavement. It is suggested that this may be the 'Dock' referred to in inscriptions, made to house a ship dedicated after a naval victory.

In 315 Alexander's general, Ptolemy I King of Egypt, gained mastery of the Aegean and once more Delos was granted independence. This was the island's greatest time of prosperity, and rich offerings flowed in from many foreign benefactors. Its fame was more than panhellenic, it was international. Half-way up Kynthos, temples were raised to non-Greek gods. In the Egyptian precinct was one temple of the healing god Serapis alone and another of Serapis, Isis and Anubis. North of this was a Syrian sanctuary of the goddess Atargatis, with a little high-walled theatre for her Mysteries and a tank for her sacred fish. The most unexpected place of non-Greek worship was a synagogue, away to the north in the area of the stadium.

In 250, the Romans arrived on Delos and their merchants soon dominated the scene. In 166 they made it a free port to curb the commercial power of Rhodes. The island of Apollo was desecrated by being turned into the largest slave market in the Aegean. His festival became a trade fair. There is a large commercial quarter south of the sanctuary with a special harbour, numerous quays, warehouses, shops, and up the hillside a theatre holding *c.* 5500, and a dense concentration of houses, among them, especially on the higher ground, elegant villas of the most prosperous merchants, with courtyards and gay floor mosaics. Near the theatre a large building decorated with theatrical masks was perhaps a hostel for visiting companies. In this and another large villa are colourful mosaics of Dionysos, ivy-crowned, and on one mosaic winged, riding upon a panther. Other villas have mosaics of dolphins and anchors, beribboned tridents, and on one, at the corners, intrepid cupid charioteers driving pairs of fierce-looking dolphins in a race round the floor. One dolphin holds a victor's crown in its jaws. Ironically, Delos is about the best site in Greece in which to study Roman domestic architecture and art.

The road up Kynthos is a regular pilgrim route, with little chapels forming 'stations' on the way. It passes the Sacred Cave on a terrace artificially constructed in a crack in the rock. The roof is made up of two huge granite blocks set like a gable, which look Cyclopean but are probably Hellenistic. The statue on the base inside was probably of Herakles. On the summit a sanctuary of Kynthian Zeus and Athena was built in the 3C, and there are many niches for votives, bases of statues, and ruins of small temples. All the inhabitants of Olympos seem to have staked a claim to be worshipped somewhere on the island. At this point the view transcends archaeology, delighting the hearts of many others than Phoebus Apollo.

The decline of Delos in the last century BC was rapid. It was sacked twice, and a Roman legate even built a wall round the city to protect it from pirates. When Pausanias visited it in the 2C AD he found no one but the temple guardians. The emperor Julian is said to have consulted also this mute oracle of Apollo. In the 5C a small Christian basilica was built at the south-east corner of the precinct, Christianizing the pagan sanctuary.

In the middle ages and later Delos was ravaged and used as a marble quarry by the successive masters of the Cyclades. In 1873 the French School began their excavations and publications and have been at work ever since, as at Delphi, shedding light on the confusing ruins of this other great sanctuary of Apollo. Delos has not the grandeur of Delphi, but it is a place of great charm.

2 City sites

Not every ancient city site gives a rewarding impression of what a *polis* was like. SPARTA, though so powerful in antiquity, has suffered the fate predicted by Thucydides, that no one would guess from its remains alone that it had ever been important. It was a collection of wooden houses, without impressive public buildings, where five villages had grown into one. The most revealing view of the site is a general one of its fertile, mountain-girdled plain, illustrating the fact that the power of a city depended initially on the amount of cultivable land that it could dominate.

Many other *poleis* are obliterated under their modern successors; and in yet others, only insignificant remains survive of perimeter walls and perhaps the bare foundations of a temple. This is the case at TEGEA, in the high plain (*c.* 600m) of eastern Arcadia. Here, though there was no convenient acropolis, the people of several villages assembled in a city, the better to fight off 6C expanding Sparta. They did so, and were admitted to honourable alliance. Later, further north in the same plain, beyond a place where it shrinks to a narrow 'waist', the people of other

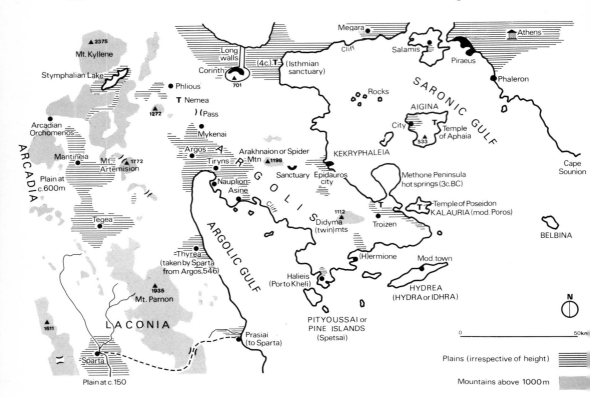

Argolis and neighbouring territories, to illustrate the distribution of city states and their plains

Arcadian villages did the same at MANTINEIA, largely to defend themselves against Tegea. The two cities fought repeated wars over border land. Mantineia, though in the 5C a member of Sparta's Peloponnesian confederacy, was liable to break away and join with ARGOS in anti-Spartan coalitions, and was more than once punished by being broken up and its people sent back to their villages; and once, when usually faithful Tegea broke away from Sparta, Mantineia is found on Sparta's side. This is typical Greek history; but for rewarding *polis* sites, we have to look elsewhere.

Argolis
Argolis is the region round the city and plain of ARGOS, though not all politically dominated by it. The Argolic peninsula, to the east, had indeed, according to Homer's list of the contingents at Troy, all formed one Mycenaean kingdom, dominated by Argos and Tiryns, and including the island of Aigina; but it is also typical of Greek history that after the fall of civilisation (or great crime-wave), when survivors or conquerors had to organize local self-defence, this one province broke up into at one time eight independent city states.

Argos (a name which recurs in several places; all, Strabo the geographer remarks, in plains by the sea) was the natural centre of the largest plain, and tried to dominate the whole area; but Sparta, having crushingly defeated Argos in 494, liberated even the now small settlements of Tiryns and Mycenae, and enrolled them as allies. As such they had their last hour of glory, in the muster roll of those who drove the Persians from Greece: 'Tiryns and Mycenae, 400' (armoured men), before resurgent Argos subdued them. Argos itself is a fine and typical *polis* site, with its sugar-loaf citadel hill, the Larisa (another recurrent name, pre-Hellenic, apparently meaning 'citadel'), and French archaeologists have made interesting finds there, including the earliest Greek suit of armour; but the city is overspread by the modern town, and the castle that crowns the Larisa is Frankish. For ancient walls, we have to go down the peninsula, where three sites represent historic Greek cities of the second rank.

EPIDAUROS

The ancient city of 'Epidauros rich in vines', as Homer calls it, is seldom visited and, though designated as an archaeological site, has never been excavated; it is eclipsed in fame by its sanctuary of Asklepios, 10km away up a valley, here treated separately. But it is an excellent example of a medium-sized coastal *polis* site, with

Epidauros: the city site

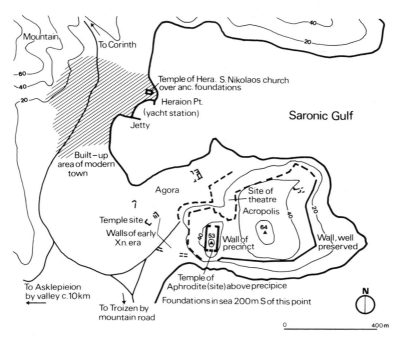

its rocky promontory citadel running out for 800m into the sea. On each side of this, the low coast is probably very much where it was in antiquity. The sea has risen *c.* 2m, but so has the land, with silt brought down from the hills. On the low ground, there may well be more remains buried than leave any trace on the surface. Even the peninsula holds enough earth, supported by the fortress walls, to carry flourishing scrub, and some patches of market garden between its main summit and a lower, landward one. The latter was surrounded by a precinct wall, and an inscription to Aphrodite suggests that, as at Corinth, her temple had here an honoured place.

Epidauros contributed ten ships and 800 armoured men to the fleet and army that repulsed the Persians; and later the walls that still stand, archaic polygonal in parts, had often to be manned. The city was a steadfast ally of Sparta, for protection against Argos; and Argos and Athens, when at war with Sparta, made repeated efforts to capture it and thus secure direct communications. In 430 Pericles, leaving the Peloponnesians (including an Epidaurian contingent) encamped in Attica, crossed the Saronic Gulf with a hundred ships, 4000 armoured men—relatively a huge force—and 300 cavalry in specially-designed horse-landing craft. They were presumably meant to cut off the Epidaurians, who lived outside the citadel, from getting into it; but the surprise failed, and Pericles, ever careful of his men's lives, called off the assault. In 419, when Athens and Sparta were formally at peace, Argos picked a quarrel with Epidauros and harried her lands; there were many skirmishes, and early in 418 the Argives, believing her exhausted, marched on the city with scaling ladders; but the walls were still stoutly held, and they, too, called it off. Later they and their allies, including Athenians, started to blockade the city with a wall from sea to sea; but all that was completed was an Athenian fort at the Temple of Hera, later surrendered under a new treaty with Sparta. The Epidaurians were a sturdy people.

TROIZEN

Troizen was a city with a larger population of prosperous farmers than Epidauros, but not so maritime. In 480–79 it mobilised five triremes and 1000 armoured men. Its acropolis, 25km south-east of Epidauros along a rocky coast, is slightly inland; a crag, rising to 313m, between two torrents, and connected to the mountains behind it only by a rocky neck. It is steep on the north-east side, and precipitous on the west, dropping to a spectacular gorge spanned by a 'Devil's Bridge'. A good deal of wall remains at the top; and at the foot, one storey of a fine Hellenistic tower stands complete, with another storey perched on top of it, in the shockingly ramshackle stonework of the late middle ages. The market place was at the foot of the same slope, with several temples and monuments recorded by Pausanias; but nothing actually remains except part of the brick walls and vault of a Roman-age bath establishment. The town extended for about 1km into the plain between the two torrents; but 'quarrying' and probably also the raising of the ground level by silt from the hills have left hardly a trace of the walls.

Troizen had a rich mythology, including claims to the sites of various events

City sites: secondary cities in Argolis in their geographical setting. Shaded areas denote plains (alluvial) irrespective of height.

famed in literature—and also claimed by other cities; for one, the place where Herakles fetched up the Hound of Hell. But its most famous legend was that of Theseus, born here, the son of Aigeus of Athens by Aithra, daughter of Pittheus the wise and good king of Troizen. A little way east of the Hellenistic tower, a large rock, mounted on a modern concrete base, is labelled as the one under which Aigeus left a sword and sandals, telling Aithra that when their son was strong enough to lift it, it would be time for him to come and find his father; and if this seems excessively 'Arthurian', it might yet be the rock shown, with this story attached to it, to Pausanias, *c.* 150 AD.

Another site connected with the Theseus legend lies *c.* 1 km to the west, beyond the torrent that descends west of the citadel. There in the plain have been exposed the foundations of two temples, of the hero Hippolytos and, further on, probably underlying the ruins of an early church and bishop's house, of Aphrodite; the reputed scene of the tragedy of Euripides' *Hippolytos* and Racine's *Phèdre*, which befell when middle-aged Theseus' wife fell in love with her handsome stepson and used to watch him secretly at his exercises.

Between the two temple-sites is a complex which was evidently a hostel: a courtyard with a large dining-hall off it, divided into compartments, where there survive some stone table-tops and the slotted stone bases for the ends of dining-couches; either for the entertainment of official visitors to festivals or, as some believe, a modest local counterpart of Epidauros' great sanctuary of Asklepios.

The Theseus myth linked Troizen with Athens. The connexion was always remembered, and was reinforced when the smaller city generously received Athenian women and children, evacuated in the face of Xerxes' invasion. This in turn was commemorated in a famous, much later inscription at Troizen (now at Athens), set up probably when the two cities were allied against Macedon. It purports to give the exact text of Themistocles' decree of 480, ordering the evacuation and mobilisation; this is hardly possible, but it may be based on a genuine tradition.

Troizen had a sanctuary of 'international' reputation, on its offshore island of KALAURIA. At a temple of Poseidon, on a saddle east of the island's highest point, there used to meet delegates from Aigina, Athens, Epidauros, Hermione, Prasiai on the east coast of Laconia (later taken over by Sparta), Nauplia (taken over by Argos) and, unexpectedly, the Minyan Orchomenos, which must have possessed a port. The distribution of cities suggests an origin of this 'league of neighbours' far back in the dark age, before the rise of Corinth. In this sanctuary Demosthenes took refuge after the failure of the Greek uprising in 322 and, cornered there by the Macedonian pursuit, took the poison that he had long carried—and walked out of the temple, so as not to pollute it by death.

Kalauria is now the holiday island of Poros, an example of the modern rise of the offshore islands of Argolis, to which we shall return.

HERMIONE
South of Troizen across the mountains, which run down to the tip of the peninsula, is little Hermione. It is mentioned along with its neighbours in the *Iliad*, and sent three ships and 300 men-at-arms to the Persian War. Between the two, it figures in Herodotos' story of a Samian naval squadron which tried and failed to unseat Polycrates, and sailed off in search of a home. They held the rich island of

Siphnos to ransom, and then bought from Hermione that of Hydrea off-shore; but they never settled there. They 'lent' it to Troizen (not to Hermione, perhaps for fear that its former owners might repent of their bargain) and sailed on to settle in Crete, near modern Khania; but their piracies brought down upon them the navy of Aigina, which, with the Cretans, destroyed them, selling the survivors as slaves. This is the first mention in history of Hydrea, now Hydra.

Hermione stood, like Epidauros, on a long peninsula with a plain, the essential economic basis, at hand. Remains of the sea walls that surrounded it survive, along with the ground-plans of two temples, all that 'quarrying' has left. In Roman times it had moved to a low hill, a new acropolis, on the mainland; and over this hill the modern town, built quite largely with ancient blocks, still spreads; for all its lack of standing antiquities, an excellent example of a small *polis* site.

HALIEIS
Near the southern tip of the peninsula, finally, was another small town, not mentioned in the Persian wars, though American excavators (the same who,

Halieis. A small Ancient Greek city

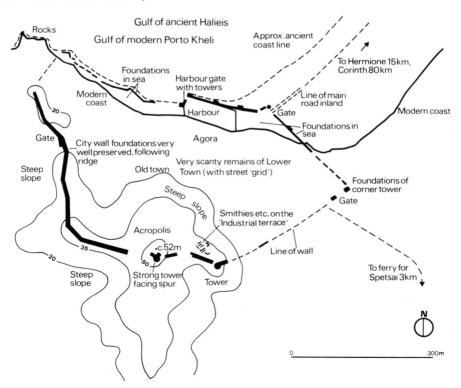

nearby, discovered the pre-neolithic obsidian blades from Melos) have shown that it existed then, perhaps a 'parish' of Hermione. Its walls and tidy streets embrace the top of a low hill, rising from an almost completely landlocked harbour. It was called, simply, Halieis, 'the fishermen'. It occupied a low hill, south-west of the shallow, land-locked bay now called Porto Kheli; a name which perhaps preserves the sound of the ancient one, even including the aspirate, though it can have a modern meaning, 'Port Eel'. With too little land ever to be important, it provided, however, a refuge for the men of Tiryns, driven out by Argos *c.* 469, and then emerges as a city state, protected by the local allies of Sparta. Down in the shallows, half submerged by the rise in sea-level, still stands the harbour gate, where a daring Spartan captured the place (presumably *before* it was given to the Tirynthians, though Herodotos does not say so), in a commando operation, 'sailing in with a merchant ship full of armed men'. It lasted on through Hellenistic times. Little remains above ground level; but the Americans' soundings have revealed a tidy, late classical grid of streets and the complete ground-plans of some small houses, each with its recessed porch, internal court and principal room off it; all in the lower town. A terrace on the hillside housed an 'industrial quarter' of workshops; but hereabout, on the way up to the citadel, no plan could be found. Clearly this was the old town, with a tangle of lanes at all angles; exactly as, in great modern Athens, the 19C planned streets and squares still surround the engaging irregularity of the old 'Plaka' under the Acropolis.

THE 'NAUTICAL ISLANDS'

Off Porto Kheli, with a scatter of rocks and islets between it and Hydra, is another inhabited island; called, with a much smaller satellite, in ancient times, Pityoussai, the Pine Islands, now abbreviated into Spetsai (the 'S' means 'to' or 'at'). This, like Hydra and Poros, now flourishes largely as a holiday resort for Athenians and foreigners; but their rise to fame has more heroic origins. In the later years of the Turkish occupation, Greek foreign trade was flourishing. The Greek trading brigs carried cannon for defence against pirates, and were often suspected of engaging in piracy themselves; and these islands were so prominent in all this that they were called the Nautical Islands *par excellence*. They had been populated by refugees in troublous times; largely, in fact, by Albanians, since the 14C the principal element in the ancestry of the modern population of Argolis and Attica. These Albanians became Orthodox Christian, and in feeling, therefore, fiercely Greek. From Troizen, the bulk of the population moved over to Kalauria, forming a town at the Crossing, in Greek *Poros*, from which Poros became the name of the whole island. On Hydra, a feature of the town is the fine houses of 18–19CC sea-captains. In the War of Independence the islands provided Greece with its indispensable naval arm and with several national heroes—even a heroine, in Bouboulina of Spetsai, who, when her husband died, commanded his ship, blockading the Turks in Nauplia. This rise of the offshore islands to prominence in modern times is a unique feature of Greek history, confined to the coasts of Argolis.

Aegean island cities

AIGINA

Aigina, the triangular island north of Poros in the Saronic Gulf, was said to be named after a river nymph, mother of its hero-king Aiakos son of Zeus, father and grandfather of heroes. His grandsons were Achilles and Ajax, the greatest warriors of the Greeks at Troy. Pindar sings of the exploits of this family in several of his ten odes for Aiginetan victors in the Panhellenic Games: 'Aigina, I am bold to speak of the descendants of you and Zeus . . .'. (*Nemean Odes* vii, 72). After his death Aiakos became one of the judges of the Underworld.

The island was, until the air was polluted, clearly visible from Athens, and her enemy in early wars. Pericles called it 'the eyesore of the Piraeus'. Occupied from neolithic to Mycenaean times and perhaps abandoned with the fall of the Mycenaean civilisation, it was settled *c.* 950 by Dorians from Epidauros. The 7–6C was the time of its greatest prosperity and expansion. Not a fertile island, it lived by its maritime power and trade, which reached to the Black Sea and Egypt. Aiginetans set up a temple to Zeus at Naukratis on the Nile. It was the first city in Europe to mint coins, and the standard of its thick silver 'turtles' (later tortoises) became common to much of the Aegean and Greek mainland. In the 6C it was a major centre of art, especially famous for sculptors in bronze.

At the time of Marathon the Aiginetans had paid homage to the Persians but were coerced by Sparta. They sent thirty ships to Salamis and distinguished themselves above all others. They later fought in the Greek muster at Plataia. After the Great War the hostility of Athens against this powerful maritime neighbour grew and the island was besieged and crushed in 457. It never recovered. At the beginning of the Peloponnesian War, Athens expelled the inhabitants and colonised it with Athenians, among them relatives of Aristophanes and Plato. The exiles returned in 403, but Aigina was never again a great power.

In the middle ages, Saracen raids (9C) caused the inhabitants, as elsewhere, to move inland. Ruins of their capital, called Palaiokhora ('Old Village'), can be seen in the numerous churches and chapels scattered about the hillside under a ruined hilltop castle, off the road halfway to the temple of Aphaia. Venice recaptured the island from the Turks in 1654 and it was one of the last Greek strongholds which she finally ceded to them again (1718). Aigina had the honour of being in 1826–8 the first capital of partly liberated Greece, and minted the first modern Greek coins, bearing the phoenix, the legendary bird born anew from its ashes.

In 1961, the first modern saint formally canonised by the Orthodox Church was the Aiginetan bishop, St Nektarios, 1840–1920. Others called 'New' saints were all martyred under the Turks. His tomb is a flourishing pilgrimage centre in a large new monastery below the mediaeval village, and his ikons are popular in boats and buses.

Pausanias (Book 2: 29,5) calls Aigina 'the most unapproachable island in Greece' because of the submerged and partly submerged rocks round its coasts.

However, its two harbours in the north-west were adequate to hold a large fleet of warships and merchantmen. The modern harbour (now enlarged) was the ancient commercial harbour. On the quay is a charming, small double chapel of St Nicholas, kept white as snow. To the north, in the ancient naval, or 'secret', harbour, the rectangular foundations of boat sheds for sixty galleys are visible, now under water. A low promontory on its northern side protects it, and this was the citadel from neolithic to Christian times. A single battered column and some foundations are all that remain of the temple of Apollo (colonnade 6 × 12) built *c.* 520–500 upon a structure a century earlier, itself over some Mycenaean houses. Fragments of sculpture from here and a selection of local pottery are in the museum, which was actually founded during the War of Independence.

A small Byzantine church, north-east of the town, called 'The Beautiful Church', is dated to 1282. Built of ancient materials, with a barrel vault, it still preserves mediaeval frescoes. It is dedicated to the two soldier saints Theodore.

The best known temple on Aigina was dedicated to Aphaia. Pausanias writes that this was the Aiginetan title for a Cretan goddess Britomartis, friend of Artemis. By classical times she appears to have become assimilated to Athena. The sanctuary is in the north-east of the island, on a pine-covered col with a fine view. Both late Mycenaean and Geometric pottery has been found there. The temple stands on an artificial terrace, 66 × 40m, in a large precinct. It was built *c.* 500: Doric, of local limestone, originally coated with painted stucco. It had a colonnade of 6 × 12 columns and two more in the porches at each end. Some of them are monolithic. Remains of semi-circular foundations of an earlier epoch project beyond the west end. East of the entrance are remains of 5C priests' houses and stucco-lined baths for ritual purification. South-east of the temple are foundations of a 5C ceremonial gateway, with those of a smaller 6C one inside close by. To the east, as usual, was a large 5C altar, superseding two smaller, earlier ones. A ramp leads from the altar to the entrance of the temple. Recent restoration helps to give a much clearer impression of the interior of a normal Greek temple. Parts of the walls have been set up, and some of the two rows of five interior columns with the smaller ones on the epistyle beam above them, which supported the ceiling. On the floor can be seen marks of the railing round the cult statue, and on the entrance columns those of a high grille door. The sculpture of the pediments, of Parian marble, found in 1811, was taken to Bavaria and is now at Munich. Fragments of a third group were found in the German excavations of 1901 and are now in the National Museum in Athens. They seem never to have been set up in the pediment, but put on a base near the end of the temple. The subject of the Munich pediments is the two sieges of Troy, in both of which the descendants of Aiakos took part—the earlier by Herakles and the later celebrated by Homer. In both, Athena, larger than the other figures, stands at the centre, a goddess above the human conflict. In the later, east pediment, she takes some part by spreading out her protecting *aegis* shawl. Round her are grouped fighting warriors, neat athletic figures, in every phase of movement, standing in close combat, falling, running up to catch the falling, archers kneeling (one is Herakles with his

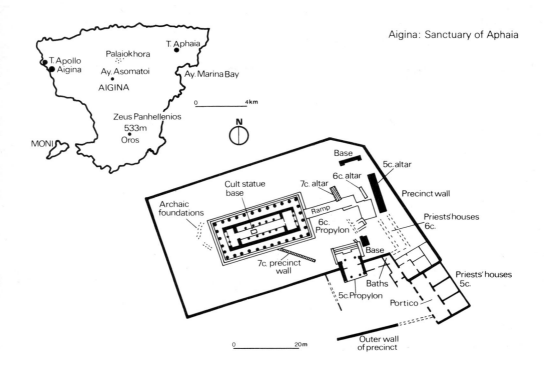

Aigina: Sanctuary of Aphaia

lion-skin cap), and in the corners lie the dying and the dead. This is the first surviving example we have of compact unity of action involving many figures, in the difficult triangular space of the gable ends. The west pediment at Olympia, c. 460, shows the developed handling of this problem. The Aphaia figures are carved in the round and mainly nude.

The principal sanctuary on Aigina was that of Zeus Hellenios (later called Panhellenios) on the summit of the only mountain (535m) in the south. In antiquity it was called Panhellenion, today simply the Oros (mountain), or Prophet Elias, whose chapel stands on the ancient foundations. The débris of ancient and modern feasts, respectively pottery and plastic, strews the slopes round about. There is a glorious view on every side. Low down on the way to it, a ruined chapel of the Ayioi Asomatoi ('Bodiless', i.e. the Archangels) is built of well-cut antique blocks from ruins known as the Naos (temple) whose dedication is unknown. Here a polygonal terrace wall was repaired in fine Hellenic masonry, of which eight courses survive. North of the summit pyramid, there was a Mycenaean settlement, reoccupied in Geometric times. Under the Pergamene kings, who held Aigina from 210–133, a typically grandiose approach was constructed. A wide stepped road led to a terrace, supported by stepped polygonal retaining walls, connected by a fine stair 7m wide to a hall, of which only

Aigina: Temple of Aphaia, showing double row of interior columns

foundations and some column bases survive; possibly a reception hall for pilgrims, below the sacred upper slopes. Cisterns above probably collected holy water. Pindar in saluting Aigina, a place he loved, calls to mind this sanctuary:

> O island of glorious name,
> Thou reignest in the Dorian sea,
> Bright star of Hellenic Zeus.

PAROS

Paros is a typical 'smiling' Cyclad, with white houses, churches and monasteries scattered over the hillside above the town. It also possesses the earliest human settlement in the Greek islands that has not been later built over. This was discovered by British archaeologists on Saliagos, a mere rock off the west coast and the north tip of Antiparos. It now extends under the sea. It is dated by radiocarbon *c.* 4300–3700 and, with the sea *c.* 6m lower, Paros and Antiparos would have been joined and Saliagos a promontory on a bay, a site similar to other neolithic settlements. Stone house-foundations, obsidian arrowheads and a marble fiddle-shaped figurine were found there. Theodore Bent, who travelled in the Cyclades in the early 1880s, deliberately excavated forty graves on Antiparos as it had not been inhabited in historic times. He discovered many marble figurines and bowls and obsidian knives. He, like a French Ambassador to the

Sublime Porte two centuries earlier, explored the vast stalactite cave on the island, which he estimated as 720ft long, 678ft wide and 360ft high. Wordsworth refers to it in a poem:

> As when the Traveller hath from open day
> With torches passed into some Vault of Earth
> The Grotto of Antiparos . . .
> He looks and sees the cavern spread and grow . . .

Archilochos, born on Paros perhaps *c.* 680 BC, was the first Greek personal poet, parts of whose poems survive, to express intense, often bitter feeling; and also some of a disillusioned anti-hero character. Without 'prospects' in his native island (being a bastard), he joined the *colony* led by his father to Thasos with its gold mines in the north. He was not ashamed to recount that he fled in battle, throwing away his shield (as dishonourable as for a modern soldier to lose his rifle):

> My trusty shield adorns some Thracian foe.
> I left it in a bush,—not as I would.
> But I have saved my life; so let it go.
> Soon I will get another just as good.

He disliked Thasos also and became a soldier of fortune, but debunks the glamour of war. Finally he returned to Paros, where he was killed fighting the Naxians. Archilochos was a great inventor of metres and his art was recognised by both Greeks and Romans, especially Horace.

The Parians, subdued by the Persians, sent one ship to Marathon. Ironically, it was on a retaliatory expedition here that Miltiades, the hero of Marathon, was mortally wounded. After 480 Paros became subject to Athens.

The sculptor Agorakritos, a pupil of Pheidias, was born on Paros. He made the statue of Nemesis at Rhamnous near Marathon. It was, according to Pausanias, made from the Parian marble which the Persians had brought with them to use for a monument of victory. Nemesis was the goddess of Fate, specially that which avenges overweening pride.

The 4C Parian sculptor Skopas worked prolifically in Greece and Asia Minor. He carved some of the reliefs on the original Mausoleum at Halikarnassos (now in the British Museum). No individual statue by him survives. He is credited with bringing a new element of emotional expression to Greek sculpture by making deeply sunken eyes.

The marble comes from quarries in the side of the island's mountain, Marpessa, now called, as are so many in Greece, Prophet Elijah (Elias). Much was quarried in tunnels, and one 91m long by 9m wide, with side chambers, can be seen. This marble was used for many statues in the archaic period. It is easier to chisel than the Pentelic marble of Attica, which was not widely used until the 5C. The Hermes at Olympia attributed to Praxiteles is of Parian marble.

A famous inscription, the Parian Chronicle (263 BC), was discovered by an

Englishman in the 17C and is now in Oxford. It is a civilised document, more concerned with poetry than politics and war, and records the births, deaths and victories of poets, and the establishment of religious festivals.

In the centre of the harbour town is a large church called Ekatontapyliani ('Hundred Gated') which is probably a corruption of Katapoliani ('beside the Town'). It is the oldest and largest in the Cyclades, but has suffered much from earthquakes and been restored and enlarged. It contains a chapel of St Nicolas on the north side of the main church dating back to Justinian (527–68), with re-used antique columns, and a very ancient baptismal tank in the form of a cross with steps leading down into it for the total immersion of adults.

Under the Franks, from the early 13C Paros was part of the Duchy of Naxos; and what the knights could do to ancient temples and other buildings is illustrated by the fort they constructed, on the ancient acropolis in the middle of the town, from the beautifully cut marble blocks and columns which they found there.

The quarries of Paros then lay unused for centuries until, in 1844, marble was taken from them for the tomb of Napoleon.

NAXOS

Naxos, 9km east of Paros, is the largest and greenest of the Cyclades, noted by Herodotos as 'excelling the other islands in prosperity' and called by Pindar 'rich Naxos'. The mediaeval and modern town, Naxia, spreads over the ancient acropolis above the harbour. It is a living mediaeval town. Narrow, twisting streets wind up to the castle. The entrance to the upper town is through a large

Naxos, Paros and Antiparos   *opposite* Paros: Frankish tower built from ruins of ancient temple

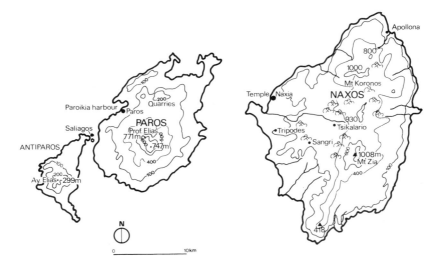

tunnel gateway, and people emerge from houses embellished with coats of arms of Venetian nobles. Mt Zia (Zeus), south-east of Naxia, rises to 1008m and a broken range over 800m extends north. The slopes are wooded.

Naxos is famous for the myth of Ariadne (the All Holy One), as the place where the Attic hero Theseus, returning victorious from Crete to Athens, abandoned this alien princess who had saved him from the labyrinth. Here the god Dionysos found her, and their meeting, in an imaginary Naxian setting, inspired Titian's masterpiece in the National Gallery, London.

A Mycenaean settlement has recently been excavated at Grotta, just outside the town to the north. It had contact both with Athens and the Dodecanese. Later, there was a small Geometric settlement at Tsikalario on the central plateau, overlooking the richest valley, adjoining a large site of twenty tumuli. Traces of a ruined apsidal Geometric house have been found on the small island of Donousa, east of Naxos.

The emery of Naxos was well known from prehistoric times and was called 'Naxian stone'. It was used for giving a smooth finish to marble. The island also produced marble widely used in the archaic period, though not as white as Parian. The importance of the early school of Naxian sculptors is known from their work at the major sanctuaries—the sphinx on its tall Ionic column at Delphi, the colossal cult statue of Apollo and another sphinx at Delos. On Naxos itself are some colossal male statues lying unfinished in the quarries—two at Flerio, 10km from Naxia, and a giant, 10m long, lying near the north-east coast, at a place called after it, Apollona. (Statues of youths were at one time assumed to be all of the youthful Apollo). It is not known why they were abandoned. There may have been flaws in the marble, or a social revolution may have stripped the patrons who commissioned them of their wealth. The latter story is told of the revolution of Lygdamis, who (c. 530) took the people's part against his fellow nobles and became sole ruler.

There are only two upright ancient monuments on Naxos. One is the fine monumental doorway of the temple, probably of Dionysos, on an islet joined to Naxia by a causeway north of the harbour, spared perhaps to serve as a seamark. In the middle ages the ruins were built into a fort, and the temple area is still called Palati (the Palace) today. The second is a square Hellenic tower, called Plaka, with a window, not far from Tripodes, said by Bent (c. 1880) to be about 15m high.

There are a number of Byzantine churches on Naxos, especially in Sangri and nearby villages south-east of Naxia, whose frescoes in part survive. The cathedral of St Mamas, dated to the 8C, is off the road in this area.

In 1207 Marco Sanudo, nephew of the Doge, equipped eight galleys to carve out a duchy in the islands of the Greek Archipelago. Seventeen islands submitted and only Naxos, with a garrison of Genoese pirates in the Byzantine castle, resisted. Sanudo landed and literally burnt his boats and captured Naxia in a few

Naxos: marble gateway to temple

weeks. His duchy included Paros, Melos and Syra. Though a Venetian, he did not pay homage to the Republic, but to the 'Latin' emperor in Constantinople. Sanudo restored the town, built the castle and cathedral, and constructed a mole on the lines of the ancient one. On the citadel his cathedral, restored in the 17C, is still used by Catholic families living in old houses round their church. It has a number of heraldic flagstones and an over life-size double ikon of the Virgin and Child standing, with a small donor crouching at her feet. Two Venetian families, the Sanudi and the Crispi, ruled Naxos for 359 years and it only fell to the Turks in 1566. Then Sultan Selim appointed as 'duke' his friend Joseph Nassi (di Nassi—of Naxos?), a Jewish banker and refugee from Portugal (d. 1569), a Rothschild of his time, who administered the island from Constantinople.

THASOS

This northern island, nearly 400km² in area, with fertile plains at the foot and even in the heart of its wooded mountains, gives the best example within the Aegean of an early Greek colonial site. It had been inhabited since neolithic times; but the Thracian natives seem to have been assimilated by the 7C colonists from Paros, led by the father of the poet Archilochos. Thracian names appear among those of well-placed Thasian citizens in inscriptions as soon as we have any.

One of Thasos' attractions was gold; though some geologists doubt the existence of gold-bearing strata, and some scholars the ascription of early mine-workings near the east coast to Phoenicians, as Herodotos was told (vi, 46). But there was certainly gold on the mainland, and there Thasians settled, mined and sometimes fought the natives, as when Archilochos threw away his shield. Thasos flourished on this and other exports, such as ships' timber and presently a famous wine. Later inscriptions show the state controlling its quality and the size of containers; and the amphoras, stamped on one handle with an official seal, are found all over the Mediterranean.

The colony began round its harbour, later protected by fortified moles and made into the naval base, while commerce was relegated to the eastern part of the bay. Foundations of moles here, too, can be seen under water. A space near the first harbour was demarcated as the market (agora), originally perhaps a rough oval of level ground; when later surrounded by porticos in Athenian style (the foundations that remain are of Roman date), it was not rectangular, but trapezium-shaped. Sanctuaries of Poseidon the sea-god and Dionysos the god of wine were established conveniently near the commercial harbour. The scanty remains of the latter, in private property, have been excavated and re-covered. On top of the ridge, which half encircles the town to east and south, were built temples of Apollo, whose Delphic oracle had directed the colonists, and Athena, goddess of cities. The foundations of the latter, identified by votive inscriptions, lie open; the site of the former has been detected under a Genoese fort built with ancient squared blocks 2000 years later. Below the summit, in an artificial grotto, is a rock-cut relief of Pan, piping to his goats, perhaps always rustic, now much worn, still charming. Artemis, goddess of the wilds and protector of women in childbed, had an open-air precinct and small temple low down on the slope, south-east of the agora, much damaged by erosion; Herakles, another chief patron of Thasos, perhaps owing something here to the Herakles of Tyre, Melkarth the seafarer, had another, to the west. Father Zeus, as Agoraios, patron of the Market and of honest dealing, had his altar inside the agora, near its seaward corner. In the south-east corner the French archaeologists, who have worked long and methodically where possible between the houses of the modern town, found the earliest of Thasos' wealth of inscriptions: written *boustrophedon*, 'as a [ploughing] ox turns'; that from the tomb of Glaukos son of Leptines, addressed or mentioned by Archilochos in several poems, set up by 'the sons of Brentis'. Burial in the agora was a rare honour, for a hero or founding-father. Nothing is known of Brentis, but his name does not look Greek. Was he a chief, or the chief, of the island Thracians, whose sons honour Glaukos for negotiating peace?

The wealth of Thasos demanded and could pay for strong walls. Soon after 500, in the crisis of the Ionian revolt, they were rebuilt in fine, polygonal masonry, some of which survives. Twice 'slighted', once when Thasos, with Persia in control of the mainland and her Phoenician fleet in the Aegean, obeyed an order to disarm, and again in 461 after a revolt against Athens, which seized the Thracian gold-mines, they were finally restored in the 4C, now in classical squared ashlar. A section on the south-west slope of the hill still stands 5m high.

Several gates were decorated with relief sculptures outside, especially towards the harbours and the plain on the west, where most people would see them. Along the sea front most of the wall has been quarried away; its line is shown – – – in our plan; but, facing the commercial harbour, two gateways survive, adorned, the first with a fine though weathered chariot scene on its west gate-post (a youthful Artemis, with her horses led by Hermes?); the second, more damaged, perhaps with a Hermes leading the Graces. Hermes was the god of trade; the reminder to traders that he, too, had his 'gracious' aspect is striking. West of the naval base the French, clearing away some undistinguished clutter of the Christian empire outside the wall, have found a gateway corresponding to the 'Chariot Gate' and, near the remains of an early Christian basilica, a piece of the wall still 2m high.

The most interesting section, however, descends from the hill, to pass west of the town. Here, on more open ground, it was strengthened with no less than ten towers, numbered by the French, from north to south, I to X. Most of them guard gates, either directly or by flanking them on an attacker's unshielded side. No. I is also called the Tower of Sotas, from an inscription of an official who supervised its reconstruction *c.* 100 BC.

From the summit, away from the grotto of Pan, ancient rock stairs descend, leading to the wall west of a gap where it has disappeared. Near its southernmost angle, west of tower X, lies a fallen block, decorated with a pair of enormous human eyes—apotropaic, defensive against the Evil Eye, envious spirits, magic perhaps. What they themselves, set high up and painted, might have done to a superstitious enemy is a matter for speculation. No one in later times took them away to build with. Nearby, still in place, an extra-large block is roughly

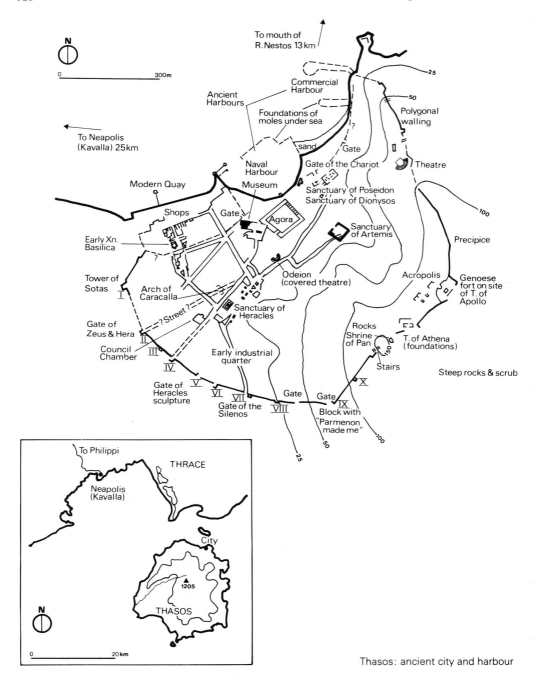

Thasos: ancient city and harbour

inscribed: PARMENON MADE ME—a tribute to himself by a proud mason. He would have been glad to think that the adjacent gate, just past the corner, which stands with its huge lintel still in place and sockets for the bar in its uprights, guarded by tower IX, is today currently known as Parmenon's.

Downhill 300m, tower VII flanks a gate famous for another relief: a giant, horse-tailed ithyphallic Silenos, 2m in height, on the left doorpost, marching into town. Companion of Dionysos-Bacchus, he carries a large wine-cup; and, while otherwise naked, he is wearing boots. Since his haunts were among the rocks and prickly scrub of the hillsides, presumably he had better. By his knees is a niche for offerings. The sculpture is a good-luck sign; and it was valued enough for 4C Thasians when re-aligning their wall and setting the gate at a higher level (250 years of occupation having raised the ground inside) to have lifted the monster slab and faithfully re-set it. Inside, the earliest occupation was industrial: a smithy. Two gold ingots (total weight c. 250g) show only that the secret of someone's safe place died with him; but the forge *may* indicate that industries involving noise and smoke were kept away from the market and residential areas. A street led off towards the town centre.

At the gate below tower V, an inscription of c. 500 names Herakles and Dionysos, children of Zeus, guardians of the city; Herakles, or a bow, his symbol, figures on many of its coins. But his archaic slab from here, a powerful warrior, wearing the skin of the Nemean Lion, kneeling to shoot outwards, is in the Istanbul Museum, and the Dionysos has been lost, perhaps on the way there. (Thasos was liberated only in the Balkan War of 1912.) Finally, at tower II the gateway was flanked by fine 5C slabs showing Zeus and Hera giving orders to their messengers, Hermes and Iris; but the latter is sorely damaged and the former broken, though fragments are in the local museum. The wall in this part is of squared marble blocks pegged together with iron; and inside, thirteen steps remain of a stair for access to the ramparts.

The last classical Greek monument to be built was the 4C theatre in the style of that of Athens, backing onto the east city wall. It has recently been restored to this form by the removal of a high fence of standing slabs set up in Roman times to protect front-row spectators, when the theatre was converted for beast-baiting!

Hippocrates, the 'father of western medicine', worked for three years at Thasos some time in the later 5C; and reverent disciples preserved, among his case-books and notebooks, in the library at Kos, a long-term report on the three years' weather, clearly from a diary, which, though too long to quote here, is of some interest.

LESBOS AND CHIOS

Three great eastern Aegean isles, Lesbos, Chios and Samos, are famous in history and song; but only Samos preserves much of its classical past.

In LESBOS, the largest (1616km²), Mytilene, the chief of its six, then only five, warring cities, is overlaid by the modern capital. In the walls of its mediaeval citadel, east of the fine harbour, ancient foundations can be distinguished by their much better masonry; and north of it is a theatre, converted in Roman times for beast-baiting. At Thermi, 15km to the north, a British expedition discovered a prehistoric settlement, with a culture related to that of Troy. Only at Methymna (vernacular Molyvos) in the north, a city which on occasions fought Mytilene, has less intensive later occupation left acropolis walls repaired but recognisably ancient, while paved alleys between clean, whitewashed houses climb up the hillside from the sea. East of the road to it, north-east of the village of Kallone ('Beauty', said to be named for the beauty of its girls), the foundations of a temple and, at least till recently, two lush foliage capitals in the style ancestral to Ionic lie in high, rough pasture; and of three smaller cities some bare foundations have been excavated. But if one would evoke the memory of 'where burning Sappho loved and sung'—Sappho, a married lady and mother, to whose house parents even from Ionia sent their girls to learn music and poetry—that is best done in the countryside, green, not without trees, full of wild flowers in spring, where she and her beloved pupils wove their flower crowns.

CHIOS (826km²), 'craggy' as Homer says, was the home of the blind singer who taught the maidens of Delos. Greeks soon identified him with the author of the great epics—and a 'school of Homer' is duly exhibited, 5km north of the town. It is the rock-cut foundation of a probably much later sanctuary. There is also a Mycenaean and early Greek site, Emborion, in the far south, abandoned in classical times for the present town site. The walls of the late-mediaeval Genoese fortress, north of the harbour, are not unimpressive; but the island's glory is the mosaic-decorated church of the 'New Monastery' (page 247).

SAMOS

Samos (491km²) is much the smallest of these three, but achieved fame by the energy of its people. It rises to high peaks; 1445m in the west, and 1140m in the centre; but the east, where the city was, though sometimes more than undulating, is not high.

The city of ancient Samos must not be confused with modern Samos, the county town, which is at Vathy, 'Deep harbour', on the north coast. Ancient Samos used to be called Tigani, 'the frying-pan'; its 'pan-handle' was the famous mole, on which more below; but when Vathy hogged the name of Samos the commune dignified itself with the name of Pythagorion, after Pythagoras, its most famous son.

The site provides all the necessities for a flourishing *polis*, for lack of which Ikaria, the neighbouring island, has hardly any history: a wide alluvial plain, where the water from hill-torrents could be tamed and drawn off in irrigation-channels; an acropolis and a harbour. Neolithic pottery has been found both west of the harbour, where the coast rises in a slight cliff, and at the other end of the plain, where an immemorial sanctuary of The Goddess, identified with Greek Hera, gained in sanctity, like many Greek Christian sites, from the finding by shepherds of a sacred image, perhaps a curiously shaped log of wood.

The famous sanctuary is at the mouth of the Imbrasos torrent, 8km from the town. Here, it was said, took place the Sacred Marriage of Zeus and Hera, prototype of all marriages, commemorated at her yearly festival. In preparation for this, her holy image was taken (as at Argos), to be bathed in a pool at the river-mouth. It was then returned to its place and bound up with withies of the *lygos* (*agnus castus*) from a sacred tree near the temple. This tree was supposed to conduce to chastity (whence its Latin name). Twigs of it were placed on their beds by Athenian ladies when observing a period of chastity before the fertility festival of the Thesmophoria, and down to modern times by some Greek monks. Perhaps at Samos, as certainly at Argos, the goddess was thus believed to renew her virginity. Then she was arrayed in her annual new robe, perhaps woven in the precincts (many loom-weights were found there), but then taken into the city, to be brought out in procession, escorted by the main force of its armoured men.

The precincts, extending east of the temple, are encumbered with a scatter of other foundations, largely of Roman age; but working between and under these and despite marshy ground, the German archaeologists who have worked here at intervals since 1910 have discovered archaic remains, including bronzes, three of a group of six stone statues signed by a sculptor named Geneleos, and the thighs of a giant male statue which would when complete have been 6m tall; the largest such statue known in Greece, except for the 'Apollo' of Naxos which never left its quarry. The huge 6C temple, 112 × 55m along its foundations, had two rows of twenty-one columns along each side, and three rows at the ends, of eight at the east (door) end and nine at the west. It was the largest Greek temple known to Herodotos. It presented a forest of columns, a 'labyrinth', as some ancients said. Today, just one column, at the south-east corner, towers above the desert of foundations, and that is unfinished, unfluted; spared through the millennia, when other marble was being burnt for lime, as a landmark for local sailors.

The old modern name of the site was 'At the Column'; north of it a wall running north-east by south-west, perhaps to keep out flood-water, was found to provide welcome shade from winter wind and summer sun, and was colonnaded, north and south: the first of the long *stoas*, later a feature of every major Greek site.

The first 6C temple here seems, as the Germans have found, to have been burnt down within thirty years. (Walls were of stone, but hangings could catch fire and ignite dry roof-beams; that, too, once happened at Argos.) It was rebuilt, even grander, half its length further west and with some re-use of materials, probably under the famous revolutionary pirate-king, Polykrates (*c.* 535–520), patron of the poet Anakreon and of many artists. It was this temple that Herodotos admired, although, despite later periods of activity, it was never finished in every detail. Herodotos has much to say about Samos (iii, 39–60, 142–9) 'because' (though he needs no excuse) 'it has the three greatest works executed by any Greeks: a tunnel driven through a mountain 150 fathoms high, . . . seven *stadia* in length, and eight feet high and broad; and along its whole length, another channel, twenty cubits deep and three feet broad, by which the water is brought in pipes into the city from a copious spring'. (His measurements are not far out: the hill-top is at 235m and the tunnel 1km long.) 'Second is a harbour-mole in water

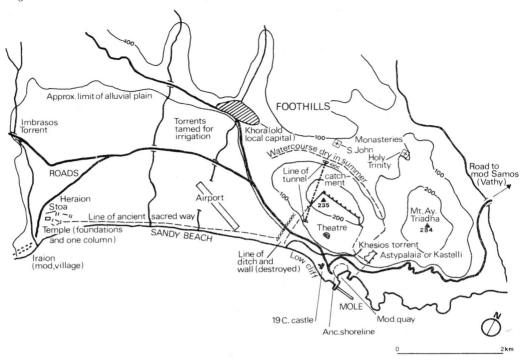

Approx. limit of alluvial plain

Imbrasos
Torrent

Torrents
tamed for
irrigation

FOOTHILLS

Khora (old
local capital)

Monasteries
S. John

Watercourse dry in summer

Holy
Trinity

Road to
mod Samos
(Vathy)

ROADS

Line of
tunnel

catch-
ment

Airport

Heraion
Stoa

Line of ancient sacred way

235

Mt. Ay.
Triadha
284

200

Temple (foundations
and one column)

SANDY BEACH

Theatre

Iraion
(mod. village)

Line of
ditch and
wall (destroyed)

Low cliff

Khesios torrent
Astypalaia or Kastelli

MOLE

19 C. castle

Mod. quay

Anc. shoreline

N

0   2 km

To Troy
40 km

TROAD

Methymna
(Molyvos)

Antissa
Eresos

Kallone

Thermi, prehist site

AEGEAN
SEA

940 Mt
Olympos

Mytilene

LESBOS

ASIA
MINOR

1280

Nea
Moni

Chios

Old Smyrna

N

Emporion

CHIOS

Teos

0   40 km

Ikarian Sea

Mod. Samos (Vathy)

IKARIA

1445

1140

Cape
Mykale

SAMOS

Anc.
Samos

479

PHOURNOI
Is.

Ancient Samos

Inset The Eastern Aegean islands

some 20 fathoms deep, and over two *stadia* long' (the modern harbour-mole stands upon it); 'and third, the greatest temple of any known to me.'

Of these the most remarkable work is certainly the tunnel, still passable were it not for a recent rock-fall, blocking the north end, and a grille at the south end to keep visitors, among the rising tide of tourists, from falling off the chipped and slippery walk-way into the water channel. The triumph of the planners—Polykrates brought in one Eupalinos from Megara near Athens, which already had a water-conduit—was that, starting from both ends, an enormous saving of labour, they met with an error of only a few feet.

The city walls run over the crest of the same 'mountain'. Of polygonal masonry in parts, the whole circuit was very likely planned by Polykrates. Much of it will have been demolished in 439, when Samos, having rebelled against Athens, was disarmed; but it was rebuilt later in late-classical ashlar. Parts still stand up to 6m high and $4\frac{1}{4}$ to 5m thick, though in other places the erosion of the hillside has brought it down. There were thirty-five towers, some well preserved, and some concealing sally-ports between the projecting tower and the curtain wall. On the east, beyond the gully of the Khesios torrent, a semi-detached fort of archaic origin, now called the Kastelli, might, one would like to think, have housed a palace of Polykrates; but when, after he had been captured by treachery and executed by the Persian satrap of Lydia, his successor, his secretary Maiandrios, fled from the Persians, he did so by way of 'a secret tunnel which he had had made, from the citadel to the sea'. *This* citadel then, it seems, must have been fairly near the sea; perhaps west of the harbour, on top of low cliffs where there now stands a 19C castle, using some ancient materials. It is that of the Greek princes, vassals of the Sultan, under whom Samos received local self-government after 1831. This was won by brave resistance at sea during the Greek War of Independence, though, being 'traded' for Euboia, Samos could not join the Greek state until the Balkan War of 1912.

Pythagorion today is a pleasant little port. Its harbour is smaller than of old, having partly silted up. The stone quay stands forward from the tree-lined sea front, and the ancient shore-line may have been still further back. Among the older modern houses fine ancient blocks, used as corner-stones, may be seen under the whitewash. A small museum houses *inter alia* a headless, seated statue with an inscription recording its dedication by 'Aeakes, son of Bruson, who taxed the spoil for Hera, according to his appointment'. The inscription is later than the statue (perhaps re-cut); but Aeakes was the name of Polykrates' father and of his nephew who ruled Samos under the Persians until liberation in 479—and perhaps of others of the family. The phrase 'taxed the spoil' is curious, but quite clear; Hera receives regular dues from the spoils of Samian piracy, which neither began with Polykrates nor died with him.

LINDOS

Lindos, halfway along the east coast of Rhodes, gives an ideal picture of an ancient *polis* site. A charming village of whitewashed houses clusters below its towering

The acropolis of Lindos

acropolis. This is on a triangular promontory, between a large, sheltered harbour and a miniature, almost landlocked one. It was occupied in neolithic times. Few Mycenaean objects have been found there, but great quantities of Geometric brooches. The sanctuary of the goddess Athena was very ancient. Lindos is a pre-Greek name, and she is always referred to as *Lindian* Athena. She was not armed, but wore a crown and garlands, and a special feature of her worship was 'fireless offerings' a custom mentioned by Pindar (*Olympian Odes* vii, 48–9).

In the 7C Lindos, the largest of the three cities of Rhodes, founded colonies at Phaselis in Asia Minor and Gela (first called Lindioi) west of Syracuse, and traded with Cyprus, Phoenicia and Egypt.

In the 6C a wise despot, Kleoboulos, is said to have ruled it for many years, and became famous throughout Greece as one of the 'Seven Sages'. A cylindrical chamber tomb on the north point across the bay is guessed to be his. He renovated the sanctuary, building a larger temple on the highest point of the rock (116m) and gave the old, wooden, seated statue a gold crown. Parts of an archaic staircase, probably of his time, can be seen under the great, late-5C monumental

Propylaia, inspired, no doubt, by those of Athens. In 342 the temple and statue were burnt down, but rebuilt on the old site. The temple (22.40 × 7.8m) was simple, with four Doric columns at the ends; it has been partly restored by the Italians. A new statue of Lindian Athena was set up, this time standing with one arm resting upon her shield, like the Parthenos of Pheidias, but retaining her crown and garlands. Lindos remained important after the unification of the island because of the fame of the sanctuary.

About 200 BC, at the height of the island's prosperity, a large, wide colonnade (88m long and 8.9m deep) stretching almost across the widest part of the acropolis, was built in front of the Propylaia, with side wings and a central flight of steps, making an even grander approach to the small temple on the summit, and an admirable use of the natural features of the site. The view on all sides is glorious. As a late poet wrote, 'Lindos rejoices in the sea'.

Lindos: the Acropolis

1 Temple	5 Commander's house
2 Propylaia (destroyed)	6 Mediaeval gateway
3 Colonnade	7 Ship Relief
4 Church of St John	8 Mediaeval fortress wall along cliff

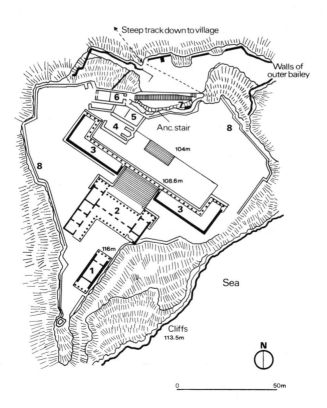

On the rock face outside the acropolis, near the base of the rock, where the Greek stairs can be seen beside and below the later ones, are the remains of a highly original monument: a detailed relief carving of the stern of a ship and part of the base of a bronze statue that stood amidships. The name, Agesandros, survives. The occasion for this honour is unknown, but the work, signed by the artist, dates from about 180 BC.

There are few remains of the ancient city below the acropolis; part of an ancient theatre set in the hillside below it, with a wall close by of well cut stone blocks, probably part of a temple enclosure and foundations of a gymnasium. Many important inscriptions have been found in the village, including the famous Lindian Chronicle, a long list of the treasures and miracles of the Lindian Athena.

In the middle ages this natural fortress needed only massive gateways, approach wall and battlements to turn it into a castle for the Byzantines, the Knights of St John and the Turks. Inside, near the tunnel entrance, is a ruined palace of the Commander of the Knights and a three-aisled church of St John.

In the village are several attractive, large stone houses of prosperous sea captains, with relief carvings round their doors and windows. Some have ogival arches. The cable pattern is a favourite motif, and it is said that the number of cables used as surrounds, or string courses, indicated the number of ships the captain owned. Some houses may belong to the 17–18C. Floor mosaics of black and white pebbles are common, even in simple modern houses.

The Western Isles

With three times the average rainfall of the Aegean—112cm p.a. at Corfu as against 37cm at Athens—the western isles are green and their plains lush. To compare their beauty with that of the white Cyclades in their blue sea is unprofitable. They are different. They are not rich in remains of classical antiquity; and the fact that the most spacious, Kephallenia (Italian Cefalonia; 763km²), was then divided between four city states helps to account for their playing no decisive part in history. The walls of Same, one of the four, on a rugged hill high above the eastern bay where ferries put in, are the best preserved in the group. But two other of these 'Ionian' islands (so called from the Greek name of the sea that washes them; with the o short, and no connexion with Iōnia in Asia Minor) will deserve more detailed treatment: Kerkyra (Corfu) for its stormy history and Ithake, English Ithaca, for its fame in poetry.

Another name for the group is the Seven Isles, a name of recent historical origin. After the shattering of the Byzantine Empire by the Fourth Crusade, they suffered so grievously from slave-raiding corsairs that they positively welcomed the protection of Venice. This was regularised in 1386, and lasted until the extinction of the republic by Napoleon. Exercised with humanity, it saved the islands, alone of Greek lands, from a Turkish occupation, and gave their culture a distinct character, seen in ikon-painting and in early 19C poetry—including Solomos' *Hymn to Liberty*, now the Greek national anthem. The Seven, from north to south, in addition to minor islets, are Kerkyra, the second-largest (719km^2); Paxos, the smallest to have its own Bishop (19km^2); Levkas, an all-but-island, with an isthmus over which ancient ships were hauled on rollers, later replaced by a canal; Kephallenia and little Ithaca (103km^2); Zakynthos or Zante, 'flower of the Levant' as Italians called it; and, far south-east off the tip of the Greek mainland, Kythera, the isle of 'Cythereian' Aphrodite, whose inclusion was due to its having been long in Venetian hands. Bandied about between France, Turkey (with local self-government which dissolved in feuds), Russia and (1807) France again, the Seven Isles passed in 1814 under British protection, and benefited in such matters as roads and piped water; but good administration did not atone, in Greek eyes, for not being allowed to join the new Greek state, recognised in 1831. Much sadness followed, until Gladstone, after politicians had deployed all the arguments later used for keeping Cyprus, saw the justice of the Greek case and delivered the islands in 1864—winning for Britain a fund of good-will which only Cyprus was to dissipate.

This is why, in the Venetian castle above the south bay of the *Isle de Cythère* one may see large bronze cannon lying, their wooden carriages long since rotted away, bearing the monogram GR.

In Homer's list of the contingents at Troy, Odysseus is lord of the Kephallenes, bringing twelve ships from Ithaca, Zakynthos, Samos or Same (presumably Kephallenia, which Homer does not use as an island-name) and a bit of the mainland coast. In the *Odyssey* the hero adds another island as part of his kingdom: Doulichion, a mysterious place (Levkas?), about which ancient scholars argued. Odysseus also says (*Od.* ix, 24) that Ithaca was furthest west of the group, which is wrong; and in the *Iliad* Doulichion and the Echinai (small islands at the mouth of the Corinthian Gulf) are under another chief, who brings no less than forty ships. Doulichion also produces fifty-two out of the 108 suitors of 'widowed' Penelope. It is evident that the saga traditions, on which poets drew in Asia Minor, centuries later, varied considerably about the western isles; which makes it vain for us, though eternally fascinating to some scholars and popular writers, to try to extract precise geography from the *Odyssey*.

ITHACA

Ithaca, the second smallest of the Seven Isles, lying north-east of Kephallenia, is an enchanting island with a great variety of landscape in its small compass of 103km^2. Its fame rests on its appearance in great poetry. Every possible detail of its Homeric geography has been lovingly identified, even with signposts, with a reference in the *Odyssey*, which gives it a fairytale dimension. Nearly all inhabited Greek islands have caves (even with a hole in the roof like the one in the *Odyssey*), coves in plenty, cliffs and springs; and identifying even the different islands from Homer's descriptions is still a problem; so these further identifications are seldom better than guesses.

Ithaca is 27km long, narrow and almost cut in two at an isthmus near the middle. North of it is the highest mountain, Homer's 'wooded Neriton' (808m).

Three sites have been excavated by the British School of Archaeology, working in the 1930s and early 1950s. One is called Polis ('city'), a cave sanctuary on the north-west coast below the main north village of Stavros. Among finds from pre-Mycenaean to the Roman period were twelve Geometric tripods of the type described in the *Odyssey*, one on wheels, and many terracotta female masks, one bearing the exciting inscription, 'vow to Odysseus'. This is late, *c.* 100 BC, but it demonstrates that among other deities worshipped in this cave, Athena, Hera, the Nymphs, there was in antiquity a local hero-cult of Odysseus. A Mycenaean house was found nearby, and many Mycenaean sherds on the slopes round the bay.

Near Stavros British archaeologists have dug on the hill of Pelikata a small early bronze-age settlement continuing into Mycenaean times, and part of a wall round the hill and a paved road beside it.

Another fruitful site is on the saddle of Mount Aetos ('Eagle') at the isthmus, where Protogeometric, Geometric and Corinthian imports were found in quantity. It would appear that there was a temple or shrine here. Ithaca seems to have been a staging post for Corinthian trade with the west in the period of colonisation.

The island plays no part in classical history. In 1185 it fell, with the other islands, to the Normans of Sicily, and in 1191 a monk of Peterborough, chronicalling the return of Richard Coeur de Lion, describes the strait between Ithaca and Kephallenia (where the suitors lurked to ambush Telemachos) as a notorious haunt of pirates. In 1479 it was devastated by the Turks and Venice resettled it from the other islands in 1504, building a village up the hill, above the modern little harbour town. Vathy ('Deep'), the deep inlet off the bay of Molo, does not appear to have been used earlier. Ithaca suffered much damage in the earthquake of 1953, but town and villages have been rebuilt.

The modern Greek poet, Kavaphes (or Cavafy), wrote a poem about Ithaca on the 'travelling hopefully', or 'the journey's the thing' theme:

> Ithaca gave you your splendid journey.
> Without her you would not have set out.
> She has nothing more to offer . . .
> You have grown so wise, with so much experience
> That you would have already realised what these Ithacas mean.

Ithaca has become, in spite of the poet's sentiments, a byword for home regained after long and perilous journeying.

KERKYRA (CORFU)

Kerkyra like Thasos entered history as a Greek colonial site; but here very little survives of antiquity. The most imposing remains are those of the Venetian fortress, with its Lions of St Mark in relief, which fought off the Turks in 1536 and, in a heroic defence, 1716–18. The name Corfu is a Venetian rendering of the Greek *korypho*, 'summit': the headland with the Old Fort, repeatedly depicted

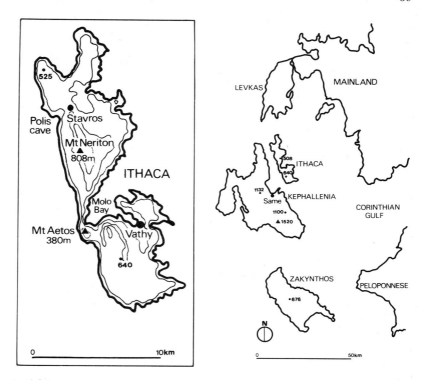

Ithaca and the Islands of Odysseus

from the south-west in Edward Lear's coloured sketches, with winter snow on the Acroceraunian mountains in Albania beyond. The Old Town crowds inside the Venetian walls like a piece of old modern Italy, between the Old Fort and New Fort, still picturesque, though sorely damaged in World War II.

Outside the Old Fort, with its salt-water moat, the Esplanade, kept open to provide a field of fire, now includes at its north end the ground of the Byron Cricket Club; a relic of the British occupation which led Kerkyra into modern times when, across the water, Byron's acquaintance Ali Pasha of Ioannina was still drowning his concubines on suspicion of infidelity and generally keeping up the middle ages.

The ancient city, fairly certainly, spread over the peninsula to the south, where scanty remains exist of three temples, a section of city wall with a gate on the west side of the isthmus, and probably a market-place inside it. (With intensive occupation nearby, the 'quarrying' effect here has been very severe.) The peninsula rises on the east to a maximum height of 69m (Church of the Ascension, a frequent hill-top dedication), dropping in steep cliffs to the sea. On the west it shelves off into the Khalikiopoulo ('gravelly') lagoon, supposed to have been the ancient Hyllaic Harbour, while the Bay of Garitsa, or Kastradhes, to the north, was the Harbour of Alkinoös. The Khalikiopoulo is today too shallow even for ancient shipping; but this may be due to later silting up.

Kerkyra was founded as a colony of Corinth, traditionally twin-born with Syracuse in Sicily *c.* 733. With one city dominating the island's 719km² (nearly as spacious as Kephallenia), it became powerful, rich in its fertile land and well placed for trade with the north and west. Corinth and Kerkyra together founded Epidamnos (Roman Dyrrhachium, later Durazzo, Dürres) and other colonies on the mainland. But after seventy years, there was trouble.

Commercial Corinth, unlike some colonising cities which merely exported their surplus population, treated her nearer colonies as daughters which, in return for protection, should submit to some direction. Syracuse was too far away for this, though she did, when in trouble, more than once appeal to Corinth for help. Strong Kerkyra was an intermediate case; she desired independence, and got it; the earliest naval battle that Thucydides knew of was one between Corinth and Kerkyra, *c.* 664. Thereafter relations were often bitter, though aristocratic family ties remained. Kerkyra was quite able to stand on her own. By *c.* 600, among the very scanty remains there are two 'firsts' in what we know of early Greek history; one, the unprecedentedly large pediment sculpture from the temple, probably of Artemis, near the known city gate centring in a truly monstrous Gorgon with her children, the winged horse Pegasos and the giant Chrysaor; the other, the inscription still *in situ* on the monumental tomb of Menekrates, of Oiantheia in Lokris, who had looked after Kerkyraian interests in his native city and been a good friend to the people (*dāmos*; Doric). He was lost at sea, presumably off Corfu, and buried by his brother 'with the *Damos*' (of Kerkyra?). Kerkyra's interests far inside the Corinthian Gulf are striking; and so is the emphasis on the *Damos* (four times in five hexameter lines), which hints at an adumbration of democracy.

Kerkyra must then have been one of the most advanced Greek states; but it was an advance to tragedy. It was a commonplace in classical Greece that the class war between rich and poor citizens could break out in bloodshed; and long after, in 427, Thucydides describes one of the bloodiest of these outbreaks, with the numerous slaves, to whom both sides appealed, mostly siding with the masses. Public violence became a cover for settling private vendettas; and the historian is inspired to his famous digression on how in a revolutionary situation even common values changed, with the ability to see both sides discrediting its holders, and 'moderation' becoming a dirty word (iii, 70–84). Kerkyra thereafter regained some prosperity, but sank to being a third-class power in Greece.

CORFU AND THE ODYSSEY

Kerkyra is not named by Homer. It was outside the Mycenaean orbit, and no traces of a bronze-age city have been found. But classical Greeks were as keen as modern writers on identifying the sites of Odysseus' adventures, and in this context Kerkyra was identified with Skheria, the island home of the civilised and

Kerkyra (Corfu): the city
inset Island of Kerkyra

hospitable Phaiakes (Phaeacians) who entertained the hero, washed up naked and exhausted on their coast, and sent him on to Ithaca in one of their magic ships. The sea-god, father of the Cyclops whom Odysseus had blinded, then out of spite turned the ship and crew into stone when they had nearly got home; and the stone, according to tradition, is still there. It is the cypress-covered islet off the Cannon Point (a French gun position of 1808–14), at the south end of the peninsula bearing the few classical foundations, and beyond the inshore islet with the convent of the Madonna of Vlakherna. The place where princess Nausicäa did the laundry and found the shipwrecked mariner is identified across the lagoon, where the copious springs of Kressidha break the coast, and the Gardens of Alkinoös (where the array of fruit-trees really is reminiscent of Corfu) north of there. The Greek colonists were proud to think of themselves as successors of the Phaeacians, who had disappeared curiously without trace; and Thucydides records their claim without comment.

Modern enthusiasts have tended to put the city of Alkinoös rather on the west coast, where Odysseus, after sailing his raft for seventeen days, with the Great Bear on his left by night, would be more likely to have come ashore. A charming site is among the rocky peninsulas of the bay of Palaiokastritsa, one of them with a monastery, where the Greeks' idea of a perfect colonial site really could be found; an all-but-island, with 'ships drawn up on each side of the road' as one went in. The Phaeacians had come there in Alkinoös' father's time, to escape the raids of the Cyclopes on the mainland. Further, it is pointed out, Odysseus narrowly escaped being dashed against fierce cliffs by the storm, but swam clear of them and into a river-mouth. A large enough river mouth would be a rarity on any Greek island, but there is one here, and it does emerge at the end of fierce cliffs: that of the River Ermones, which behind the cliffs waters the soft, green valley called locally Middle Meadow. Surely here, at least, Homer or Homer's informant had been to see?

We are sincerely sorry, but we are unconvinced. If Homer or any informant had been as far as Kerkyra, which is much further than Ithaca, he ought, for a start, to have known that Ithaca is not westernmost of its island group. It is also just too bad that Kerkyra has not yielded, at least so far, any trace of high pre-Hellenic civilisation. For that matter, hominids even half the size of Homer's Cyclops ought to have left some hefty bones in their caves; and if some were found, in a recent context, one might feel that the hunt for Odysseus was on a warmer scent. Rather, all his adventures take place in faërie, out of this world; and Homeric Ithaca itself is on the edge of it. Meanwhile, from Palaiokastritsa to the Ermones is as good a place to dream of the prototypical traveller as one is likely to find; but if one is to be rallied from dreaming, one cannot help feeling that, either from Palaiokastritsa or Corfu, and even with a mule-cart, that river mouth is an awful long way to carry all that washing.

3 Persian War Battlefields

MARATHON

> The mountains look on Marathon,
> And Marathon looks on the sea . . .

They still do. The famous plain is now planted with olives, where the Athenians must have charged the Persians in open ground; also there are many houses, including a village with hotels along the beach at the south end, not shown on our map. These obstruct the view from the Athenian burial-mound, which must mark *a* centre of the actual battlefield; but a good view can be had from a new road which now winds over the northern slopes of Mount Pentelikos to descend at the village of Nea Makri.

The Plain of Marathon

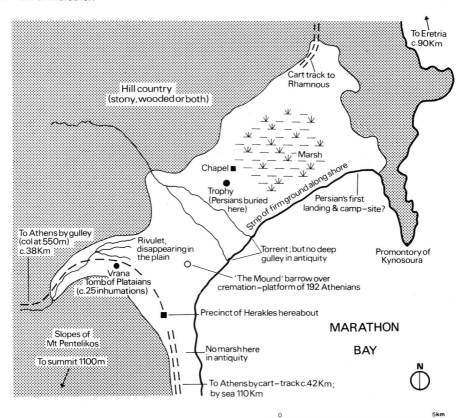

N.E. Greece, to illustrate the Persian invasions

Details of what happened here in 490 BC have long been argued enjoyably among scholars, and still are. We will see what our sources tell us, and what can be ascertained on the site, before theorising about the outstanding questions.

The Persian expedition that summer had received the surrender of most of the Cycladic islands, *and took along ships and troops from them.* It was a punitive expedition, to punish Eretria (in Euboia) and Athens for recent help to a revolt of the Asia Minor Greeks. It was clearly not an enormous force; not large enough to tackle Athens and Eretria simultaneously. Eretria stood a siege, but was betrayed after a few days by some who preferred submission to destruction. The people were deported to Asia, but not massacred. The Persians had with them old Hippias, son of the former benevolent despot Peisistratos, who still had partisans in Athens; and much was hoped from them, and from others, including the great Alkmeonid family, who well knew Persia's power. Hippias brought them to Marathon, a good place for the cavalry which they had brought in special horse-landing ships, and where he himself had landed with his father, fifty years before. Then, they had met the government levies south of Pentelikos, half way to Athens; but this time Miltiades, a great military nobleman who had been lord of the Gallipoli Peninsula—a rival of the Alkmeonidai, and high on Persia's 'wanted' list—carried the Assembly with a proposal to 'take rations and march' (a later orator quotes it); and by the time the Persians had all landed the Athenians barred their way at the south end of the plain. They were joined there by the men of gallant little Plataia; the *cliché* is justified. Athens had protected Plataia from her big neighbour Thebes, and Plataia now stood by her. Athenian HQ were in a precinct of Herakles, now located, from two inscribed stones, too heavy probably to have been moved far in later times, near the coast road; but a camp for some 10,000 armoured men, plus a probably larger number of soldiers' servants and light-armed men—some 'light-armed slaves' were killed in the battle—must have stretched far along the hill-foot. It was defended by an *abattis* of felled trees. The Plataians, on the left in the battle line, were probably camped in the Vrana valley (see map); and there, in 1970, was found the burial place, practically certainly, of their dead, later covered by a barrow. They were inhumed, not cremated like the Athenians. Half the mound (the other half being sensibly left for later checking) covered the separate graves of eleven men in their twenties, one twelve-year-old boy (someone's page, killed in circumstances that warranted military honours?), and one man of about forty, no doubt an officer. He alone had his name, ARCHIAS, carved on the rough headstone that marked each grave; and in each an early 5C food vessel was the only furniture.

The Athenians' bold move had checked any trickle of deserters to Hippias; but the dissidents were still there behind the lines. For four days the armies faced each other at a distance of about a mile; the Persians no doubt hoping that (as Miltiades puts it, in Herodotos) 'rot would set in' on the Greek side; the Athenians, for promised help from Sparta. The professional runner Pheidippides, or Philippides, who is said to have reached Sparta in two days (250km; not impossible), had set off at once, after the fall of Eretria and 'a few days' before the

Burial place of (almost certainly) the Plataian dead, who fell during the Battle of Marathon

Persians crossed over; but the Spartans had a religious festival, and a taboo prevented their marching before the full moon. (The religious scruple was no doubt perfectly sincere. Scholars who doubt it seem to forget that an *Athenian* general, Nikias, in Sicily in 413, lost a fleet and army, his own life, and ultimately the Athenian empire, because he delayed a vital move owing to an eclipse.) As it was, marching desperately as soon as the full moon was past, their leading brigade reached Athens two days too late; but the Athenians won without them.

The Athenian commander was Kallimakhos, the *elected* War Archon for the year, beginning at midsummer. Herodotos is mistaken in making him owe his position to 'the luck of the draw'; that arrangement, which reduced the War Archon to a civilian official with some judicial duties, came in only in 487. But the commander consulted the ten *Strategoi*, commanding the battalions; and one of them, Miltiades, was always considered the architect of the victory. On the fifth morning of the confrontation Kallimakhos, himself leading the right wing (a commander's traditional post), suddenly led out his armoured troops and launched them at quick step to the attack. The line ran perhaps approximately due north and south. To cover the required frontage, on Miltiades' advice he thinned his centre; but the strong wings made short work of the troops facing them (no doubt including half-hearted islanders) and then, we are told, wheeled inwards, united, and took in the rear the native Persian troops, who were (as always) in the centre, and had broken the thin Greek centre and pursued it inland.

This remarkably disciplined manoeuvre must surely have been premeditated. The Persians broke away to reach their ships; but many were cut off and driven into the marsh, an event emphasized in the near-contemporary painting of the battle in Athens' Painted Colonnade. On the edge of the marsh have been found the remains of a monument—probably the built Trophy of victory, erected at the point where the most decisive success was won; and near it, many human bones, buried unceremoniously—presumably those of the dead Persians. Others reached the sea, with the Greeks after them, 'calling for fire, and trying to lay hold of the ships.' These, however, mostly got away, with such of the fugitives as could get on board; the Athenians captured only seven, at the cost of many of their bravest men, including Kallimakhos.

It has often been complained that our accounts of Marathon ignore a serious obstacle: the deep, steep-sided, torrent bed that bisects the plain, south-west of the marsh; but here, study on the spot has justified Herodotos. The deep gulley *was not there*. Since the deforestation of the hills, thousands of tons of silt have buried much of the plain two metres deep. The rise in level has been observed round the burial mound of the Athenians; and in the banks of the deep *Charadra*, potsherds of the Christian era may be found, half-way up! At the time of the battle, the torrent was there, no doubt, but its bed was probably wide and stony.

It used also to be suggested that the marsh into which many Persians were driven was one at the far south corner of the plain. This, too, may be deleted: it was not there. In Roman times there were houses there. Its later formation is connected with the rise in sea level.

The Athenians drew breath; and then, 'when the Persians were already at sea', says Herodotos, someone was seen to be signalling to them with a shield—presumably from high up on Pentelikos. (The sun must therefore have been still well east of south.) There was, he says, no doubt about this; it was a 'public' fact; but who sent the signal or what it meant, he could not say. He adds a highly unconvincing defence of the Alkmeonidai, who were suspected at the time, saying that they had always been bitterly opposed to Hippias (quite untrue: they had, long ago, been willing to hold office under him). The *démenti* tends to focus our suspicions. The message could only have been something simple and pre-arranged, such as 'Come on, we are ready.' Probably the dissidents were not really as ready as they would have liked; but for them it was 'now or never'. The universal reaction of the soldiers at Marathon was the thought, 'Traitors!'; and through the heat of the day eight battalions, leaving the two worst mauled to guard the spoils and the wounded, beat it for home 'as fast as their legs could carry them'. They were afraid that the Persians might land at Phaleron and seize the city, held only by old men and boys. They slept that night south of the city; and the Persian generals, having arrived off Phaleron and seen them, decided to go home.

This march was the original Marathon Race; by men who had already fought a severe hand-to-hand battle, it was no small athletic achievement. To make it a *run* was the work of later Greek literature, in which the Great War story became sadly spiced with journalism. It was told that Philippides, having delivered his message to Sparta, got back in time to join his regiment (he would not have had to hurry), fought in the battle, ran home with the news, and fell dead in the market-place after gasping, 'We've won!'

It must be added that the army, like Peisistratos of old, *must* have gone by the wagon road, south and east of Pendeli. Most modern historical maps indicate the shortest way, up the Vrana valley. There is an old path that way; but those who show it as a military route have evidently not walked it. Not only is the col at 550m, half the height of the mountain; but the valley, where it rises, is V-shaped. The few hundred Plataians may have come *down* it; but for 8000 men in a hurry, no general could recommend an ascent where (unless the whole army went in single file) most people would have to struggle along with one foot higher than the other on a steep slope! Even for Philippides, *if* he ran to Athens with the news, a ten-per-cent longer route would be preferable, given a much lower ascent (there is one, south-east of the mountain), and a good track all the way.

Now we must take note of a modern theory. Herodotos says that the Persians, driven into the sea at Marathon, picked up the prisoners from Eretria, who had been left on an off-shore island, and *then* 'started to sail round Sounion, hoping to get to Athens before the Athenians'. Clearly not all the ships need have done this; if they had, they would have had little hope of winning their race. But even if some started for Athens directly after the battle, and if we assume that triremes, which could go twice as fast as hurrying infantry (with slaves carrying the shields) could keep up that speed for 110km, they still had *more* than twice as far to go. Also they had been very roughly handled, losing 6400 killed, mostly Medes and Persians. (The Athenians counted them carefully; for Kallimakhos had vowed, on behalf of the city, the sacrifice of a kid for each slain enemy.) For these reasons, it is a current theory and may well be true, that *some Persians had left secretly the night before*, including the cavalry, whose landing in good 'cavalry country' has been emphasized, but which are not mentioned in the battle. This might be accident, in Herodotos' brief account, but there is even some positive evidence for their absence. A learned, though fallible, Byzantine dictionary comments on a proverb, 'cavalry separate', referring to an ill-starred division of forces, and specifically to Marathon: Datis the Mede, general of the Persian forces, 'went off somewhere' (the dictionary does not say where) with the horse; and some Greeks in the Persian army slipped over to the Athenian lines and told them. Datis *might* have taken such a risk, because the Spartans (Hippias would have known) would be coming, after the full moon. It was again 'now or never'. It was then absolutely essential for the Athenians to smash the force left to hold them, *and* get back in time. The evidence is poor; but this theory does account for the battle taking place when it did, after four days' waiting, and just before the Spartans arrived.

THERMOPYLAI

The self-sacrifice of Leonidas, who, when his flank was turned, saved two-thirds of his army by staying with a rearguard, is known to the world; the strategy, of which that action was a part, very much less so.

Themistokles, the father of the great Athenian navy of 200 ships, a decisive factor in the defeat of Xerxes, was one of the few Greeks who, since Marathon, had been sure that the Persians would come again. He studied the topography and saw that, if the Greek fleets held the strait north of Euboia, the imperial fleet could only come at them across waters liable to storms in late summer and very dangerous to a fleet too large to draw up on the few beaches below the coastal range of Thessaly. Also, he 'sold' his strategy to the Peloponnesians, whose first inclination was to fight only at the Isthmus.

On land the allies then proposed to hold the frontier of Greece at the pass of Tempe, between Olympos and Ossa. 10,000 armoured men, implying at least as many light-armed, were sent; plenty to hold the then narrow gorge (now torn much wider open in the interests of a motor road) and the adjacent heights; but this expedition was a fiasco. The Persians, who had been preparing the invasion for years, knew much more about the region than the southern Greeks did; Macedonia had accepted their overlordship; their agents or envoys had been busy among the mountain tribes, who usually followed the lead of the Thessalians; and from Thessaly proper, the Persians had received as exiles the Aleuad clan, whose chief aspired to kingship and had been turned out by the other nobles. Also they knew, as the southern Greeks did not, that west of Olympos the land is not as rugged as might be expected. There are other passes, which only needed the clearing of a road through the forests to be practicable for an army; and indeed, as soon as the Persians reached Macedonia a third of the army was sent forward to do just that. Finding themselves with a wide front, Thessaly divided and the hill peoples indisposed to resist, the Greek army returned to its ships and went right back to GHQ at Corinth!

Themistokles had been the Athenian general on that expedition; not, as one might have expected, with the fleet. It shows how important he thought it. Now, his strategy was in ruins unless, quickly, a force could occupy Thermopylai, the last defensible position that would enable the fleet to stay north of Euboia; and time was running out. Xerxes would soon be in Thessaly; and, worse still, Greece was now preoccupied with its religious duties. The Olympic Games were at hand, held when the first new moon after midsummer was full—and at Sparta the festival of Karneian Apollo coincided with the Olympic. Many must have welcomed the excuse for postponing an unwelcome march far afield.

Leonidas, one of the two kings of Sparta, saved the situation. A constitutional monarch, he could not alone override the taboo and call out the army; but he could move himself, with his royal guard of 300, and their seven Helots apiece, 900 of whom were probably armed by the state; Helots fell in the last stand, and the Persians could not tell them from Spartans. No doubt he offered solemn sacrifice to Apollo, begging forgiveness for missing the Karneia; later tradition said that he celebrated his own funeral. He picked up volunteers *en route*, mostly poor and hardy highlanders of Arcadia, glad to find employment; 400 Corinthians; eighty men from little Mycenae, which Sparta had liberated from Argos; 4000 Peloponnesians in all (as usual, omitting light-armed), according to a contemporary

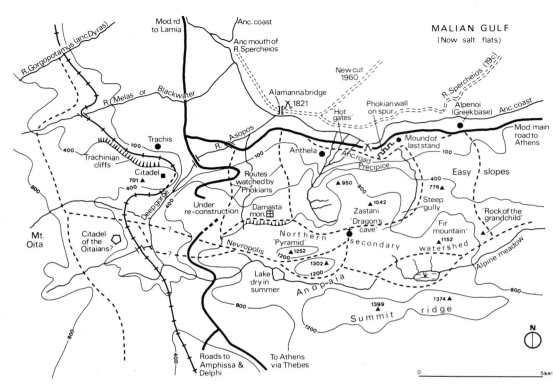

Thermopylai and Mt Kallidromos

inscription; but the figures add up right only if we count the Helots, who fought and died, at 900. With 1100 Boiotians and the local troops of Phokis and Lokris, Leonidas had about 7000 armoured men to hold the Pass between cliffs and the sea, and the rocky hills inland. It should be enough; and he had exacted promises, for what they were worth, that he would be reinforced after the full moon. But he knew that it was a dangerous assignment. For his guard, he picked not the usual 300 young men, but men in their thirties, who had sons living; whose families, therefore, would not be lost to Sparta if the not improbable occurred.

Leonidas reached the Hot Gates (so called from the hot springs, said to have been created by Zeus to refresh his son Herakles in a weary hour) in time to repair an old wall, built by the Phokians in an unsuccessful attempt to keep the Thessalians out of their country. Its probable remains are still there—though, if so, turned 'back to front' later, with stairs on the west side. They are on a small ridge, running south-west to north-east, from near the foot of the ferocious cliff that 'made' the pass, down to the modern main road, which marks approximately the ancient coast. (The silt of the Spercheios and local torrents has now pushed it far out; a visitor to the site has to 'think away' a mile of whitish salt flats, as well as the motor 'service area'.) The ancient road curved inland to a gate at the inland end of the wall; but to an enemy trying to force a passage along the beach or through the shallows, the wall stood poised above his right, unshielded flank. Counter-attacks from that direction account for the detail about Persians being 'driven into the sea' in the final *mêlée*. Herodotos mentions, as an oddity, that there is a daily tide in this bay. In most of the Mediterranean there is none; but even here, it would not be great enough to affect operations.

Herodotos seems to have gone through the pass (the coast road), going from the north into Greece, and making notes; though, probably passing the Hot Gates about midday, with the sun nearly vertical, he failed to notice that the road here is not north to south, but west to east. He noticed that there were even narrower passages before and after the battlefield, with 'barely room for a cart road'. The reason why they were not chosen for defence was that both could be turned by way of relatively easy slopes, through the woods. What made the place just east of the hot springs defensible was the great precipice inland. He noted successively the city of Trachis; the Asopos torrent (a recurrent river name), descending through a narrow gorge, past the Trachinian Cliffs; the village of Anthela, with the meeting place of the *Amphiktiones* (delegates of the local League of Neighbours, who later had a second meeting place at Delphi); the Hot Springs; the Phokian Wall; and another village, Alpenoi (or -os), which the defenders of the pass used as their supply base. Here, he notes, descended the path from above, by which defenders had been, not only on this occasion, outflanked.

The 'secret of Thermopylai' is that the top of the mountain, east of the Asopos and above the cliffs, is largely flat, with two streams flowing in opposite directions from a slight, stony watershed, amid green sward! The western one, before tumbling downhill to join the Asopos, even meanders, in deep soil, along the mountain plain called Nevropolis (evidently from Slav *polye*, 'field': there was no *polis* here). The mountain and the route 'along its back', as Herodotos says, were both called Anopaia, which may mean 'upper opening'. Later writers call it Kallidromos, the 'beautiful race-course'; an excellent description. The 'sinister possibilities' of this route, says Herodotos, had long been known to the local Malians, who had guided the Thessalians over it to outflank the Phokians; but the Greek high command (typically) knew nothing about it until Leonidas reached the Hot Gates and the men of Trachis, themselves Malians, told him. His 1000 Phokian men-at-arms (with, we may assume as usual, at least as many poorly armed light troops) then volunteered to guard the mountain.

The Persians, too, could have heard about the Anopaia easily; but they still had to reach it. A possible way is up the spur west of Anthela; but there is a cliff at the top of it, and though this can be passed at either end, these routes were rugged, and presumably held by the Phokians, in a strong position. The Trachinians themselves, who appear in a later account as '1000 Malians', probably held their citadel on the Trachinian Cliff, west of the Asopos gorge; and the Persians did not attempt that grim passage. They attacked frontally, along the coast, and were

.thrown back with heavy losses; the Greeks' armour was better, and their spears were longer. The Spartans, with their perfect training, engaged out in front of the wall, and indulged in feigned flights, drawing the enemy on, to be caught, crowded and taken in flank, in the V-shaped trap between the wall and the sea. There were enough Greeks to fight in relays; and after two days they were showing no sign of exhaustion.

Then the Persians found what, as experienced mountain fighters, they must have been seeking since their first mounted scouts arrived a week before: a Malian who could show them how to reach the Anopaia by outflanking the whole Greek mountain line: Ephialtes of Antikyra. Naturally he became in tradition the Greek equivalent of Judas Iscariot. He may have been a rogue; but one should remember that Hellas was not a state. Hellenes, like modern Europeans, often, if deplorably, fought each other, and Ephialtes owned no fealty to a king of Sparta. *If* he thought of 'his people', he would have meant the Malians, and felt that he was doing well to get the Persians moved on before they had eaten all the food in the country.

Xerxes sent the Guards, the 'Immortals', so called because there was never a vacancy in their ranks, whose march discipline might be equal to keeping up, without hopeless straggling, on hill paths at night. There was a moon—the Olympic full moon. On the other hand, the mountains were covered with oak forest. They started far out to the west, and 'marched all night, having on their right the mountains of the Oitaians and on their left those of the Trachinians; and day was breaking when they came out on top of the mountain.' *I.e.*, they went right round behind the Trachinian Cliffs. The best way up starts far to the west, where now the railway climbs up from the Dyras, modern Gorgopotamos, famous in a later war. Higher up, there is a good line on the slopes of Oita, used by a modern country road. They turned left and crossed the Asopos, either descending into a grassy basin above the gorge, or perhaps going right round it; it all depends on where the Oitaians' paths were; a rough path is much better than none. They were now on the Anopaia proper, and had to scramble up the west end of Kallidromos, which is steep but not precipitous, to reach Nevropolis. They had come some 18km by rough paths; no small feat for a column of up to 10,000 men in the August night.

Their leading companies were already up when they encountered the Phokians, alerted (one of Herodotos' graphic details) by a mysterious rustling in the forest; that of the oak leaves of many years under thousands of feet. Both sides were taken aback; the Phokians literally, while Hydarnes, commander of the Guards, had understood that he would meet no Greeks, till he was in rear of their main position. Then both reacted according to habit. The Persians loosed off their arrows, and the Greeks 'fled to the peak of the mountain and prepared to die.' 'Peak' sounds like the conspicuous rock pyramid east of Nevropolis; but, as Herodotos had only heard about the path and not been there, the Phokians may really have massed in their presumed position at the top of the north-facing cliff. But Hydarnes, quickly understanding the position from his guide, was too good a soldier to waste time on demolishing a flank guard, when by *closing up* (the typical reaction of Greek armoured troops) they had left the path open. After showering them with arrows, 'the Persians with Ephialtes and Hydarnes ignored the Phokians and started down, going fast.'

Actually, they still had some distance to go, easy going, on the flat. Just how the Persians came down is another question to exercise mountain walkers on the spot. The shortest way goes north of the main rock pyramid and passes a chapel, once that of a now deserted village with the odd name of Dhrakospelia, the Dragon's Cave. (Presumably there was a story about this, but the local shepherds say they know nothing about it. Either it is totally forgotten, or they are shy of telling strangers about a piece of folklore which their society, with village schools, has now outgrown.) Crossing a corner of Zastani, the flat top of the great precipice above the Hot Springs, this path goes down a gully to New Dhrakospelia, a later village, now deserted in turn; the people have migrated down to the main road, and renamed their village Thermopylai.

This route is actually shown in some modern books; but, as every mountaineer knows, the shortest way is not always the quickest. The narrow gully that descends from Old to New Dhrakospelia seems, like that which ascends from Marathon, unsuitable for a large body of troops, if better going can be had; and here it emphatically can. If, from Nevropolis, one goes *south* of the rock pyramid—not the obvious way, but Ephialtes would have known—immediately round the corner one finds the green sward going on, with room for thirty men abreast. There is a very slight col at the end of it, where fir forest begins instead of oak (this part is called Elatovouni, 'Fir Mountain'); here there would be a short defile; but then one emerges into the second wide, flat-bottomed valley, sloping gently down. Half an hour from the top, there is on the left a very peculiar rock, with deep hollows in it, called the Rock of the Grandchild (*Petra tou Engonou*). One suspects that the odd name might be connected with the supposed Dragon story; but again, local shepherds had nothing to say about it. From here, however, a woodcutters' road descends. The whole hillside, if one keeps well away from the Dhrakospelia valley, is uniformly easy; two American archaeological explorers, E. Vanderpool and W. K. Pritchett, have driven over the whole mountain in a 'jeep', using the woodcutters' tracks, from the west end to here.

Herodotos says that the fatal path ended at Alpenos, the Greek supply base (its mound has been identified) 'and at the stone of the Black Buttock and the seats of the Kerkopes.' The place and its peculiar rocks had their legends in antiquity too. The Kerkopes were two mischievous dwarfs who plagued Herakles when he was there; he caught them, and carried them off hanging head down from a pole, over his shoulder, but let them go when they made him laugh by saying their mother had warned them against Black Buttocks, and he was it. Pritchett has photographed, half buried in earth near the foot of the hill, another deeply pitted rock, which might have had the story attached to it.

Leonidas had early warning from watchers 'running down from the heights' that the Persians were up; and he sent away most of his Peloponnesians, to fight another day. It was necessary, since the Persians were strong in cavalry, to sacrifice a rearguard in order to give them a good start; and with that rearguard he stayed, with his Spartans and—little remembered in the tradition—the Helots and the Boiotians, whose cities were now doomed to fall.

Xerxes attacked at mid-morning, when it was calculated that Hydarnes would be at hand. Actually Hydarnes was late; one must remember the time necessary for his column to close up after the various defiles. Meanwhile Leonidas furiously counter-attacked the enemy in front, 'thrusting many into the sea', and was himself killed. When Hydarnes arrived, the exhausted remnant, with most of their spears broken, fell back to a mound at the rear of the wall. Some of the Boiotians laid down their arms; not all were spared. The Persians finished off the Laconians with arrows; and many bronze arrowheads, of oriental types, have been found in the hill of the last stand.

The sacrifice and the whole operation had not been in vain. It enabled the fleet to stay north of Euboia, where it occupied beaches overlooked by a temple of Artemis, an *Artemision*; this gave its name to the naval campaign. So Xerxes' fleet did have to risk coming at them down the coast of Thessaly in a mass, unable to draw up for the necessary night's rest on the few small beaches; and—it was old Greek weather lore that the safe period for sailing ended fifty days after midsummer—there they were caught by a violent nor'-easter, which blew for three days, and piled up on the rocks many of the ships trying to ride out the gale at anchor. A similar fate befell a squadron detached to cut off the Greeks' retreat by rounding Euboia. Heaven itself worked, says Herodotos, to bring down the Persian fleet to a level with the Greeks, or not greatly superior. But it would not have happened if the Greek fleet had not been where it was, forcing the enemy to take risks with the weather.

Nevertheless, when the storm had blown itself out, most of the imperial fleet got round Cape Sepias, to shelter in the Gulf of Pagasai. The Greeks, who had sheltered in the lee of Euboia, got back only in time to cut off a few stragglers. They were still outnumbered; moreover (Herodotos says in two passages, and the later patriotic-rhetorical tradition does not count against him) the oriental ships were nimbler, and the Greeks' 'heavier'. They fought in a defensive half-moon formation, prows out. They did some damage in two late-afternoon engagements, broken off at nightfall; but when the imperial fleet had reorganized and took the offensive, their formation, though unbroken, was heavily mauled. 'Both sides were glad' when night parted them. The Athenians reported half their ships lost or temporarily unserviceable; retreat was necessary. Leaving camp fires burning, they retired by night. A despatch boat, held in readiness, was sent to warn Leonidas; but Thermopylai had fallen that very day.

Thermopylai had delayed the Persians for a week, including four days which it took for their infantry to come up with the cavalry vanguard; a vital week, which made possible the massive Artemision operation by 327 Greek ships, with crews of over 65,000—and the storm damage to the enemy. Seldom, one may say in the Churchillian phrase, has so much been owed by so many to so few. As to tactics, Themistokles, who had the ear of the Spartan commander Eurybiadas, took all measures to ensure that next time his side should have the outside station. The northern campaign had ended in defeat; but without it, there would have been no second chance.

SALAMIS

Salamis Sound today is the outer roads of the third-busiest port of the Mediterranean; its water foul and much of its shore, even into the bay of once-holy Eleusis, occupied by shipyards and a large oil refinery. But modern times have not altered the shape of the coast, though one has to remember that the sea has risen *c.* 2m relative to the land. This is important for historical reconstruction only at one place: St George Island, inside the straits, must have been separated from Salamis island by a strait so shallow as to be perhaps even fordable, and not passable even for one trireme at a time.

Themistokles got the allies, retreating from the north, to come into the Sound, initially to help with the evacuation of Athens. Civilians had been advised to leave in good time, and some had sent their families across the gulf to Troizen; but more had hoped that it would not be necessary, and the evacuation was completed in haste and panic. Then he urged the admirals to stay and defend the straits; Salamis Island, with the Athenian government and land forces on it, was now an important military objective. Thus he hoped to provoke what he wanted: a battle in narrow waters. He persuaded Eurybiadas, the Spartan high admiral; but many of the Peloponnesians were afraid of being cut off there, and would rather have sailed to the Isthmus, where their land troops were now 'dug in' in great force. Themistokles pointed out that this would lay open Aigina and Megara, two more not inconsiderable sea powers, and that anyhow the Isthmus wall would be irrelevant if the enemy could outflank it by sea.

As it was, the Persians *could* have sailed direct for the Peloponnese; but a fleet of galleys could not keep the sea for long without access to water for the rowers. They evidently did not like the idea of approaching a hostile coast, leaving the Greek fleet still in being behind them. Damaratos, the exiled king of Sparta, still hoping to regain his throne, is said to have proposed sending a task force to occupy Kythera, off the south-east Peloponnese, and create a diversion from there; but Akhaimenes, Xerxes' brother, Satrap of Egypt and admiral of its powerful contingent, objected that after its storm losses the fleet was no longer strong enough to divide in the face of the enemy. Clearly Xerxes had nothing like the thousand ships with which the Greeks credited him, in the battle. The Persians, too, had their problems, and the Greeks on their side knew it; a few ships from the Cyclades even went over to the nationalists.

In the end, while some still advised Xerxes, whose fleet was now in Phaleron Bay, to stay there till lack of supplies forced the Greeks to come out, Themistokles helped to make up his mind by his famous false message. He informed the king of the dissensions in the Greek camp—which were real enough; and Xerxes probably knew of them, through the numerous Greek exiles and potential agents who were with him—and added, perhaps, that if attacked they would fight each other, and that he and his people would take the king's side; though our earliest source makes the message say only that the Greeks intended to escape by night. Xerxes, already anxious to make an end quickly (for it was now autumn), thereupon ordered his fleet to put to sea, where it spent the night cruising to intercept a move that did not take place, and to seek out the Greeks inside the straits in the morning.

Hence the great battle, one of the very few truly decisive battles of the world. This is not to say that the Persian empire would otherwise have conquered all Europe—it was already fully stretched—or that oriental despotism would have ruled the world till today. But the campaign could have been lost; without Themistokles and the Athenian navy, it would have been; and the victory saved 5C democratic Athens, and all that the Athenian achievement has meant to the world.

Herodotos' account, unfortunately, is disappointing; he gives graphic anecdotes, but no clear overall picture. But we have from Thucydides a remark insisting that the battle was fought *in the Narrows*; so not, as some reconstructions have it, outside their eastern entrance. For the rest, our primary source is Aeschylus' *Persians*, in which a Persian messenger reports the disaster at home; a play performed eight years later before an audience of thousands, most of whom had either been in the battle or seen it, as the dramatist probably had, among the land forces on shore. That it is poetic drama makes no difference to the fact that he cannot have mis-stated the principal, public facts.

Aeschylus gives the number of the Greek ships as 310. Herodotos gives 380; the fleet at Salamis had been reinforced by some late-comers or last 'scrapings of the barrel', which had mustered off Troizen during the northern campaign. But Herodotos' figures are totals of all the ships raised by each city during the war. He makes no allowance for the losses, which he says were heavy, in the north. The difference represents those losses. In spite of reinforcements the Greek numbers were down—but the enemy's were down by more.

As to where and how the battle was fought, Aeschylus gives two clear statements. His Messenger says that after dawn, *before* the orientals could see the Greeks, they could hear them, singing their battle hymn. (It was called *paian*, 'paean', and was sung *before* going into action. Its name, probably the first word, was a name of Apollo, as healer and deliverer; we might translate, 'O saving Lord'.) Then, says the messenger, the Greeks *came in sight, with their right wing leading*. This surely means the Greek right wing, and not the ships facing the Persian right, as some have supposed. The first statement makes it quite clear that the orientals had not infiltrated into the straits, all along the north shore, by night, as Herodotos seems to suggest, and may have (mis)understood. For the second statement, there is only one place in the straits where the Greeks could come into sight, right wing leading, and that is at the bend in the middle. The Greeks must have formed up in the ample space north of St George Island, and then come down 'right wing leading' along the friendly shore, to envelop and swarm in upon the Phoenician squadron, Xerxes' best sailors and the Greeks' deadly enemies,

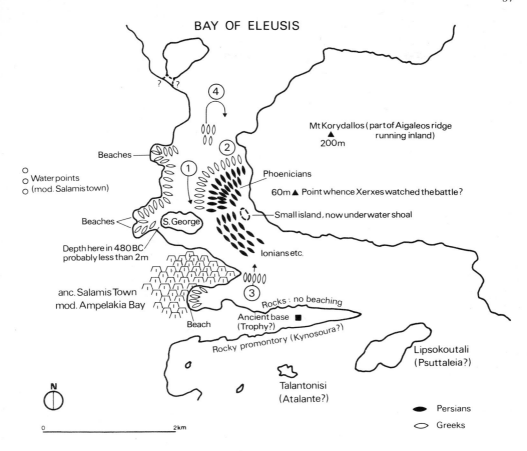

BAY OF ELEUSIS

Mt Korydallos (part of Aigaleos ridge
▲   running inland)
200m

Beaches

Water points
(mod. Salamis town)

Phoenicians

60m ▲ Point whence Xerxes watched the battle?

Beaches

S. George

Small island, now underwater shoal

Depth here in 480 BC
probably less than 2m

Ionians etc.

anc. Salamis Town
mod. Ampelakia Bay

Rocks : no beaching

Beach

Ancient base ■
(Trophy?)

Rocky promontory (Kynosoura?)

Lipsokoutali
(Psuttaleia?)

N

Talantonisi
(Atalante?)

● Persians

◇ Greeks

0 ——————————————— 2km

The Battle of Salamis

The following are detailed Greek movements, for which there is at least some evidence:
1 Greek right wing heads southward along friendly shore before engaging.
2 Athenians (left of main fleet) back water before engaging.
3 Ships of Aigina and Megara (50) posted to right of Spartans, i.e. detached (Ephoros), = 'Aiginetai lying in wait in the fairway' (Herodotos).
4 Ships of Corinth flee under sail (Herodotos, from Athenian sources); but were distinguished in the battle (Herodotos, from all other sources); i.e. a conspicuous feigned flight?

who were in the lead, when they had passed the narrowest part of the strait and were trying to fan out. The very first ship rammed, Aeschylus says, was a Phoenician, hit *on her poop*! She must have been caught turning. Then, he continues, for a time the 'torrent' of oriental ships bore up against the Greek line; but they soon fell into a hideous jam. (With the rear squadrons pressing forward, no crippled ship could get back.) 'But the Greek ships, in a circle round, kept striking in.' They, by Themistokles' planning, had the outside station this time. The end of it was that the Phoenician squadron was largely destroyed; and though the Ionian and other fleets were still numerous, Xerxes did not trust their morale. For the rest of the war, they stood on the defensive off Asia Minor; and when attacked, in the next year, they disintegrated. Xerxes himself, after a few days, returned to Asia; it was common sense, not mere cowardice; his father Darius had done as much after his setback in Scythia. Each left an army in Europe to continue the war.

There was one more act in the drama on the day of battle, to which Aeschylus seems to devote rather disproportionate attention. The Persians had landed troops on an islet somewhere in the fairway, and when the naval battle was won, the Greeks assaulted it and destroyed them. The poet says that they were Persian aristocrats, a severe loss to Xerxes, which seems most improbable; but more probably, he wanted to give some glory in his play to the armoured infantry, the class to which he himself belonged. Herodotos names the islet, Psyttaleia, but places it only 'between Salamis and the mainland', which leaves its position vague. It can hardly have been St George Island, then barely detached from Salamis, though that has been suggested. More likely (and more often suggested) is Lipsokoutali, off the east end of the strait. This position makes sense, since Xerxes expected a battle to foil a Greek attempt to escape. The curious modern name, which means 'defective spoon', could have evolved from Psyttaleia (ancient Greek y being pronounced ü, often becoming ou [oo] in place-names), by, first, the addition of an Italian article in 'Frankish' times (Greek nautical language is full of Italian words), and then an attempt to make 'Lipsoutali' mean something.

PLATAIA

Thermopylai and its mountains repay topographical study; the battle of Plataia, not so easily. It was fought south of the Boiotian river Asopos, between its tributaries and the headwaters of the west-flowing Oeroe, in gently undulating plain country, where contour lines on a map, if they are to show all the ups and downs, become so numerous as to be hard to read. Chapels and religious precincts, mentioned by Herodotos as landmarks, have disappeared and it is a guess whether churches now in the region are on their sites. Finally, the details of this small-featured terrain, where the Oeroe has, in recent geological time, 'captured' streams that used to flow to the Asopos, may have altered quite significantly in nearly 2500 years.

A difficult campaign between two armies, one superior in armoured infantry and the other in cavalry and archers, ended when Pausanias the Spartan, regent for his cousin, the young son of Leonidas, at last drew the Persians into a hand-to-hand fight, the kind of battle that suited the Spartans. In it the Persian commander fell with the flower of his army, and his allies then left the field; but all the interest of the campaign is in how things got to that point.

When Xerxes returned to Asia after Salamis, he left his young brother-in-law Mardonios to finish off the war, with all the good Iranian troops, including the

Guards. Even one division, which escorted the king to the Sea of Marmara, went back to join Mardonios afterwards. Mardonios, however, sent away the less useful regiments of all nations and languages—painted, stone-age warriors from the Sudan are mentioned among them—whom Xerxes had brought to represent the whole strength of his empire.

In 479 Mardonios, who had wintered in Thessaly, advanced, forcing the Athenians to evacuate their city again, and then, with it as a bargaining counter, negotiated with them, offering favourable terms if they would change sides. The Athenians, true to their oaths, refused, in the name of all that Greeks held dear; but they refused the offer of a home in the Peloponnese (where they would have been at Sparta's mercy), and at last, by hinting that they could not hold out for ever, got Sparta to commit her main league forces to a land campaign.

Mardonios declined to fight in Attica, where he might be cramped with his back to the hills. He retired by the eastern, more open route, right round Mount Parnes, to interpose between the Greeks and his ally, Thebes, in more spacious 'cavalry country' on the Asopos, and built a vast wooden stockade some 1800m square to enclose his camp. When the Greeks—8000 Athenian and ultimately

The routes to Plataia and Leuktra.

Mountains and rough country shaded (irrespective of height).
Plains left unshaded (irrespective of height)

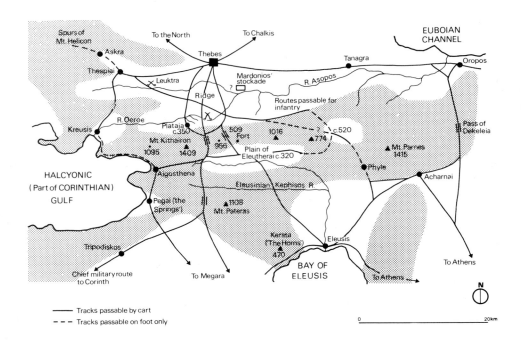

30,000 Peloponnesian armoured men, with more expected—came down over the lower hills between Parnes and Kithairon, he sent his cavalry to attack the heads of their columns; but the Greeks beat them off, killing their commander.

Pausanias then moved his line to the west, along the hill-foot, into the lands of Plataia, for better watering and camping facilities; the name, also written Plataia*i*, probably means 'the Broads'; the plain there, between the Asopos and the towering side of Kithairon, was broader than further downstream. The Greek front here ran along a low and interrupted ridge, slightly higher ground left behind between the drainage basin of the Asopos and that of the smaller, west-flowing Oeroe; and their communications, for convoys from the Peloponnese, using a natural route through the inland hills of the Megarid, were by the Plataia pass, 'called by the Boiotians the Three Heads and by the Athenians Oak Heads'. (That 'Oak Heads' is *this* pass seems to be perfectly clear from Thucydides' account of the escape of men from beleaguered Plataia in 428 (iii, 24), though G. B. Grundy, followed by several guide books, muddles it.) N. G. L. Hammond has detected traces of a 'made' road for carts here on the steep hillside.

The armies faced each other across the stripling Asopos for twelve days. They were probably not very unequal in numbers; but with their differences in armament—the Greeks stronger in close fight, but the Persians more mobile—both commanders knew well that an incautious offensive could lose the war. Persian archery stopped the Greeks watering from the stream, and forced them to rely on springs behind the ridge; this bore hardest upon the Athenians at the west-north-west end of the line, who had furthest to go. Later their horse-archers took to riding up and shooting into the Greek ranks, no doubt also 'calling them women', as we are told of the earlier encounter; not the last time that this insult has been hurled at kilted troops. (The Persians wore trousers.) But the arrows did little more harm than the insults as long as the Greeks kept down behind their shields; and Pausanias was not to be drawn. His contingents were still coming in. Meanwhile, as the troops were told, the omens were propitious only for defensive action.

Mardonios had his difficulties too. His army, though nothing like the 300,000 alleged by the Greeks, was too large to live off the country; and his convoys from Thessaly were harassed by the Phokians who, with their cities burnt, were still in arms in the forests of Mount Parnassos. He wanted a quick decision, if only it could be had without closing with the armoured Greeks in their chosen position.

On day seven he found a way to break the deadlock. The left of the Greek front line was 3km from the hill-foot; and a Theban, with knowledge of the ground, offered to guide cavalry by night, probably round that outer flank, to get at the Greeks' back-areas. The raid was a devastating success. It caught a food convoy of 500 'yoked beasts' (250 *carts*—not mere pack animals) and destroyed or drove off captive practially all of it. Moreover, having found the way, the cavalry made the back-areas unsafe by day too. The men of the next convoy were afraid to come down, and remained 'pent up in Kithairon'. There is a spacious valley head just behind the top of the pass, where one can imagine them waiting. The Greeks had

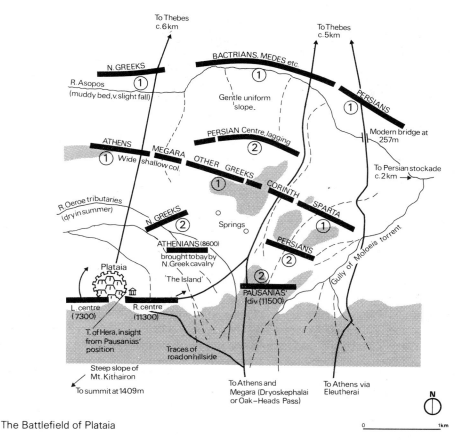

The Battlefield of Plataia

0 ————————— 1km

The one contour shown is at 330m, selected as showing the 'Asopos Ridge'; ground above this (73m above modern bridge on Athens-Thebes road) shaded.
Greek numbers are as given by Herodotos. The blocks indicating troops show (1) positions on the days before the battle, approximately certain; (2) positions which they *may* have occupied about one hour after dawn on the day of battle. It is not to be supposed that formations, especially on the move, were really so tidy.

plenty of light-armed troops, mostly javelin throwers; but while these might defend the wooded hills, they were unorganized and quite incapable of standing up to cavalry in the plain. The cavalry, growing bolder, came close up behind the Greek front line, and blocked and fouled the springs. The Greek armoured force could not be dispersed for guard duties, for fear of a general assault. After a few more days, it was clear that the position on the ridge was untenable, and Pausanias issued orders to retire by night to the hill-foot.

At the same time, trained soldier as he was, he kept in view the possibility of a counter-stroke. His orders were for the whole centre (half the army) to move back to the hill-foot and cover the descent of the food trains, and for the Athenians then to move across and link up with the Spartans. They had the only organized Greek archer regiment, and Pausanias was going to want it. As Pausanias, we are told, gained high credit for what followed, we may presume that he planned it, though his plan did not come off in every detail. The Athenians, whose movement was delayed until near dawn (perhaps according to plan), failed to complete it; and at dawn Mardonios, seeing the Spartans isolated, launched a general offensive. The Athenians were pursued and brought to bay by the northern Greeks, who had some cavalry, among the grassy undulations between the head-streams of the Oeroe. Herodotos names a place called 'the Island', where the stream parted and met again. Such a situation could never last long—one stream would 'win' and capture all the water—and it is no surprise that there is no such island there now. The Athenians were then attacked by the infantry of Boiotia, their old enemy, and held. Their failure to complete their move probably drew some criticism from their allies; and they repaid it, especially in later years, when Herodotos was in Athens and when the Peloponnesians were Athens' enemies, by laying blame on everyone else. The centre, they said, had rushed off in near panic, and gone too far; *they* should have stopped at the Island too—which is absurd; wherever and whatever the Island was, there cannot possibly have been room in it for the whole line, some 3km long.

However, even uncompleted, the Athenian move did have the effect, probably as planned, of drawing the northern Greeks, Mardonios' right or western wing, in pursuit, *across the front of Mardonios' centre*, blocking its advance. If it had been completed, the Spartans would have had the assistance of the Athenians and their archers for their battle with the native Persians under Mardonios himself; and as the Persian allies moved to join in, the whole former Greek centre, 19,000 armoured men, would have been able to come in on a flank. As it was, Herodotos says that the right-centre, headed by the 5000 men-at-arms of Corinth, moved to their right [to close the gap between the Athenians and Spartans] and the left, headed by Megara's 3000, 'advanced by the smoothest way, through the plain', but were caught on the move by the Boiotian cavalry, and suffered heavy losses. So far so good; but he adds, absurdly, that all the former centre troops only heard of the battle—taking place not two kilometres away!—when it was almost over, and contributed nothing to the victory. In fact, the cavalry whom the Megarians drew upon themselves would otherwise have been free to take the Athenians in flank. When the battle was almost over they were otherwise occupied, covering the northern Greeks' retreat. The Athenians owed much to Megara that day; but when Herodotos was in Athens, they were embittered against her; she had asked for Athenian protection against Corinth in 460 (when Sparta was fighting a revolt in Messenia), and then in 446 gone back to Sparta's side and massacred an Athenian garrison. So what Herodotos was told about Corinth (said not to have lost a man) and Megara on the field of Plataia is marred by prejudice. The only excuse that can be offered is that the Athenians on the day were fully occupied, and could not see what their allies did behind them.

The Persian centre (Medes, Bactrians and others, mostly Iranian) got left behind for two reasons. Owing to a northward bend of the Asopos, they started further back; and they had to slog up the highest part—though only about 70m high—of the ridge, while such tracks and regular fords as there were lay on the flanks. Also the Persian second-in-command, Artabazos, had not been keen on Mardonios' attempt to force a decision, which he thought too impetuous. He may not have pushed the advance very hard; and when he reached the top, he could see two separate battles going on, and nought for his comfort: in front, the Athenians stalling off the northern Greeks (of whom perhaps only the Thebans fought really hard); and away to his left, the Persians shooting into Pausanias' Spartans, crouched behind their shields, while other Persians crowded up to join in.

Crowded: that was what one should never do; but Mardonios was there, on his white horse, leading the attack, not controlling it. If the Spartans charged, it would be difficult to get away.

The Spartans did charge.

Pausanias, utilising the enemy's real successes, had 'drawn' Mardonios at last. He had got the enemy where he wanted them: in front, in a mass, the perfect objective. The final mellay was a slaughter, though the Persians fought with desperate courage, 'clutching at the spears and trying to break them.' Mardonios was unhorsed by a great stone, and killed; and when the Guards broke, Artabazos refused to compound disaster. He took his corps out of line, and right out of Greece, as quickly as he could. He has been much censured by modern historians for deserting his comrades; Mardonios' broken troops fled to the stockaded camp, and were slaughtered when the Greeks took it. But Xerxes, who was no easy master, reckoned that Artabazos had done well.

The northern Greeks went home. Thebes surrendered after a short siege, and its leaders were executed. Xerxes' invasion was over.

IV Athens and late classical Greece

1 Athens

PRE-CLASSICAL ATHENS

Neolithic men found in the Acropolis what for them, as for the classical Greeks, made up an ideal site: a defensible rock, with water. The rock was less table-shaped than now, since walls and the filling-in of the ground behind them have obscured the natural contours; but while rocks could be found anywhere in Greece, the springs were exceptional. To this day it remains surprising how much water this mass of limestone holds from the winter rains, and lets out in useful trickles even in any normal summer. There is one, down on the north side of the main western ascent, where a fountain-house and stairs down to it were repeatedly remodelled in ancient historic times: it was nicknamed the *Klepsydra* or water-sneaker; its thin but continuous flow reminded Athenians of the jars so called, with a small hole in the bottom, which were used like a sand-glass for limiting the length of law-court speeches. Earlier, this flow had fed numerous prehistoric wells, farther down the slope. Long after, the Roman-period fountain-house supplied defenders of the Acropolis in the Greek War of Independence. Further along the north face, in the stormy days of the Late Bronze Age, men found, as we shall see, an ingenious way of tapping the water supply at a higher level. In a cave on the south side there is one of the most striking examples of continuity. Round the back of it, the water was channelled behind a low, simple balustrade of blue marble slabs, installed perhaps when the healer-god Asklepios was introduced from Epidauros *c.* 420 BC, and given a sanctuary on the adjacent terrace; and there it still runs, in a cave-chapel now dedicated to the doctor-saints Cosmas and Damian (called the Penniless Saints, because they treated the poor free of charge). In 1970 an archaeologist saw a little old woman come in to burn incense; and she parked her accessories on what proved to be a classical *perirrhanterion* or sprinkler-stand. To anyone with a sense of the holy, water is holy; and this place has been venerated for at least 2400 years, and probably for over 8000. Unfortunately, it has now had to be protected by a locked grille, because tourists stole the ikons (little more than picture-postcards) as souvenirs.

Occupation of the rock has been continuous, though later ages have left little but potsherds as tangible evidence of the earlier. Athens certainly had its late bronze-age kings, though not so powerful as those of Mycenae. Eleusis and, to judge by 'beehive' tombs, Acharnai (Menidhi), only 12km north of Athens, and Thorikos near Cape Sounion, among other places, had their own kings. On the Acropolis, the probable site of the palace was on, or partly on, that of the classical

Erechtheion; both in their different ways represent the 'strong house of Erech-theus', a traditional semi-divine king, to which Athena repairs in the *Odyssey* (vii, 81). Near it a path, with built or rock-cut stairs in places, left uncovered by modern archaeologists, descends a gully to the north-east. It has been walled off throughout historic times. The main entrance to the citadel was, as ever after, from the west, where the slope is easiest, with a gate (probably an outer and inner gate) under the classical Propylaia. East of the Propylaia a section of Cyclopean wall is still to be seen. The approach was commanded from the right, an attacker's unshielded side, from this wall and from the rock bastion that now carries the Temple of Athena Nike. Recent work has removed a few blocks from the classical revetment here, so that the Cyclopean masonry may be seen inside. The Acropolis, like Tiryns and Mycenae, was being strongly forified in the mid-13C BC.

The most sensational discovery relating to this fortification work was made in 1937. Between the north face of the Acropolis rock and an enormous flake which has split off and remained leaning against it—the points of contact being masked by vegetation—there was room, with some rock-cutting, for a secret stair, used for hieratic purposes in classical times. Archaeologists of the American School, proceeding with their usual determination to get to 'rock-bottom', discovered in the lower part of the chasm, blocked by rock falls—a part unknown to classical Athens, and dangerous to work in in the 1930s—cuttings for the fitting of many more steps down to a landing, from which water could be drawn with rope and bucket out of a natural reservoir at the bottom. Getting it up would have been at best slow and laborious, and in fact the shaft was only in use for some twenty-five years. (Numerous pottery fragments found in it were all of one period.) It has now been found necessary to wall it up. However, we now know that Athens, like Tiryns and Mycenae, devised its secret access to water *c.* 1225 BC.

Athens, it was proudly claimed, never fell to invaders at the end of the Bronze Age. Moreover, Athens survived *alone*; thus becoming the capital of Attica, 2500 sq. km, a large territory for a Greek state, though Eleusis and Salamis may have been taken in only as late as the 7C. Archaeology does suggest that there was some intrusion of a new population in western Attica; and indeed myth not only tells of a separate King of Eleusis, to whom Demeter the Corn Goddess revealed the mystery of agriculture, but also of a great war in which King Erechtheus had to face northern ('Thracian') sea-raiders allied to the Eleusinians. The Pro-togeometric art style may have been created first in Athens; and 8C Geometric vases, in or originally standing upon graves in the later Agora, suggest that space nearer the citadel was by then built up.

Athenian history proper begins just after 600 BC, with the economic and constitutional reforms of the sage and elected dictator Solon; and the Acropolis

overleaf Ancient Athens, showing the line of the ancient walls, in relation to modern central streets, and the chief visible antiquities within or immediately outside the walls.

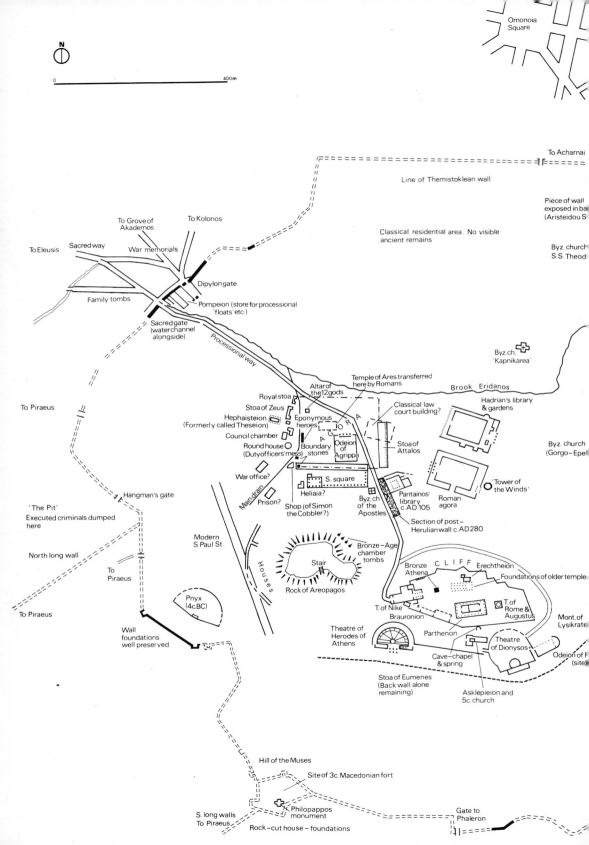

N

0   400m

Omonoia
Square

To Acharnai

Line of Themistoklean wall

Piece of wall
exposed in ba
(Aristeidou S

Classical residential area. No visible
ancient remains

Byz. church
S.S. Theod

To Grove of
Akademos
Sacred way   To Kolonos
War memorials

To Eleusis

To Piraeus

Family tombs

Dipylon gate

Pompeion (store for processional
'floats' etc.)

Sacred gate
(water channel
alongside)

Processional way

Byz. ch.
'Kapnikarea'

Brook Eridanos

Temple of Ares transferred
here by Romans

Altar of
the 12 gods

Royal stoa

Stoa of Zeus

Hephaisteion
(Formerly called Theseion)

Council chamber

Round house
(Duty officers' mess)

Eponymous
heroes

Boundary
stones

Odeion
of
Agrippa

Classical law
court building?

Stoa of
Attalos

Hadrian's library
& gardens

Byz. church
(Gorgo-Epe

War office?

Prison?

Main drain

S. square

Heliaia?

Shop (of Simon
the Cobbler?)

Byz. ch.
of the
Apostles

Pantainos'
library
c. AD 105

Roman
agora

'Tower of
the Winds'

Hangman's gate

'The Pit'
Executed criminals dumped
here

North long wall

To
Piraeus

To Piraeus

Modern
S. Paul St.

Houses

Stair

Rock of Areopagos

Bronze-Age
chamber
tombs

Section of post-
Herulian wall c. AD 280

CLIFF

Bronze
Athena

Erechtheion

Foundations of older temple

Wall
foundations
well preserved

Pnyx
(4c. BC)

T. of Nike
Braversion

T. of
Rome &
Augustus

Parthenon

Theatre of
Herodes of
Athens

Cave-chapel
& spring

Theatre
of Dionysos

Mont. of
Lysikrate

Odeion of F
(site)

Stoa of Eumenes
(Back wall alone
remaining)

Asklepieion and
5c. church

Hill of the Muses

Site of 3c. Macedonian fort

S. long walls
To Piraeus

Philopappos
monument

Rock-cut house - foundations

Gate to
Phaleron

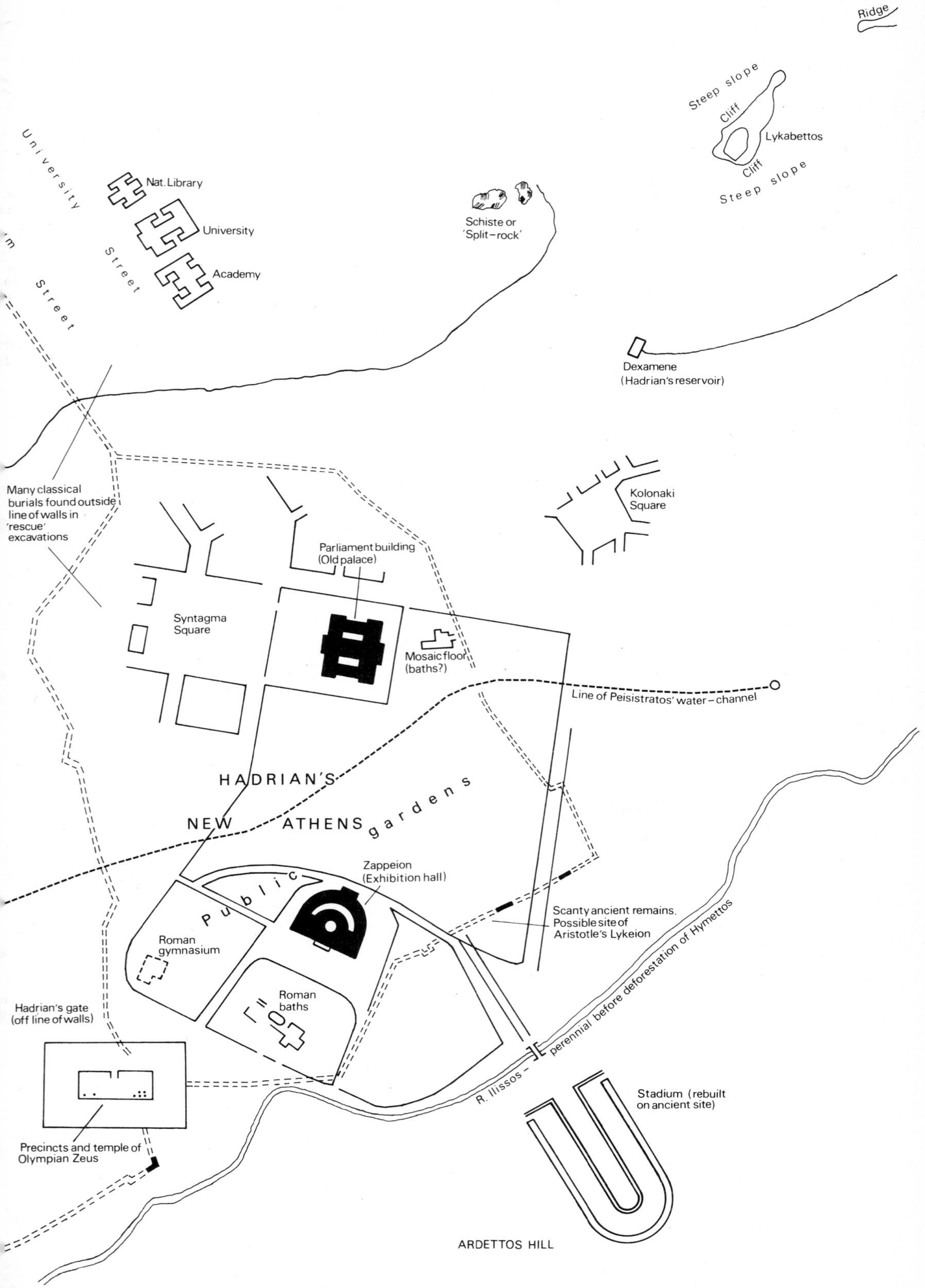

Ridge

Steep slope

Cliff

Lykabettos

Cliff

Steep slope

University Street

Street

Nat. Library

University

Academy

Schiste or
'Split—rock'

Dexamene
(Hadrian's reservoir)

Many classical
burials found outside
line of walls in
'rescue'
excavations

Kolonaki
Square

Parliament building
(Old palace)

Syntagma
Square

Mosaic floor
(baths?)

Line of Peisistratos' water—channel

HADRIAN'S

NEW ATHENS gardens

Public

Zappeion
(Exhibition hall)

Scanty ancient remains.
Possible site of
Aristotle's Lykeion

Roman
gymnasium

perennial before deforestation of Hymettos

Hadrian's gate
(off line of walls)

Roman
baths

R. Ilissos

Stadium (rebuilt
on ancient site)

Precincts and temple of
Olympian Zeus

ARDETTOS HILL

had by then long ceased to be the residence of living kings—though it was still the Citadel, which a young nobleman had recently seized in an unsuccessful attempt to make himself a 'tyrant'. The House of Erechtheus, or whatever stood there in the 7C, had become a temple.

The seat of government was now at the Areopagus, *Areios Pagos*, the Rock of the War-God; the lower rock west of the Acropolis, where met the Council of nobles, who probably called assemblies of the people only to hear what they had decided. Kings had disappeared from most of Greece during the Dark Ages, probably when they could no longer maintain war bands sufficient to overawe the other chief families. At Athens the change is said to have been bloodless; first the nobles elected a War Chief to command instead of a king who was no great fighting man; then, the decisive step, they appointed a Regent (Archon) *over* the King, for civil affairs. That left the King only the duty of conducting the chief sacrifices, with which it was safer not to meddle; the Gods might not have liked it. In fact, the *title* of King was never abolished under the Athenian republic, though its holder might be any nobleman elected by his fellow-nobles, and later any citizen chosen by lot, subject to scrutiny; he had to be married (the 'Queen' had duties) and of unblemished reputation. Six judicial functionaries later made up the full number of the Nine Archons, elected annually.

Solon's legislation, passed to allay unrest at a time when Attica, hitherto an exporter of corn, began to need imports of it, and when holders of subdivided farms were falling into debt—which could end in being sold abroad as a slave—cancelled all debts, provided for buying back those sold as slaves, and introduced a measure of popular control of the government. Archons still had to be 'knights', members of the few hundred richest families, who could afford full armour and a horse; but they had to be elected by the Assembly of all free men, and to give it an account of their actions after their year in office. Only if they then received a vote of approval did they become members, for life, of the Council of the Areopagus. And, to ensure that the Areopagus could not control the elections, Solon gave the Assembly its own steering committee, chosen by lot from among candidates of the upper and middle classes.

About this time there also took place an important piece of town-planning. The *Agora* ('place of gathering') was created: a rough square of about 130m, between the foot of the Areios Pagos and the Eridanos brook, was declared a public open space. Burials were stopped, and a few buildings already there were removed; and just west of the Agora limits (marked by inscribed stones, each declaring 'I am a boundary of the Agora') there appeared the first public buildings in the area, backing onto the low ridge called Kolonos Agoraios, 'Market Hill'. Probably, like their successors on the same site, they were for the use of Solon's new People's Council: The Council, as people came to call it for short, while the old, aristocratic one was simply called the Areopagus. As a Supreme Court, the latter kept the formidable veto power of 'Guardian of the Laws'.

The reform did not prevent the rise of a popular leader as 'tyrant'. Peisistratos, a general and himself an aristocrat (he claimed descent from Peisistratos the son of Nestor in the *Odyssey*) first seized the Acropolis perhaps in 561 and, after being twice driven out, finally consolidated his power (546?), dying old and respected in 528. No horror stories are told of him; and the economy throve. He did not live on the Acropolis; and he started but did not finish a great new Temple of Olympian Zeus south-east of it, down by the Ilissos. He also laid on piped water to the centre of the old city, south of the Acropolis, a blessing to the women, who had to carry it. His grandson, another Peisistratos, Archon 522, built the Altar of the Twelve Gods in the Agora. But there was much building activity on the Acropolis, too, during the century. The chief temple probably stood on the foundations still visible between the Erechtheion and the Parthenon; but the Acropolis Museum houses architectural sculptures and other members from more buildings, all destroyed by the Persians, than we can identify. Some, like the amiably smiling Three-Bodied Monster, still keep much of their paint. We must imagine an Acropolis with several buildings, not very large, but gay with painted stone and terracotta, before Xerxes came.

Marathon and Salamis have been described above; but it is sometimes forgotten that the Acropolis was the scene of a brave though unavailing defence in 480. Some people insisted on taking literally the Delphic prophecy that a Wooden Wall should survive when all Attica fell, and 'barricaded the Acropolis with boards and timbers'. The Persians, shooting incendiary arrows from the Areopagus, set the barricade ablaze; but the defenders still held out, 'loosing rolling stones upon those who approached the gates.' Both the stones (column drums?) and the timbers (from scaffolding?) may have come from work in progress on a great new temple that was never finished. But, that the oracle might be fulfilled, as Herodotos says, Persian rock-climbers found a way 'where there was no guard and no one would have thought that any man could get up . . . beside the sanctuary of Aglauros.' This means the cave at the bottom of the then still open part of the stair behind the Great Flake. The crack at the end of the flake perhaps helped the climbers. When they saw them already up, the defenders panicked and the Persians massacred them and 'burned all the Acropolis' (*sic* Herodotos). The red marks of fire remain on the south-west corner of the great platform, built for the projected temple and later used for the Parthenon. After the war the Athenians restored nothing. They buried the old fragments in the 'fill' required for levelling up the ground behind new walls; and large column-drums, unfluted (that work would have been done when they were in position) may still be seen, built into the north wall of the Acropolis.

EARLY CLASSICAL ATHENS

For the immediate post-war period, the centre of interest shifts to the new city wall, built in haste and against the will of Athens' late ally, Sparta. Sparta, while professing friendship, would have much preferred this teeming democracy, unrivalled in naval strength, at least to be vulnerable by land—and argued publicly that a great fortress north of the Isthmus was undesirable, lest the Persians, if they came again as was expected, might make it an advanced base.

Themistocles, the democratic leader and architect of victory at sea, as the Spartans had handsomely acknowledged, went to Sparta himself for talks, but said he was not authorised to begin them until the arrival of two fellow-envoys—who, he had arranged, were not to start until the wall was high enough to be defensible! And, says Thucydides,

> to this day one can see how hastily the work was done; for the foundations are of all sorts of stones, not even fitting well in places but [put in] as people brought them up; and many grave-stones and architectural members were built into them; for the perimeter was extended outside the city in every direction. . . .

—thus accounting for the many tombstones. Other stones came from buildings, which the Persians had systematically demolished before their final evacuation; the Athenians now 'sparing no possible source of useful material, either public or private, ruthlessly.'

Some of what Thucydides saw can be seen today in the Kerameikos, or Potters' Quarter, north-west of the Agora. The new wall bisected it, creating an Inner and Outer Kerameikos. Here the German Archaeological Institute, in meticulous excavations since 1907, has exposed some 200m of the city wall, standing to a height of about 2m. It is pierced by the Dipylon or Double Gate (inner and outer portals with a court between), whence debouched the roads both to north and south Greece and, a few yards to the south-west, the Sacred Gate, used only for the annual procession to Eleusis. Under the latter, in a separate compartment, also ran out the Eridanos brook, which, having become a main sewer, had to be covered; and between the gates was the Pompeion or Procession House, where the floats and other properties for processions were kept. Most of the Themistocleian work is masked on the outside by a later strengthening wall, and much was rebuilt; but south-west of the Sacred Gate a section, best inspected from the inside, is in position. From the foundations have come sculptures now in the National Museum: the head of a young man in low relief, upholding a discus, from a grave monument, and two square statue-bases with reliefs of young men's amusements: chariot-driving, wrestling, a dog-and-polecat fight, and two of ball-games; one certainly a team-game, and the other played with curved sticks, though, from the relaxed attitudes of the youths who are not actually 'bullying off' it does *not* look as if they expected to be engaged immediately.

Outside the new gates there developed a new Kerameikos cemetery; for it was the most frequented road out of town, and the ancients set much store by the sort of immortality that consists in being remembered, or even having one's name read. The most famous tombs were along the northern fork of the road, which passed, in a little over 1km, the sacred grove of a local hero, Hekademos, later Akademos. Here were buried Pericles, Thrasyboulos, who restored the democracy suppressed by Sparta (404–3), Zenon the Stoic, and other famous men; and here, under their memorials, lay the ashes of Athens' war dead of many campaigns. Somewhere here, then, Pericles must have delivered his famous Funeral Oration. Most of these tombs have not been found, the area being under houses, though some war-memorial inscriptions have been; but nearly a century later a new cross-road was laid out, joining the Sacred Way near the Wall to the road to Piraeus, which had its own gate further south; and along this, rich families evidently bought burial plots, in which monuments to several relatives may be found. There are twenty in the part (about 100m) which it has been possible to excavate. The previous owner(s) of the land must have made a fortune. From this 'Street of the Tombs' come the famous late-classical 4C grave-reliefs in the National Museum, replaced by casts in the original sites.

The Grove of Akademos itself—an ancient site, already surrounded with a wall by Hipparchos, son of Peisistratos—had to be saved at this time from drying up, probably through the increasing drawing off of water from the Kephisos for agriculture. Kimon, son of the victor of Marathon and now Athens' leading general, paid for re-irrigating it and laying it out (reserving, no doubt, an 'untrodden' sanctum) as a park and exercise ground; and it was here that Plato, in the next century, founded his Academy, centred in a property which he bought for himself close by, and able to use the facilities. The park, or one of its limits, has been precisely located by an inscribed boundary-stone found *in situ*. Excavations between the modern houses have also found some good pieces of 4C architectural sculpture; but the area in general is at present a dreary piece of 'subtopia'. A little better has been the fate of another famous classical site, a short walk to the north-east: the Kolonos, sacred to Poseidon as god of horses, childhood home of Sophocles and immortalised by him in *Oedipus at Colonos*, where the old, blind, fallen king finds refuge and a divinely ordered escape from this world. Sophocles' chorus sings of its dense grove and ivy, well-watered, where nightingales sing. It has passed through its subtopian stage, which distressed visitors around 1900, and the rock, the core of the ancient Kolonos, now stands, replanted with hand-watered trees, in a residential square. Its top bears stones commemorating two great scholars who died in Athens: K. O. Müller (1797–1840) and C. Lenormant (1802–59).

Kimon also surrounded the Agora with plane-trees for shade. It must still have had a country look, very unlike the Hellenistic, when shade was provided by long colonnades. Such a colonnade already existed beside the Temple of Hera at Samos, but the first Stoa at Athens was different, and an oddity. 'Stoa' originally meant 'porch' such as was formed by prolonging the side-walls of a temple, or of its predecessor, the Mycenaean chieftain's hall, past the end wall, and inserting a couple of posts to support the gable. The idea of a porch with no hall behind it would have seemed funny, though young Sophocles may just then have been making it familiar as a stage-setting. However, apparently about this time (not earlier, as was first thought), Athens built one, the first of its kind, for the King-Archon. His house, an ordinary well-to-do citizen's house, was elsewhere; but it was thought right to provide him with a place of suitable dignity for the discharge of his duties as judge of first instance in cases concerned with religion. The result was the Royal Stoa, a modest building by later standards, about 17.7m long, its open east front supported by eight Doric columns between the end walls,

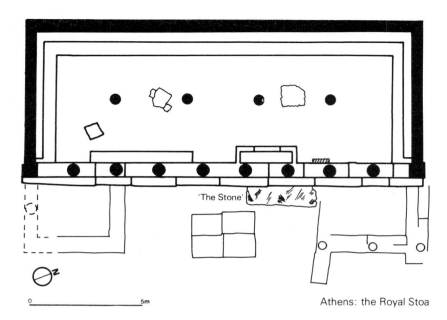

Athens: the Royal Stoa

with four more within, under the roof-ridge. Later, small wings were added in front of the two columns at each end, no doubt to shelter the inscriptions recording the Laws of Solon, which, we are told, were set up here. Slots in the stone floors to hold the ends of the inscribed slabs are visible. Facing the north-west corner of the Agora, its foundations were discovered in 1970, with the extension of the American excavations north of the Piraeus Railway cutting; and in front of it, in the angle south of the north wing, lay something visually unimpressive, but historic: a rectangular limestone slab, nearly 3 × 1m, rough-hewn, but worn smooth on top by thousands of feet. Undoubtedly it must be the 'unworked stone', or The Stone, as ancient orators often called it, on which incoming Archons stood to take their oath to observe the laws, in the presence of the outgoing King. In this place, too, Socrates waited for the formal preliminaries to his trial—and, under prosecution for irreligion and corrupting the young, passed the time, according to Plato, in interrogating and confusing Euthyphron, another pious citizen who had business with the King.

Facing south nearby—so that it would catch the winter sun, while giving shade in summer—was built, very soon after, the most famous of all stoas, from which the Stoics took their name: the Painted Stoa, so called because hung with large panel pictures by famous artists including Polygnotos, of Athenian battles; two mythical, two historical and recent: Marathon, and a success against Sparta, won along with Athens' new ally, Argos. Later the Athenians dedicated there the shields of Spartans captured in 425 on the island of Sphakteria; one of Athens' proudest moments, since it was common belief that Spartans never surrendered. One of the shields has actually been found, identified by its inscription in punched

Socrates stood here. The Unwrought Stone (top right) let into the foundations of the Royal Stoa on which men stood to take oaths. Plato's dialogue *Euthyphron* is set here.

letters—but not where it was hung. The Painted Stoa has not yet been excavated; but from Pausanias and by elimination, its foundations underlie a building north of the railway, scheduled for demolition.

Between these two stoas, continuing the road from the Dipylon, a processional way crossed the Agora south-easterly, heading for the col between the Areopagus and Acropolis. Here, below the steep slope, there stood already a temple of the Eleusinian Goddesses, and below it probably were marshalled the pilgrims about to make the procession to that sanctuary. But the most famous use of the road was by a procession uphill: that of the Panathenaia, Athena's own festival, celebrated every year, but with special splendour every four years; the procession that brought to Athena her new robe, woven by Athenian ladies, to be draped on the sacred primitive, wooden statue, said to have fallen from heaven. This is the best-known today of all high points of classical Athenian life, since we can see it all—the august magistrates, the well-born young girls carrying accessories and folding the Robe, the beasts for sacrifice; most famous of all, the aristocratic cavalry—all, by artists of the generation of Pheidias, on the Parthenon frieze. Lost, unhappily, is the transport of the Robe itself, which seems to have been spread as a sail on a wheeled 'ship'. The rest, the world still has, among the Marbles which Elgin reft from Athens, but saved from the modern smog.

South of the Royal Stoa, the foot of Market Hill was still occupied by small industrial workshops, handy for the Agora. It was only late in the 5C that they were replaced by a much grander stoa, that of Zeus the Liberator (*Elevtherios*), guardian of the city's freedom, who no doubt already had a small shrine there. His statue stood in front of it; and in it were hung the shields of war heroes killed in action. But it was more urgent to rebuild the Council Chamber destroyed by the Persians, at the south end. It too was rebuilt again later on an adjacent site, further back, cutting into the hillside, away from market noises; and the former site was occupied by rooms for the accumulating archives. These were placed in the care of the Mother of the Gods, who had a chapel close by. Next to it was the chapel of Apollo Patroios, representing in the city an ancestor cult observed on every estate. If an Athenian had to prove his descent, one question put to him was 'Where is your Apollo Patroios?'

On the other side of the Council House, at the south-west corner of the square, the ground-plan of a *Tholos* or Round House is conspicuous among the rectangular foundations. It was the Mess and dormitory for the Presidents (*Prytaneis*), or Councillors on duty. The People's Council consisted of fifty men from each of the artificial Ten Tribes (legitimised by the Delphic Oracle), into which the People had been divided after the fall of the tyranny (partly as a gimmick, thought up by Kleisthenes, Pericles' mother's uncle, to prevent conservatives from questioning the full citizenship of immigrants). Each tribe held the Presidency, in an order determined by lot, for a tenth of the year; and each day one of the fifty who had not held the position before was chosen, also by lot, to be their Chairman, a titular head of state, from sundown to sundown. He nominated sixteen of his colleagues to be duty officers with him, and they spent the twenty-four hours in or near the Council House or the Tholos, which had a kitchen and lavatory at the back. Thus, if serious news came in during 'unsocial hours', there was always a committee to receive it and decide whether to summon the full Council and the Assembly or to alert the ten Generals, who, starting as colonels of the tribal regiments, had become a standing committee of experts on defence and foreign affairs. Demosthenes describes the whole process swinging into action on the night in 338 when the news came in that King Philip had passed Thermopylai:

> The Prytaneis got up in the middle of their dinner, and some started clearing the stall-holders out of the Agora [with a view to mobilisation] . . . and others

sent for the Generals and summoned the trumpeter; and the whole city was in an uproar; and at dawn the Prytaneis convened the Council in its chamber, and you set out for the Assembly; and before the Council had done with drafting the agenda, the whole People was already seated up there.

Demosthenes, speaking in a law-court, waves his hand towards the Pnyx hill. People knew what to do. The democracy could move fast in an emergency; and the Tholos was its nerve centre.

The Generals had their own office, presumably nearby. It has been tentatively identified as a well-built edifice just to the south-west, beyond a little old cemetery which, not being *in* the Agora, was not disturbed. Across the road that led past it to the Pnyx and to residential areas, up a shallow valley, slight remains of walls may be those of other public offices, including that of Weights and Measures; but, immediately outside the Agora boundary, a couple of householders seem to have refused to be bought out. In one house a scatter of iron hobnails suggests a cobbler's shop; and the name of the proprietor may be given, scratched on the bottom of a 5C cup: SIMON. This is fascinating; for Socrates, pursuing his interrogations in the Agora, is said often to have dropped in at a Simon the Cobbler's shop, talking to customers waiting for their hand-made shoes. Pericles himself is said to have gone there (the supposed Strategeion or 'War Office' is just across the road), and to have offered Simon permanent employment in his household; but Simon said, 'I'm not selling my freedom.' He was a person of independent mind, and is even said to have been the first to write down what he remembered of Socrates' conversations. (Diogenes Laertios, ii, 122; Dorothy Thompson in *Archaeology* XIII (1960), pp. 234ff.)

Outside the shop was the wide upper opening of a main drain, covered with heavy flagstones, which carried off rainwater down the gentle slope to the Eridanos. It seems to be contemporary with the 5C buildings along the foot of Market Hill, and follows the edge of the Agora. Later it was provided with equally substantial feeders, one from the hollow below the Pnyx, while another, draining that between the Acropolis and Areopagus, was diverted in classical times from crossing the Agora, and conducted in another stone-lined channel along the hill-foot to the south-west corner. Cleared by archaeologists of the rubbish of centuries, the Great Drain is again today working perfectly.

About 50m south of this corner, the gently rising ground was terraced and levelled, and a near-square area, *c.* 31 × 26.50m internally, was surrounded by a wall, with entrance up a few steps from the Agora. It was apparently open to the sky. It is tentatively identified as the meeting-place of the Heliaia, the chief lawcourt. Under the democracy, an appeal lay to the People from any serious sentence of an Archon, or of the Council, which originally could itself try administrative cases. In practice serious charges, and also an increasing body of civil litigation, were then sent to a jury, from whose verdict, as that of the Sovereign People itself, there was no appeal unless, in a separate trial, one could prove perjury. The juries were large; 501, as in Socrates' case, was a standard number, but we hear also of 1001, 1501 (when Pericles was suspended as general and 'investigated'); even 2501. For ordinary litigation, there was soon need for more courts than one; and traces of a number of simple buildings or enclosures (no longer visible) near the opposite (north-east) corner of the Agora, have been identified as courts by the finding of a scatter of jurymen's bronze tickets and voting ballots, lost while the buildings were in use. Jury service was voluntary, but was encouraged by modest pay (one-sixth of the silver drachma earned for a day's skilled or heavy work), introduced in the mid-5C and raised (finally trebled) when food prices rose during the Peloponnesian war. This attracted chiefly the older poor citizens, who were getting past heavy work; fierce, prejudiced old men, 'Wasps' as Aristophanes calls them; but we have few complaints of corruption; there was safety in numbers.

The political Assembly originally met in the Agora; but it changed its venue to the Pnyx, just inside the city wall, ten minutes' walk up hill—partly perhaps to avoid the nuisance of having to clear away the wickerwork market stalls, which, not being technically buildings, seem to have been left by their holders in-definitely. (In the crisis described by Demosthenes, the Prytaneis apparently burnt them.) There were forty statutory meetings a year, with others when required; the routine business at the former was often dull, and relatively few people attended; so much so that the Prytaneis used to send out the Scythian slave police to 'sweep' the Agora and adjacent streets with ropes dipped in wet, red paint, to remind citizens of their duties. On the hill, 5C citizens sat on the grass or rocks, while speakers addressed them from below. The arrangement now visible, with the earthen auditorium facing the other way, supported by a curved retain-ing wall of huge blocks, and a rock-cut platform, is later; some thousands of potsherds from the 'fill' put in to level up the ground inside the retaining wall suggest the 4C BC, assuming that a very few, which are much later still, got in during maintenance work.

Dramatic performances also took place at first in the Agora, but after the collapse of a temporary wooden spectators' stand they too were transferred, to the south-east slope of the Acropolis. Here an audience could sit on the hillside, appropriately near an ancient shrine of Dionysos 'in the Marsh' at the bottom; for passion-plays of the Wine-god, in his John Barleycorn-like aspect, were said to have been the seed of drama, and his chief priest occupied the seat of honour. The stage and front seats that are there now are of the Roman age, the last of many remodellings; but when the uppermost seats were cut out of the rock, just below the precipice, we cannot say; probably in the 5C, for in the 4C similar theatres spread widely in Greece. The theatre, too, was an Athenian invention.

THE TEMPLES AND PROPYLAIA

For a generation after the Persian sack the Athenians let their ruined temples lie waste, as a witness, it was said, to the invaders' offence against heaven. But when peace was made with Persia in 449, after great victories followed by some reverses, Pericles, now the most influential Athenian, and his supporters embarked on a great building programme, for reasons at once aesthetic—to give the city a centre of unrivalled beauty; political—to assert that Athens and her League, despite being stabbed in the back by the Peloponnesians, had brought the national war to a satisfactory end; and economic—to provide employment in an economy which had been geared to war for so long that peace brought its problems.

.One great new monument already adorned the Acropolis: the Bronze Athena, so-called in contemporary inscriptions, c. 465–55, giving the accounts for its manufacture. Pausanias' statement that the glint of Athena's helmet and spear-point could be seen from off Cape Sounion, in the clear Greek air (now grievously polluted), may be accepted; facing the entrance gates from a pedestal, probably in a rock cutting still visible, at c. 40m, the statue would be seen between the buildings, and did not have to overtop them. We do not actually know how large it was, nor does any early authority name the still-young Pheidias as the master-craftsman; later, it seemed inevitable to ascribe to him all major sculpture of his age. But we can probably now see where it was cast. A large pit in the natural terrace half-way down the South Slope, near the west end, marks the site of at least a 5C foundry, clearly for some major bronze work on the sacred rock. But for a bronze Athena signed by Pheidias (Lucian says), we have to turn to some fine marble copies of one dedicated (c. 448?) by Athenian colonists on Lemnos island. Ancient critics preferred the original even to the colossal cult statue, surfaced in gold and ivory, which Pheidias executed soon after, to stand in the Parthenon; and of that, we have no good copies.

The first surviving temple to be started at this time was that of Hephaistos, the divine smith and patron of metal-workers, on the Market Hill. (It was formerly, reasonably but wrongly, called that of Theseus, which has perished. Pausanias mentions both.) Discoveries of many little industrial forges round about have now clinched the matter. Built of marble from Mount Pentelikos, with its 6 × 13 Doric columns on a foundation measuring just over 15 × 33m, it rises above the Agora with grace and dignity. But, started before the Parthenon, it was finished after it; the great state project must have drawn off the workers; and a comparison of the two shows the difference between good work of a great period and a work of genius.

Built on the highest part of the Rock, near the south side, where the adjacent ground was built up behind Kimon's new wall, the Parthenon occupied the plinth prepared for a longer and narrower temple, perhaps that which was in building in 480. The older foundation can be seen protruding at the east end. With its 8 × 17 columns, it is large; but that is the least of its virtues. The floor bulges, very slightly—it has been prosaically suggested, for the sake of drainage; but while this may be doubted, there is no doubt whatever about the other famous 'refinements' of the Doric style found here. Earlier Doric columns had bulged visibly, thickest at the bottom, giving an impression of sturdiness. In the Parthenon, the bulge has been reduced, almost to nothing; but it is still there, as can be seen looking slant-wise between the columns at a narrow band of sky. The precision of the work is no less remarkable than Iktinos the architect's conception. Other refinements,

The Parthenon

invisible to the eye and only to be proved by careful measurement, are the facts that the corner columns are a little thicker than the rest (seen against the bright sky, they *look* right); and that all the columns lean imperceptibly inwards; it has been calculated that, if produced, they would all meet, with minimal error, at a height of about a mile! Lastly, and a fact which has nothing to do with drainage, the architrave ('top beam'; the horizontal course that joins the tops of the columns) follows the bulge (not a true curve) of the floor. There is a lift of a few inches in the middle; two people, looking from opposite ends along one of the steps with eyes near floor level, cannot see each other. What it all adds up to, visually, is the apparent lightness of the whole structure, as though at a word from Athena it might fly up to heaven.

The Parthenon was essentially finished in nine years, 447–438, though the building accounts show some work continuing, no doubt on the sculptures, for a few years longer. The most famous of these shows the Procession, described above. Athens then went straight on to another typically Periclean project: to provide the Acropolis with a monumental entrance or west façade, the Propylaia. A new great architect, Mnesicles, is named; and he had no tradition, as for a temple, to guide his general design. One problem was how to harmonize the Doric columns that upheld the lintels, east and west of the entrance hall, and those supporting the coffered stone ceiling, which had to be taller. Taller Doric columns would have to be inappropriately massive, or to look spindly. In the earlier temple at Aigina, the roof was supported by small Doric columns standing upon those of the interior colonnade, which is connected by an architrave and is the same size as that outside. Mnesicles did better. Daringly in his time, he combined two styles, introducing for his interior the Ionic, scarcely seen previously west of the Aegean. Ionic columns were traditionally more slender and did not have the Doric bulge or *entasis*. Their other special feature was the capital with volutes, a classical refinement of earlier foliage capitals. With some restoration, using ancient materials where possible, the highly successful effect may be seen today.

Left and right of the entrance, Mnesicles planned two great wings, two halls, meant to be symmetrical and perhaps to be colonnaded on the outer (west) side; but only the northern was built, and its walls remained plain. It was used as a picture gallery. Two smaller halls were to have adjoined them on the east, as is shown by, among other indications, contemporary sockets for a row of beams on the exposed east wall of the existing structure; but they were not built either. In 432–1 the Propylaia were summarily finished off, as they have remained. The occasion was the impending outbreak of war; as it proved, a twenty-seven-year period of wars, ending in disaster; but an underlying cause was conservative opposition to the southern extension, which would have trenched on ground sacred to Victory, identified as a goddess with Athena; a precinct, for which Kallikrates had been instructed to plan a doorway and temple some fifteen years before. Kallikrates was perhaps Athens' regularly employed state architect; he is mentioned with Iktinos as an architect of the Parthenon.

Actually, when Athens had settled down to a state of war and her economy, despite enemy ravaging of the countryside, did not collapse, much building was again done; but not to Mnesicles' designs. Pericles was dead, and the public mood more conservative. The beautiful little Ionic Temple of Nike (Victory) was built, a free-standing structure, on its rock bastion, where it again stands, re-erected out of the original materials. Later in the war, and in part even in its last years when Athens really was in desperate straits, the Acropolis received the last of its four famous buildings: the Erechtheion, with its fine Ionic north porch and southern porch of the Maidens (so-called Caryatids; now moved under cover, after suffering sadly from atmospheric pollution). Its odd shape is due to its being built to cover a group of traditionally sacred spots; an aggregate of beautiful parts, but no very coherent whole; in execution exquisite, but in the spirit of its planning the antithesis of the work of Mnesicles.

Of some other classical buildings here, nothing remains except some rock cuttings. Some, south of the way from the Propylaia to the Parthenon, mark the site of a fence or balustrade delimiting the Athens sanctuary of Artemis of Brauron, where her temple was. At her festival young girls who had 'been to school' at Brauron danced their 'bear dance' (pp. 196ff.). East of the Brauronian enclosure was a building called the Bronze Store, *Chalkotheke*; and opposite, abutting on the north wall of the Acropolis, was a house where, every year, two still younger, seven-year-old girls lived from midsummer to midsummer under the special care of Athena and her Priestess. At the end of their service, one night the Priestess gave them packages to carry on their heads down the secret stair 'neither she nor they knowing what they contained'. They came out in the Cave of Pandrosos ('All-Dew'—a divinity mythologized as a daughter of Kekrops, first king of Athens), and by a further descent reached the enclosure of Aphrodite-in-the Gardens. Here they delivered their burden, and were given another to carry up again. Baked clay *phalloi* have been found in the Aphrodite sanctuary, and may have been the contents of the packages, wrapped up presumably by carefully purified male hands. The ritual is, then, immemorial fertility magic. Athens, even under the aegis of the virgin Athena, pays tribute to Aphrodite; and, for the spirit in which the community's fertility ritual was performed, it is significant that the deliverers of the offerings must be sexually pure; hence the little girls. They were called the *Arrhephoroi* (some think, for *Arrheto-phoroi*, 'Bearers of the Secret Things'), and their ritual was considered extremely important in classical times. Aristophanes' *Lysistrata*, a very august priestess, who in the play tries to stop the war by organizing a women's sex strike, has a chorus of privileged ladies who emphasize their duty of doing their best for the City, which has given them the best of everything; as Arrhephoroi, as 'Bears', and later as carriers of baskets in the great Panathenaic procession.

Last comer among the gods to Olympos, and to the Acropolis, was Asklepios the Healer, originally a hero, whose sons, also skilled doctors, fought at Troy. He was introduced after the great plague of 430–427, and probably after the short-lived peace of 421, from Epidauros, and was accommodated on the terrace, low on the south slope, below the cave with the already sacred spring.

Down in the Agora, the Stoa of Zeus the Liberator was built at this time. It had a Doric façade and Ionic columns within: Mnesicles' device. A much longer 4C South Stoa (*c.* 80m) was placed on the terrace at the foot of the Areopagus, between the (probable) Heliaia and, to the east, a fountain-house and what was probably the Mint. Its stout back wall of *poros* (limestone) blocks served as a retaining wall for the already ancient east–west road above. In front there was a deep, two-aisled colonnade; and behind this, a row of fifteen rooms with interior walls of sun-dried brick on poros foundations. In one of them was found a Hellenistic-age inscription which had escaped later quarriers for stone, recording the handing-over of the official weights and measures by one annual board (five commissioners and their two secretaries) to the next. Probably the whole suite served as administrative offices for the numerous boards of officials, of which we hear from Aristotle's *Constitution of Athens* and elsewhere. Much business, including all interviews with members of the public, would be transacted *in* public, as the democracy approved, at tables placed between the columns of the stoa; while the rooms are dining rooms, where the boards took their midday meals together. This is indicated by the fact that they all have their doors slightly off-centre, an arrangement which provided most conveniently for the fitting-in of dining couches, as may be seen in the much better preserved rooms of the children at Brauron. For some 250 years this simple but dignified building must have been a dominating feature, overlooking the Agora from the south. The era of the ubiquitous colonnade had arrived.

Religious continuity. The foundations of the small temple of the healer-god Asklepios (rectangle, *right*) in his Precinct on the S. slope of the Acropolis, later occupied by the large basilica-church of the healer-saints Cosmas and Damian. In the cliff, directly below the viewpoint, is the cave-chapel with a spring, sacred from prehistoric times until today (p. 164).

The economics of all this war-time building depended on the fact that the population had to be fed anyhow, and until communications with the Black Sea were cut and Athens was actually under siege, it was; and with the stone, brick and labour all available locally, it was better to pay workers for working than to keep them 'on the dole'.

LATER CLASSICAL ATHENS

No major buildings have come down to us from 4C Athens; but careful finance enabled the city to flourish without the empire, and some improvements were made. A new fountain-house was added west of the [Heliaia?]; and at the very end of the century there was attached to the north wall of the latter, visible from the Agora, nothing less than a public clock! It was a water-clock, of monumental size. Water was pumped into a vertical pipe, in which stood a float: a wooden pole with, presumably, several feet of its length showing when the pipe was full, and painted in black and white sections. The water was let out through a small hole, and as the float sank the public could read off the passing hours (a Babylonian invention) more conveniently than on a sundial. West of the Agora during the century a small shrine of Zeus Phratrios ('of the Clans') and Athena Phratria was given classical form, between the Stoa of Zeus and the Temple of Apollo Patroios; and the latter was refurbished. A pillared porch was given to the passage leading to the new Council House and in front of it the statues of the eponymous Heroes of the Ten Tribes were resited on a new base. All these dedications emphasize the nationhood and (partly fictitious) kinship of the people; and it was a place which every active citizen had to frequent, for 'in front of the Eponymoi' was where public notices were posted: texts of bills to go before the Assembly and indictments before the courts, lists of young men called up for military service, etc.

Under the financial administration of Lykourgos (338–326) the Dionysiac Theatre was also refurbished; the seating something like what we see, though the stage is of Roman date, and visibly of re-used (and clumsily re-used) materials. A square angle, cutting into the south-east corner of the retaining-wall, was probably designed in order to clear Athens' first roofed music theatre: the Odeion, with a high-pitched timber roof, built under the inspiration of Pericles c. 442, of which we know only from Plutarch.

Surviving relics of the musical, dramatic and athletic contests in which the Tribes competed with choirs and teams, are a few remnants of the 'choregic' monuments, set up by the rich men who paid for winning productions. The conventional 'cup', awarded to the sponsor, was a bronze tripod, a sacrificial cauldron; and he would dedicate it in a public place. Often it was set up on a column; and two such columns still stand at the top of the theatre seating. Others clustered, in late-classical Athens, wherever there was room for them. From the theatre they extended right round the east end of the Acropolis, along what became known as Tripod Street. A modern Tripod Street follows much the same line, dictated by the lie of the land. One example of a more elaborate monument survives, through having been engulfed in a later monastery, where Byron had it for a study in 1816. Disencumbered, it now stands in a small square 140m east of the theatre, beside the foundations of a large Roman house. This is the beautiful little Monument of Lysicrates, dated by its inscription to 334 BC, for his own and his Tribe's victory in a boys' choral and dancing competition. It is a cylindrical building, 4m high overall, standing on a 3m square base and decorated with six Corinthian columns. The so-called Corinthian column was a 4C development from the Ionic, distinguished by its rich foliage capital, with acanthus leaves between the small corner volutes. Under the Roman empire it became the prevailing style.

The absence of major buildings of this age is largely due to the fact that Athens by now had the city centre that people wanted; and rich men devoted much money to making their private houses (of which none survive) more comfortable, and competitively grand. Demosthenes in the 340s complains that some politicians 'have made themselves houses to rival the temples of the gods.' A house with a columned porch might perhaps have had some resemblance to a *small* temple!

Athens through the ages. The Acropolis, seen across the Agora area, is crowned by its classical buildings: *left to right* the Erechtheion, Parthenon (epistyle just visible), Propylaia, and Temple of Nike. Below and left of the Erechtheion, column drums, built into the wall after Xerxes' sack, must come from an unfinished temple; and below *right* modern buttresses cover the Mycenaean stair to a spring behind the Great Flake (p. 165). The tall base left of Nike Temple held a Roman charioted statue of Agrippa. In the foreground is the Stoa of Attalos of Pergamon, *c.* 150 BC (rebuilt); and *right* the Byzantine Church of the Apostles, *c.* 1020. Between them the modern road leads up to join the line of the classical Processional Way to the W. end of the Acropolis; above it can be seen remains of the rough wall built to protect the remains of the city after the first barbarian sack *c.* AD 278.

HELLENISTIC ATHENS

After 322 Athens, with her sea-power crushed, her democracy suppressed, many of the disenfranchised drawn off by the offer of land in Macedonian colonies, and a Macedonian garrison installed for long periods on the Hill of the Muses, was politically in low water; but her rôle as a university town was only beginning. The next conspicuous buildings date from the 2C, after the fall of Macedonia. Athens now received the patronage of the kings of Pergamon, emphasizing their character as protectors of Hellenism and, like Athens herself, allies of Rome. Eumenes II (d. 159) adorned the south foot of the Acropolis with a colonnade 163 × 17m, its massive back wall supporting the natural terrace and the Peripatos or Walk which extended right round the rock. Only this wall, with its blind arches, now survives, and looks very dull; but the façade of sixty-four Doric columns, of which some fragments have been found, must have been handsome. His brother Attalos II (d. 138), himself an alumnus of the Athenian schools, did the same on a grander scale with his great, two-storey stoa facing the east side of the Agora. This has been rebuilt on its original foundations, to serve as the Agora Museum, after it had been found that a projected conventional modern building in the valley beyond the south-west corner would overlie ancient foundations. (Enough fragments of the ancient columns were found to make the restoration certain in every detail; and the contents form an unrivalled museum of Athenian life, from the Bronze Age to the Romans.) Their father Attalos I had already dedicated on the Acropolis sub-life-size statues commemorating his victories over the Galatians (predatory Gauls settled in Asia); and, like the Athenians themselves after the Persian wars, he associated them with prototypes of the struggle against barbarism: Gods *vs* Giants, Athenians *vs* Amazons, and Athenians *vs* Persians. Many copies of figures from these and from his larger dedications at Pergamon survive in Italian collections, including the famous one which, in Byron's time, was called the Dying Gladiator.

Also in the 2C, Athens erected a Middle Stoa along the south edge of the Agora, and even, if we may judge by the earlier boundary stones, encroaching slightly on it; earlier buildings had kept carefully outside. This Stoa faced both ways, north and south, and some of the intercolumnar spaces were filled, not to their full height, with thin stone screens. The areas within were thus available for courts or offices. At the same time, the now old South Stoa was demolished and a new one built, parallel to the Middle Stoa and forming, with it and the Heliaia and a short connecting east colonnade, a new South Square—not carved out of the original Agora, but added to it.

ATHENS UNDER THE ROMANS

Then, in 86, came the sack by Sulla, when Athens proved unwise to have seen a liberator in Mithradates. Her leader, the last to call the people to arms in the name of democracy, was Aristion, also called Athenion, an Aristotelian and the son of an Aristotelian, though his mother was an Egyptian *odalisque*. He had already a teaching career behind him. Our sources say that he had been a slave, and became an infamous tyrant; but the detailed stories seem to refer only to wartime financial levies, punishment of deserters, and a curfew and at last short rations during the siege. No good was to be spoken of Rome's enemies!

At last, after refusing to make terms, and after a *ballista* bombardment (some of the stone 'cannon balls' have been found), Sulla overran the half-starved defenders near the Piraeus Gate, less strong than the Dipylon. There was much slaughter, damage around the Agora, where the South Square was gutted, and looting of works of art (e.g. the 'Piraeus bronzes'), though not the cult-statues; Sulla was religious. Aristion, after surrendering the Acropolis, was executed, with many other leaders. Piraeus was totally destroyed; fifty years later, there were only a few habitations round the harbour; and if Sulla otherwise 'spared the living for the sake of the dead', as he put it, it was no doubt partly for fear of the impression that destroying Athens would make on his fellow-patricians. Craftsmen set up their workshops in the ruins of the South Square. It was a diminished city, surviving on its land, its 'university' and tourist-traffic, in which young

Cicero, son of a consul, and young Horace, son of an auctioneer who had been a slave, were students when Brutus recruited them to be officers in his liberation army.

Yet, even so, Athens still attracted not only students but even money for monuments. Appius Claudius, a great nobleman known to (and heartily disliked by) Cicero, built at Eleusis; and one of Athens' most curious and original monuments is mentioned, apparently as new, by the learned Roman Varro in 37 BC: the octagonal 'Tower of the Winds', east of the Agora, which carried a weather-vane and a large water-clock, replacing that lost in the ruin of the Heliaia. The circular tank, from which water was pumped to support the float, is attached to its south side. Its ancient name was simply The Clock. Our name for it refers to the reliefs of horizontal, flying human figures representing the Eight Winds, high on its neatly-oriented sides: Boreas, the norther, wrapped up against the cold; the South wind pouring water from a vessel (rain); Zephyr, the westerly, bringing flowers; and so on. We hear the name of its architect, Andronikos of Kyrrhos (a Macedonian place-name, but also transplanted to Syria), but not who paid for it. It is a guess, though a shrewd one, that it was a gift to Athens from Julius Caesar and, consistently with that great man's intellectual interests, contained a planetarium.

With Augustus, the Roman Peace obliterated the centre of democratic Athens—the Agora, where Aristion had spoken from a platform before the Stoa of Attalos—more thoroughly than war. The great covered theatre (Odeion) donated about 15 BC by Agrippa, the Emperor's general and son-in-law, occupied the middle of the southern half (the first major building ever erected in the old, scheduled open space); and in the north-west portion was re-erected a classical Temple of the War-God, apparently brought in, stone by stone, from Acharnai, near the foot of Mount Parnes. In it, it seems, cult was also offered to Gaius Caesar, Agrippa's son, adopted by Augustus and being groomed no doubt as a new Mars, or Ares; but he died young in AD 4, after being wounded in a small eastern war. Pillared porches were added to the rebuilt Tholos and the former Strategeion. Nominally free, Athens still preserved the forms of a city-state. Meanwhile Roman subsidies enabled the Athenians to surround with colonnades a new market for commercial purposes, just west of the 'Tower of the Winds'. On the Acropolis, a charioted statue of Agrippa occupied a base which still stands outside the Propylaia, to left of the ascent; and on top, east of the Parthenon, a small round Temple of Rome and Augustus will have held that of the Emperor.

The last great building period of ancient Athens is in the 2C AD. At its beginning one Titus Flavius Pantainos donated a library, filling the middle of a block south of the Stoa of Attalos. Shops, facing the street and backing on to the library walls, may have provided endowments through their rents. An inscription lays down, rather endearingly, that books may not be taken out, 'for we have taken an oath' [so do not press us!], and that opening-hours are from dawn to noon. From not long after, there survives a piece of monumental vulgarity, but a conspicuous landmark, on the Hill of the Muses, backing on to the line of the destroyed city wall and commanding a fine view of the Acropolis. It held the sepulchre of Gaius Julius Antiochos Philopappos ('Devoted to his Grandfather'); an odd soubriquet. The grandfather was Antiochos, King of Commagene on the upper Euphrates, dethroned in 72 when the emperor Vespasian annexed the vassal kingdom, alleging conspiracy with Parthia. Since Commagene had been annexed twice before and then re-established, the Devoted Grandson may have hoped, by rehabilitating his grandfather, to obtain restoration. In this he failed; but he achieved a consulship at Rome (admission to the new Roman nobility) and was called King as a courtesy-title. Inscriptions on the tomb record his Roman honours in Latin, and his descent from the Seleukids and the ancient Kings of Persia, in Greek. He represents one type among the enormously rich grandees who battened on the economy of the Roman empire.

Then comes Hadrian, emperor AD 117–138, a passionate Hellenist, unofficially called a 'Grecian' at Rome, not as a compliment. Before his accession he had already spent a long furlough at Athens, and (as a favoured cousin of the childless Emperor Trajan) was elected Archon. An inscription still stands in the Theatre of Dionysus, recording his career, largely military, up to that date. In two more long visits as emperor he planned his great buildings. One was a library, on an imperial scale, just north of the Augustan market and covering, with its walled garden, lily-pond, surrounding colonnades and sitting-out places, an equal area, over 100 × 80m. Hadrian completed at last the huge Temple of Olympian Zeus, planned by Peisistratos and begun by Antiochos IV of Syria, respectively over 600 and 300 years before, of which seventeen tall, Corinthian columns remain. Finally, desirous to have an Athens all his own, he threw out on the east a new city wall, taking in his Olympieion, and with the street leading to it crossed by an elegant little gate, which, having been propped up by various later buildings, still stands. It bears inscriptions: on the inner face, 'This is Athens, ancient Theseus' city'; on the outer, 'This is the city of Hadrian, not of Theseus'. Completed only after his death was a more practical legacy: a water-conduit, following the south slopes of Lykabettos hill to a reservoir, which is in use today, and until 1929 was the chief one for central Athens.

An honorary High Priest of the deified Augusti at Athens in Hadrian's time was Tiberius Claudius Herodes, a very rich man (it was an expensive post to hold), with vast estates at his native Marathon and elsewhere. He had been governor of Judaea, and consul. He was a personal friend of Hadrian; the two civilised gentlemen would have agreed perfectly as to what the cult meant. His son, another Herodes, showed brilliance as a scholar, and was a protégé of Hadrian, friend of his successor Titus Aurelius Antoninus, consul, and tutor to the next emperor, Marcus Aurelius. This is the famous Herodes of Attica who, as an influential literary man and having inherited yet more wealth from another landed millionaire, Hipparchos, was one of those for whom the Antonine Age

Roman Athens. Hadrian's Gate, leading to his New Town and Temple of Olympian Zeus, seen through the arch.

really was, in Gibbon's terms, the happiest possible age in which to live. His most famous monument at Athens was his Odeion or covered theatre, commonly identified as the large Roman theatre at the south-west foot of the Acropolis. Tiles stamped HP (Greek for Her[odes]?) have been found there, but since lost. Restored but not roofed, it is used today for performances of classical drama and for concerts. He also built out and lined with marble seating the Athenian Stadium, restored by the Macedonian Greek Averoff for the first modern Olympic Games (1904).

The Odeion in the Agora had been wrecked when its roof, supported by huge beams 25m long, had, after 150 years, fallen in. It was restored, with its seating capacity reduced from about 1000 to 500, and used for lectures, while that south-west of the Acropolis—its auditorium for over 5000 perhaps 'roofed' only with awnings, as amphitheatres were—took over its original functions. That in the Agora now received its ornamental façade, with supports in the form of three Giants and three Tritons, mythical creatures with human torsos ending respectively in snakes instead of legs and in fish-tails. Three of them, having survived because their shapes did not make them useful as building-material, were re-erected in the 19C and still stand in the Agora; surely the ugliest objects that have come down to us from ancient Greece, for all that their torsos seem to have imitated those of Poseidon and Hephaistos from the Parthenon pediments.

There is a theory that 'the Odeion' (Pausanias mentions only one at Athens), thus adorned, is what Herodes built; the Roman theatre below the Acropolis, too large to be permanently roofed overall, being therefore, by definition, not an Odeion. We have in any case two major buildings, the latest in ancient Athens, one paid for by Herodes and the other anonymous; the dedicatory inscriptions on the face of each, which would have settled the matter, having disappeared. Ancient Athens had now reached its definitive form, as shown in most modern plans. It lasted for about a century.

The Herulian sack of 267 left the Agora area littered with fire-blackened ruins. The Acropolis apparently had not fallen, and the Hephaisteion and some neighbouring buildings survived. Out of the ruins the survivors built, as after the Persian sack, a new wall, using all sorts of architectural members; but since the old perimeter was far too long for defence by a home guard, even including the students, it embraced a shrunken area, incorporating the stumps of the Stoa of Attalos and, as a northern outwork, Hadrian's library, and connecting up with the Acropolis. South of the Stoa, along the Panathenaic Way, a section of its remains has been left exposed; a monument to the onset of a new Dark Age.

Yet the little university city still had 260 years to live. Our liveliest pictures of student life there come from the rhetorician Libanios of Antioch (mid-4C); and not long after his time, the men later famous as St Basil the Great and the emperor Julian the Apostate were briefly fellow-students. Pagan temples were closed by an edict of Theodosius I in 391, and the Parthenon became an empty monument; a church, only later. More buildings, new and old, outside the post-Herulian wall, were burnt, to judge by coins found in the débris, about 396, probably by the

Goths under Alaric. But still the philosophic schools continued. Soon after 400 the ruins round the old Agora were tidied up, and the area was laid out apparently as a sports-centre, or Gymnasium. Much old material was used for the necessary buildings, and in its monumental entrance the giants and tritons from the destroyed Odeion found approximately their present position. Even later, the water-flow from the west end of the Acropolis was canalised, near the line of the Panathenaic Way, to turn three water-mills. But in 529 Justinian closed the schools of pagan philosophy; and with their passing Athens sank to a market-town.

THE OLD CHURCHES OF ATHENS

Among the cities of Greece, Athens was conspicuously slow to adopt Christianity. Even the dynamic and adaptable St Paul, disputing as usual with the Jews and their followers in the Synagogue, talking informally to 'anyone he met' in the Agora and giving a special lecture to the Epicurean and Stoic professors in the Areopagus, made so little impact that he departed to Corinth, where he stayed for one and a half years. Even in 325, at the Council of Nicea, Greece was represented by only three bishops, while 200 came from the eastern provinces.

Nevertheless, there is literary and archaeological evidence for no less than fourteen early Christian basilicas in Athens in the 5–6CC, though little remains of them. One of the earliest is by the Ilissos, just outside Hadrian's city-wall, south-east of the Olympieion. Traditionally attributed to Eudokia, the Athenian wife of Theodosios II, and containing the relics of the martyr Leonidas, there remain of it only foundations and some fragments of floor mosaics, now in the Byzantine Museum. The best preserved remains, illustrating the continuity of worship on once holy ground, are those of the three-aisled basilica on the south slope of the Acropolis, beside the healing spring. It used materials from the 4C sanctuary of Asklepios and engulfed his small temple, whose foundations can be clearly seen from above. There was a small church *in* the theatre of Dionysos, another on the north side of the Olympeion, and one outside the city near Hadrian's reservoir.

The conversion of the temples into churches, in Athens as in Rome, is surprisingly late. Long after pagan worship ceased, they were left unused, as ancient monuments. The first surviving Christian *graffito* on the Parthenon is dated 694; but it may already have been a church when Constans II visited Athens in 662–3. Damage was done to the east end in constructing an apse; internal pillars were set up, dividing the nave into three aisles, and the entrance was made at the west end, in accordance with Christian practice. The temple named for the virgin goddess Athena became the Cathedral of Athens, dedicated to the All-holy Virgin Mother of God; and Orthodox worship continued there until the coming of the 'crusaders'. The Hephaisteion was converted into a church also in the 7C, dedicated to St George. Its continued use as a church has even preserved the roof, above a Christian barrel-vault, uniquely among the temples of Greece. A chapel was established in the Propylaia (the Governor's residence?), and the Erechtheion too became a church, requiring considerable alteration in the process. The city was now well supplied.

As in the empire generally, so in Athens, there was a new outbreak of building in the 11–12CC. A number of these churches survive, some disfigured by restoration and enlargement, a few largely intact. All are noticeably small compared to the early basilicas. One of the earliest (10C?) is the Church of the Archangels, commonly called Moni Petraki, set in a charming garden and now once more monastic. The sanctuary has been opened to its original form in a recent restoration. It was then well out east of the town (near the modern Evangelismos Hospital). Early 11C is that of the Holy Apostles, south-east of the Greek Agora, built on the solid concrete foundations of a Roman shrine of the (water) Nymphs at a time of expansion of the city and the visit of the powerful emperor Basil II. Cleared of later accretions and lovingly restored by the American archaeologists, it has an unusual plan, cruciform with four apses. Its careful stone and brickwork is ornamented with so-called 'Cufic' characters, adaptations for decorative purposes of an Egyptian Christian script.

Dated by an inscription as earlier than the death of its founder, Stephen Lykodemos, in 1044 is the 'Russian Church' south of Syntagma Square, restored by the Russians in 1855 (adding a campanile) and still used by their exile community. Originally monastic, it is the only example in Athens of a wide-domed church (as at Daphni, p. 251).

The other Middle Byzantine churches conform to the normal cross-in-square plan, with small central dome and many levels of roof. Two, both of much charm, stand in central Athens, their floors now noticeably below street-level. The earlier is the Kapnikarea, west of Syntagma Square, of about 1050, with slightly later west porch. Its name is mysterious; perhaps that of its founder, or of his profession (Hearth-tax-gatherer?). That of the two St Theodores, or Holy Horsemen, (foot soldiers in earlier art), further north–west, is slightly later, c. 1070.

A unique church is that commonly called the Little Metropolis (Cathedral), beside the large 19C one. It can never have been that; the Cathedral of Athens was the Parthenon; but it may have been the private chapel of the Archbishop, as is suggested by an 18C print of its surroundings. It has two dedications, to the Virgin Gorgo-epekoös ('Swift to hear') and to St Eleutherios ('Liberator'); both suggest protectors in childbirth. It is unique in its time in being built entirely of stone, and incorporates a fascinating series of re-used reliefs, from late antique to Christian, down to the 12C. Prominent among them are heraldic animal reliefs, of types common in the 8–10CC, possibly of Sassanid Persian origin and found copied on Byzantine silks. The interior has been restored to the original simplicity of an open sanctuary with a low balustrade, instead of the later-developed enclosing ikon-screen.

When in 1204 Frankish crusaders under the Marquis of Montferrat reached Athens, they viewed with bewilderment the strange figures decorating the exterior of the Parthenon. Fortunately a well-preserved metope-slab shows two draped figures, one seated, the other approaching. This they readily interpreted as the Annunciation, and took over the Parthenon as the Cathedral of Our Lady of Satines. (The prefixed S really belongs to the Greek word for 'to' or 'at'.) The Latin rite was celebrated here until the surrender of the last Duke of Athens to the Turks in 1458. The Parthenon had then been a church for nearly as long as it was a pagan temple.

A few churches were built under the Frankish occupation; but generally the Franks took over rather than built. Foreign travellers of the 17C say that Athens had as many as 300; an exaggeration perhaps, but many would be, as on the islands, small family chapels. During the War of Independence of 1821 there were still said to be 150. Some are shown in 19C prints, pressed up against ancient buildings. Many, no doubt often ruined, were pulled down when the devastated town was rebuilt; some of them, in the zeal for excavating classical remains. Only popular clamour, backed by King Ludwig of Bavaria, whose son was the new King of Greece, saved the Kapnikarea. The value of these Byzantine buildings, and their importance as part of the history and heritage of Athens, has only recently been fully recognised.

Among other small Byzantine churches in Athens is one called the 'Beautiful Church' (Omorphi Ekklesia), 12C, with an unusual portrait fresco of the Archbishop of Athens Michael Choniatis, (c. 1140–1220), who wrote a poem on the desolate state of Athens in his time, '. . . All the glory of Athens is passed away . . .' It also has some good 14C frescoes. The church is now engulfed in the northern suburbs of Athens and kept locked (key in the Byzantine Museum).

Byzantine monasteries and churches survive on the hills round Athens. One demands treatment here; the greatest (Daphni) later (pp. 250ff).

KAISARIANI MONASTERY

This monastery on the outskirts of Athens, with its late 11C church and surrounding buildings, is set in a pleasant tree-clad fold in the western foothills of Hymettos, by a spring renowned from antiquity for its cool and curative water, and a source of the Ilissos, one of the two famous rivers of Athens. There was a temple of Aphrodite nearby and the spring is mentioned by several ancient writers. The place is the scene of the sad tale of Kephalos the hunter who accidentally shot his suspicious wife Procne hiding in the bushes. Ovid in *The Art of Love* (iii, 687–94) describes the grove: 'There is near the purple hills of flowery Hymettos a sacred spring and ground soft with green turf. The wood does not make a lofty grove. Arbutus covers the grass, rosemary and laurel and dark myrtle smell sweet. Here, too, is box with thick-set leaves, and delicate tamarisk, the slender broom and cultivated pine.' All these bushes and other trees besides have been lovingly replanted here after the devastation of World War II. The famous spring, credited with fertility properties, is just outside the monastic enclosure. The spout is a much worn marble ram's head. At some unknown date it was brought out here from the Acropolis where there is a similar one; they decorated an archaic, pre-Persian war temple. A 17C Turkish writer calls this 'the place of the Ram'.

The church is dedicated to the Presentation of the Virgin in the Temple, though the feast day is on the Ascension. It is a typical small cross-in-square built of brick and stone, its small dome supported on four unfluted, Ionic columns, probably from the late antique temple. The narthex, side chapel of St Anthony and the belfry are all later. A few fragments belong to an earlier church on the site. The 16C frescoes, restored in 1956–7, give clear illustrations of some developments in the Late Byzantine period. As earlier, in the dome is the Pantokrator surrounded by angels, and in the apse the Virgin and Child enthroned between angels. Then, round the apse, are two zones of Eucharistic significance. The higher band shows the Divine Liturgy celebrated in heaven with two figures of Christ, the Great High Priest, vested as an orthodox bishop at the altar, assisted by angel acolytes carrying candles, liturgical vessels and the round fans used in the Orthodox service. Three are bowed down under the embroidered shroud carried in the Good Friday procession. Below is the Communion of the Apostles, not shown as the Last Supper, but as liturgical action. Two figures of Christ, in traditional robes, administer the bread and the wine from an altar with six apostles approaching from either side. Judas, on the extreme left, is leaving, with his halo turned black. Below these scenes are the Fathers of the Greek church, with SS Basil and Chrysostom in the centre, whose names are given to the Greek liturgies. On the vaults and highest parts of the walls is the normal selection of the main events in the life of Christ, celebrated by the Twelve Feasts of the Church.

The low-domed narthex is decorated with frescoes signed by a Peloponnesian artist, John Hypatos, and dated 1682. On the left are scenes from the childhood of the Virgin and on the right parables, and hermit saints along the west wall. At the north end is the Tree of Jesse with the Virgin and Child at the centre and the royal ancestors in the branches. Facing it is the Orthodox complementary picture of the True Vine, the spiritual posterity, with Christ at the centre and half figures of the apostles and evangelists in the branches amongst the grape leaves and clusters.

Considerable parts of the monastic buildings remain—a small refectory and large kitchen with a conical roof, a row of ruined cells, and a mill, later used as an olive press.

The unusual name is conjectured to have come from a special ikon of St Basil of Caesarea, once an object of veneration in the monastery.

The abbot of Kaisariani was the second most important ecclesiastic of Athens after the Archbishop, from whom the monastery was independent. In 1458 he had the melancholy task of handing over the keys of the city to the Sultan Mehmet II. The monastery had a school and a fine library, but the books were moved into Athens and lost in the Greek War of Independence.

2 Attica

ELEUSIS

> . . . And she was picking flowers, roses and crocus and sweet violets in the soft meadow, and flags and hyacinth, and the narcissus that Earth brought forth to entrap the flower-faced maiden, by Zeus' will, to please the Receiver of Many.

It was a wonder to behold . . . ; it had a hundred heads, and most sweet scent; and all wide heaven above and all earth laughed, and the salt swell of the sea. And she marvelled, and stretched out both hands to take the fair toy; but the broad earth opened . . . and there the Lord Receiver of Many sprang with his immortal steeds . . . and he seized her unwilling upon his golden chariot, and bore her off, crying out.

This is from the beginning of the early (7C?) long narrative *Hymn* in the metre of Homer, which tells how Persephone, daughter of Demeter the corn-goddess, was carried off by Hades, Lord of the Underworld—'Receiver of Many' is a euphemism for his awful name—and what came of it. When Demeter heard of Zeus' complicity, she struck work and ruined the harvest, and leaving Olympos, wandered on earth, disguised as an old woman. The king's daughters at Eleusis, going to draw water, found her at the well and spoke kindly to her, and their mother employed her as nursemaid to her baby son. The child throve wonderfully, and would have been made immortal, had not the Queen unfortunately woken up one night and seen the strange nurse putting the baby in the fire. Her shriek apparently broke the spell, and Demeter, annoyed at being interrupted, resumed her divine majesty and proclaimed that his chance of immortality was lost, but that because she had dandled him he would receive great honour. Then she commanded the Eleusinians to build her a temple and altar 'below the city and [its] sheer wall, above [the well] Kallichoros, on a forward rising ground'. This is an exact description of the place where the *Hymn* was no doubt first sung. The archaic temple foundations have been distinguished, among those going back to that of a small Mycenaean-age *megaron* found under the floor of the classical Hall of Initiation. The acropolis rock of Eleusis rises above, and the Well 'of the Fair Dance' may be one close by. Later it was identified with the Maidens' Well, whose well-head of massive stonework is still there, outside the Roman portals; the well where, in the story, King Keleos' daughters found Demeter sitting.

Demeter remained 'on strike' till she got back her daughter; Zeus could not let mankind perish, for the gods would then lose their sacrifices. But Hades had caused Persephone to take food in his house (one pomegranate seed); and so she was, by the laws of magic, bound to it, and to him. So for the four winter months Persephone is in the kingdom of the dead, but she returns with the first flowers.

Demeter then taught to the princes of Eleusis her holy and unutterable Mysteries, *orgia*, or things to be done—not doctrines. The *Hymn* adds,

Blessed is he of men on earth who has seen these things; but he who is uninitiate and has no part in the Rites—never has he a part in the like things even in death, down in the misty gloom.

The Mysteries of Eleusis, then, which continued for over a thousand years, offered a life after death, better than the chilly, ghost life which Homer represents as the lot of all but a few special favourites of heaven. The promise was clearly connected with the death and 'resurrection' of the corn. The myth of the Two Goddesses or Mother and Daughter, as they were devotionally called at Eleusis, was public property. Most of it was in the *Hymn*, though there was more. A fine relief, from Eleusis, though now in the National Museum at Athens, seems to illustrate a version in which the goddesses taught the young prince Triptolemos the secret of the sowing of grain, which in the *Hymn* seems to be already known. What was secret was the Things Done and Things Shown; actions no doubt first magical, then (the same actions) symbolic. It was a drunken parody of the *orgia* at a party which, when it leaked out, broke the career of the young general Alkibiades in 415. There may have been some verbal exegesis, but that was secondary, and could vary with the centuries. The result of initiation was said to be 'not learning, but an experience'; an experience, the desire for which drew thousands every autumn (at the sowing season), after preliminary rituals and purification, to undertake the exhausting all-day pilgrimage of fifteen miles, with 'stations' for worship at many chapels and holy places along the Sacred Way, before the actual ceremony by night. The final 'thing shown' at the Further Initiation, to which relatively few proceeded in a later year, was, if we may believe a hostile, Christian writer (the only possible source of evidence), 'an ear of corn, reaped in darkness'; the corn of wheat that falls into the ground and dies.

The only qualification for admission to the rites was that a candidate must be 'of intelligible speech and clean hands'. Many came from outside Attica; and slaves were not excluded. Later, Romans were admitted; Latin was clearly 'unintelligible', but they had to be placated, and anyhow many educated Romans were almost bilingual. Cicero remembered his initiation with deep reverence. 'Of clean hands' meant free from blood-guilt; to this extent at least the cult had a moral content.

The place where these impressive *orgia* took place is unfortunately the most desecrated sanctuary in Greece. Eleusis is today an industrial suburb to the west of Athens, its air and sea polluted, its rocks mauled by quarrying. Here, however, one may stand in the Hall of Initiation, as designed in the days of Pericles: nearly square, a little over 50×52m, with steps, rock-cut or built up, to serve as seating, and most of the bases for the 7×6 columns that upheld the roof. It backs, to the north-west, onto the acropolis rock; and some foundations outside the south and east corners may be for buttresses to take the thrust of roof beams. In the eastern quarter can be distinguished the foundations of the earlier hall with 5×5 columns, built under Peisistratos, and burnt by the Persians, and of its successor as restored after the war, oblong with 2×3—perhaps never completed before the grander Periclean design overtook it. Each aggrandizement of the sanctuary necessitated an artificial extension of the natural rock-shelf mentioned in the *Hymn*; and this has had the fortunate result for archaeology, that the lower courses of each superseded front wall were left undisturbed as part of the 'fill'. The latest (Greco-American) excavators have skilfully left the front in such a manner that the walls of successive ages can be seen, though to distinguish the very earliest requires skilled guidance; and an iron roof, if not beautiful, protects some mud brick upper courses of the surrounding precinct wall of Peisistratos. (When new, they would have been protected by stucco.)

Outside the precinct wall, a good deal has been laid bare of buildings not connected with the actual Mysteries, including a council chamber, gymnasium and running track; but their equivalents can be better studied elsewhere, in more agreeable surroundings. The most imposing remains are those of successive Roman ceremonial entrances. Appius Claudius Pulcher (consul 54 BC, censor 50 BC) commissioned what are now called the Inner Propylaia. Fragments of the frieze, which have been put together on the site, include a section with a rose and, next to it, a sheaf of cornstalks, symbolic of the cult.

Over 200 years later, after Eleusis had been sacked in a raid by Danubian nomads (the first to penetrate deep into the empire), the Stoic emperor Marcus Aurelius took its restoration in hand, and added the Outer Propylaia, a close replica of those of the Athenian Acropolis. The medallion bust (of him?) which still lies nearby, looking as if peeping out of a porthole, is probably from the centre of the pediment. The imperial benefactor was himself initiated in AD 176, and received the unique honour for a layman of being conducted inside the Anaktoron, the Holy of Holies, a walled chapel in the centre of the Hall of Initiation, where (probably) the Sacred Things, which were shown in the Mysteries, were kept betweenwhiles.

His were the last major buildings here; but the Mysteries continued until c. 395, when a destruction by Alaric's Goths, coinciding with the anti-pagan decrees of Theodosios, brought them to an abrupt end.

Most durable of all remains the massive well-head, almost certainly the Maidens' Well where, in the *Hymn*, the kings' daughters spoke kindly to the poor old woman who was the Goddess herself.

SOUNION

The Temple of Poseidon the Sea-God on the bold cape of Sounion, still a landmark for seafarers between Athens and the Aegean, stands on the foundations of an older one, destroyed by the Persians when they ravaged Attica and overturned the statues in its sacred places. (Hence the smashed face of the still splendid, colossal 'Sounion kouros', found here and now in the National Museum.)

The early temple was replaced in the great upsurge of temple building that started in the mid-5C; indeed, it so closely resembles the Hephaisteion, the Temple of Ares, known to us only in plan and from fragments, and that of Nemesis at Rhamnous, that all four have been attributed to one man, the 'Hephaisteion Architect'. It is built externally according to the regular, classical Doric plan, with two columns *in antis*, *i.e.* forming the centre of a porch, at each end, and the whole then surrounded by a colonnade, 6 × 13 columns, executed throughout in local white marble. The Ionic feature of a continuous frieze round the inner *cella* (as on the otherwise Doric Parthenon) was also used here. Fragments survive, of high quality, showing battles of the Gods and Giants, Lapiths and Centaurs, and exploits of the Attic hero, Theseus. The *metopes* above the colonnades were not sculptured, and of pediment sculptures only one possible fragment survives.

The temple was surrounded by a sanctuary wall with stoas and a propylon. A long fortification wall further down the inland slope of the headland, 3m thick, with eleven towers, belongs to the late years of the Peloponnesian War. Additions to it were made at the east end in the 3C, and slipways for two galleys (one ship always on guard?) were constructed in a cove on the rocky west shore.

Travellers from the Romans onward have defaced this temple by carving their names. Byron's is on the north *anta* of the east porch. But Byron at least also wrote:

> Place me on Sunium's marbled steep
> Where nothing but the waves and I
> May hear our mutual murmurs sweep;
> There, swanlike, let me sing and die.

BRAURON

Brauron (Vravron, Vraonas), a charming site on the east coast of Attica, was sacred to Artemis, Mistress of Beasts, sister of Apollo, and the bane, or, if she chose, protectress of women; and with her was associated her legendary priestess, Iphigeneia, whose tomb was shown in the cave south of the site. Iphigeneia ('Very Noble'—perhaps originally an epithet of the goddess herself?) was said in post-Homeric legend to have been a daughter of Agamemnon, sacrificed to Artemis, whom Agamemnon had offended, before the goddess would allow him a fair wind to sail to Troy. Another legend said that Artemis substituted a stag at the last moment, as in the similar story of Isaac—both tales relate to the *ending* of human sacrifice—and spirited the girl away to a far country (later identified as the Crimea, where a tribe called the Tauroi sacrificed shipwrecked sailors). At Brauron it was said that Agamemnon's sacrifice took place there (not at Aulis in Boiotia), and that the substitute was a bear, not a deer. Long afterwards, it was added, Iphigeneia's brother Orestes, pursued by Furies after he had avenged his father by slaying his mother, came to Tauris, where Iphigeneia, as priestess of Artemis, nearly sacrificed him; but she recognised him, and they escaped by the aid of Athena, taking with them the archaic wooden image of Artemis, kept at Brauron—though three other temples also claimed to have the authentic one. By this labour, Orestes won liberation from his haunting curse.

Excavation here has revealed the ground-plan of a 5C Doric temple, without colonnade, before the cave; the steps up to it are perhaps the Holy Stairs mentioned at the end of Euripides' *Iphigeneia in Tauris*. It stood upon the foundations of an older temple; and a chapel of St George now occupies the site of the altar in front of it. But what makes Brauron unique is a development, datable c. 425–415, when Attica was free from Spartan raiding: the evidence of a kind of boarding school, where girls aged about seven to eleven and, it is surprising to find, also little boys lived for some years, 'devoted' to the goddess; a substitute for ritual killing? They came from the 'best families', who kept their prestige under the democracy, and were kept in comfort, as Lysistrata's friends remember when stressing their duty to repay the City by good service. Many were commemorated by statues (now in the Museum on the site), which have upset the old modern

Brauron

1 Temple of Artemis
2 Altar under chapel
3 'Tomb' of Iphigeneia
4 Sacred cave
5 Rooms for the children
6 'Portico of the bears'
7 Enclosed courtyard
8 Blind portico, bases for
  posts for dedicated
  dresses?
9 Stone bridge over Erasinos
  brook
10 Causeway

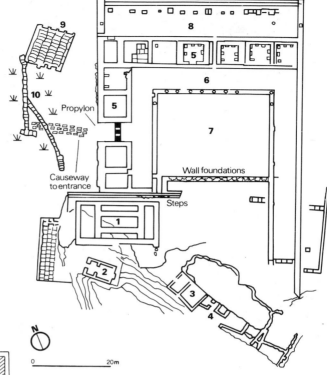

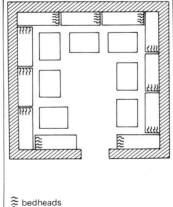

Inset Lay-out of the children's dormitory-dining rooms.

Beds are about 1·8 × 0·60m. Note doorway slightly
off-centre, to fit arrangement of couches (as in official dining
rooms at Athens).

≋ bedheads

view that classical sculptors could not or would not portray children realistically;
and some reliefs show children being brought by their parents to Artemis.

These sculptures come from a courtyard laid out north of the temple. It was
entered through a propylon from the west, by a flat, flag-stoned bridge over the
brook Erasinos, which survives complete, and adorned on three sides (not that

Brauron: colonnade with courtyard in front.

facing the temple) with Doric colonnades of local limestone, with marble capitals and metopes. Behind the north colonnade were the children's rooms (*parthenon*, 'of the maidens'); a row of six, each with seven built-in stone dining tables (several survive complete), and with bronze clamps in the floor to hold the legs of eleven small dining- and sleeping-couches. Doors were off-centre, to facilitate the arrangement, as in the officials' dining-rooms at Athens. Occupants of the middle of each of the other three walls had a table to themselves; those in the corners could eat, one from the end of a table and one from a side. The little ladies and gentlemen evidently dined with some elegance, just like grown-ups.

In the middle of the row of rooms a passage gave access to another court, and first to another, parallel colonnade, with a row of thirty-seven stone bases, slotted, as if to hold upright wooden boards. Here, perhaps, out of sight of the children, were dedicated the robes of women who died in childbirth, as Euripides' Athena prophesies. Square stone pillars stand in the courtyard, with inscriptions bearing the names of past alumnae. One is placed 5cm in front of another, obliterating it; it looks like a relic of a nasty family feud; a pity, in this otherwise dignified place.

The 'school' site had to be abandoned within a century, owing to flooding; the Erasinos brook silts up its mouth, raising the water level. Draining was necessary to enable excavation. But the flooding has yielded archaeological treasure. Under water were preserved votive objects, dedicated in a sacred spring just east of the cave and temple, including some of wood, which, since the death of the excavator, still await publication; also, now in the museum, a polished bone pipe, or perhaps half of a double flute, such as is shown on some vases. A model has been made of it, and even played.

Such, then, was the site of the annual rustic feast Brauronia, mentioned by Aristophanes, and the headquarters of the four-yearly Brauronia in Athens.

THE AMPHIARAION AT OROPOS

Amphiaraos, a legendary king of Argos, seer and healer, was one of the relatively few heroes to become a god. Persuaded against his will to take part in the expedition of the Seven against Thebes, he was miraculously saved from death by Zeus, who split the earth with a blast of his thunderbolt to swallow him up with his chariot. His oracle was first near Thebes, at a place called Chariot. There the Persian general, Mardonios, consulted it before the battle of Plataia in 480–79 (*Herodotos* viii, 133–5). The shrine was transferred to Oropos, close to a healing spring near the border disputed by Athens and Thebes, and given finally to Athens by Philip of Macedon when he captured Thebes. It became increasingly popular in the 4C and during the Roman period, to which the buildings belong. The sacred and public ones lie on the west side of the stream in a deep little valley and accommodation for officials and pilgrims on the other side.

The temple, without a colonnade, contains a base for a white stone statue, seen by Pausanias, and a table of offerings. A large piece of a colossal statue still lies there. The altar (*c.* 4 × 0.80m) stood outside, as usual. It was dedicated to a variety of gods (Pausanias i, 34:3) and had on the slope above steps for watching the sacrifices. Below was the sacred spring and a fountain and a men's bath-house. An aqueduct carried the water to other baths further along the valley. The water of the spring was too holy for purification, but the pilgrims appear to have drunk from it, judging from the number of shells found round it. Further on is a portico 108m long with a façade of forty-one Doric columns and seventeen Ionic within. This was the dormitory in which patients slept in the hope of healing dreams, a normal practice at medical sanctuaries, believed to have been instituted

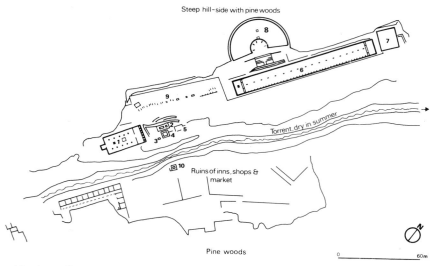

The Amphiaraion at Oropos

1 Temple	7 Women's bath house
2 Altar, steps above	8 Theatre
3 Sacred spring	9 Statue bases
4 Fountain	10 Water clock
5 Men's bath house	11 Sanatorium
6 Dormitory	

by Amphiaraos himself. Men and women were separated for this and their baths. Patients paid an entrance fee, sacrificed a ram, and slept upon its skin. Those who were cured set up *stelae* or statues and votive models of the afflicted parts, like those frequently seen on little metal plaques hung up in churches below ikons today. They also threw gold or silver coins into the spring, the place where it was said that Amphiaraos rose again as a god. About 200 BC a small theatre was built against the hillside behind the dormitory, and there was once a stadium for the widely popular four-yearly athletic and musical contests.

Across the stream bed is a bewildering jumble of ruins of houses, shops, taverns, two inns, a market and a reservoir. The most interesting and unusual object is a Hellenistic water-clock, a piece of advanced technology. The bronze plug mechanism survives.

Among numerous bases of statues of the later period are those of Ptolemy IV and his Queen Arsinoe, Greece's ravager Sulla and his wife, Mummius the destroyer of Corinth, and Brutus, honoured as a tyrannicide. Livy (xlv) mentions 'the ancient temple delightfully situated among springs and brooks', and even though these have largely dried up, the site remains a peaceful, pine-clad little valley today.

The Temple of Apollo Epikourios, Bassae

3 Late classical sanctuaries

BASSAE

The temple at Bassae ('the glens') is in a lonely setting of austere beauty and grandeur in the mountains of south-west Arcadia, remote from habitations, far above its city of Phigalia. Recent excavations have shown that it was not originally so solitary. Traces of contemporary houses have been found, as well as foundations of two earlier temples on the same site. It was built about 420 by Iktinos, the architect of the Parthenon, during a pause in the Peloponnesian war, and dedicated to Apollo Epikourios, the Helper, probably for turning away a plague. The temple, which stands nearly perfect, is unique in several features, illustrating the point that the planning of classical temples was not rigid. It is not orientated, but lies roughly north–south, like some other temples in western Arcadia. It had examples of all the three 'orders' of Greek architecture. The surrounding colonnade (6 × 15 columns) and porch columns (*in antis*) are Doric, giving a strong masculine character to the exterior. The ten inner columns are Ionic, with abnormal spreading bases and shapes of capital. They are engaged by short walls to the main wall of the *cella*. The two southernmost are set diagonally, and

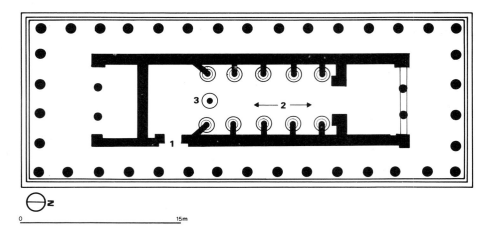

The Temple of Bassae

1 Side entrance in E. wall   2 Engaged Ionic columns   3 Corinthian capital

free-standing between them was a column with the earliest example of a Corinthian capital, now lost, but drawn by a German architect, Haller von Hallerstein, who visited the place with a British party in 1811–12. This partly broken capital shows a low ring of acanthus leaves round the base, below central volutes in relief. These three unusual columns mark off a special enclosure inside the temple, a sacred spot with the very rare feature of a small door in the side wall. It seems likely that the cult statue of the sun-god, properly orientated, was placed here, where the beams of the rising sun would illuminate it. Pausanias states that it was removed to Megalopolis (founded 370 BC) and set up in the market place. It was *c.* 3.60m high. Another feature unusual in Doric temples, but found in the Parthenon and the Hephaisteion at Athens, is a continuous frieze in the manner of Ionic decoration, but even in this Bassae was exceptional: the frieze ran round the *inner* walls of the *cella*. It shows very vigorous combats of Greeks and Amazons, Lapiths and Centaurs. It was bought by the exploration party of the Dilettanti Society and removed to the British Museum. The temple is built of local limestone and the frieze is of local marble. It had been discovered earlier, in 1765, accidentally, by a French architect, who was later murdered there for the sake of his brass buttons, supposedly gold.

THE ASKLEPIEION AT EPIDAUROS

The sanctuary of Asklepios near Epidauros, lying in a green valley-head, was the most important healing centre in mainland Greece, and is famous for the beauty of its theatre. The city, 13km away, administered the sanctuary and annually elected the priest of Asklepios with his assistants and other officials.

Originally Apollo was worshipped here as the healing god and the remains of a late-7C altar of Apollo Maleatas survive above the theatre. Mycenaean, archaic and classical finds have recently been excavated here, but no continuity of cult from the Bronze Age established—rather, a revival. The oldest (6C) inscriptions were to Apollo and Asklepios, but by the 4C Asklepios had superseded his father as the chief healing god, though sacrifices were still made to both. Asklepios is another divine hero, with a human mother, Koronis. His birthplace was disputed. In Homeric times it was believed to be in Thessaly, possibly at Trikke, and the famous medical school of Hippocrates on Kos followed this version. Asklepios came into prominence at Epidauros in the 6–5CC, and a mountain above the sanctuary was claimed as his birthplace. From here the cult spread to Athens, and oversea to Ionia and as far as Cyrene. The Asklepieia, a four-yearly festival of athletic and dramatic contests, took place nine days after the Isthmian Games, and the Athenians called the day the Epidauria, claiming that their belief in the god came from the festival.

The way into the sanctuary passes the 5C stadium, c. 190m long, lying in a natural depression, with seats partly rock-cut and partly built up. The entrance to it is by a tunnel, as at Olympia. The glory of this sanctuary is the theatre, which is, as Pausanias remarks, not the largest but the most beautiful in Greece for its composition and architecture. It was built by Polykleitos the Younger, grandson of the famous 5C Argive sculptor, c. 360–20, and holds c. 14,000 people. The acoustics are perfect. The lower blocks of seats are divided by thirteen staircases; the upper by twenty-three. The orchestra is a full circle of beaten earth with a round altar, a *thymele*, in the centre. The two side entrances have been restored. There is now an annual summer Festival of Epidauros when ancient plays are performed. Though this has somewhat spoilt the approach with the necessary provision for large crowds, the experience of sitting in this theatre, restored to its ancient purpose, filled with the mosaic of colour of the spectators' clothes, and the sun setting on the mountain scenery, is unforgettable.

Down the slope from the theatre the first building opposite is a large hostelry, like the Leonidaion at Olympia. It is a square, with four courtyards and eighteen rooms off each of them. Nearby are the small Greek baths and a large gymnasium. The Romans built a concert hall inside this, and carried out some repairs nearby.

At the heart of the sanctuary was the small temple of Asklepios, only c. 10 × 20m with a colonnade of 6 × 11 columns, which housed the gold and ivory statue of the seated god, half the size of the Zeus at Olympia. He had one hand on the head of a snake and in the other a staff, and at his side a dog. The names of both architect and sculptor are recorded. The temple was approached by a ramp, and the altar, as usual, was outside. Close by, to the north, are two adjoining colonnades, 80m in all. Owing to the slope of the ground, the west one was two storeys high. This is the *abaton*, or 'dormitory', where the sick slept in the hope of healing dreams, in which they might be given counsel, and the harmless sacred snakes crawled over them. Near this and south-west of the temple is the tholos, a mysterious and very elaborate building. It also was built by Polykleitos the

The theatre at Epidauros

Younger in the years when he was at work on the theatre. Only the six concentric walls of the sunken labyrinthine foundations remain on the site, but many decorative elements survive in the museum, with reconstructions and plans. The diameter of the building is *c*. 24m, and on a stepped base stood an outer colonnade of twenty-six Doric columns of poros, stuccoed and painted. They surrounded the circular wall, which had a window on each side of the door. Inside were fourteen marble columns with beautiful Corinthian capitals, with a small bluebell carved in the outer volutes. The pavement was chequered black and white marble, and the ceiling coffered, with elaborate carved and painted floral ornament. The cone-shaped roof was crowned with a floral centre-piece (*akroterion*). Pausanias mentions two pictures by the 4C painter, Pausias, in one of which a woman's face could be seen through a wine-glass. This rotunda was much more elaborate than those at Delphi and Olympia. Its purpose is unknown, but its position in the sanctuary and the name it was known by, *thymele*, 'altar', stresses its sacred character. It has been suggested that it was a pit for the sacred snakes, or housed a sacred spring, which has now dried up. Could it have been for an offering of incense and special prayers before the priest-doctors went on their rounds?

The propylaia are to the north of the temple area at the entrance from Epidauros town. Some of the Sacred Way through them survives.

There was considerable building in the Roman period, including a large bath establishment, and a temple to the Egyptian gods of healing. Near the propylaia is a 5C Byzantine church, with five aisles, a narthex and an atrium (courtyard).

Epidauros: the Sanctuary of Asklepios

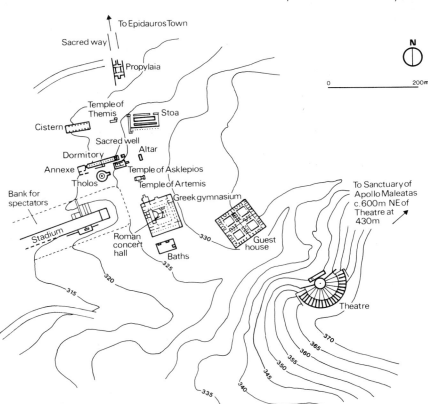

Records of cures inscribed on stone, and votive models of the afflicted parts, are in the museum. Amongst cures of an impossibly miraculous nature some cases of surgery are recorded. Faith-healing and rest in such beautiful surroundings must have effected enough cures for this sanctuary to have continued as a place of healing for about a thousand years.

KOS

Kos, the second-largest island of the Dodecanese (272km²), is long and narrow. Its east end and town lie at the entrance of the Gulf of Knidos. It is fertile and has many medicinal springs, and was renowned as the birthplace of Hippocrates (fl. c. 400) 'the father of medicine' and for the great medical school which flourished throughout antiquity.

Neolithic remains have been found at the south-west end of the island. The original chief city, Astypalaia ('Old City') was in this region. Kos was colonised c. 1000 by Dorians, it was said, from Epidauros. The new capital in the north-east (under the present town) was not founded until 366, later than Rhodes. It soon became an important maritime centre in the Aegean. After the death of Alexander it passed to the Ptolemies. Ptolemy II Philadelphos was born (309) and educated there. The first pastoral poet, Theokritos from Sicily, studied here with the native poet and critic Philetas, young Ptolemy's tutor, and set here the scene of his beautiful Seventh Idyll, The Picnic. The island later became an ally of Rome, and a favourite resort for wealthy Romans. In Byzantine times it was the seat of a bishop, and foundations of many Early Christian basilicas have been uncovered. The Saracens ravaged it in the 11C, and the Knights of St John occupied it in 1315, fortifying it with three castles as a forward strongpoint for Rhodes. It was besieged by the Turks in 1457 and 1477, and fell to them with Rhodes in 1523. It was taken by the Italians from Turkey in 1912, freed in 1945 and united with Greece in 1947.

Kos was noted for its silk by Aristotle (384–322), who writes in the *Historia Animalium* (5:19,6), 'it is said that this [silk] was first spun in the island of Kos.' It had probably been made earlier, to judge from the distinct change of fashion to transparent dresses seen in sculpture from c. 430. 'Coan dresses' were in great demand among wealthy Romans. Pure silk from the East only reached Rome in the 3C AD; Koan silk was tussore or raw silk.

After a union of the villages (366), Kos town was large, with a perimeter of 5km. Minoan-type tombs have been found outside it to the south-west, and Protogeometric and Geometric within. It has suffered many earthquakes and much rebuilding. After the last severe one in 1933, Italian archaeologists concentrated their efforts, 1935–43, on the excavation and restoration mainly of Roman buildings. The main north-south street was uncovered, with houses, shops and taverns along it, two large bath systems, and a luxurious latrine complex round a peristyle court, near the acropolis. Two large Roman houses with many mosaics were rebuilt—a miniature Pompeii. Some mosaics were taken up to adorn the palace of the Grand Master in Rhodes, which had become the Italian governor's residence.

Kos: the Asklepeion, second terrace

The covered concert hall (Odeion) south of the acropolis was partly restored, and columns of a Hellenistic gymnasium set up. A complex starting-gate of the stadium was found. Near the Odeion the church of St John the Baptist is the baptistery only of the largest Early Christian church on the island.

The Knights only fortified a small area of the ancient town, the northern side of the harbour and round the adjacent market-place. The castle is rectangular in plan with two lines of wall separated by a deep ditch. The entrance is over a drawbridge. It faces the mainland castle of St Peter at Halikarnassos (Bodrum), with an 'English tower' embellished with the arms of Henry IV and the chief noble families of England, who paid for it in lieu of actual crusading. Together these castles guard the narrow northern strait.

The curiosity of Kos town is the giant, venerable plane tree 'of Hippocrates', *c*. 12m in diameter. It cannot date from his time, but it is certainly very old.

The Hippocratic school of medicine was the first to study disease in a scientific manner and the doctors working at the Asklepieion of Kos contrasted their methods with the faith-healing or auto-suggestion practised at Epidauros and other healing centres. The Hippocratic Collection of writings on medical subjects was probably put together *c*. 300, some time after the death of Hippocrates, in the medical school of Alexandria, and attributed to him because of his great reputation. It contains admirably clear, succinct descriptions of cases, and prognoses, predictions of the course of diseases. Amongst sayings attributed to him is the well-known, 'Art is long, life is short', and the Hippocratic oath, still revered by doctors. The school of Kos provided the personal physician to Alexander and

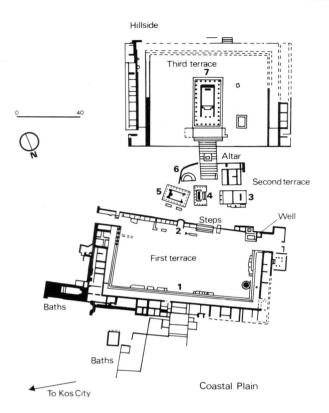

Kos: the Asklepieion

1 Entrance
2 Fountain
3 4C Temple of Asklepios
4 Altar of Asklepios
5 Roman Temple
6 Exedra
7 2C Temple of Asklepios

several Hellenistic kings and Roman emperors, including Claudius, whom Claudius Xenophon is alleged to have helped the Empress to poison. When he returned to his native island he helped financially to restore and remodel the sanctuary, after an earthquake, adorning it with statues he brought from Rome and rehousing and enlarging the library.

The Asklepieion, the principal site on Kos, is 4km south of the town, a complex of buildings mainly Hellenistic and Roman, set on a slope on four levels connected by wide steps. The Italians have carried out considerable restoration on this impressive site. The oldest temple is late 4C, but the medicinal springs are likely to have made this spot an earlier centre of healing. Roman baths of the 1C AD are on the lowest level. The next would seem to have been the Health Centre, with Doric porticos on three sides, a fountain in the massive retaining wall and several water troughs, fed by conduits from iron and sulphur springs. Patients may have lodged in the cubicles within the colonnade. From here a few steps lead to the sacred area with the large altar of Asklepios, approached by steps and surrounded on three sides by columns, outside the oldest temple of c. 300–275. It is Ionic with fine painted capitals, built of black and white marble. It once possessed the painting of Aphrodite rising from the sea by Apelles, the famous 4C painter, claimed as a native of Kos, but also by two mainland cities. Augustus removed the painting to Rome. The Medici circle would have known about it and probably proposed the subject to Botticelli, for a room decorated with pictures inspired by themes from antiquity. Behind the altar is a Roman temple set diagonally to it, with a curved stone seat behind it beside the monumental staircase, which leads up to the great Doric temple of Asklepios on the final terrace. There is a small altar half-way up the stairs. The temple, built in the 2C on the site of the original Sacred Wood of Apollo, has 6 × 11 columns, plus two in the porch. In it stood the cult statue of Asklepios and his daughter Hygieia (Health), and it contained a treasury. The threshold and the lowest step of the base are of black marble. A chapel of the Virgin, whose altar remains in place, was built inside it and a fine Byzantine capital stands there. Ionic colonnades surround the terrace on three sides. This place may have continued as a healing centre until it was shattered by an earthquake in AD 554. The Asklepieion is near the foot of Mount Oromedon (847m), a mountain of many springs. One, Vourinna, with an antique fountain-house, supplies the town by an aqueduct c. 6km long. Theokritos mentions both it and the mountain. The view from the final terrace, over Kos town and across to the coast of Turkey, is magnificent.

4 Fortifications

The best examples of mature classical fortifications date, sadly if naturally, from the wars of the 4C BC, in which the continuing power-struggles of Thebes, Athens and Sparta ended only in leaving the field open for Macedonia.

At Gyphtokastro—'Gypsy Castle', its modern rustic name—above what is now called the Old Road from Athens to Thebes, stands the best-preserved Athenian frontier fort on the Boiotian border. The south-west wall, facing the road, has been undermined and brought down by erosion; but on the other side, where the slope to a side gully is less steep, over 300m of curtain-wall, 2.5m thick, still stand up to 4m high, with eight square, projecting two-storey towers rising higher. The sentry-walk passes through them, and each has three small, square windows or loopholes in the upper storey. Wooden floors below the battlements, and much of the battlements themselves, have gone, but square sockets for the beams may be seen.

This fort was probably that of ELEUTHERAI, named after a border village down the north side of the pass, which had joined Athens before 500. From it came Myron, reckoned first of the Great Six classical sculptors, the master of the famous Discus-Thrower. The identification comes from Xenophon on a campaign in 378. In 381 a Spartan force bound for the war with Olynthos (qv) had seized the citadel of Thebes, in peace-time, with the collusion of an anti-democratic faction. This brought Sparta to the height of her power; but Xenophon, a pious man, felt that it incurred the anger of heaven. In 379 the Theban hero Pelopidas liberated his city in a 'commando' operation; so it was war. Athens, in armed neutrality friendly to

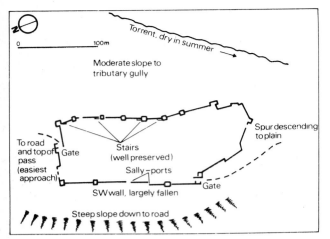

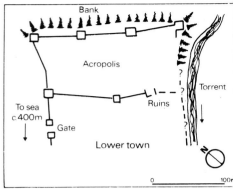

Fortifications
Above left Gyphtokastro, near ancient Eleutherai } see area map p. 159
Above right Aigosthena: Acropolis
Below Messene as founded *c.* 369 BC. From Arcadian Gate to Laconian
Gate by the road is *c.* 2.5km

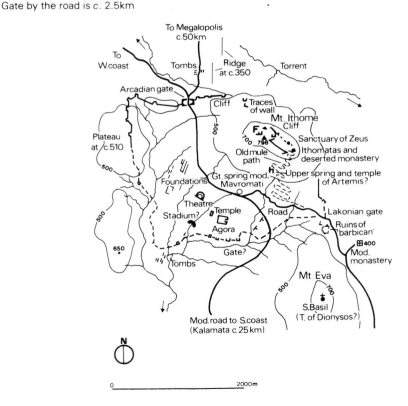

The towers of Eleutherai

Thebes, garrisoned Eleutherai, forcing the Spartans to use the road to Plataia. They took that pass, by surprise, but effected nothing decisive, and returned by the mountain track over the seaward spurs of Mount Kithairon. This led to AIGOSTHENA, a fortress of Sparta's ally, Megara, at the north-east corner of the Corinthian Gulf, and a site of 4C (or later) fortifications even better preserved than those of Eleutherai.

Aigosthena, called Porto Yermeno in early modern times, was a lonely place, at the bottom of a valley whose head is a few kilometres west of the foot of the Eleutherai pass; even lonelier in recent times, when it was a small fishing hamlet—even Baedeker never went there!—until a motor road was driven through and it became a *plage*. One wonders why it was not taken over by Athens, whose frontier was only 10km away; and may guess that it was not only thanks to its remoteness, but to the will of the local community, Doric speakers, preferring, since they were too small to stand quite alone, to belong to Megara and so to Sparta's league, rather than to a more powerful and centralised state. For a local community there was, devoted to the worship of Melampous, known to mythology as a hero and prophet who could understand the language of the birds; but at Aigosthena he was worshipped as a god (not oracular), and men were here, but nowhere else, often called Melampodoros. With determination and good walls the little place preserved its identity through the great wars; and the fine walls now visible, partly in trapezoidal blocks (5C?) but mostly in late-classical rectangular masonry, look (another guess) powerful enough to have been built with outside assistance, as a post on the Peloponnesian League's only land outlet to the north.

The area enclosed by the walls was a rectangle, running inland for some 550m and with a sea-front of 180m. At the top an outcrop of rock, which drops inland in a short bank before the inland rise continues, was chosen as an acropolis, a smaller rectangle, *c.* 180 × 100m, with an inner cross-wall cutting it off from the lower city. It is the four towers of the east wall, especially those at the corners, with another at the north-west corner of the acropolis, that have defied the ages most remarkably. They stand battlement-high, nearly 15m, while the curtain-wall between them is *c.* 3.5m. All are solid at the bottom, filled in with rubble up to the height of the curtain, and the south-east tower is solid for another 3m. Its only door is 3m above the rampart-walk, from which it must have been reached by a removable wooden ladder: the last word in impregnability. Downhill, the line of the north wall of the lower town can be traced to the sea, and the foundations of one tower remain on the beach among the modern houses; but much of the stone has been robbed; and on the south side the local torrent has carried away everything, and we can only infer that there was a parallel wall.

The Spartans in 378 did not arrive at Aigosthena in good shape. A freak wind swept down on them as they straggled along the mountain trail. Loaded asses were blown over the cliff; some men lost their grip on their shields, and saw them fall into the sea; and many at last reckoned that the shields, which caught the wind, made going too difficult and left them, with stones piled in the concave side, to be retrieved next day. Some thought, says Xenophon, that it was an omen; and the idea will have revived seven years later, when a Spartan army retreated by the same way in still more dismal plight, bearing their dead king. Four hundred Spartiate 'peers' had fallen on the dire field of Leuktra (north of Plataia), out of 700 present; a third of all that there were living, between eighteen and sixty; and that day the hegemony in most of Greece passed from Sparta to Thebes.

The Theban supremacy led to the construction of the finest classical Greek fortifications of all. Epameinondas, the victorious strategist, took steps to see that Sparta did not revive. He liberated Messenia, west of Mount Taygetos, whose people had been Sparta's helots for 350 years— and never forgotten that they were a nation; and he assisted them to fortify a capital in the theatre-like hollow of Mount Ithome, the ancient stronghold, with copious water, where Messenians behind improvised walls had held out for many years in the wars of old. He also encouraged the Arcadians to build a new federal capital, Megalopolis, a long day's march west of Tegea. Megalopolis was not an unqualified success (not least, through the jealousy of Tegea and Mantineia), and today very little of it remains above ground level; but Epameinondas' MESSENE, where the walls and line of towers stride up the *arêtes* and over the crest of Mount Ithome, remains magnificent. (ITHOME, it must be added, is the modern name of the place, the name Messene having been annexed by a large village 20km away, near the sea; a trap

Aigosthena

to travellers.) The circuit of the walls is *c.* 9km long, embracing the whole mountain 'theatre' (not, please, 'amphitheatre', so called from its resemblance to *two* theatres set face to face; a Roman invention, where spectators could watch the agonies of gladiators, captive animals or, on occasion, Christians, without risk of their escaping. A volcanic crater is the only natural phenomenon resembling an *amphi*theatre.) It would have provided a refuge for a large rural population and even their animals. Low down in the hollow, below the noble spring, the foundations have been excavated of a market-place, council-chamber (?) and temple, and, as usual rather better preserved, a theatre; but most worth seeing is the north-west section of the walls, where the road still passes through the Arcadian Gate. Between an outer and inner gateway is a circular courtyard, a trap for stormers of the outer gate; inside it a great fallen lintel-slab slants, with one end on the ground, much illustrated even before the invention of the camera. Near it on the way up the mountain two towers, though shaken by earthquakes, still keep their upper chambers. On the top a small church and monastic cells have been built with antique stone, and the view extends from Arcadia to the sea. Ithome is a place where to historic interest is added a full measure of old-fashioned romantic beauty.

These three sites and other city walls which we have described by no means exhaust the list of major ancient fortifications in Greece. In the north-west, the anopheles mosquito has probably helped to preserve extensive *enceintes* at Stratos near Agrinion, New Pleuron (late Hellenistic) north-west of Mesolonghi, and Oiniadai (of classical origin; heavily overgrown with scrub) west of the Akheloös in Akarnania. But we have selected those which, for the fineness of their masonry and their connexion with historic events, present the most interest.

V Greece and her conquerors

1 The rise of Macedonia, and after

OLYNTHOS

Olynthos, in Chalkidike, on a hill 8km north of the Corinthian colony of Poteidaia
and 3km from the sheltered bay of Torone, began as a neolithic hamlet. In 479,
after Xerxes' return to Asia, Poteidaia revolted from Persia and urged her
neighbours to join in; but Artabazos, the Persian general who had escorted
Xerxes, took Olynthos, massacred its native inhabitants and handed it and its
fertile lands over to Chalkidian Greek colonists who had not revolted. It later paid
a small tribute to Athens (two talents—Poteidaia paid six); but in 432 King
Perdikkas of Macedonia, afraid of the growth of Athenian power, encouraged a
revolt of the Chalkidians and persuaded them to concentrate at Olynthos, aban-
doning many small coastal settlements. The Athenians never took it: they took
Poteidaia, but then (429) suffered a bloody defeat in its area.

Olynthos now extended its built-up area to a flat-topped, steep-sided hill, north
across a gully from the old town, where American excavators have laid bare the
ground-plan of a whole residential quarter, town-planned as a unit. This step was
probably taken when, with Athens defeated, Olynthos emerged as capital of a
Chalkidian League, embracing most of the peninsula, and struck some of the
finest of Greek coins, with the legend, 'Of the Chalkidians'. In the 380s the League
even 'liberated' most of Macedonia, including Pella, its capital, from King
Amyntas, and seemed about to become a great power; but some of the other cities,
resenting Olynthos' 'imperialism', invited Sparta as the guardian of Greek freedom (*i.e.* enemy of any great power other than her own) to liberate them. Sparta
broke up the League. In the 360s, with Sparta defeated and Athens regaining
power, it was reconstituted; but Macedonia was lost, and in 359 Philip, the son of
Amyntas, became king of it.

Philip, during his early struggles, dealt with Olynthos with masterly diplo-
macy. Having taken Poteidaia, which Athens had retaken and colonised, he
presented it to Olynthos, along with territory on his own border, thus averting any
danger of an alliance between Olynthos and Athens until he had consolidated his
power. Olynthos, still underestimating him, harboured rival claimants to his
throne. He attacked it and, though Demosthenes persuaded Athens to forget old
grudges and send help, it was too little and too late. Olynthos was taken in 348
with the help of treachery, and destroyed. Many Olynthians were sold as slaves.

Though there were still 'Olynthians' living in the territory until Kassandros,
one of Alexander's successors, swept them up into his new city of Kassandreia on

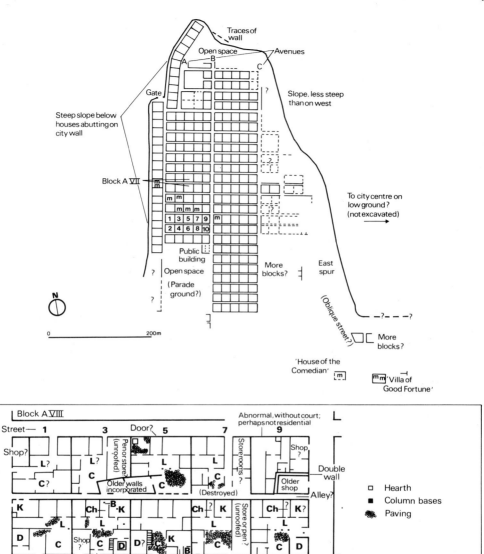

Olynthos
above North Hill residential area; m = position of mosaics
below Block A VII:

B Bath	Ch Chimney?	K Kitchen	
C Court	D Dining room	L Loggia (Pastas)	

(after A. R. Curry in *Excavations at Olynthos*, ed. D. M. Robinson, vol. VIII *The Hellenic House* by J. W. Graham, (1936)) the site of Poteidaia, and though there may have been some squatter reoccupation on the North Hill itself, the main interest of the site is that it gives a unique example (to us) of such town-planning before Hellenistic times. An area of several hectares was laid out in a grid of east–west and north–south thoroughfares, which the excavators, remembering New York, designated respectively Streets, numbered from the south edge of an open space (perhaps the local parade-ground) and Avenues A, B and C, each 20 Greek feet (*c.* 5½m) wide. Between them, each block measured 300 × 120 feet and contained ten houses, 60 feet square. So far all is very monotonous; but internally, each householder pleased himself. A prevailing feature, commended also in Greek literary sources, is the open court with, north of it, a loggia (*pastas*), catching the slanting sun in winter (south walls were kept low for this purpose) and giving shade from it when high, in summer. Off it is the *andron* or Men's Room for (all-male) dinner parties, with painted walls; a common scheme was 'Pompeian' red above a yellow dado, with a black stripe at the bottom. It was normally entered from a smaller ante-room, for the sake of privacy. Behind the loggia were the private rooms where the women gossiped and got on with their endless spinning and weaving. Traces of a footing for a wooden stair have been noticed at the side of some courts, and probably every house had one, leading to bedrooms above the north rooms, and perhaps a balcony above the loggia. Other ground-floor rooms might be stores, sometimes identified as such by the presence of large *pithoi*, or, in a corner, a stable for the donkey or an unroofed pen for sheep on the way to the butcher; or, especially at the corner of a block, a room not communicating with the interior may have been a shop, let off or, if *with* such communication both with house and street, kept by the family.

The block here illustrated shows all the above features. The five south-facing houses on street VII, even-numbered by the excavators, are typical. The courts (C), four of them with much of their cobbled flooring in place (and drains to carry off rain water into the street, not shown) lie uniformly south of the loggias (L), and in nos 4, 6 and 10 stone bases for the posts or columns (one Doric capital was found) to uphold the balcony over the loggia are *in situ*. Kitchens (K) had stone central hearths; but at least four were adjacent to small rooms which, it was thought, might have been or have contained flues to carry off the smoke (ch). In this snug environment, in the corner of that of no. 4, was found a clay bath-tub (B)—not large enough to wallow in. The Olynthian sat or stood, and sluiced himself (or had a slave do it) with a sponge or dipper. Such simple, private baths seem to have been common at Olynthos. On the other hand, there is no sign of latrines or drains for them; they must have made do with portable chamber-pots, or the open air.

These are comfortable bourgeois houses. In one, on the south-east corner of Block V (a good position), a stone record of sale shows that one Dionysios bought the house and a store, or '*pithos*-room' (there is a room on that corner, which could have been a shop) for 3500 drachmas; a sum at that time probably equal to the entire earnings of a skilled workman for over ten years. A humbler dwelling, one of the row which backed onto the city wall (apparently with back rooms whose flat roofs provided the sentry-walk) changed hands at 2000; these are the only Olynthian house prices that we have.

Across the narrow alley that divides each block from end to end—apparently only to carry off the rainwater from roofs, and not a thoroughfare—the north-side residences were clearly a good deal less desirable. In A VII, the essential courtyard and loggia are there, at least in nos 3, 5 and 7; but to get to them, the first place where one would want to arrive or bring a visitor, necessitated sacrificing space for a passage. The court had to be on the south side; and even so, even the modest height of the south houses would cut short the hours of sunshine on a winter day. There is an absence of painted dining-rooms; and the east sides of nos 3 and 7 are taken up by large store (?) rooms or possibly pens for animals. Nos 3 and 5 incorporate walls of an older building on a different alignment; how apportioned and for what purpose is obscure. Lastly, no. 9 has no evident court and was perhaps not a dwelling but an industrial workshop. It might have 'gone with' the two-roomed shop (?) on the north-west corner, but was certainly separate from the one room south of that, whose proprietor was evidently on the scene before the block was planned, and insisted on the adjacent, new building having a separate wall.

The North Hill 'housing estate' was by no means the whole city of Olynthos, which was said, probably with exaggeration, to have had 30,000 inhabitants. No temples have been found, no agora fit for a proud city. It is thought that, since the rubble-masonry foundations of the town wall (all that has been left by erosion) passed round the west and north of the top, the city may have extended far to the east, on low ground, where it would now be deeply buried under silt. Two free-standing houses or 'villas', south-east of the North Hill, may have been built when it was open country; and in these, and also in several houses in Block A VI on the Hill (though none in A VII) were found the site's chief contribution to Greek art history: pebble mosaics. With no other material than pebbles, set on end, mostly black and white, though the rarer green and red may be used to pick out details, the artists produced highly accomplished designs, abstract or even figured. The Villa of Good Fortune was named by its discoverers from the greeting AGATHE TYCHE, 'Good Luck', picked out in black on white on a floor; and in its dining-room and ante-room are the finest Olynthian mosaics: in the former, appropriately, Dionysos and his attendant rout, and in the latter the Homeric scene of Thetis bringing her son Achilles his new arms. Their names, white on black, appear beside them.

Pebble mosaics older than those at Olynthos have since been recognised elsewhere; but this is the first site where they have been found in quantity, and well preserved. Their preservation is directly due to the destruction of the city, never to be re-inhabited. Though Demosthenes exaggerates in saying that Philip destroyed it, and thirty Chalkidic cities, so thoroughly that 'one could not tell that they had ever been inhabited', that result was achieved in time. Building materials as well as furniture—pithoi and bath-tubs, doors, window-frames, beams and tiles—were desirable loot; we hear of Boiotians carrying them off in carts from

Attica during the Peloponnesian War. Portable goods were looted by Philip's soldiers; the last useful building materials probably went into Kassandreia in 316. Unprotected, the mud brick of the houses melted in winter rains, slumping down into a protective covering over floors, stone wall-foundations, and a few baths and *pithoi*, broken in the sack or in removal. Floors included the mosaics; there was no profit in grubbing them up; and some of them are now exposed, under protective roofs. They add interest to the area of streets and homes, where people shopped, gossiped and quarrelled, drank with their friends in the dining-rooms that they were so proud of—and thought themselves a match for the father of Alexander.

PELLA

Pella, the birthplace of Philip and Alexander, lies 38km west-north-west of Thessalonica on the road to Verria, in rich plainland, recently drained and purged of malaria. It is hard to realise that in ancient times it was quite near the sea, since then pushed back by silt from the Macedonian rivers, and even accessible from a navigable lagoon.

The conquest of this plainland by the highlanders of western Macedonia, driving the lowland tribes eastward, founded the Macedonia of history. Pella became its new capital, and King Archelaos (413–399) began the construction of Greek-style monumental buildings. Some Greeks made rude jokes about this 'barbarian' aping civilisation; but Euripides and his dramatist friend Agathon (of Plato's *Dinner Party*), Timotheos the 'modern' musician and Zeuxis the painter accepted invitations to his court. It is in mere hostility that Demosthenes calls Philip a barbarian 'brought up in a small and insignificant village'.

The acropolis or 'upper city' of Pella spread over two low hills north of the modern road, especially the eastern, now occupied by a village which has adopted the name of Old Pella. Excavation on the west hill has revealed truly monumental foundations in ashlar masonry of massive stones, as well as scattered pillar-capitals and other architectural members; but, on a site exposed to erosion as well as to stone-robbing, not enough to identify the palace and temples. But, on lower ground, the road itself has cut through a built-up area of palatial houses, each occupying a whole block over 45m wide and perhaps 100m long before the road sheared away their southern portions. Each was built round a series of courts, paved or planted as gardens; and what renders them unique in archaeological experience hitherto is two series of pebble-mosaics, a generation or two later than those of Olynthos, and considerably more ambitious. They have been carefully lifted and are on view in a temporary museum on the site. In the easternmost house or palace, the first to be excavated, there were also found considerable remains of the slender Ionic columns that surrounded the inner courtyard, and these have been re-erected.

Roof-tiles stamped PEL, 'Of Pella', suggest that Block 1 was an official residence. The adjacent blocks, such as Block 2 in the excavators' numbering, just north of 1, and the area south of the modern road, seem to have contained houses a good deal less grand; but the whole quarter, and probably the whole lower city,

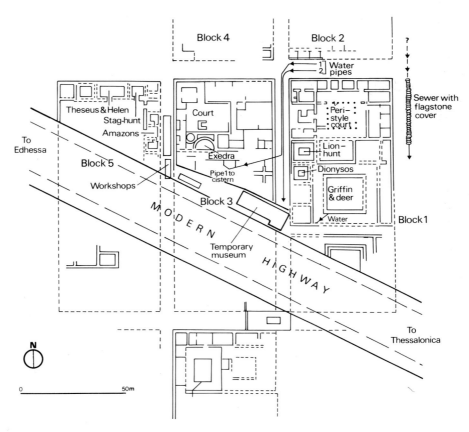

The mosaic-floored *palazzi* of Pella

was laid out on a regular chequer-board plan, with sewers (one, covered with
stone slabs, is visible east of Block 1) and with piped water laid on at least to the
great houses. Two terracotta pipelines pass north of 1 and then, together in one
trench, turn south in another street until one turns off to feed a cistern in Block 2.
It looks rather as if grandees had their private supply (though that of Block 1 has
not been discovered) while the women of more ordinary households still had, as of
old, to go to the nearest well or fountain-house. The whole city may have covered
nearly 4km² and the cost of expropriating and excavating such an area of rich
farmland would be enormous—without the likelihood that every street would be
of great interest; but soundings continue, and have lately established, for instance,
part of the line of the city wall.

Of the pebble mosaics, the most interesting finds to date, those in Block 1, show
successively a mythical griffin demolishing a deer (Greeks, as well as Macedonians, had no objection to somewhat gruesome scenes in their art); a young, nude

Pella: pebble mosaic of lion hunt

Dionysos mounted 'side-saddle' on a panther; and a lion turning upon a hunter, while a second hunter raises his heavy sword to strike the lion from behind. It may represent the hunt which the general Krateros commemorated in bronze at Delphi, in which he saved the life of Alexander. All three are thought to date from the next generation. Block 2, though palatial in size, has yielded none; but in Block 3 the northern rooms have three more, perhaps a generation later. More precise dating is a matter of argument. From south-west to north-west, we have a fight between Amazons; two hunters killing a stag; and Theseus carrying off the fair Helen in his chariot (though, as Plutarch remarks, when she was adolescent he ought to have been old enough to know better). Both series are technically more advanced, as well as richer, than those of Olynthos. Use is made of strips of lead to mark off, for instance, an arm from the body behind it. All eyes are missing; they were probably of rock-crystal or other stones which were, or at least looked, worth looting—perhaps by the 2C Roman conquerors. The mosaic art was developing, seeking greater refinement, towards the point, some time in the 2C, when artists began to work, not in natural pebbles, but in the small, square *tesserae* of stone, hard brick, or glass, which could have gold behind it—the medium of the great mosaics of the Christian era.

VERRIA (BEROIA)

Beroia, as the Macedonians wrote it, stands on an abrupt foothill of Mount Vermion (anc. Bermion), overlooking the almost perfectly flat plain of lower Macedonia. In King Philip's time it was one of the walled towns that guarded the foot of each main pass; and after him it was important enough, before the foundation of Thessalonica, for its name, like those of Edhessa and Pella, to be carried to Syria by Macedonian kings and their colonists. It was applied, in fact, to Aleppo; but the old Semitic name (Halep) has long outlasted it.

In the west, it has been famous chiefly as Beroea (the Latin spelling), the city to which St Paul retired (or advanced?) when driven by persecution from Thessalonica. There were Jews at Beroea too, and Paul's companion (Luke?) notes that they were 'more noble'—'better class'!—than those of the great port, and well read in their scriptures.

Today Verria is a booming agricultural market town, its ancient foundations buried and inaccessible; but it preserves one unique feature from early modern (Turkish) times. The Turks, like the Macedonian kings, made it a military colony from which to police the hill country; and it followed that the Greek Christian population, which hung on throughout, was in more than usual danger of persecution by rough (often Albanian) soldiers, contrary though this might be to the teaching of the Prophet Muhammad. They coped with this situation by building inconspicuous churches, behind their houses, roofed like houses; and a number of these survive in the busy modern town, commemorating surely a classical example of what is nowadays called 'keeping a low profile'.

VERGINA, THE ANCIENT AIGAI

Vergina, a village suddenly famous since Professor Andronicos discovered the unplundered tomb of—almost certainly—King Philip, father of Alexander, lies 10.5km south-east of Verria, across the river (H)Aliakmon, on gently rising ground at the foot of the Pierian mountains. The enormous tumulus, which also contains other tombs, one of them perhaps that of Philip's queen, Olympias, is near the northern edge of the village. Its sheer size probably saved it from the Gallic mercenaries of King Pyrrhos, who in 273 BC pillaged other royal tombs nearby (or perhaps, having sacked Olympias' [?] tomb, they thought they had 'done' it); and, carrying a grove of pine trees, it long deterred Andronicos himself, who had fruitfully explored many neighbouring sites. Among the rich grave-goods, now in the Thessalonica Museum, the detail that makes assignation to Philip particularly probable is a pair of richly ornamented greaves, which are of different lengths; it is recorded that Philip was lame from a war-wound. The chamber-tombs, with painted decoration, will be on view to the public when work has been completed; but as a site, perhaps even more interest will still attach to another tomb, a few minutes further up the slope, formerly known as The Vergina Tomb.

This is because, while cleared of portable valuables, no doubt by the Gauls, it preserves in perfect condition furniture, such as the living would have in perishable materials, reproduced in stone. Behind its façade, which resembles that of a small temple or a palace porch, with four engaged Ionic columns, a huge slab of marble blocked off the inner chamber. Prised out by the marauders, it now lies on the floor; but it preserves every feature of a great wooden door, with panels, large round bosses ('nail-heads'), and even a key-hole! Within are on the right a throne 1.80m high, with a footstool and with arms supported by sphinxes, and on the left

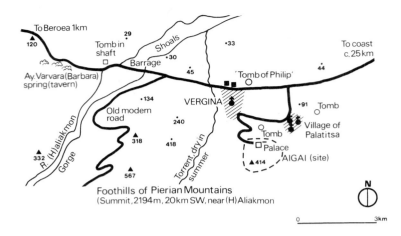

Vergina. The almost perfectly flat alluvial plain of Macedonia gives place to rugged mountains, but not, as in some places, at a tidy hill-foot. There are abrupt foothills. The acropolis of Aigai is one. Consequently, a few contour lines are uninformative, and many are confusing; a number of spot-heights (from the 1:100,000 staff map) may better indicate the lie of the land.

a low divan-bed, with all the bulging curves of soft material lovingly rendered. His late Majesty (we do not know who he was) could sit in state or, if he preferred, lie down and rest. It all gives ample scope for speculation about the ideas of Macedonian royal circles on the after-life; and if we conclude that they were a muddle—still, the real function of funerary rites is to give comfort to the living.

Among similarly façaded 'temple-tombs' in the area, which can be entered if the site-guardian is at liberty, one is just north of the (H)Aliakmon. The road from Verria crosses this on the top of a great modern barrage where the river emerges from the mountains; and the Greeks, with commendable reverence for their past, curved it back at the north end in order to spare this tomb, which can be seen at the bottom of a deep shaft on the downstream side of the road. Its chief internal feature is its plastered walls, painted in broad horizontal bands of white, black and red. Another tomb is beyond Palatitsa, an old village east of Vergina, with several old, small churches of some charm.

Palatitsa, which formerly gave its name to the area, means 'Little Palace'; but the diminutive denotes familiarity, not size. There was, in fact, a large palace, nearly 100m square a few more minutes uphill from the tomb first described, built on a convenient shelf, with some artificial levelling, at the foot of the mountains. Above it the town of Aigai rose up a steep slope, its walls climbing and converging to an acropolis; but the place has been 'quarried', like most ancient sites, and is now engulfed in pine forest. Even of the palace, which has been carefully cleared, nothing remains above the foundations, with a few courses of retaining wall on the downhill side. As 'horizontal' sites go, it is quite impressive. The main entry was from the east, from the road to lowland Macedonia. Through triple propylaia one reaches a spacious, central peristyle court, its veranda supported by pilasters,

Vergina: a royal tomb

sixteen to a side, each with twin engaged columns; and off the south side a large room, with floor of polychrome pebble mosaic in abstract designs, may have been a throne-room. The site is well chosen to catch breezes from the sea, then nearer than today; and stairs led to an upper storey. Dated by pottery fragments, the palace has been identified as that of Antigonos Gonatas, the Stoic king, grandson of two of Alexander's marshals, who, after the fifty years of turmoil that followed the conqueror's death, restored Macedonia for another century.

Aigai had its royal tombs because it was the *old* capital; and hence something must be said of its prehistory. The royal tombs were scattered, where places were available, in an area already occupied by a vast cemetery of tumuli of the early Iron Age. Most were plundered in Hellenistic times, but some remained to be investigated by archaeologists. Since just before the fall of Mycenaean civilisation in southern Greece, there was living here, as also in north-west Greece, a flourishing population, whose grave-goods (pottery and weapons) included Mycenaean imports and imitations of them, as well as weapons and ornaments that seem to show northern, even middle-Danubian origins. Their connexion with the Dorians who, according to Greek legend, overthrew the Mycenaean kingdoms, is still the subject of keen debate. There was certainly no wholesale transfer of this northern barbaric culture into the south; but these proto-Macedonians and north-west Greeks may at least have played some part in a chain reaction, ending in the invasions of the south, in which Herodotos and Thucydides believed. There was also some direct expansion into Thessaly, but rather later. So early was Pieria, the district of Aigai, with its fertile maritime plain, important. Herodotos believed that ancestors of the Dorians, living in the Pindos, were called Makednoi (i, 56); and Thucydides emphasizes that the Makedones [with a short o] included tribes further west, beyond Mount Vermion, and that the classical Macedonian kingdom was formed by eastward expansion, subduing or expelling other peoples, from the mountain-foot across the whole plain of the Axios or Vardar river, within historic times (ii, 99). Pieria was an early conquest; and if, with its back to the mountains, it looks isolated, it was not so really. The modern main road to western or highland Macedonia goes through Verria; but a practicable route, used by an old modern cart-track, climbs and follows the hills south of the (H)Aliakmon too; and the river higher up is fordable when not in spate, where it flows in a wide, sandy and gravelly bed, above the gorges.

2 Three Hellenistic sanctuaries

SAMOTHRACE

The 'Thracian Samos' was a fit Observation Post for a god watching the Trojan War: 'Poseidon . . . marvelled at the war and the battle from high on the topmost peak of wooded Samothrace. From there all Ida could be seen and the city of Priam and the ships of the Achaeans.' (*Iliad* xiii, 10ff.) The view from Mount Phengari ('the Moon' mountain: 1664m) is magnificent, east over low-lying Imbros and the Dardanelles and west to Mount Athos. The mountain and its ridges, now deforested, form the island, which has little cultivable land except at the west end near the ancient city and round the coast. A ridge descends from a secondary summit called St George (1448m) to the north-west coast and its promontory formed the starting point of the ancient harbour mole, giving shelter from the prevailing north and north-east winds. The harbour has now silted up and anchorage is often difficult off this storm-lashed island. In antiquity it was a regular port of call, as on St Paul's journey to Europe: 'Loosing from Troas we came with straight course to Samothrace and the next day to Neapolis [Kavalla] and from thence to Philippi.' (*Acts* 16, 11–12).

Sporadic neolithic and bronze-age finds have been made on the island. The latest pre-Greek settlers seem to have come from Thrace, bringing their deities, which made Samothrace famous, and a non-Greek language which was still used in the cult in the 1C BC, surviving inscribed on stone and pottery. Greek settlers arrived in the 7C, building their town at Palaiopolis ('Old Town') and importing their patron goddess Athena, whose head was stamped on their 6C silver coins. The extensive and impressive walls rising up the hills behind the town were built in the archaic period and restored in the Hellenistic. By the 5C Samothrace owned land on the mainland and sent ships to Salamis.

The special fame of Samothrace in antiquity rested on the mystery cult celebrated there. Pre-Greek in origin, with gods of alien names, the Great Gods in time became assimilated to those of the Greek establishment. The Great Mother was identified first with Asiatic Cybele, later with Demeter; a young fertility god,

The North Aegean

Inset Samothrace island

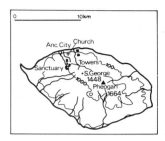

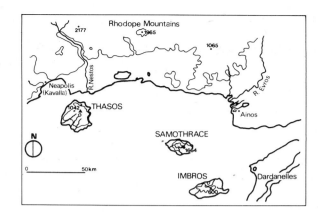

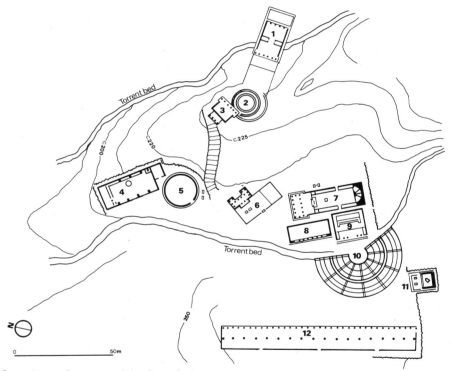

Samothrace: Sanctuary of the Great Gods

Restored sketch plan AD 1C
1 Propylon of Ptolemy II
2 Theatral area
3 Dedication of Alexander's son and brother
4 Anaktoron
5 Rotunda of Queen Arsinoe
6 Temenos (open shrine)

7 Hieron
8 'Hall of the Votive Gifts'
9 Altar court
10 Theatre
11 Fountain-house of the Winged Victory
12 Stoa

Kadmilos, with Hermes; the twin dwarfs, the Kabeiroi, also fertility gods, protected metal workers and sailors and in this last role were identified with the Dioskouroi, Castor and Pollux. They may have been Phrygian in origin, and were introduced into central Greece near Thebes.

The cult differed from that of Eleusis in being open to all, and initiation could be obtained at any time and was not tied to the annual festival. It was also possible to pass from the first grade, initiation, to the higher grade without an interval, even on the same day. The sanctuary of the Great Gods was open to all, and only certain buildings reserved for the initiated. Nearly all we know about this cult, into which Herodotos, Lysander of Sparta, Varro the antiquary, and Piso, father-in-law of Julius Caesar, were initiated, is gleaned from the buildings and inscriptions in the sanctuary, a numinous place, set in a position of wild and austere beauty, reminiscent of Delphi, but on a larger scale. Alexander's parents met here, and the sanctuary was much patronised by the Macedonian dynasty and later by the Ptolemies. Nearly all the buildings now visible belong to the great expansion of the cult in Hellenistic and Roman times, but evidence of earlier worship has been found under their foundations; remains of altars, sacrificial pits and pottery left by the worshippers. The Romans felt a link through their 'ancestor' Aeneas with Dardanos, the Samothracian, legendary founder of Troy.

The sanctuary, which grew gradually, is outside the town on a spur of the hill of St George, framed by streams east and west. There are two buildings reserved for the mysteries. The Anaktoron (Hall of the Lords), 27 × 11.58m inside, for the first stage was a simple rectangular building with a small sacristy at its south-east corner; limestone bases with cuttings evidently supported a wooden row of rising benches along the sides, and at the north end was a cross-wall partitioning off an inner sanctum, with a 'Keep Out' notice in Latin and Greek, no doubt replacing an earlier one. It seems likely that the aspirant entered by the sacristy, where he was clothed and crowned and led by the priest into the hall, where he performed first a purification rite with water and then poured a libation into a pit. He may then have been placed on a circular wooden platform and sacred dances performed round him, and then taken to the north sanctum to perform some ritual actions and shown certain symbols, which Varro said signified Heaven and Earth. All ceremonies took place by torch-light and many stones with central holes have been interpreted as stands for sconces. Quantities of small lamps, bowls and cups have also been found, and a number of lodestone iron rings, which may have been worn by those initiated. The second degree of initiation took place in another large rectangular hall, the *Hieron* (Sanctum), almost 40m long, resembling a Christian basilica. It had a double colonnaded entrance, benches down the sides for those previously initiated, and an apse at the south end with a step and, it seems, curtains. Close to the entrance are two marble stepping stones with a central one as a sconce stand. It has been conjectured that here the aspirant stood and made his confession of major sins to a priest and was absolved before entering the hall. Again, purification rites took place, and sacrifice on a central hearth. The priest then entered the apse and emerged on the step reciting a liturgy and showing sacred symbols, retiring behind the curtains to pour libations to the gods of the underworld. These details are obviously hypothetical. We know nothing of the beliefs and teaching, but this building and some features of the cult seem to have been the nearest that the Greeks and Romans came to Christian worship. Tall marble Victories (150–125) stood at the corners of the roof. One survives, except for her head, in the museum.

The most striking building on the site in its heyday must have been the huge rotunda built (289–81) by the Hellenistic Queen Arsinoe, the largest closed circular building in Greece; its outer diameter exceeds 20m and its foundations are c. 2.5m wide. A high wall of Thasian marble supported a Doric entablature outside and a gallery of Corinthian half-columns with an Ionic cornice within. The shallow domed roof was made of scale-shaped tiles, and a hole piped through the crowning finial for the smoke of sacrifices to escape. This building was probably for official gatherings of the ambassadors from all over the Greek world to attend the great annual festival in the summer. The city of Samothrace was also represented at this international gathering, when processions probably moved from altar to altar and perhaps a ritual drama was performed. This rotunda was placed very close up against the south-west end of the Anaktoron. Under the foundations the earliest remains of an altar and terrace were found (7–6CC) as well as walls of a 4C double precinct. Further south, near the Hieron, was an unaligned building, here in the heart of the sanctuary, an open-air walled shrine, open to all. An ancient sacred area, where masses of 7C pottery has been found, it was given a ceremonial gate c. 340, with three doors, a porch with Ionic columns flanked with wings, and a long frieze of dancing maidens in an archaizing style. It is possible that a ritual dance or drama was performed for the public in here. The famous statues of Aphrodite and Desire by Skopas may have stood inside. Along the west side of the Hieron stood an open rectangular building with a Doric façade called, from its contents, the 'Hall of the Votive Gifts'. South of it was an open court c. 14 × 17m, with a Doric façade and marble mosaic pavement. Steps led up to a large monumental altar. Above this, c. 200, a theatre was built into the curve of the hill. A Dionysiac dramatic contest may by then have been added to the festival. South, beyond it, was a large fountain-house, and it was on the uppermost of its two square pools that the famous Winged Victory (c. 200) stood. A French Consul found it in 1861 and it was taken to the Louvre on permanent loan. The marble ship on whose prow it stood was placed diagonally across the upper pool, and in the lower were two rocks. Reflected in the lower pool, Victory appeared to be sailing across water. This is a new and impressive form of fountain construction. Victory on the prow of a ship had been used on earlier (c. 300) coins to commemorate naval victories. Carved prows of ships, and a stern (at Lindos), had also been used as statue bases. Eleven Hellenistic ship monuments have been found in Greece; but this creation on Samothrace is a new elaboration of the theme, to relate the ship majestically to its own element of water. It has had many descendants, but no rivals in grandeur, in the numerous ship-fountains of ancient and Renaissance Rome. The wind-swept effect of the clothes of the Victory can be better appreciated when it is realised that the statue stood on a particularly wind-swept island.

On the ridge above the theatre are the foundations of a colonnade (Stoa on plan) c. 140 × 13.40m, built 300–250, with Doric columns outside and Ionic within, providing shelter from the weather. On the eastern side of the site across a ravine is a large monumental gateway (285–80) erected by Ptolemy Philadelphus, later Arsinoe's husband. It is in Thasian marble with six Ionic columns at the east end, facing the city, and Corinthian columns facing the sanctuary. A barrel-vaulted tunnel was made in the foundations to carry off the water of a seasonal torrent. Opposite the gateway are foundations of a stepped circular area of the 5C, which may have served for some introductory rites. Later, bases for more than twenty statues were set up near a reconstructed part of the steps. Slightly encroaching upon this to the north, Alexander the Great's successors, Philip III, his half-brother, and Alexander IV, his posthumous infant son, dedicated a small building, faced with six Doric columns, to the Great Gods.

The wide appeal of this cult of the Great Gods at Samothrace is shown by the dedications, from the grandiose rotunda of Queen Arsinoe to simple fish-hooks and shells in the 'Hall of the Votive Gifts'. There were groups of initiates, 'Samothrakistai', who continued to meet in their own cities, a remarkable tribute to the attractiveness of the cult. The secret of the mysteries has been well kept.

The cult came to an end in the 4C AD. An Early Christian basilica was built on the shore not far from the city, and small Byzantine churches in other parts of the island. In the 15C the branch of the Genoese Gattilusi family, who were Lords of Imbros and Ainos on the mainland, ruled Samothrace also and built three forts, one conspicuous by the sea near Palaiopolis, largely of antique stones.

Most of our knowledge is owed to American archaeologists funded by New York University, since 1938.

DODONA

'Tis mute, the word they went to hear on high Dodona mountain,
When winds were in the oakenshaws, and all the caldrons tolled.

(A. E. Housman)

Actually, Dodona itself is not *on* a mountain, but in a wide upland valley, tough in winter, as ancient Greeks said, at over 600m; smiling in spring, below Mount Tomaros, which keeps its snow till May.

Nearly all the buildings here are Hellenistic, dating from the reign of King Pyrrhos, who fought the Romans in Italy, winning battles in 280 and 279 but failing to win the war. It is dominated by his vast theatre, 135m in diameter (10m wider than Epidauros), backing onto the hillside of the local acropolis. Its stone seating is nearly all original, but, having been excavated in 1875 by the Epeirote antiquary C. Karapanos, was beginning to slip downhill until restored with modern cement. It is now again used for a summer festival of classical drama, though, owing to its position far in the north-west, with less commercial success than at Epidauros.

Dodona: the theatre

South-west from the theatre begins the Stadium or running-track, of the usual Greek form. East of this, along a terrace at the foot of the acropolis hill, passing a substantial Council Chamber, were the surprisingly modest Holy House and courtyard surrounding the Sacred Oak, centre of the oracular sanctuary of Zeus. On either side of it were even smaller chapels of other deities (not shown on the plan): Dione, his consort in a tradition older than that which wedded him to Hera; Themis, the Law of God become a person in her own right; Aphrodite, who gets in, in these austere surroundings, because doves, her birds, had some place in the early traditions of the oracle; and Herakles, son of Zeus and mythic ancestor of Pyrrhos' royal line. His temple, at the east end of the row, was actually the largest; yet only 9.5 × 6.5m. In early Christian times it was overlaid by a basilica church, later (6C?) extended by the addition of a trefoil, three-apsed sanctuary. Under its north-west corner annexe Karapanos discovered a rich deposit of bronze votive offerings (in the National Museum at Athens) buried, as usual, when it became necessary to make room for new ones.

But if the buildings are Hellenistic, the traditions of the Oracle are very old; and archaeology through its 'small finds' (bronze and pottery) supports them. Neolithic farmers settled on lower ground, in the plain of Ioannina; but their herdsmen penetrated the upland valley. In the oak forest they found one place numinous; probably a huge tree, favoured by water from the acropolis hill and on a south slope; and by the early Bronze Age (c. 2500?) there begins an accumulation

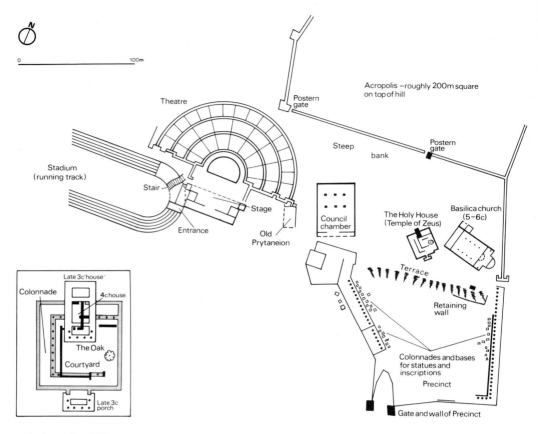

Dodona after 300 BC

Inset The Holy House
Black: foundations of first small temple and enclosure, *c.* 400 BC
Grey: foundations of 4C colonnade
White: foundations of 3C House and entrance to enclosure

of objects—pottery, axe-heads still of stone; bronze knives and axe-heads
only later—which, in this remote place, are surely votives. Even a scatter of
Mycenaean weapons and ornaments reached Dodona; and enough, in the post-
Mycenaean Dark Age, to be noticeable. A movement of tribes seems to be implied
when Achilles, whose home was in south-east Thessaly, prays for his friend
Patroklos to 'Lord Zeus of Dodona, dwelling far off'. And, he adds, 'around Thee
the Selloi, thy spokesmen, who wash not their feet and sleep on the ground'.
'Spokesmen' already suggests an oracle, needing interpreters; and Selloi (or
Helloi) may be the earliest form of the name Hellenes. The first appearance of that

name is also in the *Iliad*, among Achilles' people; and the termination *-enes* (originally *-anes*) is common among north-west Greek tribes. Not washing their feet and sleeping on the ground suggests a class of holy men (if 'priest' has too advanced a connotation), avoiding amenities that might break their contact with elemental powers.

The Oracle of Dodona, centred in an oak-tree, is explicitly mentioned in the *Odyssey*, and by Hesiod (*c.* 700). Both refer to mythical antiquity; but by Hesiod's time bronzes from the south—especially tripods, the three-legged cooking-caldrons, used at feasts and sacrifices, and later the standard 'cup' for athletic or musical victors—were reaching the place again. In 636 an ancient date-chart informs us, among names and dates of Greek colonies, that the Corinthians, then colonising on the north-west Greek coast, 'discovered' Dodona. It shows how dark the previous age had been.

Aided by its Homeric fame, the Oracle then grew in prestige. Questions addressed to it were written on tablets of lead, of which many have been found. Most are private: 'Did X steal my cloak?'; 'Will my wife bear me children?'; 'Shall I make the voyage to Y?' (One of these has on the back a negative answer.) But citizens of Kerkyra (Corfu), rent by bitter class-struggles, repeatedly ask to what god they should pray for harmony and prosperity.

The sanctuary was still without any monumental buildings. The Sky God was worshipped under the sky. The sacred oak was perhaps surrounded by a circle of bronze tripods, standing shoulder to shoulder; when the wind blew they touched, and rang. The priests then declared what the sound portended. But in the 4C the oak was surrounded by a small courtyard, with the tree near its entrance at the east corner and the first small Holy House (6.5 × 4m) entered from the corner opposite. With increasing flocks of pilgrims, it may have become necessary to protect the oak from relic- or souvenir-hunters! The ringing caldron effect was preserved by means of a dedication from Kerkyra: two pedestals, one holding a caldron and the other a bronze statue of a boy, with a whip of three thin chains, ending in knuckle-bones. The 'whip of Kerkyra' became a proverb.

The age of Hellenistic or belated classical culture here in the 'mainland' was not destined to be long. Dodona itself was sacked in 219 by the fierce Aitolians, who aspired to lead all Greece. They resented it when the Commonwealth of Epeiros, which succeeded the monarchy in 232, preferred alliance with Macedon. King Philip V, with the Epeirotes, retaliated with a raid on Thermon, the Aitolian sanctuary, and the temples of Dodona were restored out of the sale of booty; but within twenty years the Romans, victorious over Hannibal, were in Greece as allies of Aitolia, and Philip was defeated. Epeiros was caught between greater powers; and disaster came with the final conquest of Macedonia in 167. Epeiros had split during the war, the northern tribes joining the Romans, who were operating from Albania, while the Molossians, with Dodona, stood by Macedonia too long. Having decided to treat the Macedonians gently, 'liberating' them from monarchy in four republics (which the Macedonians did not at all appreciate), but wanting bonuses for their troops, the Romans decided to sell up the Molossians, literally. Detachments of troops were sent to every town and village, and given plenty of time to get there. They demanded all silver and gold, and the terrified people handed it over. Then, on a prearranged day, the troops were ordered to round up for the slave market the people on whom they had been billeted. 150,000 are said to have been sold—though the market was so flooded that prices were disappointing. Much of the land was bought up by Romans and became huge cattle ranches. A century later, Cicero's friend, Atticus, had one.

The actual sanctuary of Dodona, of course, was spared; the Romans were very pious; but we do not know who ran it. Long after, it belonged to Augustus' monstrous Victory City, Nikopolis near Actium; and a Roman presence is suggested when we find the theatre adapted as an arena for beast-baiting. A surviving inscription shows a high priest from Nikopolis presiding over the Naia, Dodona's festival, as late as AD 240–41. Julian 'the Apostate' consulted the Oracle (by messenger) as well as that of Delphi. The end came when Christians, probably in the 390s, cut down the sacred tree and dug out its roots, leaving a hole so large that its 'fill' was easily recognised by the modern re-excavators.

EPHYRA: THE ORACLE ON THE ACHERON

It is not widely known that the Acheron, familiar as one of the rivers of Vergil's hell, is really in Greece. On the coast south-east of Corfu, it and its tributary the Kokytos united to flow into a sheltered harbour, now silted up; and nearby was a small hill-town, Ephyra, where Odysseus went to get poison for his arrows. (Homer also mentions other places with the same name, of unknown meaning.) This one appears in history in 433 BC, when the great Corinthian armada put in there on its way to attack Kerkyra, a prelude to the Peloponnesian War. Mycenaean pottery had already reached it by way of trade; but it was chiefly famous for its Oracle of the Dead, housed in a building of square plan and probably pyramidal elevation, elaborated when north-west Greece (Epeiros) formed an important state in the 3C BC.

There is a cave, now with no visible entry, under the exact middle of the complex; evidently a sinister enough place to have suggested, long before, that here was an entry to the underworld, the realm of King Hades. The township occupied another hill, a few hundred yards away. What struck the excavator, Dr Dakaris of the Greek Antiquities service, in 1958 and after, is that the central sanctum, an inner square with walls over 2.5m thick, could only be reached by entering the outer building from the north and going round three sides of the square, ending with a 'Greek key' or 'labyrinthine' zigzag through chambers with probable traces of iron grilles, to reach the last, narrow, arched doorway from the south. Off it were rooms lined with at least thirty-seven great storage jars, containing perhaps largely the reserve food stores of the keepers of the shrine, but some of them, also, quantities of sulphur, which might have been used to produce a dim and sinister light in the chapel. Outside, among many fragments of the outer roof, there were none of the palmettes or other antefixes that decorate Greek temples. The place must have been made to look deliberately grim.

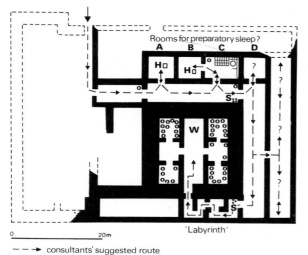

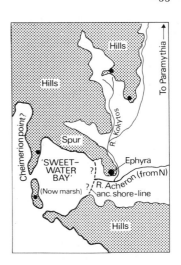

Oracle of the Dead at Ephyra on the Acheron
(Thesprotis, NW Greece)
(After S. I. Dakaris, in *Proc. Arch.Soc. of Athens*, 1961, p. 108)

A-D	rooms for preparatory sleep?	S	piles of pebbles
C	room with wash-stand	O	large jars, found broken, but in position
H	hearths	W	wheels

Dakaris did some good detective work on his finds. Rooms A, B, off the north corridor contained hearths, perhaps traces of beds, and C a built-up washstand, with drainage to the outside. 'Sleeping in' was a frequent feature of consulting oracles, in the hope of helpful dreams; and here visitors may have passed a night or nights, in perhaps dark, windowless rooms, while receiving purification against the danger ahead. Among other food remains (shells, small bones) were found many traces of certain beans which, eaten dried, are mildly toxic, producing disorientation, or even hallucinations. Thus 'fortified', the pilgrim proceeded.

To the right of the door from the north to the east corridor, and again from that into the south 'labyrinth', were found piles of smooth pebbles. Throwing away something is in magic a prophylactic against the 'envy' of hostile powers. Probably the pilgrim carried two, for discarding at these turning-points in his journey. In the east corridor, where many sheep had been sacrificed—no doubt black sheep to the dark gods, as in the *Odyssey*—the first door that he would find by the dim light of his lamp was on the left, into the outer corridor; but the sole feature of that is that it leads nowhere but to two dead ends, as in a maze. Thoroughly disoriented, he reached at last the windings of the 'labyrinth', where, on the floor, were found the fragments of many broken jugs. Was it here that he poured, like Odysseus on his visit to the dead, his offering of wine and sacrificial blood to the hungry ghosts, giving them strength to come and speak with him? The jugs were then too holy, or too dangerous, ever to use again.

But in the innermost chamber the most sensational find was made: in the north-east corner, a corroded heap of large iron wheels and, better preserved, smaller bronze wheels, some of them hook-toothed, such as might have been used in a crane worked by a windlass to prevent running back. Such an apparatus was used in Greek theatres, to let gods appear on high. It looks as though, if sugges-tion, toxic beans and wandering in the dark had not produced hallucinations enough, the keepers of the Oracle were prepared to produce real, artificial apparitions, let down from above through a slit in the wooden ceiling, in darkness, where there had been only a stone wall, and suddenly illuminated by the eerie light of burning sulphur! This is *late* Greek; and when priestcraft resorts to such (literally) brazen trickery, its society is surely 'on the way out'.

The whole experience was deliberately made terrifying, like that of visiting the (quite different) underground Oracle of Trophonios, described by Pausanias. (No remains of it are known.) After that, the visitor was given a special course of rehabilitation, before he could smile again. On the Acheron, this might have taken place in the west wing, where only the foundations of the walls remain. Clearly, one would only visit such an oracle for pressing reasons, such as to find out who had murdered one's father, or where he had hidden his gold.

This sinister place was burnt by the destroying Romans, when they harried and enslaved Epeiros in 167 BC. The burning sulphur calcined the storage-jars in the central chambers. In the 18C a Christian monastery occupied the site. It has long been deserted; but its small monastic chapel still stands, refurbished by the excavators, above the central chamber and the vaulted cave below.

3 Two Roman sites

CORINTH

The name of Corinth bespeaks prehistoric antiquity. The element 'Cor-' appears in several place-names where there is an adjacent peak; '-nth-' in the names of places, plants, and objects placed on the ground. It obviously denotes Acrocorinth, the splendid fortress, made viable by a fine spring, the Upper Peirene, below the top of the rock. Yet Corinth is not prominent in Homer. It is only in early historic times that the city rises to greatness, winning territory from Megara north of the Isthmus, colonising Kerkyra and Syracuse, and dominating oversea pottery markets in the 7C BC, especially under her famous 'tyrants' Kypselos and Periandros. As a 'bourgeois' republic she was distinguished in the struggle against Xerxes and later, as an ally of Sparta, in bringing down the power of Athens. In the 3C BC she became the centre of the Achaian federal league; but this brought upon her total destruction in 146 BC in a final struggle for Greek freedom against Rome. Of the Greek city, only the seven columns of the archaic temple, spared by the Romans but mostly demolished since, now rise above ground level. For remains of Hellenic Corinth, we have to look outside, where the

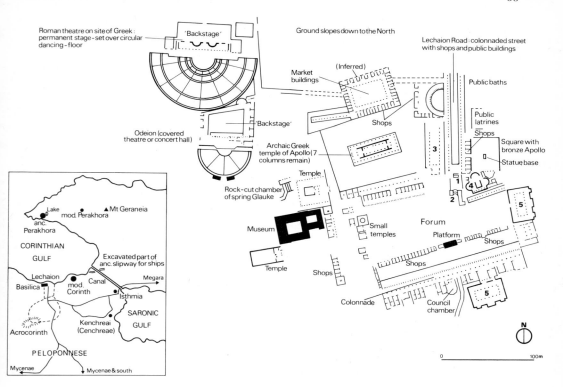

Roman theatre on site of Greek: permanent stage-set over circular dancing-floor
'Backstage'
Ground slopes down to the North
Lechaion Road: colonnaded street with shops and public buildings
Market buildings
(Inferred)
Public baths
Odeion (covered theatre or concert hall)
'Backstage'
Shops
Public latrines
Shops
Archaic Greek temple of Apollo (7 columns remain)
Square with bronze Apollo
Statue base
Temple
Rock-cut chamber of spring Glauke
3
Museum
Small temples
Forum
Platform
Shops
Temple
Shops
Shops
Colonnade
Council chamber

Lake
mod. Perakhora
Mt Geraneia
anc. Perakhora
CORINTHIAN
GULF
Excavated part of anc. slipway for ships
Lechaion
Canal
Megara
Basilica
mod. Corinth
Isthmia
SARONIC
Kenchreai (Cenchreae)
GULF
Acrocorinth
PELOPONNESE
Mycenae
Mycenae & south

N

0   100m

Corinth: central area of the Roman Colonia

1 Steps (earlier, ramp)   3 Basilica (pillared hall) with foundations of Greek temple under
2 Arched entry to Forum   4 Fountain-house of spring Peirene, repeatedly remodelled
                                                  5 Basilicas

west end of the paved 'drag-way', by which ships could be hauled across the Isthmus, has been uncovered north and south of the modern canal; and at Perakhora, across the water, by the modern lighthouse. Here the endearing stone quay of a tiny harbour and Temple of Hera, behind which was found an immense haul of archaic votive offerings, seem to mark a place where early mariners took omens and made and paid their vows, before and after their adventurous voyages to the west.

In 46 BC Julius Caesar restored the city as a Roman colony. Growing rich, and increasingly Greek, capital of the Province of Achaia, this was where St Paul was brought before the proconsul Gallio (brother of the philosopher Seneca); and Gallio's year in Greece, shown by an inscription at Delphi to have included part of AD 51, provides the first fixed date in church history.

Lechaion Street, leading up from the northern port, the site of an immense 5C basilica-church, well shows the dignity of a great Roman city. Paved, 12m wide, it

was flanked by colonnades, behind which were shops and public buildings. Half-way up on the east side, these included a set of twenty public latrines, over a sewer flushed by the overflow from the fountain, Lower Peirene, at the south end, and probably also by pipes from the adjacent public baths. The Peirene fountain-house, with remains of Roman painting, presents a complex spectacle, due to the fact that archaeological work has left visible the remains of successive façades going back to archaic times.

At this end of the street a ramp, later replaced by steps, led up to a monumental arch, the main entrance to the vast Agora, or Roman Forum, some 200m long; a centre of public life. Of the shops that lined it, many have been identified by animal-, fish- and bird-bones, as restaurants; and half-way along the south side is the Tribunal or platform, where Gallio probably sat when he refused to be provoked by a riot into taking cognizance of a religious dispute in the Jewish community: or, in the immortal words of our 17C Bible, 'cared for none of these things'.

The American archaeologists, who have worked here since 1896, have tried where possible to detect traces of the Greek city underlying the Roman; finding, for example, at the east end of the Forum, the starting-line and judges' platform of a running-track, and under the basilica or pillared hall, on the west side of Lechaion Street (3 on plan) the foundations of a Greek temple. Inside the west end of the Forum are those of six small temples or chapels of the Roman age, set up perhaps for reasons connected with business; and beyond it and the museum another older relic, the rock-cut chamber of a second spring, Glauke, 'the Grey'. But essentially what we see is Roman. We should imagine it crowded, noisy, with slender-pillared colonnades everywhere giving shelter from rain or, more often, the hot sun; full of chatter, and with food-smells, spice-smells and less savoury smells like that of leather, emerging as we pass the various little shops.

THESSALONICA

Thessalonica, to give it its 'classical' English spelling (Salonike in mediaeval Greek, and rhyming with 'Veronica' in English only since 1915), is of all Greek cities the one which best preserves structures spanning the centuries from late pre-Christian to mediaeval times.

Thessalonike was a daughter of the great Philip by one of his semi-official 'wives', married to Kassandros (Cassander in Latin), son of the general whom Alexander left in charge of Macedonia. Briefly King of Macedonia after Alexander's death, Kassandros gave her name to his new capital, to remind the world that the dynasty, which he failed to found, would be descended from the ancient kings; and parts of the walls that march over the hills behind the old town stand on his foundations.

Corinth: Lechaion Street, the Roman road from the harbour to the Agora, with Acrocorinth in the background

Thessalonica: the Arch of Galerius

The city became a capital again under Galerius, co-emperor and son-in-law of Diocletian, before AD 300, and from his time survives the triumphal arch with its rich reliefs, celebrating his victories over the revived Persian Empire: Galerius the young soldier, sacrificing in the presence of his august father-in-law, who wears civil dress; in battle, crowned by Victory; receiving the surrender of Persians, with their elephants. Originally there was a second arch to the east, forming a chamber, spanning the course of the Egnatian Way to the east. (For practical use, the Romans thoughtfully provided the city with a by-pass.) At right-angles to this, a colonnaded street led shorewards between Galerius' huge palace-complex (the massive brickwork that remains has lost its no doubt gorgeous decoration) and the Hippodrome, its site covered by modern buildings, where the Emperor entertained the people; and another northwards to what archaeologists cautiously call simply the Rotunda or Round Building, which Galerius perhaps intended for his mausoleum. If so, he never occupied it; his successor Licinius would not have him buried in the city; and ironically, very soon the Christians, whom Galerius had persecuted, had it as a church. Considerable remains, though a mere fraction of what there was, survive of the once glorious Christian mosaics of its dome and upper walls. A minaret (beheaded by lightning, not by man) commemorates the time when the Turks annexed it as a mosque. After 1912 it became again a church, St George's (not its original dedication, but found on some maps); it is now a national monument and a museum of Christian stonework from other sites.

This continuous use is typical. Philippi sank to uninhabited ruins, of interest only to specialists; but Thessalonica, on the sea, though repeatedly threatened by barbarians and more than once sacked, never lost importance. Of its other churches, one (5C?) is the only large palaeo-Christian or pre-Byzantine basilica hall-church in Greece still standing and in use, out of scores now known to have existed; though its name, 'Not Made with Hands' (*A-cheiro-poietos*), is much later,

Old Thessalonica. Modern streets follow approximately the lines of the Roman, which are shown.

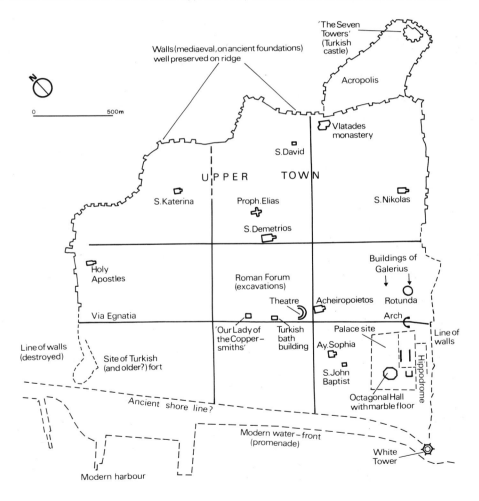

and properly belongs to an alleged miraculous ikon which found a home there. It faces west onto the Roman Forum, now laid bare; indeed, it would have faced the back wall of the theatre; but that, regarded by the Christians as a place of sin, was probably demolished. The Church of the Holy Wisdom, Ayia Sophia, with some mosaics, has next to it, partly under a modern street, a group of underground chapels including a sacred spring, still visited with much devotion. It is now dedicated to St John the Baptist, but formerly to the Nymphs. The great basilica of St Demetrios, patron saint of the city, was almost entirely rebuilt, on the ancient plan, after the great fire of 1917; but it preserves some early mosaics, including one of the Saint with two children, perhaps dedicated to his care. It partly overlies a Roman bath establishment (also regarded as a place of sin), in which (now in the crypt) the soldier-martyr was said to have been imprisoned. In the upper town, up a lane near the top of Ayia Sophia Street, the 5C (?) chapel of Osios David, an obscure hermit, had, before its early-modern adaptation as a mosque, a cross-in-square plan. It is perhaps the earliest example of this originally Syrian ground-plan in Europe; but its fame rests upon its exquisite contemporary apse-mosaic of Christ in glory. It is an apocalyptic vision, drawing deeply (as does our New Testament Apocalypse) upon the now not-much-studied visions of Ezekiel (i,ii) and Habakkuk. Christ, the young, beardless Son of Man of the earliest Christian art, sits in a mandorla of glory between Ezekiel's Four Beasts and the two prophets (Ezekiel holds a scroll, with phrases from his work), with, below his feet, the flowing waters and plentiful fish emphasized in the prophecy. The rainbow colours, green, blue, pink and gold, have defeated all the skills of colour photography. Twice covered up, in the days of the Iconoclasts, after which a monk from Egypt is said to have been ordered by God in a dream to go and rediscover it, and again under the Turks, the near-perfect preservation of this masterpiece seems itself almost miraculous. Under the plaster, near the door, 12C frescoes of high quality have also been found (1978).

With the great revival of art in the 11C, there begins the series of Thessalonica's Middle and Late Byzantine churches, with domes mounted on 'drums', and deploying a skill in patterned brickwork scarcely matched in southern Greece, save at Merbaka near Mycenae. The charming little Our Lady of the Coppersmiths (or, for centuries, Mosque of the Coppersmiths) south-west of the Roman Forum, is precisely dated, 1028, by an inscription of its donor—unexpectedly at that date, one Christopher the Lombard. It stands in a small churchyard, well below the street level, the ground having risen on an inhabited site, in a manner familiar to archaeologists, by some two metres in 850 years. Up-hill towards the walls, three later and larger churches carry on the tradition: those of the Prophet Elias, with seven domes, (though much spoiled by the necessity of shoring up its piers with cement), St Catherine, with five, and, almost in its original state, the Twelve Apostles (early 14C). Some frescoes here still await cleaning. The Church under the crumbling Empire, wrecked by the Fourth Crusade in 1204, could no longer afford the royal spendours of mosaic; but what artists under the Palaeologan dynasty could do in paint, and how far from stiff or stagnant

Byzantine art was in that last phase, has been revealed in our century by many discoveries, mostly from under Turkish-period whitewash, from Istanbul to Yugoslavia. The Italian Early Renaissance did not, it appears, take place *in vacuo*, and the 'Greek style' that Vasari so despised was already, in Greece, old-fashioned.

In Thessalonica, a notable contribution to this movement, and to its rediscovery, is made by the frescoes of St Nikolas Orphanos (better, *of* Orphanos; the family name of the founder), also dated on stylistic grounds to the early 14C, and cleared of whitewash in 1963. Though much has perished, what remains is impressive, including scenes from the life of the patron saint: a historical 4C Bishop of Myra in Lycia, whose life, much mythologized, was very popular. Here is shown, for example, the saint as a rich young man pushing gold in a stocking-foot by night into the bedroom window of a poor man who could not dower his daughters (the origin of the still-living myth of Santa 'Klaus); also that of his ship surviving miraculously a storm at sea, a tale which made him a patron of travellers, commemorated by many chapels at Greek harbour-mouths or on mountain passes. Best preserved is a section in the south aisle, with a vivid Miracle of Cana in Galilee, and part of the Life of St Gerasimos of Jordan, who cut a thorn out of a lion's paw (like Androcles). The lion stayed with him, and when some camel-riding Arabs (shown as black men) stole his horse, it chased them off, and is shown bringing back the horse, with the leading-rein in its mouth. This artist is not without even a sense of humour.

The Turks, established at Adrianople (Edirne) since 1387, took 'Saloniki' in 1387; the Greeks briefly recovered it when 'Tamerlane' crushed Bayezid at Ankara, but in 1430 came the final and violent occupation. The Turkish period, as elsewhere in Greece, is undistinguished, punctuated by the annexation of more and more churches as mosques; three bath-houses are the most characteristic monuments. Some picturesque, though poorly-built, 19C houses survive in the upper town, including the birthplace of Atatürk, near the eastern walls; but earthquakes and modern building are steadily reducing their number. The White Tower, conspicuous from the sea at the foot of the east wall and almost a 'trademark' of the city, is Turkish, no doubt on the site of a Roman structure. Before the building-out of the modern sea-front, it stood on a small peninsula. The most famous event in its history was the massacre there of the Janissaries stationed in the city, in 1826, when those famous 'New Soldiers' (as their name means), the terror of early-modern Europe, had become an ancient institution, a powerful vested interest, and a bar to a ruthless and energetic Sultan's attempts to modernise his forces.

VI Mediaeval Greece

1 Byzantine splendour

THE MONASTERY OF HOLY LUKE OF STIRIS

This great monastery lies in a vale west of Helicon, once an isolated spot, *c.* 35km from Delphi, now part of the tourist run. A turning 23km from Delphi leads in 12km through two villages, past a hillside clothed in spring with almond blossom and wild flowers, to the monastery. It is reached down a flight of steps. At the end of the terrace is the long refectory rebuilt after bomb damage, and behind it rises the restored great dome of the main church. There are two churches in the cobbled courtyard, joined at the shrine of Holy Luke, a 10C hermit saint ('Holy'—'Osios'—is the Greek title for hermits) who, after considerable wanderings, settled in this lonely place. Beside a spring he built a small chapel of St Barbara before he died *c.* 951. Living and dead he was credited with miracles of healing, and his tomb became a mediaeval Lourdes. A cross-in-square church dedicated to the Virgin was built, probably still in the 10C, with his shrine at the south-west corner of the porch. The small dome, on a drum faced with marble slabs, is supported on four columns. There is a fine tessellated floor, but no other internal decoration survives. The outer walls are a good example of Middle Byzantine patterned brickwork. A fresco on the outside wall of the porch is preserved in its original position, now inside the north transept of the larger and later church where the two overlap beside the saint's shrine. A noble armed figure of Joshua meeting the angel at Jericho (*Joshua* 5;13–15) was uncovered during restoration work in 1963, giving unexpected proof that the church of the Virgin is the older.

The great church of Holy Luke gives the best impression of a mosaic-decorated church in Greece, and is the earliest, *c.* 1020, of the three Middle Byzantine churches where mosaics survive. The coloured marble veneer of the walls, with a delicate white marble frieze above, the tessellated floor patterns and the elaborately carved chancel columns and beam supply important features which sadly have been stripped from Daphni. A far greater area of mosaic remains here (in parts restored), although the dome was destroyed in an earthquake in 1659 and the great Pantokrator surrounded with angels is missing, as also the Annunciation in the north-east niche. Out of a host of 143 saints, 131 survive.

In all its richness of mosaic this church has the fewest scenes: nine New Testament, originally four Old Testament. The choice of subject and position was made with great care. There is a classical unity of theme underlying the four pictures in the porch which was not followed in the later churches. They are

Churches of Holy Luke of Stiris *left* and of The Virgin *right*, east end

taken from the two 'Great Weeks' in the Orthodox calendar—Holy Week and Easter—and prepare the worshipper for the Liturgy to be celebrated within, the memorial of Christ's Passion and Resurrection. All are taken from St John's gospel. In the north half are the events of Maundy Thursday and Good Friday. The end lunette shows The Washing of the Feet. Christ stoops to dry Peter's feet, while Peter makes a gesture, 'Not my feet only, but also my hands and my head.' (John 13;9). Next is the Crucifixion, simply three figures, the title and Christ's words, recorded only by St John (19;26), to his Mother and John. Small red and blue circles above the dead Christ's head are the sun and the moon, placing the scene in a cosmic setting. Below his feet on a stylised rock is the mask-like skull of Adam; traditionally the place of Christ's cross was where Adam died.

South of the door is the typical Byzantine Resurrection, shown as the Harrowing of Hell. The idea that Christ descended into hell and 'went and preached to the spirits in prison' is already in I Peter 3;19, and many 2C writers refer to his

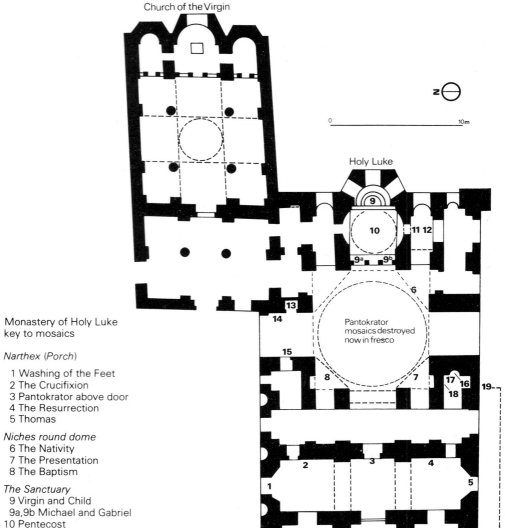

Church of the Virgin

Holy Luke

Monastery of Holy Luke
key to mosaics

Narthex (Porch)

1 Washing of the Feet
2 The Crucifixion
3 Pantokrator above door
4 The Resurrection
5 Thomas

Niches round dome
6 The Nativity
7 The Presentation
8 The Baptism

The Sanctuary
9 Virgin and Child
9a,9b Michael and Gabriel
10 Pentecost
11 Daniel in den
12 Hebrew youths in furnace

N. Transept
13 Shrine of Holy Luke
14 Fresco of Joshua, from Church of the Virgin
15 Holy Luke

Frescoes in S.W. Chapel
16 Virgin and Child
17 Christ walking towards the Baptist
18 St John the Baptist

19 to crypt

Pantokrator
mosaics destroyed
now in fresco

delivering those who had died before his Incarnation, but a whole dramatic story is in the later, 4C 'Gospel of Nicodemus'. It is recalled in the Liturgy of Easter Saturday and still on some islands partly enacted by priest and people at the great Midnight Service of Easter. Here it is illustrated simply, with only five figures, dominated by the vigorous Risen Christ, in white and gold, striding across the broken doors of hell with scattered bolts and locks below his feet, his garments windswept by his movement. He raises Adam from his antique sarcophagus and Eve stands behind in supplication. Opposite them his royal ancestors David and Solomon, believed to have foretold the resurrection, look on, amazed. There is more vitality in this picture than in the more crowded scene at Daphni. The fourth scene is The Convincing of Thomas. In the Orthodox church the Sunday after Easter is called 'of Thomas'. This subject was illustrated from Early Christian times. Thomas the doubter acclaims his Master, 'My Lord and my God', and the Risen Christ, who redeemed the past, blesses the future, 'Blessed are they that have not seen, and yet have believed.' (John 20;29). Above the door into the church is the half-figure of Christ the Almighty (Pantokrator) holding the gospel open at the verse, 'I am the Light of the world; he that followeth me shall not walk in darkness but shall have the Light of Life.' If this figure were projected downwards it would fill the doorway, recalling another text from St John (10;9), 'I am the Door'. SS Peter and Paul stand each side of the door and the rest of the apostles and evangelists on the under sides of the arches of the porch. The twelve women saints allowed in are placed at the back on the west wall. (At Orthodox services women stand at the back of the church.)

Inside, the Pantokrator in the wide dome would, as at Daphni, have dominated the whole church. The 17C frescoes are a poor substitute. This wide dome, a type only found in Greece, rests on a low sixteen-sided drum supported on arches across the corners of the square of the crossing. These give four niches (squinches) large enough for a whole scene. Three survive and are concerned with the manifestation of Christ in his Incarnation. The south-east niche contains the normal, composite Byzantine picture of the Nativity, always shown taking place in a cave, according to the early apocryphal Book of James. The Child lies at the centre, in a brick-built manger, with the rays of the star streaming down to his head. The Virgin sits behind the manger holding up his head. The haloes and rays make a great light in the darkness. Outside the cave Joseph looks on anxiously, and behind him three angels lead in the Magi, the oldest towering above the other two. At the foot of the manger is a scene always present in Byzantine Nativities: the two midwives from the apocryphal story, bathing the Child. Behind them is a group of three shepherds with their sheep and a shepherd boy piping on the hilltop. Two angels show them the way. This is the only complete Middle Byzantine mosaic we have of the Nativity.

The south-west niche shows the Presentation of the Christ Child in the Temple in Jerusalem, represented by a Christian altar with a large cross on the altar cloth and a baldacchino surmounted by a cross. In Greek this is called The Meeting—Simeon and Anna representing the Old Testament and the Virgin and

Child the New. The north-west niche has the Baptism. The hand of God appears from heaven and the Dove descends down a ray of light upon Christ's head. Angels attend, holding the clothes. Below in the highly stylised water of the Jordan is a small figure of an old man in flight, carrying a water-pot. This is the classical personification of a river god, common at all periods in Byzantine Baptisms and derived from a reference to Psalm 114;5, 'Jordan was driven back'. The small pillar with a cross at the centre of the bottom of the picture represents one set up on the bank of the Jordan, well-known to mediaeval pilgrims. Behind the Baptist is an axe laid to the root of a flourishing tree, a literal illustration of John's preaching (Matthew 3;10, Luke 3;9).

In the apse is a simple image of the Virgin and Child enthroned, the normal subject at this place in a Byzantine church. In the small dome above the sanctuary is Pentecost, with the eleven apostles and St Paul (!) seated in a circle, and the tongues of fire descending upon them from the abstract symbol of the Trinity: the Throne Prepared in Heaven with the Book of the gospels and the Dove of the Holy Spirit, above the altar where the Holy Spirit is invoked at every Mass. In the corners are groups of people labelled 'tribes' and 'tongues' to whom the apostles were sent to preach. On the great arch of the sanctuary the archangels, Gabriel and Michael, stand in Byzantine court dress, holding wands of office. In the small south chamber to the right of the altar are two Old Testament scenes of deliverance, prototypes of Christian redemption from the time of catacomb art: Daniel between two diminutive lions and the Three Hebrew Youths in the furnace beneath the delivering angel. In the north chamber there would have been other Old Testament prototypes, equally ancient in origin, probably scenes of Abraham and Melchisedek.

A great company of saints adorn the upper parts of the walls, the vaults and arches: Fathers of the Church, bishops and deacons about the sanctuary, soldier saints on the high arches supporting the dome, a crowd of monks and hermits at the west end. Among them, on a larger scale than the rest, are Nikon of Sparta and Luke Gourniotis who died within living memory. Holy Luke himself has pride of place, in the north transept opposite his own shrine, red-bearded, the only one wearing a hood.

There is a large gallery at the back and along part of the sides of the church, providing room for the women pilgrims to the shrine.

There is also some fresco decoration in the two west corner chapels of the main church, the Virgin and Child and an impressive Christ walking towards the Baptist, and more saints in medallions. In the crypt are scenes of an extended Passion and Resurrection cycle painted in the 11C, a group of monks and more medallions of saints on the cross vaults.

The mosaic figures of Holy Luke are short and sturdy, compared with those of Daphni, c. 80 years later, and the gaze from their large eyes is stern; but it should be remembered that the church was not decorated from any aesthetic motive, but was filled with a company of saints to encourage monks, 'the athletes of Christ' as they were called, to persevere in their ascetic calling.

The Nea Moni, Chios

THE NEA MONI OF CHIOS

In a wooded glen of Homer's 'rugged Chios' is the Nea Moni (the New Mona-stery—new, that is, in the 11C) above the harbour town. It is the most firmly dated of the three great mosaic churches, built in the reign of Constantine IX Monomachos (1042–54), and completed shortly after his death. The mosaics are the work of a very original artist, using sharp colour contrasts and heavy outlines, and, in two cases, a form of continuous narrative not found elsewhere in this medium at this date. As an imperial foundation it is likely that artists and their materials came from Constantinople. The church is basically the same type as Holy Luke and Daphni, but the dome was even wider, giving a great impression of space. It, with its Pantokrator mosaic, was destroyed by an earthquake in 1881, which also ruined or damaged many other mosaics.

Here it is better to begin with the scenes in the main church, since those in the inner porch (the outer is later) are more complicated and lack a coherent theme.

In the apse is the Virgin Orans, standing with arms raised in prayer, flanked in the side niches by the archangels Michael and Gabriel, in court dress, holding orbs. The mosaics of the nave depicting 'the events of the Incarnation', as an earlier emperor, Leo VI, had called the gospel scenes, are clearly placed at the same height all round the walls, in alternate deep and narrow, wide and shallow recesses. They read clockwise, beginning, as usual, in the north-east corner with the Annunciation (Gabriel only survives). The Nativity followed, but is destroyed, and the Presentation is fragmentary. The Baptism is the first in the series that is fairly well preserved. It has an engaging *genre* element in the small figures undressing and swimming in the Jordan—Christians baptised with Christ—unique at this time in mosaic. Good details survive in the Transfiguration. Over the door is the Crucifixion, with five figures about the cross, the three Marys, St John and the centurion, again an unusual composition. This is followed by a moving Descent from the Cross—the first time this scene is known in mosaic. Finally, opposite the Baptism, is a vigorous Harrowing of Hell, with Christ striding forward to raise Adam. Other scenes from the Feasts of the Church are in the porch.

High up below the dome survive SS Mark and John seated at their desks, and two great, golden six-winged seraphim at the west end. St Matthew is fragmentary.

In contrast to the clarity of the nave decoration, that of the porch is more complicated than it is in either of the other churches. It is divided into three compartments by a small fluted dome in the centre, resting on arches. The Virgin and Child are at the centre, guarded by eight soldier saints standing in the flutes. Medallions of Joachim and Anna are in the corners by the door. On the undersides of the arches are medallions of seven monastic saints on each side, and on the west wall four stylite saints looking over the balustrades on the top of their pillars. It has become a tradition that monks and hermits are placed at the west end of monastic churches. Here they surround the Virgin to whom it is dedicated. Isaiah and Daniel, prophets of the Incarnation, stand above the west door.

The two other, vaulted compartments of this porch are decorated with six more scenes. On the north wall, on the east side, is a fragmentary Raising of Lazarus, with fine heads of his sisters at Christ's feet. Along the north wall is a striking Washing of the Feet in two zones. The upper illustrates word for word the text of St John 13;4: 'He riseth . . . and laid aside his garments'—the blue cloak is shown rolled up into a large ball—'And took a towel and girdeth Himself.' Three figures of Christ are depicted, standing between the columns of the Upper Room, giving a strong vertical stress to the composition. Below there is a horizontal one, with the disciples spread out along two benches, in animated groups—the artist has taken care to avoid monotony. Christ is shown at one end washing the feet of Peter, who is making his usual gesture signifying 'my hands and my head also'. Partly on the vault and partly on the spandrels of an arch are fragments of the Palm Sunday Triumphal Entry. Here the artist has been obliged by the architecture to squeeze his picture into an awkward space. On the south wall the narrative of Gethsemane

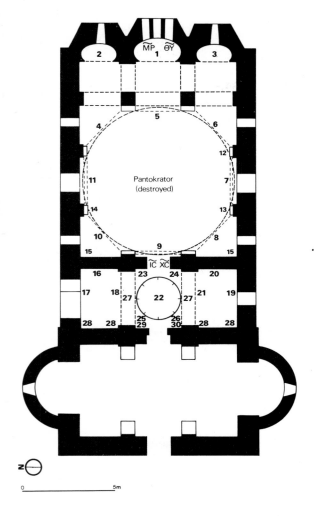

Nea Moni, Chios
key to mosaics:

Apse
 1 Virgin Orans
 2 Archangel Michael
 3 Archangel Gabriel

Dome
 4 Annunciation (fragmentary)
 5 Nativity (destroyed)
 6 Presentation (fragmentary)
 7 Baptism
 8 Transfiguration
 9 Crucifixion
10 Descent from the Cross
11 Resurrection (Harrowing of Hell)
12 St John Evangelist
13 St Matthew Evangelist (fragmentary)
14 St Mark Evangelist
15 Seraphim

Narthex: scenes from the Life of Christ
16 Raising of Lazarus (fragmentary)
17 Washing of the Feet
18 Triumphal Entry (on arch)
19 Gethsemane
20 Ascension (fragmentary)
21 Pentecost (fragmentary)

22 Virgin and Child in dome, with soldier
   saints in flutes
23 Joachim (in medallion)
24 Anna (in medallion)
25 St Panteleimon (in medallion)
26 St Stephen (in medallion)
27 Seven saints, in medallions each side
   of dome
28 Four stylites
29 Daniel ⎫
        ⎬ standing, each side and
        ⎭ above doorway
30 Isaiah ⎭

is told with the figure of Christ again repeated three times: at prayer, standing
above his disciples, and betrayed. The two closing scenes are very fragmentary:
the Ascension, where only some fine faces of the apostles and part of the halo of
glory survive, and Pentecost, lost except for two intriguing groups representing
the Nations and Tongues on the arch spandrel. The new elements of a domed
narthex, the continuous narratives on the walls and the austere beauty of some of
the individual heads, make this porch of outstanding interest, but it lacks the

simplicity of the set of lunettes in the other churches. The Nea Moni is the most remote and the least known of the three great 11C mosaic churches of Greece, but its mosaics are a major addition to Middle Byzantine art.

There are other Byzantine churches on Chios interesting for their architecture, especially the intricate patterns of their external brickwork. Other points of interest about the island are mentioned on page 130.

DAPHNI

The monastery at Daphni, on the Athens-Eleusis road, was built on the site of a 5–6C basilica, built in turn upon a temple of Apollo (of the laurel, *daphne*). An Ionic column from the temple has been set up in the side of the outer, Gothic porch, an addition, as are the cloisters, by the crusaders to this 11C Byzantine church. After doing some damage on their arrival in 1205, they gave it, in 1211, to Cistercian monks, who remained there until the Turkish occupation in 1460. The Frankish Dukes of Athens were buried in the cloister, but the arms on the two

opposite Daphni: key to mosaics

Sanctuary:
1 St John the Baptist
2 St Nikolaus
3 Aaron
4 Zacharias   } transferred to
5 St Gregory Thaumaturgos } walls outside
6 St Gregory of Agrigentum } sanctuary
7,8,9,10 Deacons

Cycle of the Virgin
Narthex, S. side:
11 Prayers of Joachim and Anna
12 Blessing of the Virgin
13 Presentation of the Virgin
N. Transept, E. wall, upper zone: 14 Birth of the Virgin
Nave, N.E. squinch: 15 Annunciation
Apse: Virgin and Child enthroned between archangels
Nave, S.E. squinch: 16 Nativity
S. Transept, E. wall, upper zone: 17 Adoration of the Magi
18 Presentation (lost)

Nave, S.W. squinch: 19 Baptism
Nave, N.W. squinch: 20 Transfiguration

Cycle of the Passion and Resurrection
Narthex, N. side:
21 Last Supper
22 Washing of the Feet
23 Betrayal
N. Transept, W. wall, upper zone: 24 Raising of Lazarus (inscription only)
lower zone: 25 Triumphal entry
E.wall, lower zone: 26 Crucifixion
S.Transept, E.wall, lower zone: 27 Resurrection
W.wall, lower zone: 28 Convincing of Thomas
Nave, W.wall, centre: 29 Dormition of the Virgin

sarcophagi there are not those of the ducal families of De la Roche or De Brienne.

Daphni is the latest (*c.* 1080–1100) of the three great 11C churches with mosaics. It is a cross-in-square with a large octagonal dome resting on squinches, as at Holy Luke. But here all the marble has been stripped off the walls, and the mosaics have suffered much damage from vandals down the ages, and also late 19C restoration. In spite of this, the composition of many of the scenes, the classical beauty of individual figures, and the only surviving 11C mosaic of the Pantokrator, the great image dominating Orthodox churches from the 9C until today, show Byzantine art at the peak of its achievement.

The dedication is to the Dormition (Falling Asleep) of the Virgin, and, out of

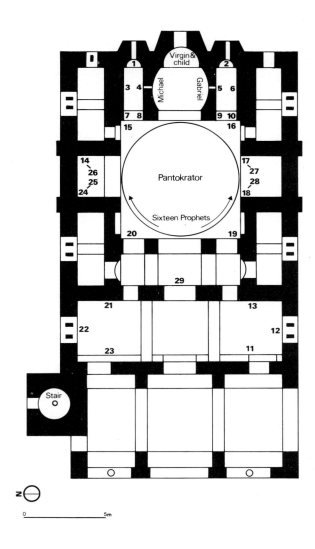

Daphni, porch S. side: the prayer of Joachim answered (detail)

eighteen scenes, five are taken from apocryphal stories of her childhood and
death. The source of the former is early, the 2C *Book of James*, which tells in detail
of her childhood. These stories of the Virgin were very popular in the east, and
later in the west, but they were suppressed at the Reformation by Catholics and
Protestants alike and the legends are little known today. Here, as a prelude to the
gospels, the Virgin's childhood decorates half the inner porch, the original
entrance of the church. There is no connexion between the subjects each side of
the door, and the unity of theme in Holy Luke is lacking. The first picture on the
right shows angels announcing the good news of Mary's future birth to her
childless parents, Joachim and Anna. Her father is seated before a hut of boughs
in a desert place; her mother at home, standing in her garden beside an elaborate
fountain with a nest of birds in a bush behind it. This double picture is one of great
charm, and has in it landscape elements that are very rare in Byzantine art.
Joachim's angel is a figure of classical beauty. The next scene is fragmentary,
showing her parents carrying the infant Mary to be blessed by the priests. The
third is her Presentation in the Temple, a very popular subject. Her parents are

bringing the three-year-old child, escorted by girls carrying candles, to the High Priest to be brought up in the Temple in Jerusalem, shown as a Christian sanctuary. (This was not a Jewish practice.) Mary walks forward with open arms, and is shown a second time seated high up within the Holy of Holies being fed by an angel. The three scenes at the other end of the porch are concerned with the events of Maundy Thursday, a prelude to the Passion: The Last Supper, the Washing of the feet, and the Betrayal.

In a centralised, domed church it is natural for the sequence of scenes to be arranged horizontally, and viewed by turning round and round. Already in the 9C the Patriarch Photios points this out, in a sermon on the earliest and most influential of Middle Byzantine churches in the imperial palace in Constantinople: 'the spectator is obliged to turn about in all directions by the colourful spectacle on all sides.'

At Daphni the whole cycle of the life of the Virgin can be read through in the scenes in the highest zone, starting with her Birth in the upper picture of the north transept, then, in the north-east squinch, The Annunciation. High in the apse, and much damaged, is the cult figure of the Virgin and Child enthroned, with archangels on the side walls. Next, in the south-east squinch, is the Nativity of Christ in a cave with the angels and shepherds, and, separately, the Adoration of the Magi high up on the wall of the south transept. Opposite, now lost, was the Presentation of Christ in the Temple. Completing the circle, on the west wall of the nave, is a large mosaic of the Dormition of the Virgin, the patronal feast of the church. Missing from the centre is the figure of Christ standing behind her bier, in the midst of the apostles, holding the soul of his Mother as a swaddled child. This closes the cycle of the life of the Virgin, the last Feast of the Church's year.

The cycle of Christ's Incarnation begins with the Annunciation, and, after the other childhood scenes, moves in the west squinches to the Baptism and Transfiguration, the manifestations of his Godhead at the beginning and the end of his ministry. The events of the Passion are gathered on the north side of the church, in the porch (see above) and, in the north transept, the Raising of Lazarus, where the inscription only survives, above an animated Palm Sunday, facing a calm and moving Crucifixion. Small flowers grow out of the rock of Calvary. The south transept in its lower pictures balance this with the usual triumphant Resurrection scenes, the Harrowing of Hell, with Christ trampling on Satan bound, and John the Baptist prominent amongst the dead, his forerunner in death as in life. (The Orthodox call him John the Forerunner.) Opposite is the Convincing of Thomas (Christ's head restored), with Christ blessing his disciples and future believers.

Over all these narrative scenes, in the great dome, is the awe-inspiring, majestic head of Christ Pantokrator (Almighty), Creator, Ruler of the Universe and Judge of all, 'He who is, and was and is to come'. It is in this image that the eastern emphasis on Christ's divinity contrasts most strongly with that of western Christendom on his humanity. Yet, though the gaze is so stern, the right hand is raised in blessing, the left hand holds the Gospels,—the story of his life on earth.

Round the drum, in pairs, are fourteen Old Testament prophets and two kings, David and Solomon, included for their prophecies in the Psalms and the Book of Wisdom, all holding open scrolls with parts of short texts believed to relate to Christ's kingdom.

As was customary, figures of bishops and deacons are grouped in, or close to, the sanctuary. Two Old Testament priests, Aaron and Zacharias, holding large incense boxes, like miniature churches, have been moved outside the side chapels and placed on the side walls. At the west end are a number of heads and busts of martyrs, including several military saints. They all hold small crosses, and do not have special attributes, as in the west, as their names are inscribed beside them.

A folk-song about Daphni runs:

> Our Lady of the golden bay trees, great is your joy
> With the mosaics, the rule, and the pearl.
>
> At Kaisariani they walk to and fro, and at Pendeli there is honey,
> And at Daphni is cool water drunk by the angels.

There is a well inside and outside the high walls of the monastery.

PATMOS

Patmos, the northernmost of the Dodecanese group, is a small, volcanic, much indented island (*c.* 35km²), almost split in the middle by two bays. The port, Skala, is in the east bay near the isthmus, and above it to the south towers the great fortress monastery of St John, a castle in excellent state of repair, with the village, Khora, of gleaming whitewashed houses clustered round its foot.

The island receives only a passing mention by Thucydides and Strabo and ancient remains are scanty. At Kastelli, on the ridge near the isthmus, are the acropolis walls, remains of three towers and, at the north end, a small chapel on the paved site of a temple. The island was one of several sparsely inhabited ones used by the Romans as a place of exile. Here, at some time during the late 1C AD, an obscure exile saw a vision which brought it world fame: 'I John, who am also your brother and companion in tribulation . . . was in Patmos, for the word of God and for the testimony of Jesus Christ.' (*Revelation* 1;9). The identification of this John with St John the Evangelist, also called by the Greeks the Theologian, is no longer universally accepted. The style is totally different from that of the Gospel and Epistle. The author wrote to the churches in Asia Minor at a time of persecution, to encourage them to stand fast, prophesying that the end of the world was near. The 'Acts of John by Prochoros', traditionally his secretary, is an apocryphal 5C work, largely concerned with miracles on Patmos, locally popular stories, some illustrated in the porch of the monastery. A cave chapel, of St Anne, and the seminary above it, halfway up the hill to the monastery, are called 'of the Apocalypse'. Curiously, Prochoros says that John wrote his Gospel in the cave and there is no mention of writing the Apocalypse there. Much later ikons follow this tradition and show the old St John seated in the cave with the young

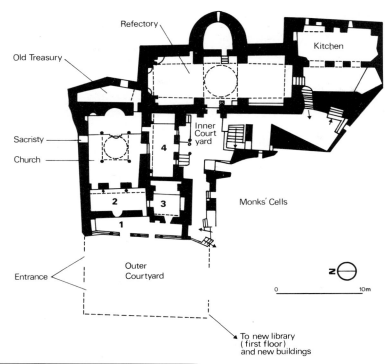

Refectory

Kitchen

Old Treasury

Sacristy

Church

Inner Court yard

4

2   3

Monks' Cells

Entrance

Outer Courtyard

1

0   10m

To new library
(first floor)
and new buildings

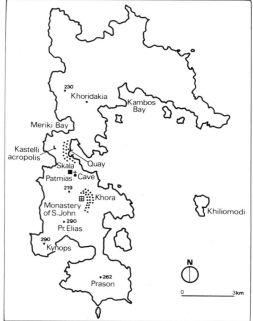

Monastery of St John Patmos
Ground plan of early buildings.
1 Outer porch
2 Inner porch
3 Founder's tomb
4 Chapel of the Virgin

Khoridakia · 230

Kambos Bay

Meriki Bay

Kastelli acropolis

Skala

Quay

Patmias · Cave

· 219

Khora

Monastery of S. John

· 290
Pr. Elias

290
· Kynops

· 262
Prason

Khiliomodi

N

0   3km

left Patmos

Prochoros 'taking down' the first words of the Gospel, and a basket of stationery (scrolls) between them.

In the 5–6CC, churches were built on the island; early architectural fragments, capitals and columns have been re-used in the monastery and later churches. The representative of the emperor Alexios Comnenos wrote of 'a little chapel in honour of the Theologian built, as the ruins make clear, in the middle of an immense and older church on the summit of the highest mountain.'

From the 7–11CC the island, like many others, was deserted owing to the raids of Saracen pirates. It suddenly comes to life again at the end of the 11C through the initiative of one man, St Christodoulos, who lived both as a hermit and an abbot. He was born in a village near Nicaea of farming stock, and lived for many years in solitary places in Asia Minor, Palestine, Kos, Patmos and Euboea. He was specially attracted to Patmos by its tradition and isolation. He wrote, 'My one desire was to possess this island', to set up 'a school of virtue.' He was a man of character and exerted influence on the emperor Alexios and the Patriarch. He went to the court, offered his lands on Kos and in Caria and obtained a charter (chrysobul) signed by the emperor granting him Patmos, and the right for the monastery and island 'to be independent and self-governing for ever'. Two more charters dealt with practical matters: he was guaranteed the free use of a ship for himself and the needs of the monastery, and exemption from all taxes. All three are dated 1088 and are kept in the monastic library.

When Christodoulos and his companions landed on Patmos it did not seem a desirable place: 'It is deserted, fallen into waste, covered with brambles and thorny scrub and because of its aridity totally infertile.' Christodoulos fell to work, and wrote, 'We began at once to lay foundations and raise the walls; we had only one desire, that of fortifying ourselves with the briefest possible delay and of raising as powerful ramparts as our strength allowed.' The difficulties were too much for his companions and taking Christodoulos with them they left for Euboea, where he died in 1093, after commanding them to return to Patmos. Surprisingly, they did. The early days were very trying and it was only by perseverance and the support of the emperor and Patriarch that his successors finally established the monastery. By the end of the 12C there were 150 monks there.

The founder's desire that the monastery should be fortified was carried out and it rose as a fortress, with vertical walls, towers and a bastion over the entrance, which originally had a heavy iron-covered gate and machicolations. The steep glacis and buttresses were added later during one of many improvements and repairs. At first the monks obliged their lay workers to live in the monastery during the week and return only at the weekends to their families, kept far away at Khoridakia in the north, so that no monk should see the women. But a 12C abbot, aware of danger from pirates in the summer, instructed: 'From the beginning of May never allow any soldier or islander to return home; let them come to the monastery and remain there to protect it; supply all bastions with stones, keep unfailing watch; fight with all your hearts,—to be pleasing to God and to ourselves.' So might a Grand Master have written to his knights. Later the rule about the families was relaxed and the peasants built a fortified village pressed up against the monastic fortress.

In the 13–15CC large estates on many of the Aegean islands, and as far away as Zante in the western sea, were bestowed on the monastery. Patmos became a centre of pilgrimage and trade such as Delos had been in antiquity. Its ships sailed everywhere from Italy to the Black Sea, under the flag of the Knights of St John. The abbots established good diplomatic relations with them and a succession of Popes, and with Venice—a rare achievement. The civilian population also prospered, and in the 16–17CC successful merchants built some fine houses, and gave their wives charming ship pendants of gold, silver and enamel, some of which are kept in the Treasury. In 1659 the Doge Morosini ravaged the island, but the monastic treasures were kept safe. The Turks (1537–1912) subjected it to fairly heavy taxes, but gave protection from barbary pirates.

In 1713 a Theological Seminary, the Patmias, was built on the hillside below the monastery. It attracted students from all over Greece, the Balkans, Austria and Russia, who returned to build up centres of Greek culture in their own countries. Its influence was considerable, since a number of the intellectuals in the movement for Greek Independence studied there, among them Emmanuel Xanthos, founder of the Philike Etaireia ('Society of Friends'), an undercover organization promoting Greek national aims as well as cultural activities. The Patmias School appeared to a foreign scholar in the 18C 'for the unhappy Greeks under the Turkish yoke what Athens had been for the ancient Greeks'. Poor students were given scholarships. The full course took seven years and comprised many other subjects besides theology.

Patmos, which had been free since the beginning of the War of Independence, was handed back to Turkey by treaty in 1832, taken by the Italians in 1912 and only united with Greece in 1947.

The monastery is a polygonal castle with the buildings inside huddled up against its walls, connected by arcades, passages and stairs, and receiving light and air from courtyards. The main courtyard outside the church is a pleasant place, usually brightened by potted plants. There is a large cistern under it. All the water collected from the winter rain is stored in cisterns. The cellars are beneath the south arcade, where corn and wine were stored, entrusted to a monk, 'who shall be chosen from amongst the most pious and most experienced, and shall have a special aptitude for the work.' The wine was kept sealed in the care of a monk, 'of sober and strong character.' The monks' cells, still in use, are upstairs opposite the entrance and in the inner courtyard. Originally the monks lived a communal life, according to the founder's intention, but later they chose to eat and live by themselves, except for worship, like the Carthusians, and as they do now.

The main church was built in the 12C, a cross-in-square, with the dome resting on four columns, two behind the ikon screen. There are two porches, whose doors and some of the frescoes are 17C; others are later. Small doors lead from each porch into the chapel with the tomb of the founder. The nave is dominated by a bulky and ornate ikon-screen. The oldest ikon, near the door, is a framed half-figure of St John, possibly late 11C, but it has suffered repainting. A number of ikons are signed by well-known 17C painters. The small treasury containing reliquaries, censers and candlesticks behind the sanctuary is not open to the public. The south door of the church leads to the light, uncluttered chapel of the Virgin, which has the earliest, 12C frescoes. In the apse, behind the screen, is the usual figure of the Virgin and Child, enthroned between archangels in court dress. Above, in the conch, the three angels entertained by Abraham (*Genesis* 18;1–8) are seated round a table with three loaves and a large bowl on it. This is a normal Orthodox symbol of the Trinity and is so inscribed here. It is also a prefiguration of the Eucharist. On the walls are Christ with the Samaritan Woman and some of his miracles, and in the lowest part standing saints. The south door leads to an inner courtyard with the refectory along the east side, a large, rectangular, barrel-vaulted room, with two long marble tables down the centre. They have decorated recesses along the sides to hold the monks' plates and cutlery. On the walls are two layers of frescoes, 12C and 13C, showing the Passion and Resurrection, the Communion of the Apostles, the Miracle of the Loaves and Fishes, and a second scene of Abraham entertaining the angels, where the emphasis is on the meal. The south door leads to the kitchen at a lower level.

A stair on the west side of the monastery leads to the magnificent Library and Treasury. Christodoulos himself created the library and impressed upon his followers the need to preserve and add to it. By the year 1200 it had 330 volumes. The earliest catalogue of both Library and Treasury dates from 1201, a rare survival from Byzantine times. There are later 14C ones. The monastery lent books to its own dependencies and other religious foundations. The list of borrowers shows how widespread was its influence.

The Library now contains between 800–900 MSS, more than 2000 early printed books and 13,000 documents concerned with the history of the monastery. The oldest MS is the 6C Gospel of St Mark, written on purple vellum in silver and gold (thirty-three leaves, the rest mainly in Leningrad, and a few elsewhere). Next is the 8C Book of Job with commentaries, and the Discourses of St Gregory Nazianzene, written in south Italy in 941. There are a number of splendid illuminated MSS. The Library also possesses a number of classical texts, some acquired in the 14C. The Treasury contains a collection of fine embroidered vestments, ecclesiastical jewelry and carved work, and more than 200 ikons. Among these is the rare miniature mosaic ikon of St Nikolas, between medallions of Christ and the Virgin, mentioned in the first catalogue, in a partly contemporary frame; a fine St Theodore the Recruit, in the fanciful Roman armour of Byzantine warrior saints, the half figure of St James, both 13C; and many noteworthy later ones.

The roof of the monastery is on several different levels. The view from here over the whole of the island and out to sea with its scatter of rocks and islands is breathtaking.

2 The Franks and later Byzantines

KARYTENA

The crusaders, after their disastrous sack of Constantinople, divided Greece into baronies, under the Dukes of Athens, the Princes of Achaia in the Morea (Peloponnese) and later the Dukes of Naxos in the islands. They built their castles often upon ancient defensive positions, though in greatly inferior masonry, but sometimes, as at Mistra, upon new points of vantage. Greece is strewn with crusader castles, and even five centuries after their departure, any western visitors

Karytena

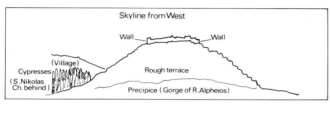

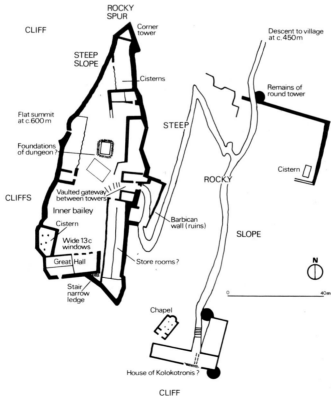

in some country places are still referred to by Greek peasants as 'Franks'. They have left their mark. As an example, we include one of the most romantically sited of these castles: Karytena in south-west Arcadia, crowning the summit of an isolated rocky hill, *c.* 600m high, surrounded by mountains. It is a formidable place, inevitably recalling the line, 'Childe Rowland to the dark tower came'. It is triangular in shape, built upon steep and, in parts, actually overhanging rocks, in a splendid position of defence against raiding Slavs from the gorges. Some scholars believe it to have been first a refugee settlement from the neighbouring Gortyna, and Karytena a corruption of that name. It was soon, in 1209, the capital of a large barony, but the castle we see was not built until 1254 by Hugh de Bruyères. His son, Geoffrey I, 'le sire de Caritaine', was renowned as a pattern of chivalry amongst his contemporaries, and his deeds recounted with a certain sympathy in the Greek *Chronicle of the Morea*. A modern novel, Alfred Duggan's *Lord Geoffrey's Fancy*, is based upon it. The castle passed by sale to the Byzantines under Andronikos II in 1320, who gave it to the rich monastery of Aphendiko at Mistra. It towers superbly above the village and the 12C Byzantine church of St Nikolaos and a loop of the Alpheios, where a six-arched mediaeval bridge, with Frankish inscriptions, still crosses the ravine beside its modern successor. A steep path, passing a small chapel of the Virgin, climbs to the single gate, with slot for the portcullis. Thence a vaulted tunnel leads into the inner bailey. There are considerable remains of a vaulted hall and gallery with Gothic windows. The water supply was from deep rock-cut cisterns, which still yawn, dangerously concealed by tall weeds and bushes.

In the War of Independence Kolokotronis, the brigand hero of the Morea, took refuge in Karytena from Ibrahim Pasha, and his house built over a bastion is still shown. He was never attacked here.

MISTRA

The hill of Mistra, a foothill of Taygetos, was not fortified in antiquity: Sparta spurned walls. Only in 1249 did William II de Villehardouin, the Frankish baron, build a castle on its summit. He was obliged to cede this, his 'most beautiful castle' (*Chronicle of the Morea*), to the Byzantines in 1262 as part of his ransom after three years' captivity. It became the HQ of the Byzantine generals for the recovery of the Morea. The emperor John VI Cantacuzene (1347–54) made Mistra its capital ruled by a governor, called the Despot, usually a son or brother of the emperor. Unlike Thessalonica, Mistra flourished for barely two centuries; but it became an important centre of intellectual life and artistic achievement. The Platonist George (*c.* 1355–1450), nicknamed Gemistos, or Plethon ('bung full'), lived and taught here for some of his long life. By his visit to Florence, and that of his pupil Bessarion, who became a Cardinal, he considerably influenced Renaissance thought, reviving the study of Plato after centuries dominated by Aristotle.

Mistra is important also for the developments in architecture and wall-painting which took place in this final phase of the Byzantine empire, at the time when Constantinople itself was little more than an island in a sea of Islam.

The hill of Mistra

The last two Despots surrendered Mistra to the Turks without fighting in 1460, and it became the seat of the Turkish governor, except during the Venetian occupation (1687–1715). In a rising in 1770 the Greeks massacred the Turkish inhabitants and in turn suffered reprisals. Ibrahim Pasha destroyed the Lower Town in 1825, in the War of Independence. The survivors moved down into the plain, to the site of ancient Sparta, and Mistra was left to fall into ruins. Much restoration has now been carried out.

Numerous small churches are scattered over the hill, many of them simple family chapels. Four of the larger churches are important for the last phase of Byzantine art. In architecture and painting there is a parallel development in complication and multiplication of detail. In the former there is a fusion of a three-aisled basilica ground plan with a cross-in-square roof. Small domes multiply round the central one, their edges curving in wavy lines over double-recessed

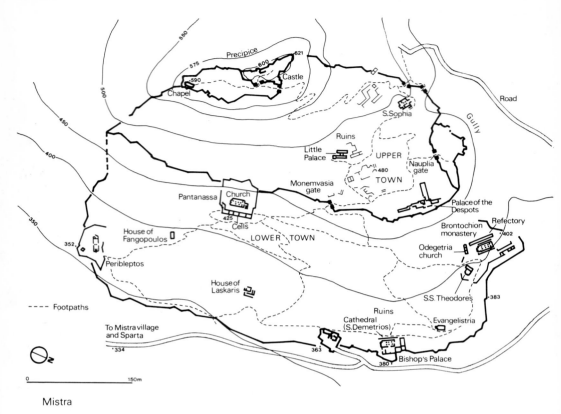

Mistra

windows. Inside are women's galleries and additional chapels placed at the corners of the church, an innovation to hold tombs of the Despots and abbots. Open porticos are added on one or two sides, and belfries, under western influence. All this could give a fussy impression, but the churches of Mistra are well proportioned and are able to carry these developments with grace. In painting there is the same tendency to elaboration, not always an improvement. The well-known scenes become increasingly crowded with 'extras' against backgrounds of fantastic architecture. People peer out of windows onto the main scene. Sometimes irrelevant but picturesque little *genre* elements are introduced. Classical monumentality and restraint and the ability to highlight the essential has gone almost everywhere, but a new liveliness, even humanism, replaces it. Colours show a great range of shades, some very delicate. Byzantine art is capable of a development that used to be denied.

The earliest churches are those of the Lower Town. First is the Cathedral of St Demetrios, in which the last emperor, Constantine XI, after nine years as Despot, received his only coronation, in 1449, perhaps on the spot where a relief of the double-headed eagle is set into the floor. Four years later he died fighting by the walls of Constantinople. This small cathedral stands in a walled courtyard with the remains of a modest bishop's palace. It is of the type described above, but here the roof and domes are a later, probably 15C addition, since they have cut off the upper part of some of the frescoes. These depict the miracles of Christ and the life of St Demetrios, and a Last Judgment on the west wall of the narthex. The most impressive fresco here is on the vault of the small south niche of the sanctuary. The ancient, abstract symbol of the Trinity, the empty Throne of God, with Christ's Cross and Gospel-book and the Dove of the Holy Spirit, is shown here against a white, star-edged halo of glory, borne by six adoring angels, whose movement enlivens this normally static subject. The marble beam of the ikon screen and arched frames for the principal ikons are good examples of the intricacy of Byzantine stone carving.

Beyond the small funerary chapel of the Evangelistria, in a large enclosure at the north-east corner of the site, is the monastery of Brontochion, the richest of all, the burial place of the Despots, who endowed it with much land and secured its coveted independence from the local bishop. There are two large churches here, among ruined monastic buildings. The first is dedicated to the two warrior saints Theodore, and the only wide-domed one in Mistra, among the latest of its kind (end of the 13C). Slightly later (c. 1310) is the Virgin the Guide, the Odegetria, also called Aphendiko ('lordly'), built from the first as a basilica with six domes, corner chapels, two porticos and a belfry. The walls have been stripped of their marble veneer. Amongst the surviving frescoes in the sanctuary is an array of full-length figures of bishops in vestments with large black crosses. They are well-known Fathers of the Eastern Church, but include in their ranks Pope Leo of Rome. In the narthex are miracles of Christ and his meeting at the well with the woman of Samaria. In the north-west chapel, where Theodore II Palaiologos is buried, below a damaged fresco showing him in his two roles of Despot and monk, is the most colourful fresco remaining: a group of martyrs in gaily coloured, embroidered cloaks. On the walls of the opposite chapel are inscribed the charters relating to the constitution of the monastery, and lists of its estates.

Chronologically, the next church of importance is the Peribleptos (mid-14C), at the south end of the site. It is pressed hard up against the rock face and is not a regular rectangle. The entrance is from the north. Architecturally it is the simplest of the churches, with a single dome, the only one in which a Pantokrator survives. Inside, it is the best preserved painted church in Mistra, decorated all over from the saints near our own level, just above the floor, to the vaults above. All the standard scenes from the gospels are here, high up on the walls and vaults. On the south side is an extended Passion cycle, and on the north the childhood of the Virgin, expanded into twenty-one miniature scenes. Noteworthy amongst the Gospel scenes is the Nativity, with the recumbent Virgin dominating the complex Christmas story, full of small figures in a landscape of stylized jagged rocks; the Transfiguration, a calm and noble Christ standing out against a complicated geometric halo; a joyous Entry into Jerusalem with a large welcoming crowd. The final scenes of the festal cycle are placed round the door: Thomas, Pentecost and an elaborate Dormition, full of detail, including the airborne arrival of the apostles on clouds to the Virgin's deathbed. In the apse the Ascension is on the vault, above the Communion of the Apostles. It is fully decorated with scenes relating to the liturgy.

The finest frescoes in this church are in the north chamber of the sanctuary. They illustrate the Divine Liturgy, celebrated by Christ, the Great High Priest, standing vested as an Orthodox bishop behind an altar, attended by angel deacons and acolytes enacting the procession of the Great Entry, the start of the most solemn part of the Orthodox Eucharist. They are clothed in white and some carry on their heads the chalice and paten under stiff embroidered cloths. They have about them a classic serenity rare at this time.

The last important church is that of the Pantanassa (the Virgin, Queen of All) convent, the most conspicuous, standing out in the middle of the site, and the only one in use today. It is also the latest. Though it was founded in the middle of the 14C, it was restored by a noble, John Frangopoulos, in 1428, and the paintings belong to this restoration. The architecture is basically that of the Odegetria, but it has even more domes, seven, as well as a conical one on the four-storey belfry. Western influence begins to appear in the trefoil patterns on the belfry and relief patterns of pointed arches and fleur-de-lys terminals on the outside wall of the apse. Two of the Palaiologue Despots married noble Italian ladies, and there was coming and going between Mistra and Italy in the 15C. The arcaded portico is another western feature. The view from it over 'the lovely vale of Sparta' to the Parnon range is magnificent.

Surviving frescoes show increased complication of detail. The Nativity is almost rococo in the restless swirling lines of the rock edges. The Triumphal Entry, near the east end, has a whole *genre* scene in the foreground, a well-house on one side, a well on the other, and children romping between. In a vault of a gallery is a graceful Annunciation, with a charming detail of a partridge drinking from a little fountain at the feet of the main figures. In the opposite gallery is perhaps the most dramatic Raising of Lazarus surviving. The detail of the man holding his cloak over his nose to keep out the smell of the corpse is quite common, but it is most realistically shown here.

Higher up the hill is the church of the Holy Wisdom (St Sophia) near the palace, the church of the nobles. It has two domes, corner chapels and belfry. In the apse is a fresco of Christ, Giver of Life. It is here that the Italian ladies are said to have been buried.

Mistra is also important for Byzantine secular buildings, since few survive elsewhere. The great ruined Palace of the Despots dominates the north side of the hill, the most extensive building on the site. It has been added to at different times. The Turks used to hold a market in the middle of it. Several partly ruined houses of noble families survive and the whole hillside is covered with crumbling walls of more ordinary ones.

The castle on the summit is largely Frankish work, but restored and added to by Byzantines and Turks. The view down the precipitous west side and into the great range of Taygetos is superb.

The spell of Mistra was still potent to hold Goethe, when, in Faust, Part II, he chose it as the meeting place of the Fair Helen, awakened from her three thousand years' sleep in Sparta, and the mediaeval knight Faust, and the place where their fair, short-lived son, Euphorion, was born and died.

MONEMVASIA

Monemvasia is a precipitous, rocky, Gibraltar-like island off the south-east Peloponnese, rising about 200m high and about a mile long, joined to the mainland only by a narrow causeway. It takes its name from its single entrance (*Mone embasis*), and gives it to the wine Malvoisie, Malmsey, known throughout Europe in the Middle Ages. It was earlier one of several places called Minoa, suggesting a Cretan connexion, but there is neither written nor archaeological evidence for its occupation in antiquity. Greek mainland refugees from Slav invaders appear to have been the first to settle on the rock in the 6C. In 1147 an attack by Normans of Sicily was repulsed. William de Villehardouin took it through famine after a three-year siege, in 1248, and gave the inhabitants honourable terms. It was one of his three great fortresses in the Morea which he was obliged to cede to Michael Palaiologos in 1262. It then became the seat of the Byzantine Governor of the Morea, tenth see of the empire, and an important commercial capital. The famous wine exported from there came mainly from Crete and various Aegean islands. There is a mediaeval *Chronicle of Monemvasia* which, in spite of its unknown date and authorship, is now more widely respected than it once used to be.

The most important Byzantine building on the rock is the cathedral of the Holy Wisdom, St Sophia, founded by Andronikos II (1287–1328), and built on a precipitous cliff in the Upper Town. It is the latest of the Greek wide-domed churches supported on squinches. It is built of squared stone and thin bricks, and has marble lintels in the narthex and a heraldic animal relief, like those on St Eleutherios in Athens. Some faded frescoes survive from under the covering of Turkish whitewash. The outer arched porch is a Venetian addition. In the inner south wall is a Turkish *mihrāb*, the prayer niche facing towards Mecca.

The castle keep, the fortifications and massive curtain walls joining the Upper and Lower Towns, the scatter of ruined buildings above and crumbling houses below, belong to the late occupations by the Venetians and the Turks. Both upper and lower gates with tunnel entrances preserve their massive iron-bound doors.

In the Lower Town the large basilica, with pointed nave arches, founded also by Andronikos, was considerably altered by the Venetians. It is called after its unusual ikon of Christ Bound, the Elkomenos.

From 1460–4 the rock became the brief possession of the Pope, Pius II, but he was quite unable to defend it, and it passed to the Venetians, for whom it was an important link in their chain of trading posts in Greece, Crete and Cyprus. They held it until 1540, and again in 1690–1715. Between and after these dates it was occupied by the Turks until the Greek uprising of 1821. The fortress, one of the last to surrender to the Turks, was the first to be freed. Five ships from Hydra arrived off the rock and nearly 1000 Maniotes, from the Matapan peninsula, who boasted that they had never submitted to the Turks, came by land. After the usual famine of a siege and the heroic exploits of three Greek Monemvasiotes, who swam under fire out to the ships as they prepared to sail away, with the news of the conditions to which the enemy was reduced, the Turks surrendered to Demetrios Hypsilantis in August 1821.

The inhabitants of this towering rock lived by, or preyed on, trade. It was alternately an important commercial centre and a nest of pirates. Its history is of periods of prosperity punctuated by months of grim siege.

In April 1941, four thousand New Zealand soldiers under General Freyberg VC were evacuated from Monemvasia to fight again in the battle of Crete.

THE METEORA

Towering above the country town of Kalabaka in western Thessaly, the Meteora ('Up in the air') monasteries are perched upon fantastic conglomerate rock pillars of various shapes, which rise in a menacing cluster from the plain of the Peneios river. This geological formation is mysterious. The way of life led on these eyries was almost as eccentric as that of the pillar saints in Syria 900 years earlier. The problem of how the first hermits ever scaled these sheer rock faces is solved by the holes in the rocks which must have been made to take beams for scaffolding. Even so, the ascent, the building of the monasteries, and the hazardous methods of descent must have presented many quick routes to heaven for those who fell off in their pious endeavours.

In the 14C this region was a disturbed frontier area between the Byzantine empire and the rising Vlacho-Serbian power. As early as the 12C it was called Great Wallachia because of the number of Roumanian speakers there. Refugees and hermits found retreats in the caves before community life developed. The earliest monastery was of the Virgin Doupiani, before 1336. Before 1400 other monasteries were founded, all of the communal (coenobitic) type. At its most developed there were fourteen monasteries and twenty smaller settlements. Many were endowed by the Serbian rulers of Thessaly and received revenues from estates on the Danube. In the 16C the Patriarch Jeremias I (1522–45) granted several monasteries the desirable status of dependence on Constantinople alone. By the 18C decline had set in, and even earlier some had been deserted. In the 19C they began to excite the curiosity of some intrepid western travellers, including Colonel Leake, and Robert Curzon, who in his *Visits to Monasteries in the Levant* gives a vivid account of his experiences here in the autumn of 1834. He was subjected to the full horrors of ascent by long rickety ladders, and being hauled up and let down in a net which spun violently round and round as the monks turned

Monemvasia, cathedral of St. Sophia

the rope round the capstan on their platform at the top. Now cement steps and a balustrade protect the visiting tourists who arrive comfortably on a well-made road. Very few monks survive, and isolation from the world has vanished.

The largest monastery, on the 'Broad Rock', is the Great Meteoron (534m high) dedicated to The Transfiguration of the Saviour. It was founded as a poor community by the hermit St Athanasios, but in 1362 the Serbian emperor Symeon Uros guaranteed it privileges, and under his son John, who retired there in 1372 as the monk Joasaph, it became rich. The main church was restored at his expense in 1387–8. The frescoes are a hundred years later and well preserved. The church was enlarged after an earthquake in 1544.

The monastic buildings of the Meteora follow the usual pattern, though adapted to the ground available. The main church may have additional chapels, there is a refectory and cells for the monks, occasionally a small garden. The frescoes are mainly late, post-Byzantine. To the regular Gospel scenes, corresponding to the Feasts of the Church, are added concepts such as 'The Ancient of Days', and 'Christ the Angel of Good Counsel', as well as vivid illustrations of the horror stories of martyrdoms and, in the porches, the Last Judgment with the manifold tortures of the damned.

The Meteora

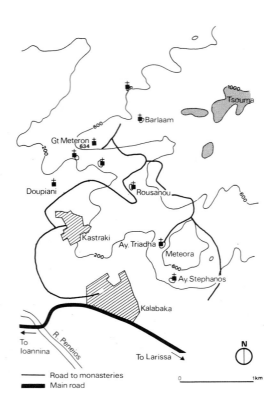

St Stephen's, Meteora. River Peneios in background

In the ravine between the Great Meteoron and the monastery of Barlaam is the highest rock of all, dedicated to the Virgin, 'the Highest in Heaven', now abandoned; but two ikons in rock niches and broken lengths of ladders bear witness to its former habitation. It was founded *c.* 1390 and given up in the 17C, probably owing to the extreme peril of the ascent by a ladder of 100 rungs.

Barlaam was called after a 14C hermit who built a church there dedicated to SS Basil, Gregory and John Chrysostom, which fell into ruins. It was refounded by the brothers Nektarios and Theophanes Asparas of Ioannina, who restored it as a side-chapel of the main church of All Saints, built in 1542–4. The date is inscribed on the wall. The carved ikon screen and frescoes are signed. The rope, net and windlass in a tower bearing the date 1536 were in use again for hauling up building materials for considerable restoration work in 1961–3. One of the surviving monks sells tickets and postcards, and a ferocious lay brother measures the length of women's skirts before admitting them.

The small monastery of Rousanou (spelt in five different ways), on a lower rock below Barlaam, was founded before 1545 by other monks from Ioannina, and later became subject to Barlaam. It has recently been reoccupied by nuns.

Ayia Triadha (Holy Trinity), on an isolated rock pillar between two ravines, is now approached by 130 steps, partly through a tunnel. The little church of 1476, dated by an inscribed tile, has been spoilt by the addition of a large, ugly narthex (1684). It has a pretty garden. It is *c.* 43m from the ground and a Swedish traveller in the 18C estimated that the ascent in a net took four minutes and the descent two.

St Stephen's, a little further on, with a good view over the Peneios valley, has the least laborious access, by a bridge across a chasm 30m deep. It was founded *c.* 1400 by Antonios Cantacuzene (probably the son of Nikephoros II, ruler, [Despot] of Epiros). The new church, rebuilt in 1798, is dedicated to the martyr St Charalambos, whose head is a revered relic. It also is now a nunnery.

Kalabaka, ancient Aiginion, was called Stagoi or Stagous ('at the saints') in registers dating from about 900, so this cannot refer, as is commonly stated, to the colony of monks who settled so much later on the heights above. Among its churches the Cathedral has a foundation inscription of the Emperor Manuel I Comnenos (mid-12C). It is dedicated to the Dormition of the Virgin and is an aisled basilica standing on earlier foundations, with some mosaics below the floor of the sanctuary. The rows of semi-circular benches for the clergy round the apse, the marble canopy over the altar, and the pulpit are all from the earlier church. The pulpit, with its long, slanting steps and fine panels of marble carved in relief, is a very rare example of this early type surviving in Greece. Near the sanctuary some of the frescoes are 12C, the others date from the 16C restoration.

MOUNT ATHOS

The monasteries of Mount Athos are not treated in this book. The Holy Mountain is an independent theocratic state and visitors are limited to men only, who must have obtained special permits through their consuls from the Ministry of Foreign Affairs. Additional letters of introduction from the Archbishop of Athens or the Metropolitan of Thessalonica are helpful.

RHODES OF THE KNIGHTS

Rhodes, capital of the Dodecanese, originally held three city states, Ialysos in the north-west, Kameiros in the west and Lindos, which had the largest territory, in the east. They are mentioned in Homer (*Iliad*, ii, 656) as sending nine ships to Troy. Both Ialysos and Kameiros had rich Mycenaean cemeteries. The cities carried on a flourishing trade, especially with Egypt. Each minted its own coinage, Kameiros first in the 6C. They became subject to the Persians, and then joined the Athenian League. In 412–11 they broke with Athens and helped the Spartans to defeat her.

In 408 the islanders united and built a new capital, Rhodes, on the northern tip. In its subsequent, chequered history, it followed a policy of appeasement of the 'great powers' in the Mediterranean, in order to protect its trade. In the wars of Alexander's successors it was long loyal to Egypt, to which it traded wine for corn. It survived a year's siege by Demetrios the Besieger who, when he withdrew, left his sophisticated siege engines. The Rhodians sold these, using the money for their world-famous statue, the bronze Colossos, Helios the sun-god, patron of the city. It was about 31 m high and stood for only sixty-six years; it broke at the knees in an earthquake in 226 and fell, causing great damage. It is unlikely that it ever bestrode the harbour mouth, as legend had it. Probably it stood on land near the later site of the church called St John 'of the Colossos'. Prostrate, it was a marvel to many. In the 7C AD the Arabs removed and sold the bronze. It was not the only Rhodian 'colossal' statue, but the largest and most famous. In the 2C BC there was a flourishing school of artists in Rhodes. The Laocoön, a signed work by three Rhodians, was taken to Rome (and admired by Michelangelo). At this time the island was, in general, a cultural centre second only to Athens. Philosophers and orators taught there and it attracted many famous Romans, including Lucretius, Cicero and Caesar.

St Paul only touched at Rhodes on his last journey to Jerusalem (*Acts* 21, 1), but by the 2C there was a Christian community with its own bishop.

The town of Rhodes was laid out on an up-to-date grid plan, and a number of the mediaeval streets follow the ancient ones. Foundations turn up from time to time after demolitions. Remains of a temple of Aphrodite lie near the Arsenal gate. On the acropolis to the west, on high ground called Mount Smith, after Admiral

Mediaeval Rhodes *c.* AD 1500

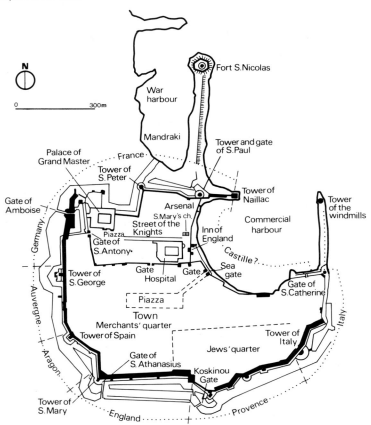

Sir Sidney Smith who lived there in 1802, are the over-restored temple of Pythian Apollo, a stadium and gymnasium.

The visible Rhodes is essentially the late mediaeval fortress town, the finest in Greece. It covers only a fraction of the ancient city; 48h (120 acres) compared with 700h, over 7km². The city walls were protected by every device known in the late 15C to early 16C. The town was divided in half, part left to the Greeks and part belonging to the Knights of the Order of St John of Jerusalem. In this stood the Grand Master's palace, or castle, largely rebuilt by the Italians during their occupation, the Arsenal, and the great Hospital, always the primary care of an Order founded originally as Hospitallers. They began in Jerusalem caring for sick pilgrims, but rapidly developed into a military order with discipline of 'Guards' quality. They were the last crusaders to leave Palestine, in 1291, after the fall of Acre. After fifteen years in Cyprus, they captured Rhodes (from the Greek Empire!) in 1308, after a two-year siege. They remained for 200 years, withstand-

Rhodes and Kos: Castles of the Knights

Rhodes of the Knights: the Sea Gate

ing two great sieges, in 1444 and 1480, when an Englishman, John Kendal, was commander of the archers. In 1522, when Turkish power was at its height, Suleiman I attacked Rhodes in force with heavy artillery and after six months the Knights, who had numbered 650, and with followers numbering only around 2000 men, were forced to surrender, but on honourable terms. One of the 180 survivors was La Valette, then aged twenty-eight. He later became Grand Master when the Knights had settled in Malta, and in 1565 successfully endured a siege as desperate as that of Rhodes. He was seventy at the time, a Churchillian character, who would never surrender.

The Knights were an international body who worked together in a community, but lived in national 'inns', or army messes, and were assigned specific reaches of the walls to defend. The Street of the Knights, above an ancient road, has a row of Inns with fairly plain exteriors, except for corbels, some gargoyles and mainly heraldic decoration. The French have three Inns, of France, Provence and Auvergne. The English Inn is separate, near the sea-gate. It was almost destroyed in 1850, but rebuilt to the original plan by an Englishman in 1919, and repaired by British forces in 1946–7. Near it is the Hospital, a large building with store-rooms below round an arched courtyard, and the main rooms upstairs. A large, airy ward occupies the east side, with a central chapel in a vaulted apse. It held thirty-two beds, with brocaded canopies, and the patients were served on hygienic silver plates. Two doctors were on duty at all times. Among the tomb slabs now preserved there is one of an Englishman, Thomas Newport, d. 1502. The hospital is now the archaeological museum.

The fortifications can best be studied from the plan, which shows the types of projecting tower developed for enfilading fire and the massive walls required to face artillery. The moat was in places over 40m wide, and had two ravelins or outworks.

The Knights continued the energetic policy of castle-building which they had pursued in Syria, and built and restored other castles in Rhodes at strategic points for coastal defence; Pharaklos, north of Lindos, originally Byzantine, was one of the strongest, and Monolithos, south of Kameiros, the most spectacular, perched on top of a precipitous rock 237m high with a single entry. They also fortified nearly all of the Dodecanese islands from Kastellorizo, 115km east of Rhodes, to Leros in the north.

Rhodes suffered over 400 years' occupation by the Turks and thirty-one (1912–1943) by the Italians. A force of Greek and British Commandos freed it from the Germans in 1945, and it was officially united to Greece in 1947, together with the rest of the Dodecanese.

Date Chart

(precise only after *c.* 600 BC)

BC 750,000	Palaeolithic men in Chalkidiki.
7000	Obsidian from Melos island used in Argolis.
6500	Agriculture in N. Greece.
3000	Metal-users from Asia in Crete and Cyclades.
2650	Early Minoan (Pre-Palace) culture in Crete.
2000	Middle Minoan (Early Palace) culture in Crete. Indo-European speakers on mainland?
1700	Second Palace period in Crete; Linear A writing (undeciphered).
1550	Rise of Mycenae.
1500–1450	Eruptions of Thera.
1450	Mycenaeans occupy Knossos? Linear B writing, read as Greek.
1400	Knossos palace destroyed (Cretan rebellion?). Mycenaean 'empire'? Warlike period (post-Palace in Crete).
1200	Widespread destruction on mainland. Impoverished Mycenae lasts till *c.* 1100. (1184, ancient computed date for the fall of Troy.) Dark Age. Refugee Greeks in Ionia (Asia Minor coast).
1000	Protogeometric pottery; *c.* 900–700 mature Geometric.
776	Ancient computed date for foundation of Olympic Games.
750?	Homer; *c.* 700 Hesiod. Greek mythology standardised.
7–6C	Colonisation in west and (later) Black Sea; Orientalising art; increasing wealth. Revolutions overthrow aristocracies in many trading cities. Personal poetry. Sparta rejects modernisation.
594–2	Solon modernises Athenian constitution. Rise of Athenian sculpture and vase-painting. Benevolent despotism of Peisistratos, finally stabilised 546–528.
546	Persia conquers Ionia; but Ionian philosophy flourishes unchecked.
508	Kleisthenes extends Athenian franchise to landless men and immigrants.
490	Athens repels Persians at Marathon.
480–79	Great Persian invasion.
478	Confederacy of Delos, becoming Athenian Empire. Age of Pericles. Classical buildings and drama. Pheidias.
431	Peloponnesian War begins.
404	Fall of Athens.
399	Execution of Socrates. Plato, 428–347. Aristotle, 384–322. Praxiteles.
371	Thebes defeats Sparta.

338	Philip of Macedon defeats Thebes and Athens (murdered 336).
335	Alexander destroys Thebes.
334–323	Alexander in Asia.
	Hellenistic Age: much Greek effort diverted to Alexandria, Syria, etc. New Comedy. Stoic and Epicurean moral philosophy.
280–75	Pyrrhos, King of Epeiros, fails to defeat Romans in Italy. Achaian and Aitolian federal Leagues, mutually hostile.
197	Romans defeat Philip V of Macedon and liberate Greece.
168	Romans destroy Macedonian kingdom and take 1000 Achaian hostages.
	Kings of Pergamos donate buildings to Athens.
146	Romans destroy Corinth and Achaian League; Province of Macedonia.
	'Cultural conquest' of Rome by Greece.
86	Athens sacked, Piraeus destroyed by Romans in war with Mithradates.
48, 42, 32–1	Roman civil wars fought out in Greece.
46	Caesar refounds Corinth as a Roman colony.
27	Province of Achaia. Athens a 'free' university-city. Augustan buildings.
AD 49–52	St Paul in Greece.
67	Nero visits Greece; plans Corinth canal.
c. 45–120	Plutarch.
117–38	Hadrian; his Gate and Olympieion.
mid-2C	Herodes' Theatre at Athens and monuments elsewhere.
c. 170	Pausanias' Guide-Book finished (up to Thermopylai).
267	Heruli sack Athens. 'Valerianic' wall built out of ruins.
324–37	Constantine removes many statues to Constantinople.
c. 355	SS Basil and Gregory Nazianzene, and Julian 'the Apostate', fellow-students at Athens.
395	Olympic Games suppressed.
	Many Christian basilica-churches.
529	Justinian (527–65) closes Athenian philosophic schools.
6–8C	Slavs settle in much of Greece.
mid-9C	Michael III subdues Slavs. Church of Skripou, 874.
823–969	Arabs occupy Crete, raid Aegean.
11C	Monastic mosaic-decorated churches (Holy Luke, Nea Moni, Daphni).
11–12C	Byzantine churches of Athens.
1080, 1147–9	Raids of Normans from Italy and Sicily.
1204	Fourth Crusade breaks up Byzantine empire. Venice takes Crete, Corfu, etc.
	Othon de la Roche, lord of Athens; Villehardouin princes in Peloponnese. Frankish castles.
1222	Byzantines of N. Greece recover Thessalonica.
1261	Michael VIII from Asia Minor recovers Constantinople.
1262	Michael VIII recovers part of Peloponnese, with Mistra.

1311   Catalan Company overthrows Franks and takes Athens. French and Italian Dukes of Athens.

1354   Turks enter Europe at Gallipoli.

1429   Turks take Thessalonica.

1430   Byzantines recover Peloponnese (Morea) from Venetians.

1453   Turks take Constantinople.

1460   Turks take Mistra.

1480   Turks repulsed at Rhodes by Knights of St John.

1522   Turks take Rhodes. Turco-Venetian wars. Venetian castles.

1571   Turks take Cyprus.

1669   Turks take Crete.

1687   Parthenon shattered in Venetian siege of Athens. Venetians hold Morea till 1715. Turks use Albanian soldiers.

1768   Disastrous Greek rising in Morea, encouraged by Russia. Greek Klephtic (resistance) ballads. Growth of Greek trade and folk art.

1821–31   Greek War of Independence. (1827, Battle of Navarino.)

1833–62   Otho of Bavaria King. Persistence of brigandry.

1864   George I (Prince of Denmark) King. Britain cedes western islands, gaining great popularity.

1866–9   Rebellion against Turks in Crete.

1881   Turkey cedes part of Thessaly, under western pressure.

1895–6   Rebellion in Crete; E. Venizelos among leaders. Crete given local autonomy but denied union with Greece.

1910   Venizelos Premier in Athens, works for Balkan alliance.

1912–13   Balkan Wars. Greece gains Macedonia, eastern islands, Crete.

1913   George I murdered by a lunatic.

1915   Constantine I refuses to support Serbia in World War I.

1917   Constantine I expelled by Allies; Greece under Venizelos joins allies, winning Aegean Thrace and Smyrna (1919).

1920   Greeks recall Constantine; allies withdraw support.

1922   Disaster in Asia Minor. Kemal forces exchange of populations.

1923–35   Republic, punctuated by coups.

1936   George II, restored, tries to support parliament but, faced by deadlock, supports dictatorship of Gen. Metaxas.

1940   Greeks defeat Italian invasion.

1941   Germans win Greece and Crete, driving out British forces.

1943–4   Communists try to monopolise internal resistance.

1944   Communists fight British in Athens.

1946   Royalist majority in elections. Rhodes and Dodecanese united to Greece by peace-treaty. Britain refuses to cede Cyprus.

1947–9   Second civil war, in the mountains.

1950–66   Parliamentary government and return of prosperity.

1967–74   Rule of military junta ('the Colonels').

1975   Second parliamentary republic.

For further reading

It is unfortunately impossible to give anything like a full bibliography in a book such as this. The most exhaustive work of reference is the *Princeton Encyclopaedia of Classical Sites* (omitting prehistoric) ed. Richard Stillwell, Princeton U.P., N.J., 1976 (£80·00).

General history: *The Pelican History of Greece* by A. R. Burn (12th imp., Penguin, London and New York, 1980).

Guidebooks: There are *two* Blue Guides, English and French, a project to produce a 'concord' having failed. *Blue Guide: Greece* compiled by S. Rossiter (Benn, London and Rand McNally, Chicago, 3rd edn 1977) is good apart from a few slips and a number of misprints; its *Crete* (enlarged) and *Athens* are available separately. The *Guide Bleu*, gen. ed. F. Ambrière (Hachette, Paris and London, Eng. trn) is scholarly, and its *Athènes* (1960), available separately, extends to Delphi and Argolis. Pausanias' *Guide to Greece* (c. AD 150–170) is available in translation by P. Levi (Penguin Classics) or by W. H. S. Jones and H. A. Ormerod (Loeb Classical Library, Harvard U.P.), with notes, maps and plans. *Wings over Hellas: Ancient Greece from the Air* by R. V. Schoder S. J. (Thames & Hudson, London and O.U.P., New York, 1974) contains 94 fine, coloured air photographs of 80 places, with key line drawings, though its historical notes are occasionally erratic.

Prehistoric sites: Vol. 1 of *The History of the Greek World* by a team of Greek scholars (Ekdotike Athenon, 1 Vissarionos Street, Athens 135, Eng. trn 1974) is excellent and lavishly illustrated. Less costly are R. Higgins, *Minoan and Mycenaean Art* (Thames & Hudson, London, 1973 and O.U.P., New York, 1967; paperback); G. Cadogan, *The Palaces of Crete* (Barrie & Jenkins, London, 1976); P. Warren, *Aegean Civilisation* [*i.e.* prehistoric] (Elsevier/Phaidon, Oxford, 1978), including Thera and Myrtos. For Thera see also the late S. Marinatos' *Thera Reports* I–VI with portfolio of colour plates (Athens Arch. Soc., 1969–74) on sale also at the National Museum, Athens.

Sanctuaries, etc: *Temples and Sanctuaries of Ancient Greece* by a team of Greek specialists, ed. Evi Melas (Eng. trn, Thames & Hudson, London, 1973; illus.) covers briefly much the same selection as this book.

On all famous Greek sites, well-illustrated 'slim volumes' by Greek archaeologists are on sale *in situ*. Some of the older ones were in bad English, but not the more recent, especially those published by Ekdotike Athenon (see above). These can also be obtained through the book trade, and include M. Andronicos' *Delphi* (1976), N. Papahatzis' *Corinth* (and district; 1977) and others. N. Yalouris' *Olympia: Altis and Museum* (1972) is from Schnell & Steiner, Zurich; Papahatzis' *Monuments of Thessalonica* (1968) from S. Molho, Thessaloniki, where other booklets (illus.) on particular churches can be obtained.

Persian war battlefields: W. K. Pritchett, *Studies in Ancient Greek Topography* (Univ. of

California Press, vol. 1 1965, vol. 2 1968); A. R. Burn, *Persia and the Greeks* (Arnold, London, 2nd imp. 1970, St Martin, New York, 1962); P. Green, *The Year of Salamis* [but including Marathon!] (Weidenfeld, London, 1970); Burn, in *Greece and the Eastern Mediterranean* (studies presented to F. Schachermeyr, ed. K. H. Kinzl; de Gruyter, Berlin and New York, 1977).

Athens: The late Ida Hill's *The Ancient City of Athens* (Methuen, London, 1953), is still serviceable, and unreplaced. For the central area the American School's guide *The Athenian Agora*, ed. Homer A. Thompson (3rd edn 1976) is indispensable.

Olynthos: See J. W. Graham, *The Hellenic House*, vol. VIII of the massive *Excavations at Olynthos*, ed. D. M. Robinson (Johns Hopkins U.P., Baltimore, 1938).

Recent work: That, *e.g.* of C. Renfrew on Melos, S. G. Miller at Nemea, and M. Andronicos at Vergina (including the sensational discovery of the tomb, probably of Philip) is still in course of publication. See, meanwhile, the annual *Archaeological Reports* on sale by the Hellenic Society, 34 Gordon Square, London WC1H OPP, to which those interested should subscribe.

Byzantine: General works: S. Runciman, *Byzantine Civilization* (Methuen, London, new imp. 1975; New American Library, New York). J. M. Hussey, *The Byzantine World* (Hutchinson University Library, London, 4th edn 1970).
     O. Demus, *Byzantine Mosaic Decoration* (Routledge, London, and Caratzas, New Rochelle, NY, 1976) is an excellent introduction to the underlying purpose of church decoration. His *Byzantine Mosaics in Greece* (Holy Luke and Daphni; Harvard U.P., 1931) is o.p. but in major libraries. D. Talbot Rice, *Byzantine Art* (Pelican History of Art, 4th edn, enlarged, 1968, Penguin, London and New York) deals with history in ch.1, mosaics in ch.5 (the 11C churches, pp 194–206, mainly plates), wall-paintings in ch.6 (Mistra, pp 291–9); extensive bibliography. M. Chatzidakis, *Byzantine Athens* (Pechlivanides, Athens) is a slim volume of excellent b. & w. photos, with brief text; it includes Daphni. Illustrated guides are available at all the chief Byzantine sites, except the Nea Moni on Chios, which seems doomed to remain unpublished for the lifetime of the veteran personage who has for some fifty years held the exclusive rights. D. Nichol, *The Meteora: Rock Monasteries of Thessaly* (Chapman & Hall, 1963) is now among Variorum Reprints (1975). S. Runciman, *Mistra* (Thames & Hudson, London, 1979; Thames & Hudson Inc. New York, 1980).

The Franks: W. Miller, *The Latins in the Levant* (Benn, London, 1928; repr. AMS Press, New York, 1976), still the most comprehensive account of a complicated, exciting and disastrous period. Chr. Karouzos, *Rhodes: a Guide to the City and Museum* (Esperos, Athens), available in English since 1973. E. Bradford, *The Shield and the Sword* (Fontana pbk, Collins, London, 1974), a succinct history of the Knights of St John; and E. Brockman, *The Two Sieges of Rhodes, 1480–1520* (Murray, London and Allenson, New York 1969), a stirring account of the end there.

A book on 'Old Churches and Monasteries' of Greece (*Alte Kirche und Klöster*) ed. Evi Melas (see above under 'Sanctuaries') has appeared in German, but not yet in English. It is to be awaited.

Glossary

abacus (Gk *abax*, a board): the square slab above the ornamental capital of a column.

acanthus (*akanthos*, thorn): ornament of broad, spiky leaves on Corinthian (*qv*) capital.

adyton ('unentered' by the public): the inner 'holy place' of a Greek sanctuary.

agora: 'place of gathering', political or for market.

akroterion: figure or other ornament on corner or end of roof-ridge of temple etc.

architrave ('top beam', Latin *trabs*): the horizontal course supported on columns and supporting the end of roof-beams.

atrium: central open courtyard of Roman house; later, also ceremonial forecourt of early Christian churches.

Byzantium: the older, classical name of Constantinople, commonly used by Byzantine writers.

cella: main body of a temple as distinct from the portico and the shrine.

Corinthian column: one with Ionic (*qv*) shaft and base, and acanthus and volute (*qv*) capital. Hence 'C. order' of architecture.

Doric column: one with no ornamental base, thickest at bottom and with slight bulge (*entasis*) in the shaft and plain 'cushion' capital, refined in classical times into section of a cone. Hence 'D. order'.

epistyle ('upon the columns'): Gk for architrave (*qv*). Now used of the beam, often of carved stone, crossing the top of a church iconostasis (*qv*), resting upon pillars standing upon the stone balustrade.

exedra ('sitting-out place'): a semi-circular seat, such as, in stone or marble, survives at Kos, Olympia, Delphi, etc.

gymnasion: place, usually an open field, for athletic exercises.

iconostasis: the screen concealing the sanctuary in a late or post-Byz. church; so called because the chief ikons are set in it as panels.

ikon (Gk *eikon*, image, likeness): a sacred picture, usually on a panel.

Ionic column: one of uniform thickness, with ornamental base and volute (*qv*) capital; hence 'I. order'.

megaron: a hall, esp. main room of a Mycenaean palace, with central hearth.

metope: in Doric architecture, the space between beam-ends resting upon the architrave; then decorative member put in to keep birds out; pre-classical, a painted terracotta slab; classical, a slab of stone or marble, often sculptured in relief.

Morea: mediaeval name of the Peloponnese.

narthex: the west interior part of a church, to which penitents and the un-baptized were confined; divided by a wall from the nave.

odeion ('Odeum', literally 'song-hall'): a covered theatre.

palaistra: a wrestling-school or training-place.

pendentives: triangular segments of a sphere, filling upper corners of the square centre of a church, as a support for the dome. Their concave inward faces provide limited space for decoration, often occupied by figures of the four Evangelists writing.

pithos: a large storage-jar, 1–1.80m high, Minoan and later.

propylaia ('front portals', plural): a monumental, columned entrance-complex. The singular form is scarcely used, being replaced by the following:

propylon: a columned gateway, usually of moderate size.

ravelin: in mediaeval fortification, an outwork of two walls forming a salient, in front of the main line.

squinches: a method, less sophisticated than pendentives (*qv*), of poising a wide dome over a square space; arches are built across the corners of the square, and filled in, providing surfaces wide enough to contain a whole scene of the Gospel story.

stoa: any columned portico, especially those which lined late-classical and Roman city-centres, often with shops or offices behind.

strategeion: office of the Athenian *strategoi* or generals; 'Defence Ministry'.

tholos: any round building.

triglyph: ('triple-grooved'): in Doric architecture, originally the projecting beam-ends, roughly carved; later represented by stone or marble divisions between the metopes (*qv*).

trireme: a 150-oared (later 170-oared) classical Greek war galley, with the oars grouped in threes.

volutes: the outward and downward curling features of an Ionic (*qv*) column-capital; a classical development from earlier, originally Asian, forms of foliage-capital.

Index

Not indexed are passing allusions (e.g. to Hannibal, never directly concerned with Greece); also names appearing only once, unless judged to be of some interest.

Spelling Most ancient Greek names are directly transliterated, not filtered through Latin (e.g. Plataia, not Plataea); but those which have become familiar in English are left in their familiar form: Aeschylus, Socrates, etc. 'Long' signs (a stroke over a vowel, ē, ō) and accents are given in this index where it is thought that they may be useful, to reveal the fact, e.g., that all Greek place-names in -sos accent on the last syllable; so Knōssós, not Cnossus or (as the Romans themselves often wrote) Gnosus. Any form of rigid consistency becomes intolerable; even the most inveterate 'Romanists' blench at calling two eminent Athenians Cimo and Solo; nor has 'Simon' ever lost his final -n.

The same applies to modern Greek names, with the added complication that few foreigners are acquainted with the Greek official code. Names of sites only recently famous are given as the discoverers left them; so Phylakopí, but Foúrnou Korifí; while ancient famous names are transliterated, with exceptions as above. On Thessalonica we have finally settled for the spelling made 'classic' in English by the King James Bible.

Vowels should be pronounced more or less as in Italian; modern Greek pronunciation, which uses eight different vowels and diphthongs for the sound EE in seen, is certainly far from the ancient; it is, for example, an obvious fact that Athenians of the Periclean age wrote all names ending in -ES with an epsilon, rhyming with NESS, not with KNEES.